HOME FROM THE WAR

HOME FROM THE WAR

Learning from Vietnam Veterans

*With a new Preface and
Epilogue on the Gulf War*

ROBERT JAY LIFTON

Beacon Press *Boston*

Beacon Press
25 Beacon Street
Boston, Massachusetts 02108-2892

Beacon Press books
are published under the auspices of
the Unitarian Universalist Association of Congregations.

99 98 97 96 95 94 93 92   8 7 6 5 4 3 2 1

Text design by Irving Perkins

Library of Congress Cataloging-in-Publication Data

Lifton, Robert Jay, 1926–
Home from the war: learning from Vietnam veterans; with a new
preface and epilogue on the Gulf War / Robert Jay Lifton.
p.   cm.
Originally published: New York: Simon and Schuster, 1973.
Includes bibliographical references and index.
ISBN 0-8070-5505-0 (paper)
1. Vietnamese Conflict, 1961–1975—Veterans—United States.
2. Vietnamese Conflict, 1961–1975—Psychological aspects.
3. Veterans—United States—Mental health.   I. Title.
[DS559.72.L54   1991]
959.704'3373—dc20   91-39232

FOR

Abbie	*Harvey*
Al	*Hy*
Andy	*Jack*
Arthur	*Jan*
Bob	*Jo*
Bob	*Joe*
Bob	*Mike*
Ed	*Paul*
Ernie	*Peter*
Felix	*Randy*
Florence	*Steve*
Harry	*Wayne*

and Hoang (a surviving child of My Lai)

Contents

Preface to the 1992 Edition

During the last decade of the twentieth century, America is still haunted by Vietnam. In 1990, a definitive study of the Vietnam generation revealed astonishing psychological costs of the war, still affecting veterans themselves and reverberating throughout much of American society 15 years after the last American combattant had left Vietnam. The study found that 15.2 percent of all male Vietnam theater veterans, 479,000 of the 3.14 million men who served there, *currently* suffer from posttraumatic stress disorder. For women the percentage is 8.5, or 610 current cases (a figure some consider low because of underreporting [see Epilogue]) of the 7,200 women who served there. An additional 11.1 percent of male veterans and 7.8 percent of females—350,000 men and women—suffer from "partial post-traumatic stress disorder."

At one time or another over 960,000 men and 1,900 women, between a quarter and a third of all who served in Vietnam, have had the full-blown disorder. Rates are particularly high in hispanic and black veterans. Moreover, those with posttraumatic stress disorder are prone to other profound effects: they frequently experience various psychiatric illnesses; they are five times more likely than those without the disorder to be unemployed; 70 percent have been divorced; almost half have been arrested or in jail at least once; and they are two to six times as likely to abuse alcohol or drugs. A particularly notable finding was the extent to which people close to troubled veterans have themselves become casualties. Spouses and partners report their own emotional difficulties, children manifest behavior problems; after all the years that have passed, "the suffering of these families is only now being recognized" (See Richard A. Kulka et al., *Trauma and the Vietnam War Generation*, New York, Brunner/Mazel, 1990). What the study tells us is that no aspect of American life has escaped the continuing pain of Vietnam. This book is about early expressions of that pain and efforts to overcome it.

The Gulf crisis also began in 1990. And when President George

Bush ordered large numbers of American troops to the Persian Gulf, everyone thought of Vietnam—the Vietnam veterans themselves and all who came into contact with them, decision makers planning military action, and millions of ordinary Americans. That preoccupation was a bit strange because the two situations were in so many ways quite different. The Vietnam War evolved slowly, over years, even decades. It began with a struggle against French colonialism led by Ho Chi Min, a nationalist leader respected throughout the world, and the American part of the war, while including extensive airstrikes, mostly took the form of counterinsurgency operations that were indecisive, confusing, mired in atrocities against civilians, and unsuccessful to the point of clear American defeat. The Gulf War, in contrast, came upon us quite suddenly and involved a cruel dictator viewed with contempt by most of the world. The American-led fighting, although including a very brief ground operation, took place almost entirely from the air, using weapons of the highest technology which virtually eliminated personal contact with the enemy.

Yet so powerful were the memories, the searing images of Vietnam, that they came close to dominating Gulf War thinking. From the beginning, in fact, Vietnam seemed to provide much of the impetus for fighting the Gulf War aggressively, and for fighting it at all. President Bush and everyone else insisted that "this will not be another Vietnam," meaning that American forces would be positioned in sufficient numbers with sufficiently overwhelming fire-power to assure quick victory and to eliminate the prolonged frustrations of Vietnam. Vietnam so decisively inhabited American thinking not only because it was our last war (not counting, of course, Panama or Grenada) but also, and more importantly, because its memories were so painful and, for many, unacceptable. Vietnam had become our "bad example" of war and death. Our leaders found a new survivor mission of their own in reversing that bad example by displaying American military power once more in a remote part of the world, this time in a way that would gloriously succeed.

A key element in the Vietnam reversal was information control. The American public turned against the Vietnam War because of increasing knowledge made available to them about what the war was really like, what was actually happening to Vietnamese and American human beings. Policy makers made sure that no such information would become available during the Gulf War. Censorship arrangements were the tightest ever applied in an American war, as were the extreme restrictions imposed upon television and print journalists concerning access to the human consequences of the war.

What resulted for the American public was a relationship to the war that was both unprecedented and bizzare. The communications revolution, epitomized by CNN 24-hour coverage from the war zone, as well as from Washington and other places throughout the world, provided instant images of war-related activity in a manner not yet possible with Vietnam. Yet at the same time, viewers, listeners, and readers were, psychologically speaking, further than ever from the war.

The new generation of high-tech weaponry used in the Gulf War contributed enormously to American information control. Rather than be exposed to ugly suffering and dying, the American public was offered a continuous television seminar on our advanced military technology. Indeed the weapons themselves, as brilliant robots, became the "heroes" of the war: the advanced F-117 Stealth Fighter-Bomber with its infrared nighttime equipment, the bomb released from it "smart" enough to seek the air shaft of a specific building; the Tomahawk cruise missile, able to "see" even in darkness by means of a tiny television camera mounted on its nose; and the M1A1 tanks, fitted with state-of-the-art "reactive armor" to direct explosions outward, especially those coming from chemical warheads.

Television correspondents seemed themselves awed by these robot-heroes. They respectfully turned to experts—mostly retired generals and admirals as well as geopolitical theorists—to explain the technical details and larger significance of these new military entities. The weapons gurus often used elaborate audio-visual aids, thereby creating an antiseptic classroom atmosphere.

In contrast with Vietnam reporting, where corpses, burning villages, and suffering civilians made their way onto the screen, the televised message of the Gulf War was one of elegant technology. Viewers responded by becoming conscientious students. We gained entry to technical areas that, to many of us, had previously seemed impenetrable. We could even feel ourselves transported to an esoteric realm, made privy to the secrets of a mystery cult. We were dazzled by the achievements—the precision and "pin-point accuracy" of our robot-heroes.

More than that, we became vicarious participants in the war. Always available to everyone were charts of Baghdad targets, demonstrations of the new talents of our aircraft, missiles, and tanks, and shots of the magnificent desert sand. We could warm to the enthusiastic descriptions of American pilots of "fantastic" bombing runs over Baghdad, likening the scene to the most brilliant Fourth of July fireworks display. We could plunge into the excitement of war, its heightening of existence in the face of death, without experiencing anything in the way of personal risk, that is, without the death. We could be swept into a kind of technological euphoria that served as a substitute for more humane emotions.

Inevitably, however, some reality broke through. We first witnessed the terror evoked by Iraqi Skud missiles in Americans, Israelis, and others. A little later we saw the suffering on the faces of captured American pilots who, under extreme duress, mouthed the platitudes that enabled them to survive. And finally we saw Iraqi corpses, hundreds of ordinary people killed in a civilian air raid shelter somehow mistaken by our military leaders for a command post. But before we could pause to reflect on such matters, we were once more inundated with demonstrations of how our technological marvels unfailingly protect us and equally unfailingly strike enemy targets.

That technological euphoria undoubtedly distracted Americans from recognizing that, over the course of the bombings, there had been virtually no Iraqi resistance. As a taxi driver said to me at the time: "This ain't no war. It's just us dropping bombs and killing people." And the ground war turned out to be not much different. It consisted mainly of our tanks moving rapidly through Kuwait and Iraq, their advance delayed only by arranging custody for the enormous number of enemy soldiers seeking to surrender. The contrast with Vietnam could not be greater.

Since our side seemed to be doing almost all of the fighting, a number of Americans began to wonder whether "war"—which suggests a struggle between two armed forces—was the right term for what was occurring. We did actively engage in the mass killing from the air of fleeing Iraqi soldiers. With our cluster bombs, as one pilot put it, "we hit the jackpot." Another described the slaughter of a column of soldiers twenty to thirty miles long by waves of fighter-bombers as "close to Armageddon." No matter how overwhelming a military attack, how swift a *blitzkrieg*, there is supposed to be, in a war, some attempt at resistance. If not a war, what was the nature of our project in the Gulf?

A large number of Americans, also influenced by Vietnam, had thought it wrong for us to embark on the war in the Persian Gulf. Indeed, significant opposition appeared much earlier than in the case of Vietnam. Polls taken over the course of our buildup suggested that about half of all Americans opposed military action. There was, to be sure, unanimity about turning back Iraq's invasion of Kuwait. But to many if not most Americans, the way to do that was the policy of strict economic sanctions which had been quickly agreed upon by most of the nations of the world. Sanctions had the added advantage of providing a new, nonviolent model for combating an act of violence. Only when President Bush invoked, with some exaggeration, the danger of Iraq's imminent acquisition of nuclear weapons, did he succeed in gaining an American majority for military action. And even after that, he barely overcame Congressional resistance to granting him the power to make war.

Vietnam was very much a factor in my own response to the Gulf crisis. I found myself deeply troubled by the enormous buildup of American troops in Saudi Arabia, quickly transforming a defensive posture into a formidable offensive force. Reminiscent of Vietnam were the contradictory American statements justifying this shift. These in turn suggested another misreading of an alien environment, an unreflective impulse to employ military force, and an erroneous series of projections concerning the consequences of American war-making.

During the buildup I initiated an informal meeting of concerned friends and colleagues on the Gulf crisis and the danger of war. The group quickly cohered and became the Ad Hoc Committee for Peace. We met regularly to explore ways of opposing the approaching war. In a surprisingly brief period of time we were able to extend our support and raise sufficient money for a full-page advertisement in the *New York Times*, which eventually ran in February 1991, just prior to the ground war. It bore the title, "Is there nothing left but the killing?" In response to that advertisement we received more than a thousand letters with additional substantial contributions. Soon after the war ended, we were able to run a smaller subsequent advertisement on problems of peace, to organize a public evening on the war and its aftermath, and to put together a book-sized collection of "Peace Pieces" by members of our own expanding group and many others. We collaborated with a number of other groups, including Veterans for Peace, among whom there were many who served in Vietnam. We also worked with the Military Families Support Network, which lent moral support to Americans in the Gulf while opposing the enterprise they were part of. At this writing we are making preliminary plans to continue the group in order to explore and combat the international war system.

This all suggests a broad spectrum of opposition and doubt, influenced by Vietnam, concerning the Gulf War and American policy contributing to that war. Yet everything changed, as it always will, with the first shots fired against Iraq. Doubt and opposition were surpressed as Americans suddenly found themselves afflicted with war fever, with an impulse toward absolutizing our virtue and heroism and the enemy's evil and cunning. The process was furthered by a prior tendency toward rendering Saddam Hussein, bad enough in his human actions, a less-than-human demon.

A national flag fetish was expanded into a yellow-ribbon fetish. Originally a demonstration of support for hostages held in Iran in the late 1970s, then for relatives in the Gulf War zone, the ribbons became an added focus for the national war fever. The militarization of public events was such that the ultimate American football contest, the Superbowl, became a vehicle for displaying to an enormous national television audience war-related patriotic fervor—the message was that the American men and women serving in the Gulf, not the football players, were the real heroes. In virtually all sports, more and more teams were encouraged or required to wear flags sewn onto their uniforms. This is the kind of aggressive patriotism that celebrates not love of one's people and homeland but the most narrow and deadly definitions of "us" and "them."

Consider, for instance, the case of the athlete at Seton Hall, a small college with a big-time basketball program. His principled refusal to wear the flag on his uniform brought about first admonitions, then boos from fans and general ridicule, then harassing telephone calls at various hours of the day and night, and finally death threats. He decided that he, his wife, and small child had better leave the country. His refusal to wear the flag had to do with his being an Italian Christian pacifist who opposed war in general and the Gulf War in particular.

The sequence of events not only reminds us of Samuel Johnson's depiction of patriotism as "the last refuge of a scoundrel," but suggests that certain kinds of patriotic outbursts can at least temporarily "scoundrelize" much of a nation. And this national excess seems related to Vietnam, at least indirectly, as a compensation for the tainted, inglorious national imagery associated with that war. But I must add that just as a significant number of Americans spoke out in opposition to Vietnam wrongs, so did many express concern and outrage about the Seton Hall incident and our overall Gulf War patriotic excess.

With the quick and decisive victory, patriotism turned automatically into triumphalism. The legitimate desire to welcome warmly men and women returning from the Gulf—in contrast, as many publicly pointed out, with the cruel reception often given Vietnam veterans—was marred by accompanying celebrations of a glorious and heroic American victory. Flags were everywhere, and plans were announced for enormous parades in most major American cities. But perhaps most troubling in all this triumphalism was the occasion of President Bush's victory speech before a special session of both houses of Congress. Everybody who was anybody in government was there, and just about all of them seemed to be wearing flags on their lapels. Greeted in the fashion of a monarch, the president (according to the *New York Times*) "basked in the atmosphere of triumph, which produced cheers at his every mention of the military." Worse, the president held out our "achievement" in the Gulf as a model for future American accomplishment. I can recall no public event that made me feel greater shame as an American.

The national Memorial Day ceremony, coming just a few months after the war's end, included triumphal images from Desert Storm brilliantly packaged for television: American troops silhouetted against sand and sunset and warmly greeted by Kuwaitis celebrating their liberation. And Vice President Dan Quayle declared the military outcome to be "a victory of good over evil, freedom over tyranny, of peace over war."

Did Americans believe him? Not entirely. Evidence soon appeared of ambivalence concerning the displays of triumphalism. While people cheered at the sidelines, many Americans began to wonder at the appropriateness of sexy drum majorettes, aggressive military hardware, and stirring victory marches. A leading television talk show even focused on the question "Are we having too many parades?" There was good reason to suspect that some of the public enthusiasm for the war and the victory was an attempt to overcome inner doubts about the entire enterprise. In any case, the celebratory atmosphere was relatively short lived.

For one thing, it became quickly evident that the war had hardly solved the problems of the Middle East. All kinds of strife remained, including the brutal suppression by the Iraqis of a Kurdish uprising that had been called for, then abandoned by, our leaders. Americans were confused by President Bush's apparent desire to keep in power none other than the man we had declared a demon, Saddam Hussein. That position was all too reminiscent of our pre–Gulf War support for Saddam as a buffer against Iranian fundamentalism. Also troubling to Americans was the extraordinary cost of the war, the hundreds of thousands of casualties, mostly Iraqi, and the extreme environmental damage. There were shades of Vietnam here once more, as there were in emerging reports of deliberate American official "misinformation" on such things as the size and capability of the Iraqi army.

But it was President Bush's immediate response to the victory that best revealed the psychological centrality of Vietnam for the whole Gulf enterprise. His most ringing words were not of heroic warriors—on the order of Churchill's "Never have so many owed so much to so few"—but of a declared release from a set of attitudes: "By God, we have kicked the Vietnam syndrome once and for all!" What did he mean? By the Vietnam syndrome he was referring to a constellation of images: military frustration and defeat; our unwillingness to "go all out" to destroy an opponent; and our subsequent reluctance to involve U.S. troops in faraway conflicts. For George Bush, then, the Vietnam syndrome is equated with American weakness.

But there are other possible readings of the Vietnam syndrome. One has to do with individual posttraumatic stress reactions once referred to in many quarters as "post-Vietnam syndrome." Another reading, which I put forward in this book, is of the "syndrome" as an expression of wisdom. This study records how an impressive number of Vietnam veterans, in probing the sources of their own trauma, found meaning only in asserting the very meaninglessness of their war. They were expressing precisely that bitter insight in their memorable act of public theater on the Capitol steps in 1971, when they literally threw their medals back in the face of those who had awarded them. They were making a statement not only about the Vietnam War specifically but also, by implication, about similar wars that might occur, and indeed about war in general.

That reading in turn sheds further light on what President Bush was saying. By kicking the Vietnam syndrome, the President was "once and for all" reinstating the good name of war. He was asserting an American military prerogative to "kick ass," as he likes to put it. Is that prerogative to become the "Gulf syndrome"?

This embrace of decisive war-making power is part of a psychological and political struggle to ward off a troubling sense of American decline. Vietnam contributed much to that sense of decline, as subsequently did Watergate and a variety of intractable domestic difficulties (problems of the economy, cities, education, health care, drugs, and so on) as well as international humiliations (Americans held as hostages in Iran and elsewhere in the Middle East, a sense of diminishing technological and economic status as compared with Japan and Germany, and a decreasing ability to provide a clear democratic model to other nations). That sense of diminishing empire has been articulated by a number of historians and political observers, sometimes labeled as "declinists." Inevitably they are attacked by those who claim (and generally advocate) American hegemony and who speak of a revival of national power and influence. Such "revivalists" have seized upon the Gulf War as demonstrating Joseph Nye's dictum that "where America leads others follow—this year, next year, and for the next generation." Such assessments, however, tend to include claims of American social and ethical health, whatever the evidence to the contrary. The power-revivalist position, then, depends on collective psychological patterns of denial (what is happening is not happening) and of psychic numbing (what is occurring is not experienced). The process can then come full circle when denial and numbing are reapplied to memories of the American experience in Vietnam.

That psychological and political context was ready-made for the Gulf War, which could then make its own contribution to the greater American pattern of denial and numbing. Americans were told to embrace their military success as a way of "feeling good about themselves again," rather than feeling weighed down by problems that will not go away or by burdensome truths about decline.

Only some weeks after the end of the war did accurate knowledge of its conduct and consequences begin to reach Americans. We learned some of the details of two types of war-making, both almost entirely from the air. The first, the annihilative, was directed mainly at Iraqi soldiers. It consisted of massive carpet bombing and made use of new rocket and missile systems as well as fuel-air explosives whose vapor clouds produce fireballs of such magnitude that they can engulf everything and asphyxiate all human beings within several hundred square yards. Michael Klare, an authority on this weaponery, tells us that it was designed "to produce nuclear-like levels of destruction without arousing popular revulsion." Certainly its use suggested a disturbing narrowing of the gap, at least in destructiveness, between nuclear and "conventional" weaponery.

The second form of American war making, aimed at cities, consisted of the much-heralded "smart bombs." They were indeed sufficiently precise to leave most of Baghdad standing while completely destroying limited targets. Those limited targets, however, included Iraq's national electric power production and transmission grid, its telecommunications system, and its fuel-refining capacity. As a result, water could not be pumped to the population, emergency generators could not function, nor could telephones or computers. As H. Jack Geiger noted during a visit to Iraq sponsored by the Physicians for Human Rights, "Health officials cannot even count the sick." That group and other medical teams observed large numbers of serious gastrointestinal conditions, with fatalities highest in young children. Large-scale epidemics of cholera, typhoid, and possibly polio are still feared as part of what Geiger calls a "slow motion catastrophe" in a "bomb now, die later" war. Overall, American casualties were about 200, while Iraqi casualties, impossible to ascertain accurately, have been estimated between 50,000 and 200,000.

These two draconic forms of aerial attack, together with tight control of information, constitute a new form of war making. The Gulf War thus becomes a model for future American military enterprises in the Third World, in response to governments or groups or individuals considered a threat to our interests. While racism can always be a factor, it need not be a dominant one. More significant is the emerging military "hi-techism": a relationship to our advanced military equipment that enables us to view our individual lives as more valuable than those of people without such technology. This pattern reflects and perpetuates high-tech nationalism and an ideology of American hegemony.

We therefore risk seeing ourselves not only as a blessed country but also as the agent of an all-powerful technological deity. Militarized high technology becomes equated with absolute virtue, and as possessors of that virtue we have the duty to be the most powerful of world police. We can claim the added virtue of restraint because we maintain this status without military use of nuclear weapons. The technical superiority that had so confused matters in Vietnam—we depended on it there too, but it didn't quite work in a counterinsurgency war—becomes, in a different kind of war, both strategically effective and a psychological rallying point. Rather than worry about guerrilla units, we destroy the infrastructure of cities and annihilate enemy troop concentrations, all with minimal psychological or moral reverberations.

But Vietnam taught us that such projections can be fallible. War making depends on holding to certain casts of mind, certain forms of dissociation, among American soldiers and civilians. Dissociation, in essence, is the separation of one part of the mind from the rest of the mind, or from consciousness—in this case the always dangerous separation of knowledge from feeling. For much of the American population, that dissociation may take the form of psychic numbing, a diminished inclination or capacity to feel, as happened for a considerable period of time in relation to Vietnam. And for those most centrally involved in war making—in the creation and use of devastating high-tech weaponry—the dissociation may take the form of doubling: the formation of a relatively independent, functional second self associated with the killing project while one's prior, more humane self continues to maintain its standards of decency in everyday life. Yet there are always cracks in the dissociative process, openings toward feelings and truth.

During the Gulf War, friends told me about their four-year-old child, George, who was afraid that missiles would come out of the television set and get him. George was telling us something about the extraordinary role of television in the war and its possibility for conveying danger and other unpalatable truths. Like all of us, George and his family were inundated with the images and sounds of war, with the television set a third party in the parent-child dialogue. Through it, George became aware that missiles kill human beings. Because children have less developed defense mechanisms, they can be more vulnerable to these shadowy images, even if they then incorporate them into their play. George was thus able to imagine something adults were largely surpressing: that the weapons in the Gulf War—ours and theirs—were not innocuous, that they endangered human life.

We may suspect that adults too, whatever their more advanced defenses, were not entirely immune to such fear and recognition. Indeed, one of our valuable evolutionary achievements as human beings is our moral imagination, our capacity to connect fear and threat not only with self-protective measures but with empathy or feeling for others also subjected to fear and threat. Dissociative processes, to be sure, undermine that empathy. But they do not easily destroy it altogether. We are capable of finding ways to reassert it, as occurred in relation to the Vietnam War. This book is an exploration of how a vital part of our humanity may be lost and how with enormous effort, with fits and starts, it may be regained.

ROBERT JAY LIFTON
Wellfleet, Massachusetts
September 1991

Preface to the 1985 Edition

It is in place now, known simply as "The Wall." It is a V-shaped structure of polished black granite, 400 feet long, sunk into the landscape next to the Lincoln Memorial, and containing the names of 57,939 Americans killed or missing in Vietnam. It is a very quiet memorial, stark and heartbreaking. In its tabulation of death and pain, and nothing else, it could not be more appropriate. Vietnam veterans go there to acknowledge dead comrades and in that way reassert their own lives; they go there to mourn. For them it is a wall of healing.

That is as it should be. By the time the memorial was completed in 1982, the great majority of Vietnam veterans had long re-entered American life, whether as working people, professionals, or elected officials. A decade or so from their war, their pattern has been one of reconciliation with their society.

The other truth about Vietnam veterans is their high percentage among hospital patients and prison inmates, and the legacy of significant inner pain even in those who seem externally to be holding their own. That pain has been documented all too clearly in recent psychological studies, and in the experience of the national Outreach Program for Vietnam veterans. Much of their suffering stems from conflicts described in this book, conflicts having to do with the sense of absurd killing and dying associated with their war.

Their healing and reconciliation are in no way enhanced by the contemporary political temptation toward historical and psychological falsehood: the image of the Vietnam War as a "noble American cause." Here we need to make sharp distinction between the nobility and bravery of individual men in facing death or saving comrades, and the dreadful, filthy, unnecessary war they were asked to fight. Indeed, the reader will find special nobility in the manner in which some Vietnam veterans were able to confront the searing truths of their war during the early rap groups described here. Those of us involved in the groups learned much very quickly about the healing power of truth and mutual caring, and take pride in the extension of those principles to thousands of Vietnam veterans in Outreach Program groups modeled largely on our experience.

Healing, yes. But what have we learned from the pain and loss? In the begining pages of this book I discuss the legacy of warrior mythology, of the Hero as Warrior; and of socialized warriors in all cultures in whom the original heroic quest has been replaced by cultivation of professional skills in killing and dying, skills all too easily and destructively called forth by political leaders.

The entire warrior ethos is now being radically questioned, and none too soon. Vietnam has much to do with that questioning, and so does the nuclear threat. Yet in this book I found myself using the term "antiwar warriors" to evoke the militancy with which some Vietnam veterans came to oppose their war. Now, twelve years later, I believe that the concept of the antiwar warrior has relevance for everyone on this earth.

Consider once again that extraordinary Washington scene in April 1971, when a group of Vietnam veterans returned their medals to the leaders of the country that had honored them. These veterans did not appear politely at the office of a senator or a general; they did not return the awards quietly. Rather, they threw them at the Capitol steps the way one might throw a baseball or a football, or, yes, a hand grenade, but with greater anger. They were still warriors, and their behavior reflected some of the commendable characteristics of the warrior ethos. One of those was courage, traditionally expressed in battle, but now in daring to reveal to their people what only they could reveal. Another was loyalty, traditionally a willingness to serve country and flag, now in the insistence that their country confront its own descent into evil and return to its professed principles. Still another characteristic of the ethos is love of one's fellow warriors, still present in their angry remembrance of dead comrades as they cast away their medals. And another is love of one's people, now revealed in the demand for its return to truth and honor. And finally, there is the warrior-hero's commitment to the higher purpose of collective renewal, always murky in war but never more luminous than in Vietnam veterans' denunciation of war.

Vietnam veterans were not entirely unique. Mahatma Gandhi and Martin Luther King were also antiwar warriors, as have been leaders of most great spiritual and social movements. What was special about Vietnam veterans was the stark and revealing drama of their shift from direct involvement in war to the stance of antiwar warrior. Equally remarkable was the accompanying critique of a number of components of their own maleness, which many found necessary to making that shift.

With nuclear weapons, traditional expressions of the warrior ethos become not just more dangerous but potential vehicles for human extinction. Yet those warrior qualities of courage, loyalty, love, and revitalization, along with the aggressive and potentially destructive impulses with which they may be expressed—all these are still with us, and their transmutation is needed more than ever. Put simply, we may say that the noble goal of maintaining the continuity of human life now requires the mobilization of vast legions of antiwar warriors: men and women committed to the struggle against nuclear holocaust and the reassertion of immortalizing human connection, their own and everyone's. Vietnam veterans know something about this. Can we learn from their example?

Not fast enough, it would seem. In America we witness the calling forth of tired if not hypocritical expressions of the warrior ethos for destructive Vietnam-like missions in our own hemisphere. But now there is resistance to these missions, in political circles and throughout the American consciousness. That resistance is related to the Vietnam experience. If we have not learned enough from those antiwar warriors, we have at least learned something. We are capable of learning still more, and there lies our hope.

This book is an expression of that hope, whatever the pain and evil described. It is a book much less about a war in Vietnam than about the extraordinary transformation experienced by a group of young men and its meaning for the rest of us now.

ROBERT JAY LIFTON
Wellfleet, Massachusetts
August 1984

Acknowledgments

Kenneth Keniston, David Riesman, and Erik Erikson, close friends and colleagues over decades, contributed greatly to the dialogue around this book and made valuable suggestions about the manuscript. I am grateful also to Robert Liebert for sensitive comments on the manuscript, to participants in the 1971 meeting of the Wellfleet psychohistorical study group for their discussions of the work as then presented to them; and to Eric Olson, research assistant, friend, and collaborator. Lily Finn prepared the manuscript with profound care and compassion. Alice Mayhew's dedicated editorial work improved the manuscript greatly and made it possible for all concerned to maintain a sense of authenticity throughout the publishing arrangements. My wife, Betty Jean Lifton, not only did all of the things that loving spouses can do to sustain one another through difficult enterprises, but was originally responsible for introducing me to Vietnam and has been infusing my responses to that country ever since with her humane insistence that we pay attention to the suffering of its children.

The entire effort depended upon the Vietnam veterans whom I interviewed, talked with informally, and met with in rap groups; they taught me a great deal, and we shared more than mere psychological exchange. The same is true of fellow psychological "professionals," with whom I discovered a new dimension of colleagueship: Chaim Shatan, Florence Volkman Pincus, Arthur Egendorf, Betty-Jo League, Peter Lawner, Abbie Adams, and Robert Schapiro. Richard A. Falk, peace colleague, collaborator, and warm friend, has taught me much about the political and historical aspects of the war.

I have altered certain identifying details to protect the anonymity of veterans without affecting the psychological currents involved.

Throughout the book I employ two forms of quotation: conventional inverted double-commas to portray words others have used (such as "What am I doing here?" or "identity crisis"); and single inverted commas to suggest ironic meanings or some other form of special emphasis I wish to convey (Company C's 'survivor mission' at My Lai, their 'play' in kneeling down and firing).

Prologue: Engaging the Affliction

Well, there've always been people going around saying someday the war will end. I say, you can't be sure the war will *ever* end. Of course it may have to pause occasionally—for breath, as it were—it can even meet with an accident—nothing on this earth is perfect—a war of which we could say it left nothing to be desired will probably never exist. A war can come to a sudden halt—from unforeseen causes—you can't think of everything—a little oversight, and the war's in the hole, and someone's got to pull it out again! The someone is the Emperor or the King or the Pope. They're such friends in need, the war has really nothing to worry about, it can look forward to a prosperous future.

—Bertolt Brecht

The distant Trojans never injured me.

—Homer

Man creates culture by changing natural conditions in order to maintain his spiritual self.

—Otto Rank

As I complete work on this manuscript, something called "The Vietnam War" (more accurately, "the Indochina War") approaches the state of permanent national affliction. To trace my own involvement I must go as far back as 1954, when my wife and I made our first visit to Indochina, she as a journalist and I as a neophyte psychiatric investigator taking a respite from work in Hong Kong. At that time the United States was replacing France as the Western presence in that country, taking over from her the white man's burden there. I remember French correspondents telling us then, "You'll see what will happen. You will make the same mistake as we did. The same thing will happen all over again." As opposed as we were to American policy, the prediction seemed absurd. It was late in the day for colonialism, and besides, that was European stuff. Like most Americans, we had a lot to learn. But we stayed long enough to become impressed with the psychological and historical energy of the Vietnamese Revolution—my wife, in fact, was in Hanoi with other journalists when Ho Chi Minh and his followers (then called the Vietminh) triumphantly reclaimed their old capital.

Over subsequent years, as I explored psychological dimensions of totalitarianism, social change, nuclear weapons, and (more generally) death and the continuity of life, that war stayed very much with me as it progressed (for the majority of Americans) from unpleasant background rumbling (1954-64) to nasty foreground obsession (1965 to 1973). During that time I developed two strong commitments. One was to psychohistorical investigation, to developing new theory and method for applying psychological principles to historical events. The other was to opposition to nuclear weapons and to the war system in general, and through a

15

deepening involvement in peace-movement activities, to the war in Vietnam in particular. I struggled to find ways to bring together the two commitments, to bring passion to investigation, and scholarship to political and ethical stands. There were difficulties, but I became convinced that keeping these pursuits separate was by far the greater danger. The crucial experience for me was my work in Hiroshima in 1962; one could hardly be neutral on the subject of the atomic bomb.

My Lai came as no great surprise to anyone familiar with the American project in Vietnam. Extensive information about American atrocities there had long been available for those who cared to know. But My Lai shocked nonetheless, in its concrete details and its dimensions. It brought about an abrupt change in my own relationship to the war, and in my life in general. I recall the shame and rage I experienced when reading an early account of My Lai in the *New York Times* in November, 1969, (while on an airplane taking me to Toronto for a talk on psychohistory and a radio broadcast on nuclear weapons). The rage was directed partly toward the warmakers in power, and partly toward myself for not having personally done more to confront or resist American slaughter of Vietnamese. I expressed these feelings at the beginning of my talk at the University of Toronto, and have remained preoccupied ever since with the overall issue of American war crimes in Vietnam and the atrocity-producing situation that created them.

Part of my response to My Lai had to do with what I knew to be its close relationship to much of my professional-investigative experience. I had served as an Air Force psychiatrist in Korea in 1952, had later done extensive interviewing with American prisoners of war repatriated from North Korea, and had been generally concerned with individual experience in extreme situations. But most of all I felt reverberations of Hiroshima, of holocaust and of the psychology of the survivor. I sensed that what I had learned in Hiroshima about immersion in death had great bearing upon My Lai. Probing these questions more deeply in connection with antiwar activities felt right and natural for me—as a "psychohistorian" and as a human being. One makes such decisions precisely out of this sense of fit rather than out of any kind of altruism or special moral virtue. If one is to grasp holocaust from a distance, one must, at some inner level, decide to become a 'survivor' of that holocaust, and take on the 'survivor mission' of giving it form in a way that contributes to something beyond it. In any case I sought out more information about My Lai, wrote and spoke about American war crimes in Vietnam in association with several groups focusing upon them, and eventually edited, together with Richard A. Falk and Gabriel Kolko, a collection of readings on the subject entitled *Crimes of War*.[1]

Throughout, I considered myself primarily an investigator. But an invitation to testify before a Senate subcommittee on veterans on the psychological effects of the war gave me an opportunity to put this investigative function to direct ethical and political use. I had already begun talking informally to returning GIs and veterans, and to a number of other people who had gathered extensive information on the subject. I also drew upon the work of Murray Polner, a historian who did an interview study of returning veterans of diverse political views,[2] while myself beginning to meet with groups of antiwar veterans to discuss the nature of their Vietnam experiences. In January, 1970 I drew up a statement for the Cranston Subcommittee[3] in which I tried to set forth ways in which the special features of the Vietnam War brought about in GIs advanced states of brutalization and psychic numbing, and made massacres like My Lai inevitable. I came to speak of this kind of work as a form of "advocacy research,"[4] in which intellectually rigorous investigation is combined with commitment to broader social principles, causes, or groups.

A short time later I was able to conduct a series of intensive interviews, totaling ten hours, with a GI who had been at My Lai and had not fired. From this profoundly illuminating encounter, I became further convinced that, despite all of the American writing on Vietnam, very little was understood about what either GIs or Vietnamese really experienced there. In December of 1970 I helped initiate a program of weekly "rap groups" at the New York office of the Vietnam Veterans Against the War (see Chapter 2), and met regularly with one of those groups over a period of two years. I continued to conduct individual interviews, mostly tape-recorded, and talked more informally with Vietnam veterans at a variety of meetings, at which I often shared platforms with them. In all, I spoke to about four hundred veterans, spent more than one hundred and fifty hours in rap groups (forty-five meetings), and eighty hours in individual interviews.

This intense coming together with antiwar warriors led me to larger questions concerning the mythology of war and warrior-heroes, and the relationship of this mythology to militarization of American society. It is sometimes said that Vietnam is of little significance compared to these larger American military-institutional problems. But I would say, to the contrary, that the concrete American experience in Vietnam provides a very special opportunity to examine our changing national relationship to what could be called the 'psychomythology of war-making.' To grasp that opportunity, however, we have to get beneath most of what is said about the war and open ourselves, in ways that few Americans have as yet been willing to do, to its special human actualities.

Not that these actualities are unrelated to those of other wars. I found echoes of many things I have heard Vietnam veterans say in J. Glenn Gray's *The Warriors* and Guy Sajer's *The Forgotten Soldier* (on World War II); in Alastair Horne's *The Price of Glory*, Erich Maria Remarque's *All Quiet on the Western Front*, and the poems of Wilfred Owen (all from World War I); in Leo Tolstoi's *Sebastopol* (from the Crimean War), Alfred de Vigny's *The Military Necessity* (from the Napoleonic and earlier wars), and even in Bertolt Brecht's *Mother Courage and Her Children* (on the Thirty Years' War of the seventeenth century). Not surprisingly, World War I writings came closest, especially battlefield recollections by Europeans of their responses to that war's dreadful combination of slaughter and meaninglessness.

I am suggesting that we keep constantly in mind a dialectic between the specificity of the Vietnam War and its relationship to all war. As always, the particular is the only path to the general, but cannot itself be comprehended outside of the general. In this dialectic I am convinced that the extremity of psychological and moral inversions in Vietnam can be uniquely illuminating —but only if we examine those inversions in their individual and collective expressions.

There is a related question about the special qualities of the group of men I have worked with. Almost all of them belong to the minority of Vietnam veterans who emerge with an articulate antiwar position, as opposed to the great majority who are much less clear in their views or the other minority who support the war. Most have seen active combat, again in contrast to the larger number of veterans who held noncombat assignments. I made no attempt to gather data from a "representative" group of veterans. For I was in no way undertaking a comprehensive study of the reactions of American GIs to the Vietnam War on the model of my earlier study of Hiroshima survivors. Nor is this book simply a report on the rap groups or individual interviews with veterans, though these provide most of the data on which it draws.

Rather, it explores certain remarkable feelings and images brought back from the Vietnam War, and their bearing on both the nature of the American involvement in that war and of war in general. Above all it depicts a process of individual and collective transformation from war to peace, and of radical subversion of the warrior myth. The book also examines new kinds of group and individual relationships on behalf of shared social and therapeutic goals, which, in turn, connect with struggles throughout the society to create new institutions or to restructure old ones. The book is concerned with our general understanding of psychological change, and develops a model for such change taking place not in childhood or adolescence but in young adulthood. Finally, it is about psychiatry (and by extension, other healing professions, psychological and theological), its corruptions as revealed in the Vietnam War, and its possibilities for a transformation of its own. In short, the book deals with what is probably man's oldest and most fundamental theme, that of death and rebirth, suffering and realization.

The conceptual model I bring to the study is that of death and the continuity of life, a model I have elsewhere suggested as more appropriate to contemporary experience than the existing psychoanalytic model of instinct (primarily sexual instinct) and defense (mainly repression).[5] Of great importance here are issues surrounding the psychology of the survivor, as developed in my Hiroshima study, though I have had to reconsider certain of these, notably the 'animating' possibilities of guilt. To conceptualize the central issue of transformation I refer back to earlier work on open personal change, as well as to an evolving theoretical perspective on individual and historical continuity or 'symbolic immortality.' It is no surprise that prior images of continuity are shattered in these men. What is remarkable, and of the greatest importance, is the capacity of many of them to form new connections, however vulnerable they are, all the more so since many of these connections are based on insights that the larger society finds antagonistic.

My way of understanding these matters has evolved over eighteen years of psychological investigation of historical issues, an enterprise which about halfway along, came to be known as psychohistory. As in the past I am working with shared themes,[6] with a group of people who have undergone a common historical experience. As in earlier work, I see that experience within a trinity of psychobiological universals (in this case, such things as the potential for guilt and the need for connection and continuity); specific cultural emphases (such as the long-standing American preoccupation with technique and the American sense of national virtue); and recent or contemporary historical forces (the collision of the post-World War II American image of exterminating communist evil with a fifty-year-old Vietnamese revolution combining nationalist, anticolonial, and communist ideology). This last, contemporary-historical element of the trinity, generally neglected in psychological work, is extremely important here as it suggests some of the source of the malignant bind into which American GIs were helplessly thrust. Though I call upon many earlier concepts of my own and others, the special problems under study, both in their newness and neglected oldness, require that previous concepts be modified, reformulated in a psychohistorical frame, or simply replaced by new principles.

Some of these principles follow directly upon the evidence, while others require me to be speculative. My belief is that intellectual responsibility in a subject of this kind requires carrying one's ideas beyond the immediate data, while anchoring that speculation in concrete observation. Some of what I suggest about transformation from war to peace not only goes against the traditional grain but defies socio-historical odds as well. I do so not out of easy optimism or even wishfulness—neither the content of the study nor my previous investigative experience allows for either. Rather, I want to raise the question of the significance of an important change undergone by a relatively small group of men for a larger change in human consciousness now sought from many sides.

Finally, I must serve warning that this will not be a book written by a phantom researcher: I will be there—too much there, some might claim—throughout. Articulated subjectivity, the use of the self as an investigative instrument, has become an increasingly important principle for me, as it has for others involved in psychohistorical work. That principle plus the advocacy I have already mentioned would render a denial of subjectivity—a claim of being a "neutral screen"—both hypocritical and, in the broadest sense, unscientific. I cannot say that I underwent the same transformation as the Vietnam veterans I describe, but I did not emerge from this study unchanged.

ROBERT JAY LIFTON

Wellfleet, Mass.
November, 1972

CHAPTER 1

The Hero Versus the Socialized Warrior

It is a joyous thing, is war. . . . You love your comrade so in war. When you see that your quarrel is just and your blood is fighting well, tears rise to your eye. A great sweet feeling of loyalty and of pity fills your heart on seeing your friend so valiantly exposing his body to execute and accomplish the command of our Creator. And then you prepare to go and die or live with him, and for love not to abandon him. And out of that there arises such a delectation, that he who has not tasted it is not fit to say what a delight it is. Do you think that a man who does that fears death? Not at all; for he feels so strengthened, he is so elated, that he does not know where he is. Truly he is afraid of nothing.

> —Jean De Bueil (in *Le Jouvencel*,
> fictionalized fifteenth-century recon-
> struction of service under Joan
> of Arc)

Humanity is mad! It must be mad to do what it is doing. What a massacre! What scenes of horror and carnage! I cannot find words to translate my impressions. Hell cannot be so terrible. Men are mad!

> —Alfred Joubaire (second lieutenant in
> French Army at Verdun,
> May 23, 1916)

The hero-deed is a continuous shattering of the crystallizations of the moment. . . . Transformation, fluidity, not stubborn ponderosity, is the characteristic of the living God.

> —Joseph Campbell

THE WARRIOR has always laid claim on our emotions. He has been celebrated by virtually all known cultures for his individual courage, and for the collective glory he makes possible. The quest for such glory is, in turn, part of man's general struggle, in the face of inevitable biological death, for a sense of immortality.

In an earlier work I described this principle of symbolic immortality as the need to maintain an inner sense of continuity with what has gone on before and what will go on after one's own individual existence. From this point of view, the *sense* of immortality is much more than a mere denial of death though man is certainly prone to that denial; it is part of compelling, life-enhancing imagery, through which each of us perceives his connection with all of human history. The sense of immortality may be expressed biologically, that is, by living on through or in one's sons and daughters and their sons and daughters (or, via an expanding bio*social* radius, in one's community, nation, people, or species); theologically, in the idea of a life after death or, more importantly, of the spiritual conquest of death; creatively, through works and influences, large or small, that persist beyond biological death; through identification with 'eternal nature' and its infinite extension into time and space; or through a feeling-state of 'experiential transcendence'—so intense that time and death disappear.[1]

The warrior's courage in killing becomes associated with one or more of these modes, so that his immortality, his glory, becomes Everyman's. If so, our present weapons technology renders that kind of immortalization a contradiction in terms: the warrior-linked quest for the eternal makes problematic the existence of the immediate future. But before we accept the inevitability of either nuclear or conventional immolation, we do well to make some distinctions.

When we consider the significance of the ancient mythological theme of the Hero as Warrior we discover that something more than technology has gone wrong. For, as Joseph Campbell tells us, the mythic image of the warrior is that of merely one of the "thousand faces" of the hero. The Hero as Warrior—like the Hero as Saint, World Redeemer, Artist, Emperor, Tyrant, Lover, etcetera—follows the heroic life-trajectory of the call to adventure, the crossing of the threshold into another realm of action and experience, the road of trials, and eventually the return to his people to whom he can convey a new dimension of wisdom and of "freedom to live." Campbell goes further in describing this transformative function of the hero and tells us that "the sword edge of the hero-warrior flashes with the energy of the creative Source; before it fall the shells of the Outworn."

For the mythological hero is the champion not of things become but of things becoming; the dragon to be slain by him is precisely the monster of the status quo. Holdfast, the keeper of the past . . . the enemy is great and conspicuous in the seat of power; he is enemy, dragon, tyrant, because he turns to his own advantage the authority of his position. . . . The mythological hero, reappearing from the darkness that is the source of the shapes of the day, brings a knowledge of the secret of the tyrant's doom. . . . The hero-deed is a continuous shattering of the crystallizations of the moment. The cycle rolls; mythology focuses on the growing point. Transformation, fluidity, not stubborn ponderosity, is the characteristic of the living God.[2]

The symbolism is that of killing in the service of regeneration: "the great figure of the moment exists only to be broken, cut into chunks, and scattered abroad." And the Hero as Warrior, like his religious or artistic counterparts, acts in the service of man's spiritual achievement: "the ogre-tyrant is the champion of the prodigious fact, the hero the champion of the creative life."[3]

The nature of the wisdom, redemption, or enlightenment the hero brings to his people has less to do with the Oedipus complex and the son's confrontation with the father, as the early psychoanalytic interpretation had it, than with man's perpetual confrontation with death. Death is not eliminated, or wished away, but rather transcended by a newly envisaged enduring principle, by an activated sense of being part of eternal forms. The deeds performed by the Hero as Warrior thus reawaken a people's sense of its "immortal cultural and racial substance,"[4] or what we spoke of as the biological or biosocial mode; as well as that of lasting achievement (the creative mode); and, in many cases the most intense form of psychic exhilaration (the mode of experiential transcendence). The hero in any myth becomes the giver of immortality. And the Hero as Warrior incarnates this symbolic quest; he kills not to destroy life but to enlarge, perpetuate, and enhance life.

But warriors and their myths are readily absorbed by specific societies, to be recreated in their own hierarchical, power-centered image. We then encounter the phenomenon of the warrior class, or what I shall call the socialized warrior. Now the allegedly heroic act, the killing of the enemy with whatever accompanying ritual, is performed to consolidate and reaffirm the existing social order. The socialized warrior thus easily lends himself to the corruptions of patriotic chauvinism, or to the spirit of slavishness which Karl Liebknecht called "the obedience of the corpse."*[5] We may extend that term to include the common "deadness" of both the robotized soldier and his enemy-victim.

This has been the way militarized states have rendered their conquests scared, and invested their socialized warriors with the mantle of the hero. The process began, as Campbell points out, with "the warrior-kings of antiquity [who] regarded their work in the spirit of the monster-slayer," and has continued ever since so that "This formula . . . of the shining hero going against the

---

* "The obedience of the corpse" is the literal translation of the German, *kadavergehorsam.*

dragon has been the great device of self-justification for all crusades."[6] Even the great Athenian statesman Pericles was prone
to this "self-justification," no less than the Spartans he opposed:
In 431 B.C., he urged that his countrymen go to war and "be
determined that, whether the reason put forward is big or small.
we are not in any case going to climb down or hold our posses-
sions under a constant threat of interference"; and a year later,
in his celebrated funeral oration for fallen Athenian warriors, he
asked that the parents of the dead recognize the "good fortune"
of their sons who were able to "end their lives with honor" in a
way that "Life was set to a measure where death and happiness
went hand in hand."[7]

But that expression of Athenian democratic imperialism was
still a far cry from the kind of glorification of the socialized warrior that existed in other ancient societies, as described and
condemned by Aristotle: the ancient law in Macedonia "that he
who had not killed an enemy should wear a halter"; a custom
among the Scythians that "no one who had not slain his man was
allowed to drink out of the cup which was handed around at a
certain feast"; and a practice of the Iberians of indicating the
number of enemies a man has slain "by the number of obelisks
. . . fixed in the earth round his tomb."[8] Here the worth of the
socialized warrior comes to be measured by concrete acts of
killing, and by a still more concrete "body count." Through
killing he achieves honor, fellowship, something close to a state
of grace. Only through killing can he connect with, and reinforce,
the immortalizing currents of his society and culture.

To reach the desired psychological state, the socialized warrior
has always required some kind of initiation process, a symbolic
form of death and rebirth that may coincide with his attainment
of adulthood. In that rite (now called *basic training*), his civil
identity, with its built-in restraints, is eradicated, or at least
undermined and set aside in favor of the warrior identity and its
central focus upon killing. Only through such a prescribed process can the warrior become psychically numbed toward killing and

dying, shielded from complexity, and totalized in his commitment to the warrior role.[9]

An energizing force in the socialized warrior, and in his "patriotic" citizen-followers, is what Josiah Royce called the "warspirit." Royce spoke of this spirit as a "fascinating and bloodthirsty form of humane but furious ecstasy."[10] It is the feeling of being "transported," or what we have referred to as "experiential transcendence." The word "humane" is paradoxical but not entirely inaccurate; it has to do with the "love of the group," the "blood bond" of those who kill, defend, or survive together. In other words the socialized warrior has an "as-if" relationship to the mythological hero. He too confronts, and at times seems to conquer, death. But in the end his specific acts of killing and dying are not transcended in a way that provides a new vision of existence; rather these acts are revered in themselves, and in the service of group aggrandizement.

The socialized warrior thus becomes a distorted, literalized, and manipulated version of the Hero as Warrior. The larger purpose of the heroic quest gives way to cultivation of skill in killing and surviving. That skill can combine courage, loyalty, and technical proficiency (as, for instance, in the case of the gunman or "gun" of the early American West), but its relationship to the immortalizing principle is dubious and strained, if not falsified.

There are, of course, many in-between experiences. Revolutionary guerrillas are a case in point. By subsuming their acts of war (and the courage and skill required for those achievements) in a political-ethical vision for their people, they enter directly into the hero myth. But once they achieve social power and sometimes even before that they, too, tend to become converted into, or replaced by, more narrowly gauged socialized warriors.* If

---

* Twentieth-century China is a good example of this process. The Cultural Revolution of the late 1960s can be understood as an attempt to sustain the heroic aura so magnificently achieved by the guerrillas (the early revolutionaries themselves), almost two decades after power had been achieved and these guerrillas had given way to "socialized warriors" or their equivalents in political and cultural realms. Hence my title, *Revolutionary Immortality*, for the study I made of these events.

there is such a thing here as a lesson of history it is that the forces of entrenched power much prefer manipulable socialized warriors to more unmanageable heroes who are dedicated to principles which go beyond either themselves or their country's rulers. The result has been the murderous missions of socialized warriors. I have elsewhere suggested that the victimizing impulse can be understood as an aberrant quest for immortalization, one in which the victimizers require a contrast between their own group which 'lives forever,' and that of their victims, which is death-tainted and must die.[11]

Yet there have been dissenting voices—those who have freed themselves from the powerful cultural pseudomythology to take a hard look at the killing and dying. Those critics of the cult of the warrior have insisted that we feel the pain of the warriors' victims. They reject the conventional image of noble killing and insist upon calling it collective murder; and the individual warrior's death becomes absurd rather than heroic.

High technology brings further strain upon the warrior ethos. Automated weaponry is not conducive to the idea of glory. People no longer look for an ultimate meaning in the specific feats of heroes of war. To be sure, the military proliferates everywhere; but the warrior ethos becomes increasingly weak as a fountain of immortalization. Where versions of it remain psychologically viable, as in the case of militant revolutionaries, war and killing are experienced as means to social revitalization—and the warrior ethos gives way to the myth of the hero.

But old pseudomyths do not die easily, especially when they make contact with basic human emotions. As in the case of reactions to so many symbols and images undermined by new historical forces, there is confusion and ambivalence rather than full rejection or genuine replacement. In the United States we can observe a particularly excruciating conflict between a still predominant effort to hang onto, and technicize, the cult of the socialized warrior, and a heretical, disorganized, but nonetheless enlarging effort to replace it with an immortalizing cult of peace and peace-makers. Yet little is really understood about how such a shift can be achieved on a scale large enough to matter.

No wonder, then, that the country has been fascinated by the phenomenon of 'antiwar warriors' (or former warriors). I refer of course to those Vietnam veterans who, publicly and militantly, turned against their own war. For this to have occurred while a war was still in progress is unprecedented. They raised questions not only about America's but about everyone's version of the socialized warrior and the war system and exposed their country's counterfeit claim of a just war.

Antiwar veterans generate a special kind of force, no less spiritual than political, as they publicly proclaim the endless series of criminal acts they have witnessed or participated in, contemptuously toss away their hard-won medals, reenact the Vietnam War by means of "search-and-destroy missions" in various American towns and cities—or, with bitterly ironic symbolism, occupy the Statue of Liberty or the Lincoln Memorial. Charles Oman, in his classic study of war, spoke of the veterans of the battles of the Middle Ages as "the best of soldiers while the war lasted . . . [but] a most dangerous and unruly race in times of truce or peace."[12] Can we say that war veterans have not changed? Or is there a new and significant quality in their "unruliness"—a quality that has to do with a transformation of the human spirit?

CHAPTER 2

America's New Survivors: The Image of My Lai

> A blot
> Amongst the bushes
> Of a ridge—a slot
> Of dryness—
> The head of a pin
> Nowhere to go,
> Nowhere to begin.
>
> —Burrows Younkin (from *Winning
> Hearts and Minds: War Poems
> by Vietnam Veterans*)

If it's dead it's VC. Because it's dead. If it's dead it *had* to be VC. And of course a corpse couldn't defend itself anyhow.

> —GI remembering My Lai

What am I doing here? We don't take any land. We don't give it back. We just mutilate bodies. What the fuck are we doing here?

> —GI recalling his feelings during a moment in Vietnam

THERE IS SOMETHING SPECIAL about Vietnam veterans. Everyone who has contact with them seems to agree that they are different from veterans of other wars. A favorite word to describe them is "alienated." Veterans Administration reports stress their sensitivity to issues of authority and autonomy. This group of veterans is seen as having "greater distrust of institutions and unwillingness to be awed by traditional authorities," so that "they are less willing to be passive recipients of our wisdom." The individual Vietnam veteran, it is said, "feels an intense positive identification with his own age group" and is part of "an unspoken 'pact of youth' which assures mutual safety from threats to their sense of individual identity."[1]

Even when sufficiently incapacitated to require hospitalization on a VA psychiatric ward, Vietnam veterans tend to stress the issue of the generation gap and of larger social problems rather than merely their own sickness. And there is evidence, confirmed by my own observations, that large numbers of them feel themselves to be "hurting" and in need of psychological help but avoid contact with the Veterans Administration. They associate it with the war-military-government establishment, with the forces responsible for a hated ordeal, or with their suspicion (whether on the basis of hearsay or personal experience) that VA doctors are likely to interpret their rage at everything connected with the war as no more than their own individual problem. The result has been (again in the words of VA observers) "degrees of bitterness, distrust, and suspicion of those in positions of authority and responsibility."

To be sure, these patterns can occur in veterans of any war— along with restless shifting of jobs and living arrangements, and difficulty forming or maintaining intimate relationships. These precise tendencies among World War II veterans, men who had "lost a sense of personal sameness and historical continuity," led Erik Erikson to evolve his concepts of "identity crisis" and "loss of 'ego identity.' "[2]

But these men give the impression of something more. Murray Polner, who interviewed more than two hundred Vietnam veterans of diverse views and backgrounds concluded that "not one of them—hawk, dove, or haunted—was entirely free of doubt about the nature of the war and the American role in it." As a group they retain the "gnawing suspicion that 'it was all for nothing.' " Polner concluded that "never before have so many questioned as much, as these veterans have, the essential rightness of what they were forced to do."[3] Beyond just being young and having been asked to fight a war, these men have a sense of violated personal and social order, of fundamental break in human connection, which they relate to conditions imposed upon them by the war in Vietnam.[4]

Some of the quality of that war experience is revealed in the following recollection of My Lai by a GI who was there, and whom I shall henceforth refer to as "the My Lai survivor":

The landscape doesn't change much. For days and days you see just about nothing. It's unfamiliar—always unfamiliar. Even when you go back to the same place, it's unfamiliar. And it makes you feel as though, well, there's nothing left in the world but this. . . . You have the illusion of going great distances and traveling like hundreds of miles . . . and you end up in the same place because you're only a couple of miles away. . . . But you feel like it's not all real. It couldn't possibly be. We couldn't still be in this country. We've been walking for days. . . . You're in Vietnam and they're using real bullets. . . . Here in Vietnam they're actually shooting people for no reason. . . . Any other time you think, it's such an extreme. Here you can go ahead and shoot them for nothing. . . . As a matter of fact it's even . . . smiled upon, you know. Good for you. Everything is backwards. That's part of the kind of unreality of the thing. To the grunt [infantryman] this isn't backwards. He doesn't understand. . . . But something [at My Lai] was missing. Something you thought was real that would accompany this. It wasn't there. . . . There was something missing in the whole business that made it seem like it really wasn't happening.*. . .

The predominant emotional tone here is all-encompassing absurdity and moral inversion. The absurdity has to do with a sense of being alien and profoundly lost, yet at the same time locked into a situation as meaningless and unreal as it is deadly. The moral inversion, eventuating in a sense of evil, has to do not only with the absolute reversal of ethical standards but with its occurrence in absurdity, without inner justification, so that the killing is rendered naked.

This overall emotional sense, which I came to view as one of *absurd evil,* is conveyed even more forcefully by something said in a rap group by a former "grunt." He had been talking about the horrors of combat and told how, after a heavy air strike on an NLF unit, his company came upon a terrible scene of dismembered corpses. Many of the men then began a kind of wild victory dance, in the course of which they mutilated the bodies still further. He recalled wondering to himself:

What am I doing here? We don't take any land. We don't give it back. We just mutilate bodies. What the fuck are we doing here?

Whatever the element of retrospective judgment in this kind of recollection, the image was characteristic. During another rap group discussion about how men felt about what they were doing in Vietnam, a man asked: "What the hell *was* going on? What the fuck *were* we doing?"

* Note a similar passage from a description of World War I: "How long has it been? Weeks—months—years? Only days. We see time pass in the colourless faces of the dying, we cram food into us, we run, we throw, we shoot, we kill, we lie about, we are feeble and spent, and nothing supports us but the knowledge that there are feebler, still more spent, still more helpless ones there who, with staring eyes, look upon us as gods that escaped death many times."[5]

These questions express a sense of the war's total lack of order or structure, the feeling that there was no genuine purpose, that nothing could ever be secured or gained, and that there could be no measurable progress. We may say that there was no genuine "script" or "scenario" of war that could provide meaning or even sequence or progression, a script within which armies clash, battles are fought, won, or lost, and individual suffering, courage, cowardice, or honor can be evaluated. Nor could the patrols seeking out an elusive enemy, the ambushes in which Americans were likely to be the surprised victims, or the "search-and-destroy missions" lashing out blindly at noncombatants achieve the psychological status of meaningful combat ritual. Rather, these became part of the general absurdity, the antimeaning. So did the "secret movements" on this alien terrain, since, as one man put it, "Little kids could tell us exactly where we would set up the next night." The men were adrift in an environment not only strange and hostile but offering no honorable encounter, no warrior grandeur.

Now there are mutilations, midst absurdity and evil, in any war. Men who fight wars inevitably become aware of the terrible disparity between romantic views of heroism expressed "back home" and the reality of degradation and unspeakable suffering they have witnessed, experienced, and caused. One thinks of the answer given by Audie Murphy, much-decorated hero of World War II, to the question put to him about how long it takes a man to get over his war experiences. Murphy's reply, recorded in his obituary, was that one never does. What he meant was that residual inner conflicts—survivor conflicts—stay with one indefinitely. These conflicts, as I was able to generalize from my Hiroshima work, have to do with anxiety in relationship to an indelible death imprint, death guilt inseparable from that imprint, various forms of prolonged psychic numbing and suppression of feeling, profound suspicion of the counterfeit (or of "counterfeit nurturance"), and an overall inability to give significant inner form—to "formulate"—one's war-linked death immersion. This impaired survivor formulation undoubtedly was a factor in Murphy's repeated difficulties and disappointments after his return from his war, as it has been in the unrealized lives and premature deaths of many war heroes*; and, indeed, in the paradox quoted earlier (from Charles Omen) about warriors during the Middle Ages being "the best of soldiers while the war lasted . . . [but] a most dangerous and unruly race in times of truce or peace."

Yet veterans have always come to some terms with their war experiences though some formulation of their survival that permits them to overcome much of their death anxiety and death guilt, diffuse suspiciousness and numbing. Crucial even to this partial resolution of survivor conflict is the veteran's capacity to believe that his war had purpose and significance beyond the immediate horrors he witnessed. He can then connect his own actions with ultimately humane principles, and can come to feel that he had performed a dirty but necessary job. He may even be able to experience renewed feelings of continuity or symbolic immortality around these larger principles, side by side with his residual survivor pain and conflict.

But the central fact of the Vietnam War is that no one really

---

* A more extreme parallel is the case of Sergeant Dwight W. Johnson, who won a Medal of Honor in Vietnam for racing through heavy crossfire to rescue a close buddy from a burning tank, and then, when the tank had exploded killing the rest of its inhabitants, hunting down and killing face-to-face, in retaliatory rage, five to twenty Vietnamese soldiers. He required psychiatric hospitalization immediately after the episode, as he did later on back in the United States, when he was thought to be suffering from "depression caused by post-Vietnam adjustment problem." He never got over his persistent "bad dreams," his guilt over having survived while his buddies died—or, as one psychiatrist put it, for "winning a high honor for the one time in his life when he lost complete control of himself," which made him wonder: "What would happen if I lost control of myself in Detroit and behaved like I did in Vietnam?" Three years after his heroic episode, he was killed, at the age of twenty-four, by the manager of a grocery store he was alleged to have attempted to hold up at gunpoint. All this was recorded in a *New York Times* obituary of May 26, 1971, as was his mother's concluding comment: "Sometimes I wonder if Skip [Sergeant Johnson] tired of this life and needed someone else to pull the trigger."

believes in it. The larger purposes put forth to explain the American presence—repelling outside invaders, or giving the people of the South an opportunity to choose their own form of government—are directly contradicted by the overwhelming evidence a GI encounters that *he* is the outside invader, that the government he has come to defend is justly hated by the people he has come to help, and that he, the American helper is hated by them most of all.[6] Even those who seem to acquiesce to these claims do so, as Polner's findings suggest, with profound inner doubt, and in response to tenuous and defensive "psychological work."

Nor do many actually fighting the war take seriously the quasi-religious impulse to "fight the communists." Rather, their gut realization that something is wrong with this war is expressed in combat briefings (often by lieutenants or captains) as described to me by a number of former GIs:

I don't know why *I'm* here. *You* don't know why *you're* here. But since we're *both* here, we might as well try to do a good job and do our best to stay alive.

This is the very opposite of calling forth a heroic ideal or an immortalizing purpose. And while it is true that survival is the preoccupation of men in any war, this kind of briefing is not only a total disclaimer of any purpose beyond survival but a direct transmission of the absurdity and antimeaning pervading the Vietnam War. That transmission has a distinct psychological function. It inserts a modicum of out-front honesty into the situation's basic absurdity, so that the absurdity itself can become shared. And the way is paved for the intense cooperation, brotherhood, and mutual love characteristic of and necessary to military combat. In the end, however, everybody feels the absence of larger purpose. Hence the deadpan professional observation by a Veterans Administration psychiatrist, in response to a query from his chief medical director concerning the special characteristics and problems of the "Vietnam Era Veteran": "Vietnam combat veterans tend to see their experience as an exercise in survival rather than a defense of national values."[7]

The distinction is important. Huizinga, in discussing the connection between play and war, speaks of the concept of the "ordeal," its relationship to "the idea of glory," and ultimately to the warrior's quest for "a decision of holy validity."[8] This theological vocabulary conveys well the immortalizing appeal battle holds for the warrior. But in Vietnam one undergoes the "ordeal" or test without the possibility of that "idea of glory" or "decision of holy validity." There is all of the pain but none of the form.

What we find instead is best understood as an *atrocity-producing situation*. It is created by a special combination of elements that Jean-Paul Sartre has described as inevitably genocidal: a counterinsurgency war undertaken by an advanced industrial society against a revolutionary movement of an underdeveloped country, in which the revolutionary guerrillas are inseparable from the rest of the population. Those elements in turn contribute greatly to the draconian American military policies in Vietnam: the "free-fire zone" (where every civilian is a target), and the "search-and-destroy mission" (on which everyone and everything can be killed, or as the expression has it, "wasted"); the extensive use of plant defoliants that not only destroy the overall ecology of Vietnam but, if encountered in sufficient concentration by pregnant women, human embryos as well; and the almost random saturation of a small country with an unprecedented level of technological destruction and firepower both from the air and on the ground. These external historical factors and military policies lead, in turn, to a compelling internal sequence that constitutes the psychological or experiential dimension of the atrocity-producing situation.

My Lai provides a grotesque illustration of that sequence, and makes clear that *the psychology of the survivor is central even to the killing process*. I was able to reconstruct events at My Lai on the basis of my interviews with the veteran who had been there, additional informal talks with several writers who have investigated various aspects of the atrocity, and descriptions of the event in various articles and books.[9] My assumption, based upon all this (and much other) evidence is that My Lai is exceptional only in its dimensions, and that these very dimensions reveal the essence of the atrocity-producing situation.

Many forms of desensitization and rage contributed to My Lai, some of them having to do with specifically American aberrations around race, class, and masculinity. But my assumption in speaking of an atrocity-producing situation is that, given the prevailing external conditions, men of very divergent backgrounds—indeed just about *anyone*—can enter into the "psychology of slaughter."[10] This assumption is born out by an examination of the step-by-step sequence by which the American men who eventually went to My Lai came to internalize and then act upon an irresistible image of slaughter.

During basic training, the men encountered (as did most recruits) drill sergeants and other noncommissioned officers who were veterans of Vietnam, and as such had a special aura of authority and demonic mystery. From these noncoms the recruit heard stories of Vietnam, of how tough and "dirty, rotten, and miserable" (as one remembered being told) it was there. He also heard descriptions of strange incidents in which it became clear that Vietnamese civilians were being indiscriminately killed —tales of Americans creeping up to village areas and tossing grenades into "hootches," of artillery strikes on inhabited areas, and of brutal treatment of Vietnamese picked up during patrols or combat sweeps. Sometimes pictures of badly mutilated Vietnamese corpses were shown to him to illustrate the tales.

Here and later on there is a striking contrast between the formal instruction (given rotely if at all) to kill only military adversaries, and the informal message (loud and clear) to kill just about everyone. That message, as the My Lai survivor put it, is that "It's okay to kill them," and in fact "That's what you're supposed to do"—or as a former marine received it: "You've gotta go to Vietnam, you've gotta kill the gooks."[11] The process resembles the Japanese use of *haragei* or "stomach talk"—perhaps more accurately translated as a "gut message"—in which what is really meant and acted upon is the opposite of what is actually said. Thus, Japanese statesmen, toward the end of World War II, publicly proclaimed that Japan must fight to the last man; the meaning intended—Japan has no recourse but to surrender—was considered too dangerous to state directly because of the threat of right-wing assassinations. Not surprisingly, there was considerable confusion about what the words were actually supposed to mean.[12] Similarly, American leaders would find it politically inexpedient, and morally unacceptable (to themselves as well as to others) to state outright that all Vietnamese (or "gooks") are fair game; instead they turn the other cheek, undergo their own psychic numbing, while permitting—indeed making inevitable—the message of slaughter.* In both cases the stomach talk reflects profound moral contradictions—something close to what we shall later speak of as a counterfeit universe— as well as deep-seated ambivalence all around. But in contrast to the Japanese ambiguity, the American version is all too clear, the message unmistakable.

Thus the message of slaughter becomes inseparable from the death-and-rebirth process of basic training. The coercive desym-

---

* Sometimes the informal message of slaughter can be conveyed by such crude symbolism as what the marines came to call the "rabbit lesson": On the last day before leaving for Vietnam, the staff NCO holds a rabbit as he lectures on escape, evasion, and survival in the jungle. The men become intrigued by the rabbit, fond of it, and then the NCO "cracks it in the neck, skins it, disembowels it . . . and then they throw the guts out into the audience." As one marine explained: "You can get anything out of that you want, but that's your last lesson you catch in the United States before you leave for Vietnam."[13] Prior to the exposure of My Lai, very little was likely to be said about those provisions of the U.S. Army Field Manual, "The Law of Land Warfare," which define as war crimes various forms of massacres and atrocities including the killing or harming of civilians and specify that "members of the Armed Forces are bound to obey only lawful orders."[14] And when these principles were taught, *that* unconvincing lesson was likely to be treated as "stomach talk" for the more compelling rabbit-lesson principle.

bolization of basic training, its "systematic stripping process" in which the civilian self is "deliberately denuded" so that the recruit can "reject his preexisting identity . . . envelop himself instead in the institutional identity of the military organization . . . [and] accept his impotence in the face of military discipline and recognize the crushing recrimination it can inflict if he should seek to challenge it"—all this becomes a means by which he is not only "acculturated to the military system" but also acculturated, in an anticipatory sense, to the atrocity-producing situation awaiting him in Vietnam. The "masculine initiation rite" of basic training and the "manly status"[15] acquired in it become inseparable from what is best called the *machismo of slaughter*. That machismo is in turn directly associated with simple fear, with the message that *any* Vietnamese—man, woman, or infant —may be setting the booby trap that will kill you; the implication being that to survive you must "kill them all."

For many at My Lai the message was reinforced in concrete racial terms by the special environment of the "Jungle Training Center" at Schofield Barracks in Hawaii: facsimile Vietnamese village with booby-trapped huts and slant-eyed dummy targets. There Charlie Company of the Americal Division, initially in disarray, was taken over and revitalized by an able and on the whole well-liked commanding officer, whose somewhat over-zealous inclinations earned him the nickname "Mad Dog Medina." The by now specific image of slaughter became more intense and immediate shortly after the company's arrival in Vietnam. They quickly became aware of random killing: "If you can shoot artillery and bombs in there every night," one of the men was quoted as saying, "how can the people in there be worth so much?"[16] Still more graphic was the sight of a troop carrier driving by with "about twenty human ears tied to the antenna."[17] The men were at first shocked ("It was kind of hard to believe. They actually had ears on the antenna"), but not long afterwards some of the men, having spotted a few Vietcong and called in artillery, came back with an ear of their own, to the approval of their commanding officer: "Medina was happy; it was his first kill."[18]

Others began to mark their estimated kills with notches on their rifles. The imagery is that of the hunt. The 'animals' one shoots serve merely to provide trophies, evidence of one's prowess.

But the men were hardly relaxed in their 'sport'—the company spent its first ten weeks in Vietnam in a confusing, fatiguing, and frightening combination of construction work, patrols, and fruitless maneuvers. The men underwent a gradual but profound process of numbing, reflected in their increasing callousness and brutality toward Vietnamese. They justified their behavior by the unpredictability and 'unfairness' of an environment in which friendly gestures toward a particular village were no guarantee against sniper fire: "We give the medical supplies and they come and kick our ass."[19] This image of justified slaughter was furthered by the resentful observation that South Vietnamese troops seemed to be "laying around doing nothing," causing the men to wonder, "Why should I fight for them?" Still stronger feelings could be expressed on a similar basis, as quoted to me during an individual interview: "I'm gonna go out and get me a gook—because those bastards are responsible for me being here."

And there is the perpetually enraging elusiveness of the enemy, as described by the My Lai survivor:

No matter how much effort you put into it, you can't find him. You can't lay your hands on him. And the fact that he also might be anywhere, you know . . . as though you were hunting a specific deer and you don't know which one it is and there's a deer herd all over you.

There is, in other words, confusion and reversal within this hunting image: the invisible enemy, being able to track down the GI, becomes the hunter, the GI the hunted.* The only possibility

---

* The "deer" in the image suggest a sense of one's enemies as relatively gentle creatures, as does a good deal of additional imagery in which genuinely human contact with the Vietcong and North Vietnamese is sought. But they can also be seen as tough, determined, and strong; and where there has been evidence of mutilations by them, as brutal.

for overcoming this combination of helpless passivity, bitter impotence, and general terror lay in a real confrontation with the enemy—in getting him (as some of the men would put it) "to stand up and fight like a man." For the men of Company C that idea of a true battle—of a *genuine ordeal*—became something of a dream, no doubt both wishful and fearful.

The combat they actually did experience over the next month hardly lived up to that dream. Instead of a proud ordeal, they experienced only a series of hit-and-run blows and losses. There was the first death, always a profound event for men in combat, shattering the myth of group invulnerability and thrusting the men into the conflicts of the survivor. Each inwardly asks himself the terrible survivor question—"Why did *he* die, and not me?" Each struggles with the unconscious sense that his own life was purchased through his buddy's death, with the variety of ways in which he feels responsible for that death. One must make it up to the man killed, do something that gives significance to his death, in order to justify one's own survival and avoid the experience of overwhelming death guilt.[20] In combat that means getting back at the enemy, and in most wars there are prescribed forms for doing that—battlefield rituals in which one can demonstrate courage and initiative that take their toll on the enemy. In the absence of such forms, and for the most part of a visible enemy, the men were left with their acute survivor grief, with their sense of guilt and loss, which could in turn become quickly transformed into rage.

Hence, Company C's first death—that of a GI named Bill Weber—was "the turning point. Suddenly we realized a guy could get killed out there. So let's get our revenge before we go." Their lieutenant also changed: "He was no longer a GI [preoccupied with petty regulations]. He got to be a savage too."[21] After several additional ambushes in which men were wounded, the company experienced its greatest blow: a minefield disaster in which twenty percent of the men were incapacitated—four killed and twenty-eight severely wounded (another report had six killed and twelve severely wounded). Now survivor guilt became much greater: "There were men dying," as one of them later put it, "and you weren't one of them." More than guilt, there was the sense that the company as a unit—virtually the entire universe the men then inhabited—had been annihilated. Extreme images were needed to reconstruct self and world, and these, not surprisingly, took the form of absolute revenge. Fantasies previously held by individual men now were pooled, as the My Lai survivor recalls, into open discussions of "wiping the whole place out," or what he called "the Indian idea . . . the only good gook is a dead gook." The idea of the enemy, though increasingly hazy, was also broadly extended to include "anybody but them, anybody but an American soldier."*

Finally, there was Sergeant Cox—blown to pieces by an artillery shell he found in a booby trap he was attempting to dismantle. These hidden, hand-set, and grotesquely deadly arrangements, released by either direct touch, a timing device, or (through wiring) by the hand of an outside observer, contributed greatly to the combination of helplessness and terror the men felt. The name given to the devices suggests the sense in which they not only maim the victim but make him into a hoodwinked fool—they are "trap[s] for the booby."[22] The men had special feelings toward Cox, an older person with extensive war experience whom many of them leaned on for emotional support. His grotesque death exacerbated their sense of loss, their fear, and above all their rage. The next day a memorial service was held for Cox and for the others recently killed. The importance of the occasion was marked by the presence of a chaplain, but the main state-

* The My Lai survivor claimed that there was strong evidence that the mines had been set, not by Vietcong, but by our Korean allies who had encamped in that area a short time before—which would place much of the responsibility with higher American headquarters, since they would presumably have been notified about the mines by the South Koreans. In any case, he noted that the men resisted this idea and preferred to place all the blame on the Vietcong (or "the gooks") so that their imagery of revenge could remain justified.

ment made was the combination eulogy-pep talk delivered by
Captain Medina, the Company Commander.

Eulogies have the function of extending the significance of the
life just ended; survivors can then justify remaining alive by
taking on the mission of perpetuating that life, by carrying on
the dead man's work. There are many versions of what Medina
said that day, but all accounts agree that he spoke movingly
about Cox and the other men who had been killed, brought his
listeners close to tears, and provided them with a compelling survivor mission. It was something like:

We lost a lot of guys. Pinkville caused us a lot of hell. Now we're
gonna get our revenge. Everything goes.[23]

Or, as the My Lai survivor recalls Medina saying, "Here's our
chance to get back at them. . . . There are no innocent civilians
in this area"—so that the men listening could conclude: "We
were supposed to wipe out the whole area—waste it." Others
remembered similar phrases such as "kill everything in the village" or "destroy everything with life"[24]—the message somewhere in-between exhortation and military orders, and perhaps
received as both. There was also the strong impression (according to the My Lai survivor) that "he wanted a big body count
. . . [because] this was a chance to go out and really show the
brigade that we're something." Whatever Medina's actual words,
his eulogy-pep talk provided the men with a concrete 'survivor
mission' that gave significance to deaths being mourned. Now
they had a psychological link between the deaths that had so
overwhelmed them and the actions they could take in order to
reconstitute themselves.

Medina apparently did not give a direct order to kill women
and children. Rather, he combined "combat orders" from
above,* his own impulses as a zealous officer, and an appeal to

---

* Later investigations of My Lai revealed that Medina had attended a higher-
level briefing earlier that day, at which a similar "pep talk" had been given by

the shared emotional state of his company—which, within the standards prevailing in that environment, resulted in a logic of slaughter. His talk was both command and release—as the My Lai survivor put it, "more or less permission . . . just sort of like, 'You can do it. . . . Whatever you do is up to you.'"

Medina's talk also enabled the men to form a rather strong psychic image anticipating their actions the next day, the day of My Lai.† The nature of that image undoubtedly varied, and in many cases contained elements of actual combat; but it mainly had to do with diffuse destruction and killing. Thus, one of the men recalled that, as he listened to Medina talking of burning huts, destroying livestock and food supplies, and poisoning wells, another man leaned toward his ear and said: "It's gonna be a slaughter, you watch."[26] The My Lai survivor described his own anticipatory image, which, significantly, was in the third person:

They could run into a bunch of ARVNs and wipe them out—or Koreans and wipe them out . . . or they could run into a bunch of civilians. I thought one way or another somebody is going to get shot to pieces and it would just as soon be civilians. . . .

Following an artillery and gunship assault, the men landed from their helicopters at about 8:00 A.M. on the day of My Lai, fully armed for combat. The killings started almost immediately —some of them seemingly random and individual, but the larger number performed en masse, after 'herding' together groups of

---

Colonel Oran K. Henderson, who had just taken command of the brigade. Henderson was quoted as saying that he wanted to "get rid of [the Vietcong unit located in that area] once and for all," that he wanted the three companies to "get more aggressive." The Task Force Commander, Colonel Barker, also spoke and was reported to say that he "wanted the hootches burned, and he wanted the tunnels filled in, and then he wanted the livestock and chickens run off, killed, or destroyed."[25]

† This kind of anticipatory image is of enormous importance, as it has a great deal to do with the kind of behavior that follows. One can in fact say that all behavior occurs in response to some form of anticipatory image, which is in turn continuously modified on the basis of past and immediate experience. These issues are discussed at greater length in *The Broken Connection*.

men, women, and children, and then firing into them. Some Vietnamese were first manhandled; several of the younger women were raped and then killed; homes were set fire, and livestock were shot. The killing was consistent with the men's anticipatory image of slaughter; it was exacerbated by the direct zeal of certain individuals—as for instance, the by now well-known orders of Lieutenant William L. Calley to "take care of" and "waste" large groups of captured Vietnamese. There was at no time any opposition, and no Vietcong were found. Most of the killing was done during the first two hours. By the time the company took its lunch break at about 11:00 A.M., between four hundred and five hundred residents of the village were dead. It later turned out that an additional hundred Vietnamese were killed that morning in a neighboring village by another company from the same task force, involved the same "combat operation."[27]

During all this killing the men behaved in many ways *as if* they were in a combat situation. The My Lai survivor noted that they kneeled and crouched while shooting—"like some kind of fire fight with somebody." For, as he went on to explain:

If you're actually thinking in terms of a massacre of murder, going in and shooting a bunch of defenseless people, why crouch? Why get down? Why do any of this? You must have something else on your mind. You must be thinking there's a possibility that you're going to get it yourself . . . that they pose some kind of a threat to you. . . .

He went even further in emphasizing the confused perceptions of the men (his continued use of the second person suggesting that he himself shared some of this confusion): "Because your judgment is all screwed up . . . they actually look like the enemy, or what you think is the enemy." What this, along with much additional evidence, suggests is that there existed in American soldiers at My Lai (and at other scenes of atrocity) the illusion, however brief, that, in gunning down old men, women, and babies, they had finally "engaged the enemy"—had finally got him to "stand up and fight."

One could say that the men sought to make this their "baptism of fire." The term is used for a soldier's first experience of actual combat conditions and is associated with the idea discussed earlier of an immortalizing ordeal. The combat conditions the men had already experienced—humiliating skirmishes and dev-astating encounter with mines and booby traps—lacked sufficient nobility or possibility for glory to qualify for this general cate-gory. So they sought their baptism, their beginning ordeal, at My Lai, and when that did not qualify either they acted as though it did. They were engaged in a double level of 'play': military combat, in any case, is a male game and they were engaged in a particularly murderous *imitation* (as-if rendition) of the game of combat. Even the play element, in other words, was degraded and desymbolized.

I thus encountered conflicting descriptions about the kind of emotion Americans demonstrated at My Lai. Some recollections had them gunning down the Vietnamese with "no expression on . . . [their] faces . . . very businesslike,"[28] with "breaks" for cigarettes or refreshments. Yet others described the men as hav-ing become "wild" or "crazy" in their killing, raping, and de-stroying. The My Lai survivor described one GI engaging in a "mad chase" after a pig, which he eventually bayoneted; and others, in uncontrolled ways, tossing grenades or firing powerful weapons into the fragile "hootches" that made up the village. There is psychological truth in both descriptions. The business-like demeanor of the men had to do with their advanced state of psychic numbing, a state enhanced by their (partial) sense of carrying out orders and of thereby being engaged in a 'profes-sional' military endeavor. The wildness and craziness had to do not only with the actual nature of what was going on (and the capacity of an observer to separate himself sufficiently from the situation, then or later, to contrast it with normal behavior) but also with the passions that lay beneath the numbing: the force of the 'survivor mission,' propelled as it was by death anxiety and death guilt. Thus, as they killed, the men were said to have shouted such things as "VC bastards, you dirty VC bastards," and "that's for Bill Weber," and "Cry, you dirty gook bastards, cry like you made us cry."[29] They were 'bearing witness' to the deaths of their buddies; only later could many come to understand that it had been *false* witness. Underneath the combination of numbness and passion in each man was the central or controlling image of slaughter energizing the actions of virtually all of them.

To be sure the image was accompanied by doubt ("We only had a half-assed idea of what we were supposed to do"[30]) to the point of emptiness: "The people didn't know what they were dying for and the guys didn't know why they were shooting them."[31] Yet that very emptiness and absurdity served as a further impetus toward killing—toward pressing the logic of slaughter to the very end, until some kind of meaning could be squeezed from it. The illusion—the as-if situation—is pressed to the limit, until one has no choice but to see it as real.*

For example, one very confused young soldier remembered, in the midst of the My Lai holocaust, trying to make up his mind whether or not to kill a dazed little boy with one arm already shot off. He remembered thinking that the boy was about the same

---

* The process of rendering the as-if situation real, by means of accelerating slaughter, is described by another GI in relationship to a different atrocity:

. . . wondering and peeking around between hootches and inside hootches we realized we were just in a village . . .and they were going about their tasks, hardly noticing us until we came in strength. That is, fifteen or twenty of us showed up at once. And then all of a sudden they . . . got a little excited . . . pretty soon . . . a couple of the NCOs were shouting orders to "take those two and put them over here and this one and put him with those two." And pretty soon we had a crowd of people there, all yelling and screaming and kicking and wondering what's going on. . . . Pretty soon . . . a shot or two'd go off and somebody would yell: "You dirty Vietcong bastard!"—you know, something like this. . . . I fired into the crowd myself in the excitement. And I saw a few people go down. . . . It was horrifying to me at the moment. But in order to justify it I did it more, you know. It doesn't seem logical, I guess. But as you do something absurd sometimes you . . . add to it, or maybe do it repetitively just to make that appear to be . . . some part of your makeup. . . .[32]

age as his own sister, and found himself wondering, "What if a foreign army was in my country and a soldier was looking at my sister just as I'm looking at this little boy. Would that foreign soldier have the guts to kill my sister?" He decided, "If he'd have the guts then I'd have the guts," and pulled the trigger.[33] So strong was the collective image (and now, program) of slaughter that intimations of wrongdoing or absurdity had to be subsumed by it, explained away within that image. By means of this bizarre criterion for guts or courage, the murder of a child is turned into a test or an ordeal. One met the test and stamped out inner doubt by carrying out the most extreme moral inversion and seeing the whole thing through to the end.

There was both compulsion and satisfaction in doing so. The My Lai veteran spoke of the killing as "scratching an itch . . . it's going to drive you nuts unless you do it." And he went on to explain:

You have a need to explode . . . and . . . like in Korea . . . and in World War II you could do it. When they used to have those battles I imagine a lot of guys were really tremendously relieved. . . . [At My Lai] they could just sit there and mow them down. And that's what I guess they wanted to do.

He admitted experiencing a similar impulse, which he consciously restrained:

It's a matter of controlling it, you know, saying, "Well . . . no, I can't do that. That's not right. I'd sure like to.". . . I think I can understand the men in the company because the things that were working on them were working on me too.

Another GI compared the situation to "the first time you masturbate. . . . You feel guilty because you think you shouldn't do it, yet somewhere you heard that it's perfectly natural and anyhow it's irresistible, so what the hell."[34]

Beyond this masturbatory imagery, there is sexual innuendo

throughout the descriptions of My Lai—the sense of men who had been inactivated and rendered impotent suddenly asserting a form of violent omnipotence. The pattern is epitomized by the rape-murders which took place. In one of these, as described by Gershen, a GI finds a girl alone outside of a hut, forces her inside, tears her clothes off, and just before mounting her has the following thoughts, paraphrased by Gershen:

. . . you dirty bitch you killed Wilson and you killed Weber and Cox and Rotger and Bell, and you got me out here and look what you're making me do and look what my buddies are doing, and I hate this war and it's your fault that I'm here.[35]

Though she resisted him at first, according to the account, she gradually showed pleasure and sexual passion. But the GI, still in a state of rage and confusion, shot her and burned the hut, "Because [still in Gershen's paraphrase] he knew he hated these people and he didn't know why he was doing it." The rape scene undoubtedly lent itself to distortions in its re-creation, but the way in which the rape itself is subsumed to the false witness of the survivor mission of "revenge," and ultimately to the overall image of slaughter, is nonetheless significant.

Some experienced a more general sense of satisfaction. Paul Meadlo, who did considerable firing and killing, much of it in compliance with Calley's on-the-spot orders, said (during a television interview eighteen months later) that immediately after My Lai he "felt good." He explained that feeling more fully on another occasion:

I lost buddies. I—I lost—I lost a good, damn buddy, Bobby Wilson. And it was on my conscience. So after I done it I felt good. But later on that day, it kept getting to me.[36]

Meadlo also said (during the same television interview) that "It seemed like the natural thing to do at the time"* "Natural"

* Later Meadlo's public position hardened, undoubtedly because of both legal and psychological pressures. During the Calley trial he pointedly used the term

here (as in the earlier reference to masturbation) means that slaughter was the norm in that situation; that it was psychologically necessary and felt psychologically right (however temporarily). In this sense the whole massacre was a "natural" consummation of the collective 'survivor mission' and accompanying image of slaughter. Once begun, the slaughter was self-perpetuating; each expression of it confirmed and strengthened the overall image. Carrying the massacre through to the end was related not only to completion or consummation but also perhaps to an impulse, at whatever level of consciousness, not to leave survivors to tell the tale. (As it turned out, there were survivors, both Vietnamese and American, who did just that.)

The sense of their survivor mission having been accomplished gave the men, almost for the first time, a sense that their efforts —their very deaths—had significance: "Until now, we were dying uselessly,"[38] was the way one of them put it. Men who had been extremely tense and distraught since the minefield incident now (according to the My Lai survivor) "more or less loosened up" and "seemed more relaxed." More than that, the company "became more effective."* Moreover, right after My Lai the Vietcong "disappeared," company casualties dropped, and "It seemed . . . there wasn't any threat anymore." Though he knew that there were other reasons for these developments, such as better awareness of minefields and the NLF's hit-and-run tactics, the overall psychic effect was that My Lai "almost made some kind of sense." He compared the situation to "baking something," using the wrong formula and the wrong ingredients and yet having it

"Vietcong" as interchangeable with My Lai villagers, and when asked about having joined in shooting women and babies sitting on the ground, he answered: "I assumed at every minute that they would counterbalance [counterattack] . . . [by means of] some sort of chain or a little string they had to give a little pull and they blow us up, things like that."[37]

* He thought that replacements the company received could have been helpful as well. In any case this new "effectiveness" was, at best, short-lived—before long the units involved at My Lai were broken up, and the entire Americal Division was disbanded.

"work." And since "Everything seemed to fit. . . . it made my arguments [against what was done at My Lai] sound a little bit hollow."

Buoyed by their new confidence, he explained, the men went on to find justification for what they did, claiming "They were all VC anyhow, and VC couldn't get along without their support" —even down to the killing of infants: "Well, they'll grow up [to help the VC]." Unlike higher military authorities, the men in no way sought to cover up what they had done—at least not to one another. On the contrary, they seemed pleased at their change in fortune: "Now instead of discussing the horrors of the mine-field incident, My Lai was the new thing they had to talk about." They compared notes, often boastfully, in the manner of men looking back at a battle:

How many did you get? . . . It was really something terrific. . . . How many I got . . . the record and all this other stuff. One guy was very proud of the record. It was over one hundred. . . . There were probably a lot of exaggerations.

There were also extensive and admiring discussions about technical functioning of weapons—the damage done by grenades, forty-five-caliber automatic pistols, and the extent to which a seventy-nine artillery shell will blow someone to pieces. In all this they were recreating My Lai, treating it *as if* it were a great battle and a noble victory, and themselves *as if* they were all-powerful warrior-heroes who had magnificently carried out their ordeal.

This kind of post-slaughter rationalizing and boasting was partly in the service of suppressing doubts about whether My Lai qualified as that kind of immortalizing event, doubts that could lead to the kind of guilt Paul Meadlo referred to when he said, "Later on that day, it kept getting to me." The next day Meadlo accidentally triggered a mine that blew off his right foot. Since he was quoted at the time as saying "God punished me" and as angrily informing Lieutenant Calley that "God will punish you for what you made me do," it was quite possible that self-punitive components of his sense of guilt contributed to this accident. For residual guilt was undoubtedly strong in many of the men, and was to emerge in various forms later on.* More impressive, however, and much more disturbing, is the extent to which guilt could be at least temporarily refused or sloughed off by means of the advanced numbing and perverse meaning extracted from the many levels of 'as if' pervading the environment. The most malignant actions can be performed with minimal guilt if there is a structure of meaning justifying them, even an illusory pseudo-formulation of the kind existing at My Lai. Only when achieving a certain independence from that environment and its pseudo-formulation can one begin to experience an appropriate sense of guilt. This way of avoiding guilt can render extremely dangerous any group of more or less ordinary people (that is, devoid of any diagnosable psychiatric illness) who happen to possess lethal weapons, while themselves possessed by lethal (and numbed) impulses toward false witness.

This state of numbed false witness was the norm at My Lai, as it has been for Americans throughout Vietnam. One had to be a bit exceptional or, in that situation 'abnormal,' in order to avoid taking part in slaughter. The My Lai survivor, who did not fire at My Lai, was heard muttering during the killing, "It's wrong, it's wrong." But he had long been 'maladjusted' to the combat situation—not in the sense of being unable or unwilling to fight, as he believed in his country and was a soldier of outstanding size, strength, and ability—but in his mounting disapproval of the way the men in his unit were treating the Vietnamese, and his increasing alienation from them on that basis. Well before

* Gershen describes the men in Charlie Company whom he visited more than eighteen months after My Lai, as "frightened, conscience-stricken, terrified kids." One of them "still sees bodies in front of his eyes at night," another "feels terribly guilt-ridden," two more "have had nervous breakdowns," and at least four have difficulty finding or holding or concentrating at jobs. Nor did refraining from killing at My Lai prevent one from feeling guilty later on, as we shall see in the case of the man we have been referring to as the My Lai survivor.

My Lai he had reached the point where "I often got along better with the Vietnamese than with the guys in my outfit."

While it is difficult to know exactly why he was able to join the handful of men who stepped out of the norm and did not participate in the firing, three long-standing psychological patterns seemed significant. First, he had sensitive access to guilt on the basis of particularly strong feelings of right and wrong imbued by family and by protracted Catholic religious training. Second, his lifelong inclination to be a loner, to engage in activities that kept him both physically and psychically separated from others, helped him to maintain a certain degree of autonomy from group influence and from the atrocity-producing situation itself. Third, he had an unusually strong sense of military pride and identification, a form of warrior ethos stressing honor; in Vietnam, and especially at My Lai, he felt both the code and himself to be violated.

After My Lai, he was further isolated from the others by his sense of disappointment in the few men he had been close to: "I'd seen people I thought I could depend on . . . that were going ahead and shooting, shooting people up like that." By joining in, in other words, his friends had failed to give further support or reality—had, in Buber's sense, failed to "confirm" him in his own autonomous stand. Moreover, such were the group pressures that the few others who apparently did not fire tended to hide that fact. As one man, who concentrated on killing animals in order to avoid shooting at people explained:

I didn't do it [kill people]. But nobody saw me not doing it. So nobody got on me.[39]

As the only one in his unit publicly identified with opposition to My Lai, he felt himself somewhat ostracized. This made him uneasy, and he was himself sufficiently sensitive to group pressures to speak cautiously about the event and hide much of his revulsion. Moreover, all this, and the continuing 'as-if logic' and illusion surrounding the event, caused him to experience strong doubts about his own critical views. Eight months later, just before leaving Vietnam, he encountered Ronald Ridenhour, an acquaintance (from earlier days in the unit) who had not been at My Lai but had heard stories of the slaughter and was gathering information for his eventual exposure of the incident to the American public. The My Lai survivor spoke to Ridenhour at length, contributed much to that store of information, and at the same time experienced great personal relief. For the encounter convinced him that

I wasn't the only nut. . . . I wasn't really crazy. [Condemning what happened] was the right thing.

He was finally confirmed in his own previously isolated ethical imagery. Yet his words ("I wasn't the *only* nut") suggest that even then he was by no means fully liberated from the inverted morality—and inverted sanity (he still had a partial image of the rest of the men as the sane ones and Ridenhour and himself as the "nuts")—of the My Lai illusion.

A key to understanding the psychology of My Lai, and of America in Vietnam, is the body count. Nothing else so well epitomizes the war's absurdity and evil. Recording the enemy's losses is a convention of war, but in the absence of any other goals or criteria for success, counting the enemy dead can become both malignant obsession and compulsive falsification. For the combat GI in Vietnam killing Vietnamese is the entire mission, the number killed his and his unit's only standard of achievement, and the falsification of that count (on many levels) the only way to hold on to the Vietnam illusion of noble battle. Killing *someone*, moreover, becomes necessary for overcoming one's own death anxiety. We have seen how, at My Lai, killing Vietnamese enabled men to cease feeling themselves guilty survivors and impotent targets, and become instead omnipotent dispensers of death who have realized their mission. Only killing, then, can affirm power, skill, and worth.

And there is a way of measuring: one counts, scores points, competes with one's fellow soldiers, or collectively with another unit, for the highest score. One kills "for the record."[40] Indeed, there is now considerable evidence confirming earlier suspicions that My Lai was largely a product of the numerical (body count) ambitions of high-level officers. That "record" could determine their promotions and profoundly affect their future careers. For instance, Colonel Oran K. Henderson, a non-West Pointer who had previously suffered a number of frustrations in his efforts to become a general, "followed the usual commander's practice of emphasizing body counts"; as did the Task Force Commander, Colonel Frank A. Barker, an unusually aggressive and ambitious officer, whose units were known for their high body counts and their capacity to "gun down a lot of people."[41] The hunger for a high body count on the part of these two officers, and of course on the part of their superiors as well, was passed along to Medina at the earlier briefing, and so on down the line—everyone, from President of the United States on down to the lowliest GI caught up in this malignant mix of pressure and need.

There was a troublesome disparity between body count and the number of captured enemy weapons, a disparity which, if honestly evaluated, would have made it clear that bodies counted were mainly those of civilians. Instead, Colonel Henderson, during his briefing, attributed the disparity to GIs having been insufficiently aggressive in the past in "closing with the enemy," thereby permitting women and children in the area to pick up the weapons before the GIs "arrived to where they had killed a VC."[42] Again illusion is more compelling than actuality. In different men and in different degrees, the illusion is sustained by genuine self-deception, conscious lying, or, probably most common, a kind of "middle knowledge" within which one both knows the truth about body counts (the reason for the disparity between bodies and weapons) and does not know—resists knowing—that truth.* But the image of women and children picking up the weapons of dead VC also contains still another informal message that killing women and children was, therefore, "okay." The body count illusion thus carries its logic full circle—the falsification of the evidence that civilians were being killed leading in turn to a further reason— and motivation—for killing still more civilians. All this happens because so much rides on the body count: the conquest of death anxiety, one's sense of skill, worth, and manhood—and for many, one's future as a professional soldier and long-range claim to the immortalizing status of warrior-hero.

The official body count that day for Task Force Barker (of which Charlie Company was a part), operating in and around My Lai, was "128 Vietcong." Nobody seemed certain just how that number was arrived at, but a discussion Calley recalled, in his testimony at his trial, between himself and Medina gives us something of a clue:

CALLEY: He asked me about how many—basically what my body count—how many people we had killed that day. And I told him I had no idea and for him to just go on and come up with an estimate, sir. . . .

DANIEL (prosecuting attorney): Just any body count? Just any body count, is that what you are saying?

CALLEY: Basically, yes, sir.

DANIEL: Captain Medina could just put in any body count that he wanted to put?

* The term "middle knowledge" was used by Avery Weisman and Thomas Hackett[43] to describe the state of mind of fatally ill patients in relationship to their impending death. Within the psychoformative perspective of this book, we may say that middle knowledge becomes necessary where one can neither find a place for the painful death-linked truth within one's overall formulation of self and world nor deny the pressing evidence of that truth. The problem is solved by evolving (at least) two contradictory images, the extent to which the accurate one can be covered over by the illusory one depending largely upon the degree to which the environment supports illusion.

CALLEY: Any body count that was reasonable. I would imagine he
would put in the highest acceptable body count that he would. . . .

DANIEL: Did he give an actual count?

CALLEY: Yes and no. I don't remember exactly what it was. I remember that I took fifty, sir. . . .

DANIEL: Did you tell Captain Medina that you had shot the people
in the ditch?

CALLEY: Yes sir, I did. . . .

DANIEL: How did you tell him about it?

CALLEY: He asked . . . what the percentage of civilians was.

DANIEL: What did you tell him?

CALLEY: I told him he would have to make that decision, sir.[44]

Calley and Medina, in other words, were groping for the maximum figure that could be considered "reasonable"—that could
be constructed or rationalized from the events of the day—that
could support the logic of illusion. Calley thus made an estimate
"off the top of my head" that came to "between thirty and forty,"
but Medina preferred fifty. Medina then radioed an overall body
count (for all the units) of 310,[45] but somewhere along the line
this was pared down to the figure of 128.

Again the disparity between body count(128) and weapons
captured (3)* was troublesome, this time to the GI in the public
information office who had to write up the action. One form of
compromise was combining the figure of "128 Vietcong" with
that of "24 civilians." The "middle knowledge" of the situation
was reflected in the duality of response to the final figure. On the
one hand there was "great excitement" at the base area because
it was "the largest for the task force since it had begun operations
forty days earlier." On the other, there was a certain amount of
embarrassment and uneasiness reflecting considerable awareness

---

* One might ask why there is not more falsification of the number of weapons
captured as a way of eliminating the disparity. The answer is probably that the
captured-weapons figure is much more difficult to falsify, because one is dealing
with concrete, gathered objects concerning which accuracy or falsification can
readily be proven, as opposed to corpses that, in their repellent distance, lend
themselves to every kind of admixture of exaggeration, fantasy, and falsification.

of what had actually happened—as expressed in such comments as "Ha ha, they were all women and children," and in what one observer called "a general feeling that this was a bad show, that something should be investigated." To examine the complex web of cover-up and pseudoinvestigation is to be impressed with the sustaining power of the My Lai illusion. While the cover-up, as Seymour Hersh[46] has demonstrated, can be attributed to specific high-ranking officers, it must also be understood as part of a vast military and civilian collusion to maintain the war's justifying fictions of order and nobility in the face of its fundamental corruption, false witness, and absurd evil.

In the end, Charlie Company was credited with only fourteen of the 128 "kills," and the majority of these attributed to "artillery fire" as a way of giving the incident a greater aura of combat. The official report referred to "contact with the enemy force," and the colonel in command of the task force was quoted as saying that "the combat assault went like clockwork."[47] We may thus say that the body count serves the psychological function of making concrete the whole illusionary system; it is the locus of falsification.

One learns more about this phenomenon from other impressions of how the bodies were counted. The My Lai survivor told me that the prevailing standard was:

The ones that could walk they counted as bodies. The ones that couldn't walk they counted as, you know, sort of, they didn't count them. Because they couldn't have been Vietcong. They thought about this later.

He went on to say that he had heard talk of a body count of over 300 (undoubtedly the early count made by Medina) and was never clear about why it was reduced to 128. But the distinctions he describes, the informal attempts to impose a standard according to which one counts some bodies and not others, all this suggests the need to hold on to fragmentary aspects of actuality and logic in the service of the larger illusion.

Needless to say, these standards varied greatly. I heard descriptions of totals inflated in every conceivable way: by counting severed pieces of corpses as individual bodies; by counting a whole corpse several times on the basis of multiple claims for credit (by the man or unit doing the killing, the patrol encountering the body, the headquarters outfit hearing about the killing, etcetera); and by counting murdered civilians, animals, or nonexistent bodies according to the kinds of need, ambition, and whim we have already encountered. Once a corpse has been identified (or imagined) it *becomes* that of a slain "enemy," and, therefore, evidence of warrior prowess—as the My Lai survivor makes clear:

If it's dead it's VC. Because it's dead. If it's dead it *had* to be VC. And of course a corpse couldn't defend itself anyhow.

He went on to place the body count into a frame of corrupt competitiveness—a company commander "obsessed with the body count" who "wanted a body count that would just beat all," that would "satisfy him . . . [and] satisfy higher headquarters . . . even if he knows this body count is a big dirty old lie." For, "Probably higher headquarters knows also. So they're fooling each other and theirselves as well." The whole thing, as he goes on to explain, resembles a cheater's golf game:

There was A Company over on the other side. They were counting bodies too. . . . He [the Company Commander] did sort of envy those people counting their bodies, keeping score. . . . Expressing sort of a disbelief that they had actually got that many. Which is like playing golf with somebody and carrying your own strokes and having some guy say, "I'm on [the green] in three." "You're on in *three?*" If it didn't matter to you how many *you* were on in, it wouldn't matter to you how many *he* was on in.

I am convinced that the ethically sensitive historians of the future will select the phenomenon of the body count as the per-

fect symbol of America's descent into evil. The body count
manages to distill the essence of the American numbing, brutalization, and illusion into a grotesque technicalization: there is
something to count, a statistic for accomplishment. I know of no
greater corruption than this phenomenon: The amount of killing
—any killing—becomes the total measure of achievement. And
concerning that measure, one lies, to others as well as to oneself,
about why, who, what, and how many one kills.

The atrocity-producing situation, the illusions that surround it,
and the military arrangements that further it—all these have
their origins in a malignant spiral[48] of parallel illusion, deception, and self-deception surrounding the entire American relationship to the war in Vietnam.

By extending the analysis outward in a psychohistorical direction, we recognize that the murderous false witness of GIs in the
Vietnamese countryside results directly from a more extensive
false witness on a national scale. Propelling that false witness is
a totalistic cosmology—reaching its height during the post-World
War II Cold War years but persisting even now—that contrasts
absolute American purity with absolute communist depravity.
Joining that cosmology, indeed becoming part of it, is an equally
pervasive technicism that leads Americans to view Vietnam as
no more than a "problem," a "job to be done" by applying "American know-how"—and to ignore psychological and historical
forces surrounding the long-standing Vietnamese struggle against
Western invaders, and Chinese invaders before that. When the
"problem" persistently resists the American "solution," when the
job will not get done, the assumption is that still more "know-
how" is needed—greater fire-power, more "scientific" computer-
ized studies of "safe hamlets," better "techniques" for improving
the always-inadequate South Vietnamese military "leadership."
This marriage of totalistic cosmology and all-pervasive technicism, amply documented in the Pentagon Papers, has prevented
fundamental questions from being raised, while perpetuating

three overall psychohistorical illusions around which the war has been pursued.

The first of these illusions concerns the nature of the war, and converts a fifty-year-old anticolonial revolution, nationalist and communist from its inception, into an "outside invasion" of the South by the North. The second concerns the nature of the government we have supported, and converts a despotic military regime without standing among its own people into a "democratic ally." The third illusion, partly a product of fatigue over maintaining the first two, holds that we can "Vietnamize" the war (leave and still keep the present government in power in the South) by turning it over to a regime that lacks legitimacy and an army that has shown little will to fight—through a program that is American rather than Vietnamese, and one that few if any Vietnamese really want to implement. Bound up with this last illusion is a seemingly pragmatic Machiavellian effort (which may itself turn out to be infused with illusion) to create in Vietnam an urbanized "consumer society" under American and Japanese corporate hegemony. In all, it is not too much to say that the illusions surrounding an aberrant American quest for immortalizing glory, virtue, power, control, influence, and know-how are directly responsible for the more focused My Lai illusion.

This new version of American "manifest destiny" has been rudely subverted, not by a formidable adversary, but by people of no standing in the world, small people from a tiny, obscure, technologically backward country, employing hit-and-run guerrilla tactics that not only frustrate and defeat American military power but at the same time mock in the extreme the vision of American grandeur. Most humiliating of all, those very guerrillas —defined by official America as the carriers of the communist infestation—emerge (for most of the world, including many American civilians and soldiers) as the anointed ones of this war. Only they can be said to have approached the myth of the warrior-hero—in their ability to relate killing and dying to an immortalizing vision as well as in their extraordinary prowess and continuous sense of ultimate victory. Americans, in contrast, have suffered from the absence of both cause and sense of victory. For victory in itself tends to *feel* immortalizing, and has been perceived since antiquity as a favorable judgment of the gods, a confirmation of anyone's virtuous quest and equivalent of manifest destiny.

In earlier work, I found that survivors of the Hiroshima holocaust experienced what I described as "a vast breakdown of faith in the larger human matrix supporting each individual life, and therefore a loss of faith (or trust) in the structure of existence." The same is true not only for large numbers of Vietnam veterans but, perhaps in more indirect and muted ways, for Americans in general. This shattered existential faith has to do with remaining bound by the image of holocaust, of grotesque and absurd death and equally absurd survival. Even Americans who have not seen Vietnam feel something of a national descent into existential evil, a sense that the killing and dying done in their name cannot be placed within a meaningful system of symbols, cannot be convincingly formulated. The result is widespread if, again, vague feeling of lost integrity at times approaching moral-psychological disintegration.

What distinguishes Vietnam veterans from the rest of their countrymen is their awesome experience and knowledge of what others merely sense and resist knowing, their suffering on the basis of that knowledge and experience, and, in the case of antiwar veterans, their commitment to telling the tale. That commitment, especially for rap group participants, meant asking a question very much like that of Remarque's hero in *All Quiet on the Western Front:* "What would become of us if everything that happens out there were quite clear to us?" "Out there" means Vietnam, their own minds, and in the end, American society as well.

As part of their survivor mission, antiwar veterans seek understanding of and liberation from the political and military agents of their own corruption. Their constant probing of these and other aspects of American society is less in the spirit of calm reflection than of anxious and pressured need. Amid their confusions and touchiness, they have shared with one another a bond of brotherhood around their holocaust, their corruption, and their struggle against both. There is a sense in which they can fully trust only those who share their experience and their mission—though in each this trust may live side by side with suspicion toward one another, related to suspicion of oneself.

They are loath to judge other veterans whose corruption has been much greater than their own. I recall a very tense moment during a psychiatric meeting at which a group of veterans described some of their experiences. When they had finished, a questioner from the floor asked them what they thought of a promise made by Lieutenant Calley (who was then still on trial) that, should he be acquitted, he would go on a speaking tour throughout the country on behalf of peace. The men visibly stiffened and answered in a series of terse phrases, such as "I can't judge him," "I have nothing to say about him," and "It could have been any of us." They knew too much about their corruptibility and everyone's within that specific atrocity-producing situation to be able to pass judgment upon a man in whom the disintegrative process had gone still further. They were not only trying to cope with their own guilt (see Chapter 4) but with their overall formulation of their holocaust.

For they have taken on a very special survivor mission, one of extraordinary historical and psychological significance. They are flying in the face of the traditional pattern of coping with survivor emotions by joining organizations of veterans that not only justify their particular war but embrace war-making and militarism in general. Contemporary antiwar warriors are turning that pattern on its head and finding their survivor significance in exposing precisely the meaninglessness—and the evil —of their war. They do so, not as individual poets or philosophers (who emerged, for instance, from World War I) but as an organized group of ordinary war veterans. The psychological rub in the process is the necessity to call forth and confront their own warlike selves, or, as they sometimes put it, "the person in me that fought the war."

For a number of them, and at varying intervals, political activities become inseparable from psychological need. Telling their story to American society has been both a political act and a means of psychologically confronting an inauthentic experience and moving beyond it toward authenticity. For such people not only is protest necessary to psychological help—it *is* psychological help. At one moment one sees confused youngsters struggling to put together their shattered psychological selves— at another, young people with premature wisdom. As one of them expressed this uneasy combination to me, "I feel bitter because I'm a pretty young guy and the things I had to do and see I shouldn't have to in a normal lifetime." Still, they feel they have come to difficult truths that adult American society refuses to face. Indeed, in their eyes most of adult America lives in illusion. They describe others saying such things to them as, "You're different from other people," or "You seem to know things that other people don't know." Since that knowledge has to do with death and pain, they have a double view of themselves in another way as well. They see themselves sometimes as a victimized group unrecognized and rejected by existing society and sometimes as a special elite who alone can lay claim to a unique experience of considerable value in its very extremity and evil.

There is an additional paradox as well: that of an antimilitary group creating itself around its military experience, an antiwar group made up of those who fought the war now opposed. This means that their war-linked death anxiety and death guilt are constantly at issue. Merely to be in one another's presence is a reminder of the conflict and pain around which their group takes shape. No wonder they are wary of their own identity as antiwar veterans. As one of them said during a rap group: "Our life is being against the war. When the war ends, then we end as people." While ostensibly referring only to his antiwar organization, he unconsciously revealed his own sense of depending totally upon—and being consumed by—the identity of the antiwar warrior.

By a number of criteria, the group I have worked with represents a small minority of Vietnam veterans. For one thing, most saw active combat, as opposed to the majority of men stationed there in support assignments. For another, they emerged with an articulate antiwar position, in contrast to the majority who take no public stance on the war, and to another minority who emerge strongly supporting it. Concerning the first issue, my impression was that the intensity of residual conflicts were roughly parallel to one's degree of involvement in (or closeness to) combat, but that the sense of absurd evil radiated outward from the actual killing and dying, and that every American in Vietnam shared in some of the corruption of that environment. Hence, Polner's finding that no Vietnam veteran was free of doubt about what he had been called upon to do.

Similarly, even those who later come to insist that we should have gone all-out to win the war—should have "nuked Hanoi" or "killed all the gooks"—are struggling to cope with their confusions and give some kind of form and significance to their survival. There is much evidence that antiwar and prowar veterans (the categories are misleading, and the latter hardly exists in a public sense) are much closer psychologically than might be suspected—or to put the matter another way, take different paths in struggling to resolve the same psychological conflicts. Clearly the great majority of Vietnam veterans struggle silently, and apolitically, with that specific constellation of survivor conflict associated with Vietnam's atrocity-producing. situation. So that one antiwar veteran could comment:

I hear a lot of people say, "We know Vietnam veterans and they don't feel the way you do." My immediate reaction to that is, "Wait and see. If they are lucky they will. If they are lucky, they will open up."[49]

The likelihood is that relatively few of the three million Vietnam veterans will be able to "open up" in the way he means. Yet there is a very real sense in which those few are doing symbolic psychological work for all veterans, and indeed for all of American society.

CHAPTER 3

Rap Groups

What would become of us if everything that happens out there were quite clear to us?

—Erich Maria Remarque
(in All Quiet on the Western Front)

Here was the first opportunity that I really had to talk with guys who had gone through the same thing. They were having the same doubts about themselves, you know, and digging inside themselves—and you didn't want to do that with just anybody. . . . I said, Wow! you know, you got something here.

—Former Army sergeant, remembering his first rap group

RAP GROUPS came into being because of antiwar veterans' sense that they had more psychological work to do in connection with the war. The groups evolved from correspondence and telephone discussions between Jan Barry, then president of the Vietnam Veterans Against the War, and myself. In his first letter to me (November, 1970) Barry spoke of "two perhaps separate projects which we are trying to bring together as one": the first, doing something about "the severe psychological problems of many Vietnam veterans because of their experiences"; and the second, countering "the military policy of the war which results in war crimes and veterans' nightmares." As part of this second point, he invited me to participate in the Detroit Winter Soldier Investigation (January, 1971), one of the first and certainly the largest of the public meetings at which veterans have given testimony on American atrocities in Vietnam—and I did eventually become a panelist at that memorable gathering.

Barry was less specific about the first matter, a psychological program for veterans. He asked about circulating a statement on the brutalization of GIs I had made earlier that year to a Senate subcommittee, and about the possibility of my preparing further commentaries for, and exchanging ideas with, a number of the veterans. But from the beginning of our discussions, in his mind as well as in my own, the political-ethical and psychological-therapeutic components were inseparable.

I called in Dr. Chaim Shatan, a psychoanalyst at New York University with whom I had worked previously on issues surrounding American war crimes; when he and I sat down with Jan Barry and several others from VVAW, we all met in antiwar colleagueship. The veterans told us how intensely VVAW

members "rapped" with one another in the office—about the
war, American society, and their own lives—and how they felt
they would like to have people around with greater psychological
knowledge. I suggested that we form more regular rap groups,
which seemed to be what the veterans themselves had in mind.
What evolved, then, was initiated by the veterans, and had
direct continuity with informal processes already taking place
among them.

It also seemed natural for us to schedule meetings at the
VVAW office—on the veterans' own turf—where the group I
have been part of met regularly for two years. Though the place
was modest and its facilities cramped, the occasional suggestion
that we meet at some more comfortable place—a university or
an office of one of the professionals—was either vaguely rejected
("It's easier to meet here") or ignored. Another group did make
such a move, but only after a good deal of trust and cohesiveness had developed after six months of weekly meetings, and
that move could have been a factor in the group's later demise.
Otherwise, all meetings have continued to take place at the
VVAW office (the rap groups moving with VVAW when it
changed its office site) as one of the kinds of personal involvement for veterans made available at that office.*

We made plans for weekly two-hour sessions. But the atmosphere in those early groups was so charged and so compelling
that nobody left at the appointed time, and we got into the habit
of continuing the meetings for three hours or more. The explo-
sion of feeling that occurred, associated as it was with a war
whose pain pervaded all of our lives, rendered those first meetings unforgettable in their emotional power and poignancy.

* In November 1972, when VVAW had to give up its New York office our
group meetings were switched to a room in a seminary, with the expectation of
moving to the new, much smaller VVAW office as soon as a section of it could
be divided off to afford a degree of privacy. There was some ambivalence about
that prospective move, however, because by then one or two of the participants
had come to prefer the seminary's separation from the office tensions of an increasingly conflicted and fragmented VVAW organization.

Mostly through Dr. Shatan's efforts, we quickly formed a panel of professionals from psychological and psychiatric colleagues in the New York City area. From the beginning he and I had a sense of groping toward, or perhaps being caught up in, a new group form. Though far from clear about exactly what that form would be, we found ourselves responding to the general atmosphere by stressing informality and avoiding a medical model. Hence, we called ourselves "professionals" rather than "therapists" (the veterans sometimes discarded both and referred to us as "shrinks"), and the meetings "rap groups" (which stuck) rather than "group therapy." The casual, first-name basis on which we had come together extended directly into the groups, as did the fluidity in boundaries between professionals and veterans. Another part of the group's evolving ethos was the requirement, at first unspoken and later discussed, that everyone put a great deal of himself or herself on the line—a process that seemed natural enough to the veterans but was a bit more problematic for the professionals. As people used to interpreting others' motivations, it was at first a bit jarring to be confronted with hard questions about our own, and with challenges about the way we lived. Not only was our willingness to share this kind of involvement crucial to the progress of the group, but in the end many of us among the professionals came to value and enjoy this kind of dialogue.

As in certain parallel experiments taking place, not only in psychological work but throughout American culture, we had a clearer idea of what we opposed (hierarchical distancing, medical mystification, psychological reductionism that undermines political and ethical ideas) than of what we favored as specific guidelines. But before long I came to recognize three principles that seemed important. The first was that of *affinity*, the coming together of people who share a particular (in this case overwhelming) historical or personal experience, along with a basic perspective on that experience, in order to make some sense of it (the professionals entered into this "affinity," at least to a certain extent, by dint of their political-ethical sympathies and inclination to act and experiment on behalf of them). The second principle was that of *presence,* a kind of being-there or full engagement and openness to mutual impact—no one ever being simply a therapist against whom things are rebounding. The third was that of *self-generation,* the need on the part of those seeking help, change, or insight of any kind, to initiate their own process and conduct it largely on their own terms so that, even when calling in others with expert knowledge, they retain major responsibility for the shape and direction of the enterprise. Affinity, presence, and self-generation seem to be necessary ingredients for making a transition between old and new images and values, particularly when these relate to ultimate concerns, to shifting modes of symbolic immortality.

Things did not always go smoothly. Confusion was greatest at the beginning, but throughout the experience there has been much divergence of opinion on goals and on what was actually happening. For the first few Saturday afternoons we met as one expanding group, consisting not only of veterans (who heard about the project either through police scuttlebutt or notices sent out to VVAW membership) and a few professionals, but also occasional journalists interested in the veterans, who had arranged to be invited by one or more of them. The atmosphere became so informal, and the open door policy so open that, as one of the veterans put it a bit later when the door had been closed a bit, "We felt like monkeys in a zoo." This early confusion and experimentation, however, in no way diminished the intensity of these meetings.

The group's first crisis came a month after it was formed, during which its size (fifteen to twenty veterans and three to five professionals) had increased to the point of becoming unwieldy. The idea of dividing into two groups had been mentioned repeatedly and then put aside because of the unwillingness of the veterans to make the separation. Finally a definite decision was made to divide the group, but all efforts to agree just how to do that ended in excruciating impasses. The "old-timers" (men who had been in the rap group from the beginning) insisted upon sticking together, causing the "newcomers" to feel bitterly rejected. The situation was finally resolved by an arbitrary suggestion on the part of one of the professionals that those sitting to his left constitute one group, and those to his right another. Later, in looking back on how painful the division had been, the veterans could recognize their need to hold onto whatever intimacy they could achieve, and connect that need to the extreme precariousness of all intimacy in Vietnam and to their subsequent difficulty in becoming, or remaining, close to other human beings.*

Of the two smaller groups thus formed, one ran for about eight months, and the other (the one I have been associated with) for more than two years (and is still going as of January, 1973). Each of the groups consisted initially of about twelve veterans and three to four professionals. In my group the professionals checked regularly with one another to make sure that at least one or two would be present at each session, but this usually proved

* But as far as I know there was no comment in either group about the resemblance between the way in which we split up the groups and certain procedures conducted by first sergeants in the military ("I want all you guys on this side to line up over here, and all you guys on that side to line up over there"). It is difficult to say how much this kind of military habit and expectation was operating, how much that particular professional sensed that the men wanted (or would at least respond to) an arbitrary suggestion almost resembling a command. The veterans' simultaneous aversion to such authority would have caused them to react negatively had they not perceived the request to be a constructive solution to a seemingly insoluble dilemma. What one probably can say is that, at that early stage, they had not yet found their individual or collective voices sufficiently to explore and decide upon the matter in a way satisfactory to themselves. Prior to the arbitrary suggestion by the professional, the grumbling over time wasted on the decision and the rising bitterness threatened (in the retrospective opinion of a number of us) to end the rap group experiment almost before it had begun. Yet one might also speculate that, had the professionals been able to interpret more sensitively to the veterans what was happening in a way that could have facilitated their coming to their own decision about the group division, this might have contributed to still greater self-generation on their part throughout the subsequent rap group program.

quite unnecessary as all of us were profoundly drawn to the group, and on most occasions three or four of us would be there. But the style of the groups, for both veterans and professionals, was one of relatively fluid comings and goings. In my group, for instance, over a two-year period, there have been about thirty-five veterans who have participated intensively, a third of them for a year or more, another third for a minimum of ten to twenty sessions (thirty to sixty hours), and the remainder for a minimum of five sessions (fifteen hours). There have been about eighty additional veterans who came to just one to four sessions (three to twelve hours). We have had six professionals, of whom I have been the only one associated with the group throughout its life, though for periods of time some of the others have been more regularly involved than myself. A veteran-coordinator with some psychological training has had a central part in maintaining the group's continuity.*

This fluidity was partly a reflection of the "open door policy" of the rap groups: from the beginning they were open to all Vietnam veterans, and, by practice, to any veteran of the Vietnam era and even to active-duty GIs when they turned up. A newcomer who expressed doubts about eligibility or a sense of belonging was likely to be told by one of the men, "You're our brother." In this sense the rap groups resembled various forms of street-corner psychiatry. Also contributing to their fluidity was the style of life of the veterans—many of them traveled a great deal throughout the country, either working for VVAW or just on the move, very few had regular jobs, and their general sense of restlessness was a constant subject of discussion. Among professionals, fluidity had to do with time available and depth of

* The other original group has parallel statistics, with roughly half the number of veterans in both the intensive and more transient categories. In addition, there have been at least thirty referrals for individual psychotherapy made through the veteran-coordinator of the program, often with individual therapists who agreed to do a certain amount of work without fees or with minimal fees. Professionals in the rap-group program, in other capacities, have undoubtedly made at least that number of additional referrals.

interest, as well as with the evolving tradition within the groups combining intensity and flux.

But the groups differed from street-corner psychiatry in their second function, important from the beginning, of probing the destructive personal experiences of the Vietnam War for eventual dissemination to the American public. This investigative-publicizing function could come into conflict with the other goal, that of individual healing and change. While there was still just one large group, a television network asked to be permitted to record a rap session. After extensive discussion, the request was refused, but a compromise arrangement was made in which the group gathered round a television camera right after a rap session and, in response to questions, discussed the kinds of concerns and feelings it had just been talking about behind the closed door. The smaller groups then more or less formalized this kind of compromise, specifying that no one, other than veterans and designated professionals, would be permitted to sit in on the rap sessions themselves.

There was, then, a tension between openness and closure, between a bond of brotherhood extending to anyone interested in sharing something about the negative impact of the war and more focused concentration upon individual needs. The sudden appearance of new people could be jarring, and sometimes led to frustrations among regular group members who wanted desperately to talk about their own struggles. The very intrusion, however, could serve to reawaken the group's sense of being part of something much larger than itself. This openness completely disappeared in the other of the two original groups when it moved to the office of a professional, and it continued to function for only a month or two after that. In my own group, the openness was diminished somewhat, though by no means eliminated, when a decision was made (after the group had been in operation about six months) to change the meeting time from Saturday afternoon to Thursday night. The reasons governing the change had to do with scheduling problems on the part of both veterans and professionals and a general feeling that, with the warm weather, people tended not to be around on weekends. But since Saturday afternoon is always a time of more comings and goings in the VVAW office, an element in the decision might well have been the impulse, on the part of some veterans and professionals, to sequester the group a bit, and achieve sufficient closure to focus in more on intense individual experience. On the whole, that is what happened during the year following the move, though a number of new people came and a certain amount of fluidity was retained.

This issue of openness and closure—really one of boundaries —reflects a fundamental theoretical question about the groups, felt particularly keenly by the professionals, one that has never been and perhaps cannot be resolved. It had to do with two conflicting views of the nature of the groups. Most of the professionals took the position that what we were doing was group therapy: the psychoanalysts, psychiatrists, or psychologists in the group were offering necessary therapy to the veterans who were, in effect, our patients or clients. The minority view, for which I was an active spokesman, was that we were trying to create a new institution, involved in an experiment with a new community, and that although there were definite elements of group therapy, the process could better be described as a dialogue between professionals and veterans, beginning from a common stance of opposition to the war, each drawing upon special knowledge and experience. The first understanding permitted sharp role definitions: the veteran was there to be helped, the professional to help. If we abandoned the group therapy model, the argument went, the veterans would be denied what they most needed, and in a sense cheated. But the second understanding placed greater emphasis upon sharing of roles, upon ethical and political commitments of professionals no less than veterans, and upon a generally open-ended attitude toward group norms and boundaries. This view stressed the uncertainty of the appropriateness of our psychological procedures for what it was the veterans sought, and the need for professionals to open *themselves* to change.

The disagreements, friendly but continuous, were expressed at several special meetings of professionals involved in the program and extended into the rap groups themselves. Some professionals were concerned that, if the second view of the groups were adopted, we would find ourselves prescribing "correct" political opinions as a prerequisite for group acceptance. While agreeing this would be highly undesirable, I found myself arguing that our shared antiwar position was inseparable from our capacity to contribute to the psychological well-being of the veterans, and that, since political and ethical views inevitably affect and to some extent define therapeutic encounters, we would do better to examine these relationships openly.

Despite the continuing disagreement, the professionals too tended to be drawn into the common bond of brotherhood, largely I suspect through identifying with the veterans' death immersion and survival experience. But those of us who held a more radical view of the groups tended to outlast the others in the general program—both because we were more at home with the unorthodoxy and unpredictability of the situation, and also, I suspect, more politically committed to it. Moreover, a number of the more traditionally minded therapists leaned toward the more radical-experimental view, as we all came to recognize that whatever it was we were offering attracted only a limited number of veterans, no more than enough to keep two or three groups going at any one time.

Each of the professionals tended to retain a certain personal and professional style, for which he or she became more or less known. In my group, another male professional had a keen eye for physical-spatial patterns in the group and for immediate group process. A female professional had a particular talent for exposing tendencies to avoid or cover over real feelings, often related to early family experience. Another female professional was sympathetically sensitive to seemingly bizarre behavior, which she could not only make sense of but connect readily with ordinary experience. And a third female professional had an extraordinary capacity to combine keen interpretation with warm involvement at every level. I became known for connecting individual emotions with general social and historical trends, and for my sensitivity to issues of death and survival. I also was thought of as something of a "mediator"—less likely to initiate confrontation than to express understanding for divergent positions.

Most of the veterans came into the experience knowing relatively little about group process. On the whole they tended to favor the more experimental, open-ended idea, but they had no definite collective position about the two competing visions of the group. Their reactions could be complex, however, in ways that revealed the impossibility of attributing absolute "correctness" to either of the two views. For instance, they encouraged one of their number to coordinate group arrangements, as well as referrals for individual therapy when these were sought by a veteran or recommended by a professional. Through him the veterans, in effect, ran their own program. But this same coordinator was occasionally criticized in the group for what one of the men called "training on us": for using the group for his own educational purposes as the aspiring psychologist he in fact was. They were sympathetic to the idea of an experimental community, but not at the expense of their own dignity or psychological needs.

Behind the rap group program was Vietnam, and over the course of time one could observe an evolution in the relationship between the men and their war. During the first few meetings there was a direct focus on the war and a rush of resentment, horror, and atrocity. At times these meetings had some resemblance to public hearings such as the Winter Soldier Investigation, the important difference being that the men focused on themselves, upon their own guilt, pain, and rage. Emotions came in a great flood, and the strange rendition of purgatorial corruption, and commitment to growth beyond that corruption, had a profound impact on everyone present. Yet after a while the men themselves detected a tendency to "tell war stories" as a means of *avoiding* personal feelings. And after a few months there was a shift, as one of them put it, "from war stories to ourselves"—with increasing focus on here-and-now psychological struggles. Having achieved that focus the veterans could then return to the war, as they repeatedly did, but in a way that connected it to their immediate lives. Memories and images of the war then became bound up with but also subsumed in a deepening self-exploration—with subtle combinations of "war" and "now" often emerging in the dreams the men described.

Sometimes the war seemed almost forgotten during weeks of exploring conflicts in love relationships or jobs, only to reappear suddenly with the entrance of a newcomer who had been attracted to the rap group precisely because of painful preoccupations with things that happened in Vietnam. At the beginning of the meeting the newcomer was usually introduced around by the coordinator and then left alone for an hour or two if he chose to do some listening, as was frequently the case. Then, finally, someone would turn to him and ask him gently about himself and why he had come. He might then talk directly about the war, or about almost anything else—feelings of loneliness, "hassles" with the Veterans Administration, or desperate thoughts of suicide. The group was always solicitous and responsive. The other veterans would, in fact, manifest striking, previously hidden sensitivities. They conveyed the impression that any man who shared their catastrophe had claim on their energies. What is more, a newcomer had special value because (as one of the veterans pointed out after a year of meetings) "he brought us back to the war."

The men were not without their ambivalence to this continuous reactivation of war conflicts. But they sensed that repeated reexamination of those conflicts, along with therapeutic help to others less far along, contributed greatly to their own transformation. There are important parallels here to Alcoholics Anonymous and drug addiction programs run by former addicts. But here the habit one is kicking is war, and the commitment includes not only staying off the drug, but making a basic political and social realignment, becoming a different kind of person.

Discussions moved quickly from present struggles to war experiences to prewar conflicts, but each meeting tended to be dominated by one or two general themes: a pattern of guilt or violence, the struggle for love and intimacy, counterfeit versus authentic situations, the ambiguities and limitations of being an antiwar veteran, the appropriateness of emotion and the capacity to feel. The themes intertwined in endless ways, as the rest of this book suggests. Yet each, in the form it took, was directly bound up with the special kinds of death immersion, survival, and struggle for meaning associated with the Vietnam War.

The combination of ultimate questions and experimental arrangements gave all in our group the feeling that we had to call upon new aspects of ourselves, become something more than we had been before. Central to this process were the changing relationships between veterans and professionals. The veterans who came regularly became increasingly sensitive to currents in the group process and began to assert themselves more and offer forthright judgments on the professionals. For instance, on one occasion several veterans strongly praised one of the professionals for having pressed them toward self-examination and away from "telling war stories." But when that same professional, perhaps partly in response to their praise, continued to assert individual-psychological (and past-oriented) interpretations that diverted a few of the veterans from other immediate issues they were bent on exploring, one of them (with a little background experience in psychological work) angrily rebuked her for insisting upon a narrow perspective under the guise of neutrality and for being too conventional in her psychological approach. True to form, I found myself mediating—agreeing with the veteran and saying so, but also affirming the professional's good faith in seeking to illuminate suppressed conflicts.

Looking back now, I realize that this kind of mediating on my part probably perpetuated some of the ambiguity of the group —I neither rejected her conventional, somewhat reductionist approach out of hand nor insisted upon its complete replacement by the model of a new community. But in mediating in this fashion I was reflecting both the dual feelings of the veterans themselves and my own struggles toward responsible forms of professional and political radicalism and advocacy research.

During that same meeting one of the veterans began to describe, with considerable ambivalence, the images of me he held—that of an eminent professor and writer who sent him a letter on elegant Yale stationery (implying a mixture of distance, resentment, and admiration), and that of an ordinary fellow named Bob who was regularly in the group and with whom he felt easy. Toward the end of that session, one of the more quiet and self-effacing veterans suddenly came out with a still sharper comment: "You can disagree with her [referring to the conflict with the other professional], but at least she is here in the group with us. What about Bob Lifton—taking all those notes? Is he really in the group?" During earlier discussions of purposes and motivations I had told the group of my efforts to combine investigative, therapeutic, and antiwar commitments, and of my intent to do some writing about the rap group experience, all of which had apparently been well accepted. I had taken some notes in the past, but that day I had been taking particularly extensive notes and was jarred not only by the sudden confrontation but by my immediate feeling that there was much justice in the criticism. I responded by both affirming my intention to write on the subject (which again nobody objected to), and at the same time admitting a certain insensitivity and distancing in taking extensive notes (which is what they *had* objected to).

The professional who had been criticized earlier then complimented the veteran on his "courage" in confronting me—adding that she had felt like saying the same thing on a number of occasions but had not had the nerve to do so. To which I commented that the veterans, lacking professional training, had less to unlearn. At the end of the session, another of the professionals told me, gently but definitely, that she too had been uncomfortable about my taking notes, and offered to sit down with me and pool our memories if I wished to reconstruct exactly what had gone on in a particular meeting.

After thinking about the matter, I decided simply to cease taking any notes at all—which was briefly and favorably noted in a later session. I found I could reconstruct most of what went on—including key phrases used—by jotting down recollections right after the session and dictating a detailed summary a little later. And although I had always felt myself to be actively immersed in the group process, my involvement became a bit more intense and personal. Sometime later I discussed that particular confrontation with a colleague, who was critical of the veterans for what he viewed as the kind of exaggerated demand for concrete, personal encounter so characteristic of young people today, and who thought I should have held to my investigator's prerogative and continued taking notes. But I saw the matter differently. What had been at issue was the veterans' pride and emerging confidence in shaping their own group pattern: they could accept a wide variety of styles, motivations, and conceptual positions on the part of professionals, but demanded full "presence" from them. Aware that much of what was happening would eventually reach beyond that small room, their sense of dignity nonetheless required that they reject any arrangement that could be construed as making them into mere objects of study.

On the whole the fluidity of boundaries between professionals and veterans encouraged feelings of relaxed camaraderie. Members of the rap group came to see me about plans of one kind or another; I wrote recommendations for a few of them; and on one occasion I prepared a statement relating a veteran's conflicts to his war experience for use in a minor court procedure. On a number of occasions I drove between New York and New Haven with veterans in the rap group, or had meals or drinks or coffee with them, in connection with various psychological and political meetings we participated in together. Yet the boundaries by no means disappeared: what we have been able to do together has depended upon our distinctness and separateness from one another as well as upon intense common concerns.

My impression has been that this dialectic between "presence" and separateness has generally been well understood and mutually comfortable. But not always. At one meeting I did not attend, at which there were only two veterans and two professionals (word had gone out to most of the others that the meeting would be canceled because of an organizational action on that day, but those who came decided to go ahead with a rap group anyway), an issue came up during which a professional, in response to a veteran's prodding, agreed to "get out of my therapist's bag" and "mix it up." Which he did, in the process telling one of the veterans that he very frequently thought him "full of shit." At subsequent meetings the veteran expressed his hurt and anger, and pursued the question of what the whole incident had meant. Reviewing the sequence of the exchange, it became clear that the professional had become irritated with the veteran's attempt to assume a therapeutic stance toward others as a way of avoiding his own emotions. But another important element was the increasing alienation from the group on the part of that professional, who had earlier been central to its function. The meetings had become problematic for him, partly because of their changed time, but also for other reasons that could well have been related to conflicts over roles and boundaries. In any case his little outburst was a kind of parting shot, as he did not again appear. The matter was never fully resolved, but the veteran could readily accept my own comment that professionals, in "getting out of their therapist bags" and "mixing it up," were as capable as anyone else of losing their balance, showing bias, being less than perfectly controlled.

This was the only incident of its kind, and one could probably say that the veteran and professional concerned expressed rather bluntly the kind of feelings that often exist but remain unsaid in various therapeutic or partly therapeutic situations. Yet much of the veteran's hurt had to do with the degree of mentorship and interpretive power vested in the professionals. Without saying so, the effort on the part of everyone in the group was to avoid classical forms of "transference," in which patients are expected to revive and project onto therapists infantile feelings originally experienced in relationship to parents; and to create instead an atmosphere in which the professionals' undoubted therapeutic authority could coexist with genuine mutuality and individual autonomy. But I do not think that kind of atmosphere can be created without significant tensions from both sides—professionals rendered anxious by less role structuring than they are used to, and veterans touchy about professionals' therapeutic authority, both wanting it to exist (which is why they called professionals in) and resenting any suggestion of infringement upon their own autonomy.*

The rap groups brought together unconventional combinations of people in terms of backgrounds as well. The participating veterans have been bright and articulate but with varying educational backgrounds—some no more than high school, a few attending training institutes, and a considerable number attending local colleges (on veterans' benefits), often with interruptions of one kind or another. Most came either from the lower middle class or the working class, though there were also a few from relatively comfortable or even well-to-do families. Concerning religious backgrounds, I had the impression that the number of Catholics (usually lapsed) was rather high, though this may be partly because Catholics were particularly prone to bringing up psychological issues related to early religious training. But all—Catholics, Jews, Protestants, and one who declared himself

---

* The veterans' concern with autonomy paralleled my own prior emphasis upon dialogue in both research and therapy, as well as work by Halleck, Szasz and others in stressing both the pitfalls of "transference" and the central importance of the principle of autonomy.

a Buddhist (on the basis of studies made in Vietnam under the mentorship of a fellow GI)—tended to be strongly critical of the institutional arrangements within their religions.

Racially the rap groups, like VVAW itself, have been predominantly white, though including as active participants a number of light-skinned blacks and a few men of combined black and Puerto Rican backgrounds. The virtual absence of veterans one would refer to as simply black was often commented upon regretfully but looked upon as more or less unavoidable at this historical moment. On one occasion, about six months after the rap groups had begun, three dark-skinned blacks came in—and although one was a girlfriend of one of the men, causing a certain amount of muttering, the group did not require her to leave. As it turned out she and her boyfriend left in the middle of the session, while the third black remained until the end. He watched with quiet intensity a rather dramatic scene in which the group built a protective ring around another newcomer, a light-skinned black, who had recently attempted suicide—with different members gently probing his difficulties, telling of conquering their own suicidal inclinations, inviting him to stay in the group, suggesting arrangements for individual therapy, and offering places to stay in their apartments as well. When finally the dark-skinned black was himself addressed, he said such thing as "I liked being here" and "I liked what happened here." He went on to talk feelingly about white racism and also about his own inner struggles against diffuse antiwhite feelings. But when enthusiastic invitations to return to the group were expressed, he paused for a moment and said slowly, perhaps slightly reluctantly, yet quite definitely, "I guess I have to do my work 'uptown' "—meaning, with other blacks.

The professionals in the rap group program have included psychiatrists, psychologists, and psychoanalysts, most with university affiliations but mainly involved in clinical work with patients, including active work with groups. I was exceptional in being primarily involved in research, though I have had considerable clinical work and a certain amount of group experience in the past. But my research and teaching had focused upon various experimental approaches to interviewing, dialogues, and seminars, and I had given some thought to the kind of radical social experiment we found ourselves in the midst of. We varied greatly in our intellectual commitments—most could probably be categorized as neo-Freudians, and I had my particular psychohistorical inclinations—but the divergent views about group process mentioned earlier could not be directly correlated with specific psychological schools of thought. As in the case of the veterans, we had all religious backgrounds (except Buddhist) represented, with Jewish professionals outnumbering the others and most active in organizing and reorganizing the rap group program.

In general, our group was made up of people who would not otherwise have come into ready contact with one another. But for the war and, one suspects, the antiwar movement, most of the veterans would not have sought out professional psychological help—because neither their social-intellectual backgrounds, nor their degree of psychiatric disturbance, would have inclined them toward such help. Nor would the professionals have encountered either the veterans or each other in such intensive group interplay. In this serendipitous mix, everyone's preexisting assumptions were challenged: the veterans' notions of what "shrinks" were like, and how much of self and society had to be examined in order to make a genuine break from the war; and professionals' ideas about neutrality and advocacy, the efficacy of standard psychological practice for unstandard situations, and how to risk a bit more of oneself in one's work than one was accustomed to; and on both sides, about dealing with uncharted situations growing out of catastrophic war and rapid social change.

Not long before completing this manuscript, I was informed of another discovery. A month or so before, a dark-skinned veteran, whom we took to be either part American Indian or possibly Puerto Rican, appeared in the group and spoke articulately and feelingly about personal struggles involving a recent divorce, his own responsibility for his infant child, everyday issues around work, and a new relationship with a girlfriend. He came again the following week but abruptly left about fifteen minutes after the session began, and one of the other professionals had the impression that he had only come into the rap group that night because she had encountered him in another room of the VVAW office and asked him if he planned to be there. We wondered about his behavior, until three weeks or so later when he appeared again at VVAW to confess to one of the officers that he had come as an FBI informer, but had liked everyone he met and felt very badly about the whole thing. Efforts to seek him out again and talk to him more—one of them following a chance meeting with a member of the rap group on the streets—were to no avail. Several themes predominated in our subsequent discussion of the matter in the rap group: curiosity about whether the FBI imagined that subversive plots were being hatched in the rap group and had specifically singled it out as an object of study, or whether (as is likely) the informer was simply sent to the VVAW office, as had a number of others in the past; our sense that the informer had been telling us about genuine personal conflicts and had become quite involved with us, despite his mission; a certain amount of small satisfaction that this involvement with us and others at VVAW had led him to reveal himself to us; a feeling of rage, particularly on the part of a few veterans, at having been "had" (again betrayed), violated in a very special way in having our receptivity and openness so abused; and most of all, an icy contempt for the FBI that had also to do with feelings toward official America in relationship to the war.

What of the fate of the rap groups themselves? As of January, 1973 one of the two original groups, the one I have mostly described, remains active. The other, though no longer functioning itself, provided the inspiration and a nucleus of two members for a new rap group forming in a different borough. And there is still another group in a third borough largely inspired by our program. Three additional groups ran for varying periods of time; and we have heard, through inquiries about our experience made to me, to other professionals, or directly to the VVAW office, of rap groups springing up in various parts of the country. On the one hand, we must say that rap groups have not really taken hold on a large scale within the organization. We have had a sizable panel of professionals ready to participate but have lacked interested veterans in larger numbers. Only a small minority of veterans has been willing and able to undergo the sustained psychological discipline required, and that group of veterans has derived very great personal benefit from them.*

On the other hand, we may say that the rap groups as an available resource have had considerable symbolic significance within and without VVAW far beyond their number of participants. They have achieved a small tradition in New York and elsewhere and have stood for a continuing search for integrity. They have, moreover, given rise to other experiments, the most notable of which has been a program of three theme-centered workshops conducted at the New York office in March and April, 1972. The themes themselves—"How much of John Wayne is still in us?" (masculinity, violence, and male-female relations), "How deep did the war reach?" (mostly on varieties of guilt), and "Where do we go from here?" (conflicts and possibilities of

---

* During late 1972 and early 1973 many veterans' rap groups have sprung up throughout the country—in association with VVAW chapters, with other Vietnam veterans programs, at universities, and in prisons. During this period of time Dr. Chaim Shatan (whose op-ed column on the subject in the *New York Times* was a major stimulus to this process), the veteran-coordinator of the rap groups, and I have corresponded with people from about thirty such groups —not counting those in Veterans Administration hospitals, where they have also proliferated. We are now in the early stages of forming a "Vietnam Veterans Psychological Information Service" to serve as a clearing house for psychological materials and information about rap groups and related programs.

the identity of the antiwar veteran)—and the inspiration and leadership of the workshops came directly out of the rap groups. Each of the workshops involved about fifty veterans, who were divided into smaller groups with one or two professionals but led by a veteran. Indeed, in the entire workshop program, as well as in more recent rap groups, there is an increasing tendency for veterans taking over interpretive-psychological as well as organizational responsibility.

We are certain about nothing, but we anticipate continuing and enlarging the workshops, and revitalizing the rap group program.

The rap groups have represented a struggle on the part of veterans and psychological professionals to give form to what is, more than most realize, a common survival—for the veterans of a terrible death immersion, for the professionals of their own dislocations in relationship to the war and beyond. During our most honest moments, we professionals have admitted that the experience has been as important for our souls as for theirs.

CHAPTER 4

Animating Guilt

Reconciliation . . . to overcome the consequences of my guilty action. . . . this can happen . . . only out of the core of a transformed relationship to the world, a new service to the world with the renewed forces of the renewed man.

—Martin Buber

Starkly I return to stare upon the ash of all I burned.

—Wilfred Owen

I felt sorry. I don't know why I felt sorry. John Wayne never felt sorry.

—Former infantryman remembering
feelings after killing an NLF
guerrilla with a knife

THE AMERICAN SURVIVOR of Vietnam carries within himself the special taint of his war. His taint has to do with guilt evoked by death. His most disturbing images are of particular encounters with the dead and dying; his harshest self-judgments emerge from these encounters and concern not only what he did or did not do but his sense of the overall project he was part of.

In the rap groups the men frequently talked of their resentment of others viewing them as "monsters," "beasts," and "murderers." But before long they made it clear that these were their own self-judgments as well. A typical sequence was that of one man who described being unable to take a steady job after returning from Vietnam largely because of what he took to be negative attitudes of prospective employers:

They would think, "There's a murderer, a monster." I sometimes still think that myself.

One man in our group told of being spat upon by an anonymous greeter at the airport when he returned, an experience referred to so often by veterans as to become a kind of mythic representation of a feeling shared by the American people and the veterans themselves: an image of Vietnam as a war of grunts immersed in filth (rather than one of noble warriors on a path of glory) who return in filth to American society. They have fought in an undeclared and therefore psychologically illegitimate war, without either ceremonies of departure or parades of victorious return. Rather, the men speak of "sneaking back" into society, just as they were "sneaked" into Vietnam by higher authorities spinning (and caught in) a web of deceptions about whether

American troops were to go to Vietnam, how many, how long they would stay there, and what they would do there. The relatively few ceremonies held to welcome returning heroes have been abortive, and, as in the case of the war itself, nobody believes in them. Hence, they can have the effect of actually intensifying the veterans' guilt. This was true of the former GI who had experienced a great deal of guilt over the rape-killing of a Vietnamese girl and the participation in random killing of civilians in general. On a radio broadcast he recalled feeling a certain amount of relief and even pleasure when, resplendent in dress uniform and medals, he was greeted at the airport of his home town and told by an old lady in the group that he was "the cream of the crop." For a while he went about basking in this glory, but very soon the falseness of the situation impressed itself upon him "and then I started feeling even more guilty because I realized that I was playing on—I was almost using—the people I had killed or hurt for this good, glorifying feeling."[1] In his case death guilt mounted until he felt so much in conflict with American society and its war—and with himself and *his* war—that he decided to desert, flee to Canada, and work against the war from there.

There is a bitter paradox around the whole issue of wrongdoing that is neither lost on these men nor fully resolved by them. Sent as intruders in an Asian revolution, asked to fight a filthy and unfathomable war, they return as intruders in their own society, defiled by that war in the eyes of the very people who sent them as well as in their own. Images and feelings of guilt are generally associated with transgression—with having crossed boundaries that should not be crossed, gone beyond limits that should not be exceeded. Here the transgression has to do with two kinds of death; that which they witnessed and "survived" (deaths of buddies), and that which they inflicted on Vietnamese. Though the two involve different experiences, they merge in the absurdity and evil of the entire project. Hence the men feel themselves to have been part of a killing force not only in the literal military sense but in a moral-psychological sense as well. Above all, they are survivors who cannot inwardly justify what they have seen and done—and are, therefore caught in a vicious circle of death and guilt. Memories of deaths witnessed or inflicted, which I have elsewhere categorized as the death imprint,[2] evoke disturbing feelings of guilt, which in turn activate that imprint. The resulting death guilt, at whatever level of consciousness, is the fundamental psychological legacy of this particular war.

Hence the touchiness of the veterans, revealed especially during early rap groups, about certain questions frequently asked them upon their return, especially by children: "Did you *kill* anyone over there? How *many* did you kill? How did you *feel* when you killed someone?" The veterans felt badly used by their questioners, saw them as deriving some kind of pleasure from hearing about killing, and interpreted these questions as proof that people in America, even children, were "programmed for violence." But they quickly came back to their own struggles about how much to condemn themselves for having killed or helped with killing, and for having remained alive. They explored the realization that they could kill, did kill, and only partly accepted the justification they themselves put forth, namely that it was necessary to kill in order to survive. Much of those early meetings were taken up with the men testing one another—and finding themselves wanting—by setting up virtually impossible moral choices: "If you had to kill someone again in order to survive, would you do it?" "If you had to kill an innocent person in order to survive, would you do *that*?" "If you had to kill a child in order to survive, would you do *that*?"

In stating these dilemmas they were groping for a moral and psychological "position" on what they had done. They were performing a kind of psychic *danse macabre* around their own death guilt, moving gingerly back and forth, toward and away from it. At times they seemed to pass judgments of total evil: on all men or on "human nature" (the idea that anyone would kill anyone to save his own life); on American society (its demand that everyone be violent); and ultimately on themselves (their willingness to kill, sometimes even with pleasure, having revealed them to be, at bottom, nothing but murderers). But one could also perceive a search for an alternative to total evil, for a better way to recognize and confront their own guilt.

The response of professionals in the rap groups was very much part of the equation. On the whole we did not say too much during these discussions, our silence perhaps an expression of our all too apparent limitations when faced with some of the most fundamental questions surrounding human existence. I remember experiencing great discomfort not only at the idea that men had been put in the situations they described but at my own inability to muster sufficient wisdom to be the healer I wished to be. When I did speak, I stressed, as did other professionals, the entrapment of the situation itself. We discussed together how, in that setting, combinations of fear of death and responses to deaths of buddies could have caused virtually anyone—psychiatrists and psychologists like ourselves included—to do the same thing. We were, of course, conveying our sense of the atrocity-producing situation —trying to do so, at least in my own case, without denying an irreducible element of individual responsibility. I felt the men themselves to be groping toward that kind of dialectic between entrapment and responsibility, and found myself and other professionals not dismissing but, in a very real sense, sharing their guilt.

In connection with issues mentioned earlier, I talked a little about the fascination death and killing hold for everyone, especially children, as part of the struggle to come to terms with the realization that one's own life could and would be at some moment snuffed out. Rather than stressing my professional relationship to these questions (the men knew I had done work bearing on them) I told of a recent personal incident in which two Vietnam veterans came to my home and were introduced to my nine-year-old son, who immediately asked them the very questions that had so angered the men in the group ("Did you kill anybody over there? How many did you kill?"). We could then discuss more concretely ways in which American culture aggravated and distorted this universal fascination with violence. Still on the subject of children and parents, I spoke of my son's early interest in guns and the conflicts this evoked in my wife and myself, both of us deeply involved in antiwar causes, and she, a children's writer, specifically committed to the principle of toy disarmament. The veterans questioned me further, and I told of grudging compromises my wife and I made, intent as we were in conveying on the one hand our disapproval both of the weapons and their romanticized aura in American society, and on the other hand recognizing that our son, well aware of having lived in Hiroshima for six months as an infant, was struggling, through play, to cope with all too real issues of violence and death, and that sustained prohibition threatened to convert his interest into irresistible fascination. The group could then talk about the national American preoccupation with the gun in ways that connected with, rather than covered over, individual struggles around violence. We thus came full circle: their original idea that "kids were programmed for violence" had been partly confirmed, but in a way that neither explained away the personal guilt they sought to explore nor denied them the psychic leeway they required for that exploration.

In all this the veterans struggled toward a new relationship to their guilt. They sought from the very guilt that seemed to hold them in static 'deadness' an energy for 'coming to life.' Indeed their entire relationship to their antiwar organization was bound up with this quest. There were two important images involved. The first had to do with their transgression, their having caused (in Buber's phrase) "a wound in the order of being," their having 'killed' someone or something. The second was an image of a world beyond the transgression itself. That is, to transcend the conditions of the transgression (the atrocity-producing situation) one had to open oneself up to the larger "order of being" one had injured.

During rap groups and individual interviews the men frequently called forth one particular memory which, in starkly condensed form, stood for the whole of their struggles with death and guilt. When encountering this kind of memory in Hiroshima survivors I spoke of it as an "image of ultimate horror."[3] In Vietnam veterans, one could speak of an *image of ultimate transgression*—of having actively violated the human order beyond anything resembling acceptable limits. One such image was the description, in Chapter 2, of GIs cavorting around mutilated bodies: the transgression depicted was the killing of Vietnamese without purpose, the grotesque destruction of human beings beyond mere killing (by airplanes), and the further mutilation of corpses (by the GIs on the ground). Still more fundamental to that image was what had happened to the GIs themselves— their bizarre war dance among pieces of former human beings.

This 'joy in transgression' was expressed still more vividly in a novel by a veteran who had served as a medic in Vietnam:

Threat made me threatening. And I came to be fascinated by my threatened life and to enjoy the immediacy of it, and yes, to hate it too and to hate myself for enjoying it. The eye lusted after what it saw. My soul lusted after its feeling no matter what it felt. . . . I was two of myself, one human and the other inhuman. . . . I delighted in the destruction and yet was a healer. . . . I was, God forgive me, pleased at the ugliness of what I saw and was and lived. And I do not understand why. And I am polluted by my knowledge. I liked it. I enjoyed death. God, how awful![4]

The atrocity-producing situation encouraged whatever inclination one possessed for experiencing this feeling of transcendence in connection with killing and mutilating; it could become the only way to "feel alive." This same writer expressed to me personally his further views on atrocity in Vietnam:

It wasn't all weakness, you know. There was also a kind of strength—but a very perverted kind. Something like a Dracula movie. . . . Whatever you psychologists call it, there is only one word for it—evil. . . . At a time like that you find out what man is like. You learn that this is what man is.

The ultimate transgression is joy in killing and mutilating. The veteran who described the scene of mutilated bodies was able (over the course of many rap groups) to explore that kind of memory in association with principles beyond it and to see behavior in Vietnam as only a part of the broad gamut of man's possibilities. In contrast, the writer so appalled at having enjoyed killing, remained isolated with his memories, which became for him the entire truth about man. Partly because of prior psychological tendencies, and perhaps partly for creative purposes, he so totalized evil and guilt that they defined for him his own—and man's—condition ("this is what man is"). He therefore remained locked in a state of perpetual transgression and killing: he could say to me, "If I had a chance to push the button that would blow up everything, I would push it." Evil of that magnitude can only be killed by destroying everything.*

The transgression, however, could also take the form of simply remaining alive while a buddy dies. The same veteran who described the scene of the mutilated bodies had another recurrent memory: crawling away from a terrible ambush with the corpse of his closest buddy, who had saved him from death not long before, on his back—after the rest of his squad and most of his company had been wiped out. He remembered "wishing for my death—I wanted to die." And he implied that there was a sense in which he did die: "I was the worst ghost they ever had out there." He expressed the fear that "I've used up my luck."

His reactions suggest the soldier-survivor's sense of having betrayed his buddies by letting them die while he stayed alive

---

* It must be said that another side of him sought to counter this totalized guilt and evil by means of a gentle concern with love and nurturing in his personal life.

—at the same time feeling relieved and even joyous that it was *he* who survived, his pleasure in surviving becoming a further source of guilt. Nor can one feel that it was logical or right for him and not others to survive. Rather, he becomes bound to an unconscious perception of organic social balance which makes him feel that his survival was made possible by others' deaths: if they had not died, he would have had to; if he had not survived, someone else would have.[5] His transgression, then, lies in having purchased his own life at the cost of another's. In a very real psychological sense he feels that he has killed that buddy. In the man described above, death anxiety and death guilt were reflected in extreme fearfulness (particularly of intimacy of any kind), explosive rage, and marked restlessness and instability. Those symptoms diminished without ever disappearing over the course of eighteen months of rap groups (and weekly individual therapy as well), and at times he could show a considerable talent for living. During one of his happier moments he declared: "You know, I don't really believe I'll *ever* die." He was expressing the other side of the survivor's death imprint—the sense of having defeated death and been rendered invulnerable to it—of having crossed over and returned. This feeling of invulnerability, in him as in others, was fragile, and masked a more powerful sense of heightened vulnerability underneath.[6]

His ghost metaphor suggests this mixed imagery. It evokes the principle of the "homeless dead" found in primitive and folk cultures—spirits or ghosts of people who die suddenly, through suicide or violence, while on a journey far from home, through violating a taboo, or else in some kind of unfulfilled state (either lacking biological posterity or being denied the proper death rituals). The homeless or living dead are said to be condemned to a miserable transitional existence, and are considered dangerous to the living. One can see in this general imagery structured cultural forms for expressing the death guilt of survivors, who consider themselves responsible for the plight of the "homeless

dead." But in our example, it was the survivor who saw *himself*
as the ghost. He had, so to speak, already died—so powerful were
his death imprint and his death guilt. Yet the other, life-affirming
side of the metaphor was his sense that, in his particular form of
rejection of the war, he was haunting the anonymous "they,"
who "had" him "out there," and gaining a measure of psychic
strength in the process.

The veteran struggling with these transgressions finds that
the two forms—killing and surviving—have merged into a
diffuse sense of death guilt associated with his involvement in
the overall evil of the military project. He must explore his condemnation, contempt, and disgust for the project, and tease
apart his self-condemnation, self-contempt, and self-disgust at
his part in it. Our experience was that a veteran could never
isolate all guilt around one or two particular actions and then be
done with it—guilt is simply not manageable in that way. But
recalling specific images of death guilt enabled him to explore
pressures contributing to and images beyond his actions, and
then, gradually, alter his relationship to guilt in vitalizing ways.

There were many such examples over the course of the rap
groups. One veteran, generally rather quiet, jarred the group
one day with an urgent description of three memories: the first of
going out on a meteorological mission with an enormous, highly
inflammable hydrogen balloon, coming under heavy fire, and
waiting in terror that the balloon would be hit and he himself
"burned to a crisp"; the second of coming close to death when
enemy shells suddenly fell very near a tent in which he was rest-
ing; and the third, the most disturbing to him of all, of an incident around a small dog he had befriended. His first sergeant,
who had disciplined him previously and consistently baited him,
insisted that the dog be surrendered to be killed because there
were "too many stray dogs around the place," threatening him
with the stockade should he refuse. He complied. We then discussed, in the group, his sense, conveyed in all three images, of
profound helplessness and impotence—or stasis—in the face of

the threat of death. The last memory in particular symbolized, through the dog, his guilt over lives he felt forced to "sacrifice" in order that he might survive, psychically as well as physically. It was an image of imposed collusion in killing, of imposed corruption and death guilt.

Prior to the kind of sustained self-examination that took place in the rap groups, the men tended to experience a three-step sequence in their awareness of guilt: first, fleeting images of self-condemnation directly after killing or surviving (this initial awareness of guilt is more widespread than generally recognized, despite the advanced state of numbing and brutalization during combat); next, further desensitization, both sudden and sustained, that comes to dominate psychic life sufficiently during the time in Vietnam (and often for a considerable period afterwards) to ward off and minimize periodic flashes of guilt feelings; and finally, a sustained post-Vietnam confrontation with individual and shared forms of guilt.

The deserter who had taken part, with three other GIs, in the rape and murder of four Vietnamese girls, told a radio interviewer how at the time he felt "just plain guilty" and experienced "an immediate feeling . . . almost religious . . . like I was supposed to be punished." Then, in adapting to the atrocity-producing situation he found, very quickly, that "I didn't feel anything about it" and looked upon it as "just an incident—another weird incident on our patrol." But his guilt feelings reasserted themselves periodically in unguarded moments, as on one occasion when he and another man who had participated in the rape-murder were both "stoned in a bunker" (he later explained that "grass tends to magnify emotions"). When back in the United States his awareness of guilt became strong and sustained, and played a fundamental part in his decision to desert, in psychiatric difficulties he experienced, and in his deepening commitment to antiwar activism.[7] One can say that guilt becomes the fulcrum on which the psychological destiny of the Vietnam survivor turns.

The men directly relate the desensitization to the deaths around them. As one veteran wrote in a brief antiwar pamphlet:

A very sad thing happened while we were there—to everyone. It happened slowly and gradually so no one noticed when it happened. We began slowly with each death and every casualty until there were so many deaths and so many wounded, we started to treat death and loss of limbs with callousness, and it happens because the human mind can't hold that much suffering and survive.[8]

The numbing could be reinforced by other desensitizing processes, such as applying oneself to military tasks, being proficient on patrol in a way that had survival value for one's whole company, keeping one's weapon clean and functional, or concentrating on the workings of whatever technology, from rifle to artillery to detection devices, was at hand.

Fundamental to the desensitization process is fear—of the enemy and the overall hostile environment, of being killed or wounded, of the military authority above one. Conquering fear is, above all, a group experience; one kills and survives with the men in one's unit; one merges with them on a basis of shared psychic numbing. This collective psychic commitment to avoiding guilt, or at least an awareness of it, protects one from potentially fatal ostracism on the one hand and the specter of military punishment on the other. The latter fear was conveyed in the men's recollections of being "terrified of L.B.J.," the half-mocking way of relating a notorious stockade (Long Binh Jail) to the President who had become so personally identified with the war. The other side of the psychic commitment to avoiding guilt is the psychic investment in the desymbolization and deformation of the numbing process—the blockage and distortion of inner forms of response to overwhelming external experience. In other words, to cast off numbing and confront guilt would render one vulnerable to every kind of assault from without and within.

Only after leaving the atrocity-producing situation does the veteran's investment in desensitization diminish sufficiently for him to be able to afford, psychically speaking, to confront his guilt. And even then only a small minority is able to pursue that most difficult of psychological enterprises. Precisely this confrontation with death guilt (usually but not always with the aid of an organization like VVAW) distinguishes the articulately antiwar veteran from the rest of his former military compatriots who either remain silent (in Polner's term, "haunted") or outspokenly combative against the enemy. Men in the last two groups carry their desensitization process over into American assignments and civilian life. Their numbing, however, often fails to ward off disturbing symptoms around guilt, as revealed again by Polner's work and by reports of widespread guilt-linked psychiatric breakdown among veterans throughout the country.

But many antiwar veterans also resist that confrontation, and struggles around it—struggles to feel guilt—created some of the tensest and most important moments in the rap group, as the following experiences of two men over the course of two sessions suggest.

A former infantryman, though bitterly opposed to the war and increasingly committed to the rap groups, repeatedly insisted "I just can't *feel* any guilt." By insisting upon this inability whenever the subject came up, he gave the strong impression that he thought he *should* feel guilty. As an example of what he meant, he told of an incident in Vietnam in which he saw a grenade he had placed blow a Vietnamese apart so that pieces of the corpse flew fifty yards into the air, at which time he remembered "just laughing out loud." When others in the group suggested that his laughter might have been a way of covering up his feelings, especially feelings of guilt, he merely shrugged his shoulders inconclusively.

But a few minutes later he reported a rapid series of disturbing dreams, including the following three:

I was riding on some kind of vehicle—a bus I think—down Fifth Avenue. Somehow it turned into a military truck—and the truck got bigger and bigger, until it reached an enormous size. I was a soldier on the truck—and . . . I fell off . . . and was killed.

I was riding on a subway—underground—and somehow [along the course of the ride] I seemed to turn into a soldier in uniform . . . there was a lot of confusion and then there was a battle with the police . . . in which I was killed.

I was in Vietnam and off in the distance there was a firefight. One of the guys near me panicked and kept telling me he thought he heard something . . . acting very scared. . . . I was so disgusted with him that I said, "Why don't you light a flare?" Anyone who's been in Vietnam knows that that was ridiculous, and that I was only kidding him—because it would be crazy to light a flare since that would locate where you were for the VC. But this guy didn't know any better, being new in Vietnam, so he actually lit the flare. . . . There was firing and he was killed.

He quickly explained that the third dream recreated an incident that had actually taken place in Vietnam, differing from it in just one detail: in real life the GI who lit the flare was not killed, and no harm had resulted from the kidding. He also revealed that he very frequently had dreams similar to the first two, in which, starting out as a civilian, he would somehow be pulled back into the military and be killed.

The group responded actively to the dreams, most comments having to do with the dreamer's fear of the military (the idea that they were not through with him yet), and especially his guilt (the idea that he had done something wrong and had to be punished, killed). I related the three dreams to the psychology of the survivor (referring to Hiroshima and the Nazi death camps), and particularly emphasized two themes: the idea that *he*, psychologically speaking, was not finished with the military or the war, that he still had important psychological work to do in connection with them; and that the dreams contained a rather specific message from the underground (or the unconscious) that had to do with the question of guilt, and that seemed to contradict his surface (conscious) insistence that he wasn't experiencing any. To which his response was, "Maybe I don't *want* to feel guilty—maybe I'm afraid to"—because, as he explained, he already was burdened with violent impulses toward people in American society and feared that feeling guilty would make things much worse, to the point of actually losing control. But he seemed to respond to my reassurance that recognizing guilt could have the reverse effect: that by getting in better touch with one's feelings one would have less inclination toward random violence. He then moved closer to a recognition of guilt by re-calling another incident in Vietnam—the death of a close buddy while he himself was in Hong Kong on R and R (Rest and Recre-ation leave), and his sense of "helplessness" at not having been around to do anything to prevent it. But he still did not quite reach the point of *feeling* guilt.

At the same time another member of the group, a former Ma-rine sergeant and a forceful man with an aura of masculine strength, expressed considerable antagonism to the idea of guilt. The following week he again spoke at length on how foolish and unnecessary an emotion it was, how "guilt is just plain useless." He said that this stress on guilt was the one thing he resented about antiwar veterans, and went on to insist:

I had no reason to feel guilty. . . . I didn't kill in anger. I felt no malice toward the people I killed. . . . I saw my buddies dead and that's why I killed. . . . I killed nineteen of them—yes, you can count them.

The group was skeptical but did not press him. He then went off on a seemingly different tack, speaking self-critically about his lifelong tendency to be a con man. The group probed gently into what he said, and we questioned him about the kind of secrets he was trying to hide as a con man. He then abruptly switched back to Vietnam and the "mistakes" he made there, now speaking in more pained and bitter tones than he ever had before:

Yeah, I did make some mistakes in Vietnam. I made one very big mistake. I made the mistake of trusting somebody I shouldn't have trusted. I told him exactly where to set up the patrol, but he didn't do what I said. He wanted to sleep dry. Well, now he's sleeping dry.

As platoon leader he had chosen twelve of his best men for a patrol, and for reasons not entirely clear—partly because he allowed an unfit person to lead the patrol, perhaps, partly because he had not given sufficiently precise orders himself—they were ambushed and killed in extremely violent fashion. He later came upon the scene of bodies strewn about in pieces:

Some of the men we couldn't even find—they were buried under bunkers. . . . You know, when you see dead men—whether they're round-eyes or gooks, they're all the same. Their faces are screwed up —they're all fucked up. . . . I don't know why it all happened—there was the damned fool war—and maybe I just wasn't old enough to have responsibility for so many men.

After saying these things he got up and darted out of the room, explaining to another group member (who followed him to see if he was all right) that he just wanted to sit quietly by himself for a while.

Just then, the other veteran struggling with guilt (whose dreams were quoted above) spoke up again, now in tremulous tones:

You know, I'm shuddering. . . . I'm shaking all over . . . because what he said hit me hard. . . . Before . . . we talked about guilt . . . but I didn't feel too much. But now I really feel remorse. I feel very badly about what I did in Vietnam—and it's a terrible feeling.

Through clearly anxious and upset, he also seemed relieved. This marked the beginning for him of a forthright exploration (over many subsequent meetings) of guilt and responsibility that left him feeling freer in all aspects of his life, and conveyed the impression of a man liberating himself from a heavy burden.

After a few minutes the other veteran returned to the group, telling us he had to be off by himself for a few moments because "it was too much for me." He, too, seemed both miserable and relieved. At the next meeting he spoke of having cried a great deal over that week, and conveyed the sense that he too was moving toward much greater awareness of feelings around guilt. Then, during a videotaping session held right after the rap group, he and others went on to clarify some of their attitudes toward guilt, expressing resentment over the idea that only the men who fought in Vietnam were singled out as the "guilty ones." He took a very active part in the extensive discussion of issues of guilt and responsibility that followed both on and off camera, and virtually amounted to a second rap session.

He went on to tell of the uneasy feeling he and the men in his platoon had when they removed belongings from dead Vietnamese. They found letters they could not read, but the accompanying pictures of parents, girlfriends, wives, and children made them think. "They're just like us." But he did not romanticize his former adversaries either, and still ruminating on issues of guilt and recalling "the things [mutilations] they did to my men," he asked quietly and rhetorically: "I wonder whether *they* feel guilty." We explored the universality of atrocity, the possible psychological differences between American soldiers and those of the NLF and NVA in relationship to a sense of purpose in fighting and killing; and we asked ourselves how NLF and NVA soldiers might have felt upon removing letters and pictures from American bodies.

But in the end he could not quite cope with the subject—he did not return to the group. One of the members of the group visited him subsequently and found him still very much preoccupied with the men he had sent out on patrol to their annihilation. He had initiated a confrontation with his guilt in a way that undoubtedly had psychological and moral value for him, but he felt the need, at least temporarily, to retreat from that confrontation.

Guilt is experienced even—perhaps especially—by those who struggle against atrocity. It then becomes associated with transgressions one failed to stop—as the following two experiences suggest.

The My Lai survivor, having witnessed only a portion of the shootings, questioned other men after the atrocity about what took place:

I was asking questions not because I wanted to know what happened but because I wanted to make sure it really did happen. . . . I was hoping that I could doubt my own senses. I couldn't but I was hoping I could.

He seemed to be describing an inner struggle between numbing and denial on the one hand and an insistent actuality on the other. Actuality won out, so much so that he became an outspoken survivor-witness to the event. For he felt himself very much in it, and his guilt demanded that he do no less:

There's just no way I can actually . . . feel that I was separate from this whole thing, especially when I didn't do anything to stop it myself. . . . You feel sort of responsible. . . . A part of it. . . . Especially with the war being the way it is, if you're not against it you're for it. If . . . you weren't against that company, you were for it . . . that's the way you think. You'd rather be somebody else looking at it from a distance or from a helicopter or watching it in a movie theater or something like that.

He could not, in other words, consider himself to be looking in at the event from outside, even though at the time of the actual slaughter, by keeping his gun pointing downward and not firing, he had been something of a spectator. For we recall his telling us that "I think I can understand the men in the company because the things that were working on them were working on me too," and that at the time he felt that "I'd sure like to [shoot]." Just as My Lai could be considered an 'as-if combat engagement,' he felt himself to be something like an 'as-if murderer.' Not being able to separate himself psychically from My

Lai right after the event, he considered doing so physically by deserting. He imagined running away and going off to hide in the Rocky Mountains, where he could separate himself not only from My Lai and the military but from everyone and everything, including perhaps his own guilt—

because, you know, you could walk from one end to the other, from down in that range in Mexico all the way up to where it ends up in Alaska, without seeing anything or anybody.

A man who had earlier embraced the military, and, in fact, was able to refrain from firing at My Lai largely because he felt the true soldier did not do such things, now asked himself: "Is there anything in [the military] that's worthy of anything . . . worthy of me . . . that I should stay in, that they should have me?"— conveying the impression that in his own eyes neither he nor it had lived up to acceptable warrior standards.

He remained haunted by inner questions of what he should or could have done to stop the massacre:

Every day I think of something else. What if I'd done *that?* What if I'd done *that?*

He always concluded that "nothing would have worked," and yet knew that "I'll always wonder if there wasn't something I could have done right then and there on the spot."

He went on to speak of a profound loss of faith in both ordinary men ("I'll never trust people like I did before") and in leaders (". . . before that I thought . . . people who had the power had enough sense, you know . . . [that] they couldn't make mistakes, at least big mistakes"). He had difficulty extricating himself from an abyss of infinite evil: "I used to think that there was a certain limit to what [people] do." Underlying everything was his realization that *"I could have been one of those who did the shooting."*

He faced another pitfall as well. Telling the truth about My

Lai made him feel guilty toward his buddies because "even though you may be trying to help them they will think that you're hurting them—and you don't want to have them think that you're hurting them."

He remained confused, longing always for the kind of precise, authoritative (and authoritarian) self-judgment—the definitive survivor formulation—that kept eluding him.

If only I could find out exactly what I should have done . . . and then say, well I didn't do it . . . I goofed on that one. . . . Or else if I find out something that I should do, do it and then get it over with and just forget about the whole thing—because . . . I have a feeling this is going to follow me all around.

Much of his residual conflict is between loyalty toward palpable human beings who, whatever they did, were his buddies midst the intimacy and threat of combat, together with intense prior loyalties to the military and to America itself; and a more hazy loyalty, emerging from bitter disillusionment with that entire earlier category of loyalties, to a higher principle of responsibility to life and to the "order of being." What is probably most remarkable is that he came out, on the whole, on the side of the latter. But he had to remain plagued by the ultimate contradiction:

You get stuck in Vietnam . . . expecting that you're doing the right thing, and all along you're doing the wrong thing.

Nor were public responses to his revelations about My Lai psychologically helpful to him:

They think I either must be a martyred Jesus or else a communist subversive, one or the other. Right? No, wrong!

When an organization sought to bestow upon him an ethical award, he felt embarrassed, refused the award, and fled. He remains restless, confused, articulate, resourceful, and guilt-ridden.

He had been sufficiently sensitive to guilt, and to constructive alternative images that could animate that guilt, to avoid firing at My Lai. But he had not been able to sort out issues of guilt and responsibility with sufficient inner clarity (or sufficient freedom from earlier susceptibilities to self-lacerating guilt) to sustain an animating relationship to issues of guilt and responsibility. Thus as much as he had come to hate the war, he could not commit himself to a specific public position or course of action against it—any more than he could to a plan for his own personal future.

The phenomenon of the "forgotten atrocity" can also take on great importance in the changing relationship to guilt, as the experience of another veteran suggests. A former Army sergeant, after listening to others' recollections of painful war experiences at the first rap session he attended, suddenly remembered an incident he had "completely forgotten for thirteen months." It involved a group of Vietnamese woodcutters, mostly old men, women, and children, who would gather daily at the perimeter of his base to gather bits of branches and scrub brush. One day an underground tunnel was discovered nearby, apparently dug by NLF infiltrators for explosives that could have blown up a portion of the base, and the GIs suspected that the woodcutters must have cooperated with the infiltrators in hiding their movements. An air strike was then called in, which destroyed the tunnel, and when the woodcutters next appeared they were greeted with large amounts of tear gas and herded toward the base. Under orders from the commanding officer and a platoon leader, a squad of GIs opened fire on the unarmed Vietnamese, at first aiming above them, then hitting them in the legs and arms, and finally simply mowing them down and killing a great number of them. The veteran described pleading with an officer and an NCO to have the men stop, only to be contemptuously dismissed with such words as, "What are you, a communist? Do you like these fucking gooks or something?" He later reported these events to his commanding officer, despite the fact that the latter had once told him that, "The only good gook is a dead gook." Now he was told that, "I would be in the brig if I didn't shut my yap."

He remembered being appalled by the whole incident at the time. But as a skilled technician in artillery and radar performing delicate and crucial work, he was also aware of how much he depended upon cooperation both from officers above him and the men he was in charge of, in order to maintain respect and authority as well as effective function.

So I knew there was no chance of ever having anything done and I was just jeopardizing everything and didn't want to get hassled or thrown into the brig . . . so I just forgot it and I didn't do anything more about it. . . . I just tucked it away in some dead space . . . and went on functioning.

Indeed he focused ever more single-mindedly on the technical challenges confronting him.

He told me later that he experienced guilt at the moment of recalling the event:

I was very pissed with myself . . . for not having stopped it and for not, you know, screaming about it through the rest of my tour. . . . Like that's one thing that I can't forgive myself for.

But his guilt undoubtedly antedated the recovery of the memory. The woodcutter incident had been for him an act of ultimate transgression; as in the case of the My Lai survivor, he could neither prevent nor separate himself from the event, despite his condemnation of it at the time. But the extensive numbing around the image had rendered it inaccessible. When he was asked during the rap session why he had not spoken publicly about the atrocity (as others in the group had), he was quite surprised by the question and answered, "Because it wasn't liv-

ing in me as an atrocity." Guilt had been living in him right
along, however. A lapsed Catholic, he reverted to an idiom from
his extensive religious training in describing his present dedication to antiwar work as "doing penance" and a "kind of absolu-
tion." It was more than that. After recalling the atrocity during
the rap session, he went through a period of intense pain—for
several weeks he was frequently tearful and easily upset—giving
way to a sense of relief and then to increasing confidence and
energy in living and working as a veteran-activist—all this part
of a strong overall subjective sense of growth and change.*

Death guilt takes on a special kind of intensity when experienced directly toward the enemy. A veteran appearing at a rap
group for the first time told of a frightening recurrent dream,
in which an NVA soldier would shoot and kill him. The figure
in his dream was the same NVA soldier he had actually confronted in what was, literally, face-to-face combat: as each of
them shot they could see one another clearly. The veteran was
wounded in the leg, and, without quite making things clear, gave
us the impression that the NVA soldier had been killed. The
combat incident had occurred a year earlier, but the recurrent
dream together with diffuse anxiety had been intensified by two
forms of symbolic reactivation—the veteran's increasing involvement in antiwar protest, and his having been surprised by a
mugger near his home in Manhattan a short time before.† In
the midst of these associations to his dream one of the other
men suddenly asked him, "Do you feel guilty about being alive?"

* He later told me, in a tone combining self-condemnation with pride in additional insight, that he had actually done even less to stop the killing than he
originally reported. He had protested little or not at all to the officer and NCO
involved, but had quickly retired to his bunk. He had come to this clarifica-
tion—a further stage of recovering his 'forgotten atrocity'—at a "men's group"
containing a number of veterans.

† Anything that makes psychological contact with the survivor's constellation
of death anxiety, guilt, and loss can serve as a symbolic reactivation of his original death immersion. The death immersion (in this case the war) can itself be
viewed as a symbolic reactivation of earlier "survivals"—of childhood experiences
—small "holocausts" associated with separation, disintegration, and stasis.[9]

He answered without hesitation: "Yes. You're supposed to be dead."

Right after that another veteran reported a brief but pointed dream of his own:

I was arguing with myself. Then there were two separate selves, and one of them finally shot the other, so that I shot myself.

The dream, and a few associations to it, epitomized the survivor conflict: an inner split that is both guilty and deadly; a simultaneous transgression and retribution—the self murdering the self. It also suggests the classic literary and mythological theme of the double, in which one self can represent life (sometimes immortal life) and its replica death (or mortality).[10] Above all, it is the starkest of images—at the same time concrete and metaphorical—of being both victim and executioner.

No doubt dreams like the above two have been experienced by men returning from other wars, or, in the case of the second one, by people who have not gone to war at all. But with the Vietnam War the disbelief in the entire symbolization surrounding "the enemy" makes such dreams particularly likely to occur, and excruciatingly infused with guilt. One man put the matter rather simply when, in the course of a discussion about these matters, he told of killing a Vietcong soldier with a knife, and then added rather softly:

I felt sorry. I don't know why I felt sorry. John Wayne never felt sorry.

That is, one was supposed to be tough and numbed, but one was not—at least not entirely—given the extent of disbelief in "the enemy" and in one's right to kill him.

These three responses are reminiscent of Wilfred Owen's lines:

> Foreheads of men have bled where no wounds were.
> I am the enemy you killed, my friend.
> I knew you in this dark . . .[11]

"The enemy" becomes simply a man the soldier-survivor has killed, who now returns to haunt him. And the question the Vietnam veteran must ask—"Was *he* an enemy?"*—harkens back through man's entire war-making history. More than that, the veteran is subject, at one time or another, to the psychologically devastating idea that it is "the enemy" who is fighting the "just war," as was the case with a former marine:

One time [in] Vietnam I came to realize that the people I was fighting were right, the Vietcong were right, the NVA were right, and that I was wrong. And when I realized that, then I hated myself for not stopping. I despised myself.[13]

Perhaps only a veteran of Vietnam could rephrase the Twenty-third Psalm with these words:

> Yea as I walk through the valley of death
> I shall fear no evil
> For the valleys are gone
> And only death awaits
>
> And I am the evil.[14]

One suspects that warding off precisely that judgment is the purpose of still another version of that psalm that is much better known in Vietnam, and has been widely displayed as a marine slogan:

> Yea as I walk through the valley of death
> I shall fear no evil
> Because I'm the meanest son-of-a-bitch in the valley.

* This is the question asked by an old soldier described by Alfred de Vigny[12] who, in the dark of a surprise bayonet attack, discovers he has killed a fourteen-year-old child ("one of those fourteen-year-old officers, so numerous in the Russian armies") before the eyes of the child's father. As the child dies he drops a malacca cane, which falls into the soldier's hands, "as if he were giving it to me." The soldier vows right then "never to carry any other weapon," and instead carries the malacca cane with him everywhere as a kind of talisman and perpetual reminder of guilt. To the surgeon attending him for a wound soon after the incident he says, "I'm tired of war."

For many the "I am the evil" is inwardly more convincing.

The psychic field underlying guilt—the field in which "Foreheads of men have bled where no wounds were"—is one of war divested of its religiosity, of its grandeur and glory, and, above all, of its honor. The combat briefing mentioned earlier (*"I* don't know why *I'm* here. *You* don't know why *you're* here. But since we're *both* here, we might as well do a good job and do our best to stay alive") is a call to a battle divested of its sacred images and equally sacred combat rituals; killing loses its "higher purpose," its contribution to the "divine order" for which any war is ostensibly being fought.[15] No longer conducted within structure or ritual, killing becomes random, suffused with guilt, an expression of general disintegration—as in the following representation of the men at My Lai:

And so they cursed and they yelled and they laughed and they cried and they killed and they raped, and deep down in their hearts they felt it was wrong. But on another level of their minds they felt they were right and war is wrong and the death of their buddies was wrong and being in Vietnam was wrong and protesting the war in the United States was wrong and who the hell knows what's right and what's wrong.[16]

Here the victims were noncombatants. But where chaos and antimeaning reign in the total absence of significant ritual for sacred purpose, all killing is transgression. All killing touches upon atrocity.

Just as the absurdity of the Vietnam War environment, with its fiercely irreconcilable antimeaning, includes but goes far beyond man's existential Absurdity (facing death in a world without God)—so does its evil differ from more institutionalized Evil. The latter, as epitomized in the Catholic church, for instance, places wrongdoing within a larger system: Evil has a place in the symbolic universe, and is therefore knowable, describable, expectable, and to an extent permissible. Evil can even be the focus, as in imagery of the Devil, of a negative pole of immortality. Above all, there is a ritual structure within which

one can repair or atone for what one has done—one can proclaim guilt, overcome guilt feelings, and reconstitute the self
within the established forms of a particular religion, culture, or
world view. At its best, Evil can even possess the virtue, so to
speak, of illumination.

But the kind of evil encountered in Vietnam has little place
in anyone's cosmology: it is unformed, chaotic, inchoate, and,
on a number of levels, unspeakable. It comes under the category
of what theologians speak of as "surd evil," meaning evil closely
related to chaos, and (according to the *Encyclopedia of Religion*) "in which there is no principle of improvement; its only
function is to be endured, rejected, conquered, or passed by."
That chaos is associated theologically with death, or the existence
of the universe prior to life; and the word "surd" derives from
the Latin *surdus*, meaning deaf, silent, mute, dumb, inaudible,
or insufferable to the ear.* The *sense* of absurd evil, then, suggests a relationship to a realm that is incongruously bad and
deadly, and the guilt derived from that sense, at least initially,
has a parallel absence of structure, a chaotic nakedness. Unlike
guilt that has a clear place within a religious or cultural system,
this guilt must be supplied with form and direction. The men
provide such form and direction first by placing themselves in
the categories of both victims (thrust into an atrocity-producing
situation deadly to all) and executioners (who dealt with their
situation as expected, by killing), and then by moving beyond
and rejecting both of these roles. Instead of the "brave warriors"
who become "more than themselves" (immortalized) in battle,
these men felt diminished, deformed, dishonored. Yet despite all,
a few have been eventually able to discover a "principle of im-

---

* *Surd* is now used in mathematics to mean "of a number or quantity that cannot be expressed in finite terms of ordinary numbers or quantities," that is "irrational"; and in phonetics to mean nonvocal or voiceless (*Oxford English Dictionary*). "Ab," meaning "off," intensified the "surd" and suggests something not
only "insufferable to the ear" or (particularly in music) "inharmonious" or
"jarring," but actively incongruous.

provement" where there had appeared to be none, ways of eventually becoming "more than themselves" after having first been so tainted and diminished.

The particular evil and taint of the Vietnam War finds appropriate, if tragic, symbolism in the "heroin epidemic" among American servicemen. There has been no doubt about the actuality during the early 1970s of widespread heroin addiction in Vietnam—probably related to such factors as the easy, low-cost availability of the virtually pure drug, the drying up (at least temporarily) of marihuana supplies, the death-linked corruptions of the environment, and the related apathy of those who were (in one journalist's words) "at the butt end of a bad war." Yet despite that actuality, the drug epidemic takes on a near mythic quality. The men are sent to war and encounter evil; they take on the taint or sickness of that evil in the form of "the heroin plague" (the mass media term); the society that sent them becomes terrified of them, lest they carry the "plague" back home; a system of forced "testing" and "decontamination" is set up before the men can be permitted to reenter the society (including sudden urine checks in the middle of the night, required "treatment" under sometimes coercive conditions, etcetera); but the system does not always work, the fear of contagion remains acute, as do images of the infected men returning to spread their plague throughout the mother country. Now the addicts, instead of the war itself and the way we are fighting it, become the locus of evil.[17] The "problem," when finally acknowledged, becomes drug addiction, and that, we are told, is what must be overcome. The fact that American political and military machinations are largely responsible for the problem in the first place* is further

---

* American responsibility for the heroin epidemic includes not only our pursuit of the war itself but our complicity in maintaining the conditions under which opium is grown, and at times in the opium trade itself. Hans J. Spielmann, in a knowledgeable article about the "Fertile Triangle of Southeast Asia"—Thailand, Burma, and Laos—where two-thirds of the opium source of heroin originates, discusses the complicated levels of economic pressure and corruption involved, including extensive participation by United States Special Forces and the CIA in

evidence of the relationship of the "heroin plague" to the deeper and profoundly cruel mythic truth about the "surd evil" we perpetrate in Vietnam.

Freud saw the idea of parricide—the son murdering or wishing to murder his father*—as at the center of the idea of guilt. I am suggesting that we retain the image of guilt as related to the sense that one has 'killed'—but extend the paradigm beyond parricide and the Oedipal complex to that of death and the continuity of life. This is the principle of Buber's association of guilt with a "wound in the order of being." One experiences a sense of guilt because one feels that at some level one has killed or destroyed—whether one's victim has been another person, a principle, or oneself.

We have been discussing two general forms of guilt that can be designated as *static* and *animating*. Static guilt is characterized by a closed universe of transgression and expected punishment, in which one is unable to extricate oneself from a death-like individual condition. One form we have seen it take is that of

opium traffic in the recent past ("for, to be sure, political reasons"), and concludes that the governments involved view United States objections as "in the main window dressing" because "the U.S. spreading involvement in the war meant that its chief concern was stability in Southeast Asia. And if this meant the continued production of opium in the sensitive areas, say in the fertile fields where Laos, Burma and Thailand come together—that was all right with the U.S." Alfred McCoy has confirmed all that and much more in a more recent, exhaustive study.[18]

* In *Civilization and Its Discontents*[19] Freud insists that "We cannot get away from the assumption that man's sense of guilt springs from the Oedipus complex and was acquired at the killing of the father by the brothers banded together." Freud believed that this primal guilt has been carried over in man's unconscious from prehistoric times through images genetically transmitted over the generations; and that it is reactivated and added to by guilt-producing experiences of the individual. I shall return to the general question of guilt in Chapter 13; here I wish only to introduce a perspective on guilt that emphasizes its more general relationship to death—and to related themes of separation, statis, and disintegration encountered anew by each individual rather than genetically transmitted.

numbed guilt, in which one's 'deadened state' seems to be a literal form of retribution for one's own act of 'killing': the "punishment fits the crime."

Numbed guilt resembles what Freud called an unconscious sense of guilt—but I use the term to emphasize the extent to which the entire being is frozen or desensitized, in order to avoid feeling the "wound" (or 'death') one has caused (or thinks one has caused), leaving one anesthetized from much of life itself.

Numbed guilt includes a vague feeling of badness, of having transgressed, in the absence of a form or even a clear-cut emotional structure within which to articulate that guilt. Unable to confront what one has done, or even to feel clearly guilty, one is instead plagued by an unformed, free-floating discomfort with oneself, which is likely to be associated with touchiness, suspiciousness, and withdrawal.

Self-lacerating guilt is another form of static guilt, in which, rather than a sustained 'deadening,' one performs a perpetual 'killing' of the self. That is, the *mea culpa* of self-condemnation takes the form of a repetition-compulsion, and the very insistence upon one's own unmitigated evil prevents actual 'knowledge' of guilt. The as-if situation here is that of continuous reenactment of the retribution, continuous killing of the self. Guilt accompanying clinical forms of depression, and what we speak of more generally as "neurotic guilt," tends to be of this self-lacerating variety.

In both of these forms of static guilt one is cut off from the life process—held in a state of separation and inner disintegration as well as stasis—that is, in a death-dominated condition.

Animating guilt, in contrast, is characterized by bringing oneself to life around one's guilt. This requires, as we have already suggested, active imagery of possibility beyond the guilt itself. Animating guilt and image beyond the guilt are in a continuous dialectical relationship, the one requiring the other. Thus, animating guilt propels one toward connection, integrity, and movement. But for this self-propulsion to occur, one requires prior internal images of at least the possibility of these life-affirming patterns, imagery that can in turn relate to something in the external environment. In this sense the imagery of possibility antedates the animating guilt, but it is also true that animating guilt can activate the individual to the point of virtually creating such imagery.

Central to the principle of animating guilt is the energy it engenders, an energy of aspiration emanating from a sustained and formative dissatisfaction with both self and world (if the focus is entirely on one to the exclusion of the other, it is doubtful that the guilt can be animating). Above all, animating guilt is a source of self-knowledge—confirming Buber's dictum that "Man is the being who is capable of becoming guilty and is capable of illuminating his guilt."[20] In illuminating one's guilt, one illuminates the self; not a part but the entire self-process is involved. Nor is animating guilt merely "restitutive," though it can certainly be that. Rather, it presses beyond existing arrangements, toward new images and possibilities, toward transformation. Above all, animating guilt is inseparable from the idea of being responsible for one's actions—so much so that we may define it as the anxiety of responsibility.

To be sure, these three kinds of guilt do not separate out as precisely as this schema might suggest; they, in fact, overlap and probably never exist in pure form. But I have observed in a considerable number of veterans a relationship to guilt so animating as to be a form of personal liberation. The discovery of one's animating guilt can, for such men, be nothing less than rediscovery of oneself as a human being. The deserter quoted earlier, for instance, remembered his dramatic recognition that "I was somebody with feelings who had done something wrong and I— I was not an animal or some kind of killing machine." Guilt itself becomes a source of relief and renewed self-esteem: "I physically felt satisfaction, knowing that I felt guilty. Meaning that I was not a murderer." And such animating guilt, once em-

braced, propelled him toward continuous growth: "I'm still trying to qualify as a human being . . . still trying to get positive
judgments on me, I guess."[21]

Clearly these forms of guilt operate in ordinary life as well.
Static guilt is more associated with neurosis or with a generally
numbed state of "normal" existence. But animating guilt undoubtedly operates in enlivening ways that have not been much
appreciated. Given the necessity of imposed moral sanctions on
the part of parents, there is no such thing as a childhood totally
devoid of guilt. But there is much more to be said about the way
in which parent-child transactions lead to choices and habits of
either static or animating guilt. The choice is probably never
absolute, and even those accustomed to static forms of guilt can,
under certain combinations of pressure and opportunity, trans-
form that guilt in an animating direction—as was true of a number of Vietnam veterans. At any time during the life cycle, a
focus on animating guilt means less numbing, less in the way of
repetitious self-condemnation, and more in the way of feeling,
constructively critical self-evaluation, autonomy, and change.*

---

* What is at issue is one's *relationship* to guilt, which becomes inseparable
from the way in which one uses or lives with that guilt. I choose the word "animating" because, in its derivation from the Latin *anima*, meaning breath or
soul, it suggests the idea of infusing with movement, energy and life. In speaking of these various forms of guilt, I mean to include related forms of shame.
In earlier work I have stressed that guilt and shame are variations of a single
fundamental theme, having to do with self-condemnation for one's responsibility
in the breakdown of human connection and order. With guilt, as evolved mostly
in the Western cultural idiom, that breakdown or 'killing' is associated with
the idea of sinfulness or evil and the expectation of appropriate retribution or
punishment. With shame, as evolved mainly in non-Western cultural idioms,
the breakdown or 'killing' has to do with the failure to live up to group standards, and the idea of being exposed in one's failure, with the expectation of
banishment from the group, of being considered beyond the pale. But there is
much overlap, and no culture is devoid of either. Variations of shame and guilt
are, in fact, intrinsic to all communities, not only as sanctions for wrongdoing,
but as part of the very cement of culture and human relations. As parallels to
what I have described for guilt, *numbed shame* would be a form of avoiding
exposure (or self-exposure) through desensitization; *self-lacerating shame* would
take the form of blindly compulsive self-condemnation for one's failures without

War, especially war perceived as absurd and evil rather than heroic, can offer a grim opportunity for the embrace of animating guilt. Commenting on the extraordinary World War I poetry of Wilfred Owen, C. Day Lewis notes "the suddenness of his development from a very minor poet to something altogether larger. It was as if, during the weeks of his first tour of duty in the trenches, he came of age emotionally and spiritually."[22] From Owen's own letters, we learn of a crucial combat experience, after four months on the line, in which a shell exploding near him blew him into the air and left his "brother officer" covered with earth, [where] "no relief will ever relieve him, nor will his Rest . . . be a nine days—Rest." Incapacitated for several months after that, Owen's condition was variously diagnosed as a concussion, shellshock, and neurasthenia, but he understood better:

You know it was not the Bosche that worked me up, nor the explosives, but it was living so long by poor old Cock Robin (as we used to call II/Lt. Gaukroger [the man killed]), who lay not only nearby, but in various places around and about, if you understand. I hope you don't!

His death guilt enabled him to look critically at his war and all war:

. . . I am more and more Christian as I walk the unchristian ways of Christendom. Already I have comprehended a light which never will filter into the dogma of any national church: namely that one of Christ's essential commands was: Passivity at any price! Suffer dis-

---

illumination; and *animating shame* would involve probing the roots of failure, exposing the self to the self, on behalf of narrowing the gap between what one sees oneself to have been and what one would be. In the end, however, Vietnam Veterans' feelings of being "ashamed" of what they had done were inseparable from their guilty sense of wrongdoing. More basic than the distinction between guilt and shame, I believe, is that between an animating as opposed to a static relationship to either.

honor and disgrace; but never resort to arms. Be bullied, be out-
raged, be killed, but do not kill.

*And am I not myself a conscientious objector with a very seared
conscience?*[23] [Italics mine]

A year later he could apply that same animating guilt to an
illumination of the "death in life" state—the numbed, static
guilt of "Mental Cases":

> —These are men whose minds the Dead have ravished.
> Memory fingers in their hair of murders,
> Multitudinous murders they once witnessed. . . .
> —Thus their heads wear this hilarious, hideous
> Awful falseness of set-smiling corpses.
> —Thus their hands are plucking at each other;
> Picking at the rope-knouts of their scourging;
> Snatching after us who smote them, brother.
> Pawing us who dealt them war and madness.[24]

No wonder that Vietnam veterans sometimes express strong
identification with certain veterans of World War I—more so
than, say, with those of World War II. Wilfred Owen died a
week before his war ended, having already put his death guilt
to powerful use in the moving "survivor formulation" contained
in his poems. Now we see a vast segment of an entire American
generation doing the same, not through poetic talent (though
a few poets among them are beginning to emerge)* but through
a fierce articulateness of their own, energized by their animating
guilt. The inner imagery is: "I killed or let die—wrongly designated 'enemies,' my buddies, part of myself—for which I have
been punished by a 'deadening' within me; now I must make
things live, renew life, come alive myself." They teach us much

---

* Two notable collections of poetry by Vietnam veterans have now appeared:
one by Michael Casey has just received the Yale Younger Poets Award for
1971;[25] and another with contributions by more than forty poets, entitled *Winning Hearts and Minds*,[26] published successfully by the veterans themselves.

about the relationship of guilt to the survivor's struggles with dying, killing, and living.* Their own struggle to achieve an animating relationship to their guilt takes on special importance during an age of numbing, holocaust, and transformation.

The antiwar veterans, however, encounter a larger society intent on maintaining its numbed guilt—concerning the Vietnam War, and much else as well. And while most Americans came to detest this humiliating and unresolvable war, and while they sensed there was much about it that was unusually ugly, they nonetheless resist the full revelations of the veterans' animating guilt. For these threatened their own symbolizations around national virtue and military honor.

In the past, the warrior as hero could be a repository for broad social guilt. Sharing in his heroic mission could serve as a cleansing experience of collective relief from whatever guilt had been experienced over distant killing, or from the need to feel any guilt whatsoever. But when the warrior-hero gives way to the tainted executioner-victim, not only is this repository taken away, but large numbers of people risk a new wave of unmanageable guilt and a profound sense of loss, should they recognize what their warriors have actually become.

Not surprisingly, then, the antiwar veterans' demand that the people of their society join in transforming their guilt to an animating dimension is often ignored or actively resisted. For to do what the veterans ask would mean confronting the responsibility of the society as a whole, and of its leaders in particular, for the killing and dying. It would require the most intense exploration of shared forms of guilt as well as revitalizing images beyond that guilt. Many find it easier to lash out at those who ask for the confrontation. There can even be a desperate insistence, despite all evidence to the contrary, in the continuing purity

---

* Note Buber's idea that experiencing guilt can provide "real insight into the universality of lived time, a fact which shows itself unmistakably in the starkest of all human perspectives, that concerning one's own death."[27]

and guiltlessness of American warriors, and of the society as a whole. We see this kind of phenomenon in some of the canonization of Lieutenant Calley, and the temporary popularity of a song, "The Battle Hymn of Lieutenant Calley."

And yet there are stirrings here and there in American society in the direction of animating guilt, of the society's renewing itself by means of illuminating what it has done to others and to itself, what it has perpetrated and survived. And there does exist much in the American past, religious or otherwise, that can provide ethical images that encourage one not only to "feel sorry" (like the veteran quoted earlier) but to alter the tainted political and military course of the society. And beyond a specifically American experience, there is evolving, during the latter half of the twentieth century, a worldwide ethical impulse toward feeling the pain of abused people everywhere, a tendency for the executioner to feel his own victim's suffering. Or to put the matter another way, there is an increasing breakdown of the old forms of social equilibrium within which victimizing patterns and manageable forms of guilt (or of avoidance of guilt) could be maintained. Like everything else, these arrangements are out of joint, and every executioner faces the possibility of being at least confronted by the suffering of his victims.

It is sometimes said that people no longer feel guilty the way they used to. That may be true, but it is also likely that a reservoir of guilt still exists within most societies—the problem lies in converting the numbed and self-lacerating versions of guilt that predominate into more animating forms. I believe this is what was meant by one antiwar veteran who, during a discussion of the desirability of amnesty for draft-resisters and deserters, turned to me and said rather softly, "I want amnesty for all of us." He was not asking to be "forgiven," or that society "forget" what he and others did—much of his life, in fact, was devoted toward seeing that such things were remembered. Rather, he wanted everyone to join in a process of altered definitions of honor, based in turn upon the transformation of guilt.

CHAPTER 5

Zones of Rage and Violence

Fuck you—fuck you one and all.

—GI upon awakening in a postoperative
recovery room in Japan, and
discovering that his leg had been
amputated (from Glasser, *365 Days*)

Take the war out of the T.V.s and put it in the complacent streets
Kick Amerika awake
Before it dies in its sleep.

—Charles M. Purcell
(from *Winning Hearts and Minds*)

UNRESOLVED DEATH GUILT can also be expressed through feelings of rage and impulses toward violence. These are prominent in survivors of any war, but the binds, betrayals, and corruptions experienced by the Vietnam veteran fuel those tendencies to the point where they invade large zones of his psyche. Bursts of anger were very frequent during our rap sessions, and it was more or less taken for granted that rage close to the surface was the normal state of the Vietnam veteran. The important question was what one did with the rage. During individual and group sessions, three different patterns of rage and violence seemed to emerge.

There was first what could be called the habit of violence. In war, violence becomes a quick and absolute solution to whatever seems to threaten or intrude, all the more so when there is great confusion about where danger lies and who is the enemy. Beyond that, the veteran can become habituated to the survivor mission of revenge (for buddies killed and other forms of suffering) and extend his false witness to the civilian environment. Static forms of residual guilt can serve as a stimulus to such continuing false witness. Similarly, residual anxiety of a more general kind serves to maintain the habit of violence around a lasting image of killing or destroying as a means of ridding oneself of the fear of death.

A number of veterans told how, when brushed by someone on the street—or simply annoyed by something another person had done—they would have an impulse to "throttle" or kill him. And they would directly associate this impulse with patterns of behavior cultivated in Vietnam: with "wasting" whoever passed for the enemy, with the numbing and brutalization underlying that behavior, but also with the rage beneath the numbing. As one man put it,

In Vietnam you're mad all the time—you wake up mad—you're mad when you eat, mad when you sleep, mad when you walk, mad when you sit—just mad all the time.

He was undoubtedly overemphasizing the awareness of anger but probably accurate about the extent of its inner existence, even if defended against. (His use of the word "mad" could also unwittingly infer "craziness.") In any case an important segment of a generation of young American men built identities and life-styles around the rage and violence of a war environment as absorbing as it was corrupting. The guilt-linked sense of these inner zones of rage and violence is precisely what causes a man to retain the image of himself as a "monster."

Others have observed a similar preoccupation with violence in Vietnam veterans. Charles Levy, who has done extensive interviewing and "rapping" with working-class marine veterans, observes that "the thinking of these veterans seems to be dominated by a fear of their own violence." Moreover, they were prone to give expression to random violence toward relatives, friends, or strangers. Levy recognizes that some of these men had violent tendencies prior to Vietnam, but believes that "the level of violence has now changed," and that "Now it has no boundaries." We can say that the guilt-linked habit of violence cultivated in Vietnam undermines earlier controls and distinctions around violence—as evidenced in observations like Levy's and in reports of violent crimes by Vietnam veterans.[*1]

Simply by coming to the rap group, the men I worked with

---

* Out of Charles Levy's original sample of sixty men he interviewed, a total of seven have been accused of murder (two) or attempted murder (five), which comes to a total of more than ten percent. Of course much more extensive statistics on a national basis are required, but a greater potential for random violence in Vienam veterans than in veterans of other wars would be consistent with their particularly intense survivor conflicts.

were, in effect, taking a stand against random violence. Not that they lacked such impulses, often in complicated form. One veteran, somewhat prone to violence from childhood, spoke of his post-Vietnam struggles to overcome "the beast in me," by which he meant an inclination to attack other people suddenly while in a dreamlike state in which he was hardly aware of what he was doing. For some time after his return from Vietnam he worked as a milkman on a night route, where he could avoid other people and express his rage by periodic screams into the night. He spoke about his violent impulses in a repetitious, self-enclosed fashion, as though protecting himself from something underneath the violence. One of the professionals helped the group break through this protective armor by pointing out the profound fear behind each situation of violence the veteran described, to which he quickly responded:

Yes, sometimes I think I'm still back with those thirteen guys [in my squad]. . . . It's like going out on a mission and waiting for the first shot.

He was, in other words associating his violent impulses with death anxiety. The imagery he used was reminiscent of a tendency described by Levy for veterans to experience, at the moment of their violence, what they themselves referred to as a "flashback" to Vietnam—to a situation either of combat or the killing of civilians.*

The veteran quoted above told how, when in Vietnam, he and other GIs sometimes played a contemporary version of Russian roulette, in which one man would pull the pin of a grenade, which would then be tossed back and forth among the men until

---

* There is some evidence that this post-Vietnam violence is most likely to occur where the victim can be relatively easily viewed as "inhuman," as the equivalent of a "gook." (See Chapter 7) In any case, the "flashback" experience has been identified in many situations in which veterans have been accused of violent crimes which have been brought to the attention of our group of psychological professionals.

one of them made a decision to throw it off safely just before it exploded. Such a game combines violent and suicidal impulses as a response to overwhelming fear of death. In them, the men are able to recreate in playful-fearful microcosm—and thereby mock—the threat of *absurd* death characterizing the larger war.

Over the course of more than a year's involvement in the rap group, this veteran's violent tendencies greatly diminished. He could then confess that he had been much less violent in Vietnam than he had implied. He had previously given the impression that he had killed many people there, whereas in actuality, despite extensive combat experience, he could not be certain he had killed anyone. After overcoming a certain amount of death anxiety and death guilt, that is, he had much less need to call forth his inner beast to lash out at others or at himself.

A second form of rage and potential violence occurred around the theme of betrayal, the veterans' sense of having been victimized, badly used, or as they often put it, "fucked over," in having been sent to fight in Vietnam. They spoke about having been misled, put in a situation where they both slaughtered people and suffered for no reason, and then abused or ignored on their return. There was sometimes talk of contemptuous treatment from employers or prospective employers, in which "coming from Vietnam didn't mean a damn thing" (though they also realized that on many occasions, it was they, the veterans, who resisted the jobs). In this and other ways they expressed victim's rage, which could extend to virtually every area of living.

Such a chain of perpetual victimization and accompanying rage was described by a former marine who had fought at Khe Sanh:

. . . talk to anybody was going through Marine Corps boot camp . . . the dehumanizing process is just hard to describe. I wish somebody had a record of suicides that go on at these places . . . [and] the beatings that go on daily. Boys are turned not into men, but beasts— beasts that will fight and destroy at a moment's notice, without any regard to what they are fighting or why they are fighting, but just fight. I have seen men fight each other over a drink of water when there was plenty for both of them. . . . [Then in Vietnam] I got so disgusted that I put a picture of L.B.J. up in my tent and I had "Wanted for Murder" underneath it. . . . [resulting in his being transferred to combat and sent to Khe Sanh] and I spent the next seven months getting shot at. . . . When I came back home I was very much antiwar, and yet there was a hostility in me toward other people. . . . If someone irritated me, my first impulse was to kill the fucker. . . . I'd catch myself and I'd think of another alternative to deal with whatever the problem was. . . . I started an antiwar group at the University. . . . I was busted for possession of marijuana. There was half a gram of marijuana involved; and five months after I was arrested, I was convicted . . . and received a ten-year [suspended] sentence. . . . While I was in jail on a $10,000 bail, a man killed his wife and was put in jail and was released the next day on $1500 bail. So that lets you know the priority of capital crimes in Texas. I'm still on probation because of that sentence. And if anything happened to me right now, I could start serving that ten-year sentence. While I was in jail, I realized it was no longer a case of my government and I having different ideals . . . but . . . of a life and death struggle between me—[and] not *my* government but *their* government. Today there is still a lot of hate in me—a hatred that makes it difficult to form . . . relationships with anyone. I am working on that. There was a time when the red, white and blue meant something to me and I loved this country, but I can tell you now that a country that burns yellow babies and starves black babies is a blood-sucking whore whose death I hope to live to see.[2]

When this kind of statement was made in the rap group, as it sometimes was, the men would support the indignation and rage at what they (and I) saw as very real experiences of victimization. At the same time the group was sensitive to, and would critically explore, tendencies to remain immobilized around extreme suspicion and a paranoid outlook, or imagery of "destroying everything" (American society, the people in it, etcetera).

For just as the men rejected the imposed role of executioner, so they rejected that of victim. It was always a matter of a particular person and his behavior, actions, or decision—never a mere victim—however duped and badly treated by the all too real forces of victimization. These external forces (the government and military pursuing the war, the police and courts imposing absurd penalties for marijuana use as a way of suppressing a political militant, etcetera) were taken seriously as part of the equation; there was never a reduction of all rage to childhood resentments, though these too were examined. Rage and indignation were too much respected for that: they were looked upon as significant, at times painful and self-destructive, but often appropriate and valuable emotions.

The rage could be directed toward any figures or symbols of authority, especially official authority—political leaders, the Veterans Administration, representatives of the establishment or ordinary middle-class society, or of the older generation. Specific leaders and symbols were also discussed at length, so that psychological judgments could be informed by critical perspectives on normal social arrangements. But there was a special kind of rage reserved for the military.

The men expressed fantasies, old or current, of violent revenge toward those in the military who had abused them, especially toward "lifers" (regular Army men) who seemed much more hated than anybody officially designated as the enemy. These images could be relatively focused, or they could take on the diffuse, impotent, quality of a recollection of the deserter who was referred to earlier:

I wanted to become a communist. I wanted to assassinate the president. I wanted to organize some kind of uprising that would swoop down on the Pentagon—save the world from the imperialistic United States, etcetera, etcetera.[3]

More frequently the men would describe a gradually mounting bitterness at being hassled and ultimately betrayed by the military. That betrayal could take the form of a variety of small indignities, broken promises, bad assignments, lack of recognition, or brutalization by specific officers or noncoms—but always at the end of the road was the ultimate betrayal of Vietnam. Those most embittered toward the military were the ones who had initially believed in it and given themselves to it. Their resentful critique could extend far beyond the Vietnam War to corruptions throughout its structure, but they would always return to the war as both reflecting and furthering the poisoning of an institution they had admired, and within which they had, for a time, flourished. For them the betrayal was greatest.

The reaction of the veterans to others' violence within the military revealed much of the quality of their rage. During one rap group meeting there was an extensive discussion of an incident reported in the newspapers, in which an army major was shot and killed by two black GIs after having apparently reprimanded them for conducting too noisy a party in their barracks. A few of the men admitted an immediate feeling of pleasure upon reading about the incident; others wanted to know more details about what the major had said to the soldiers and the kind of relationship he had with his men prior to the incident; but overall, the men tended to bring their struggle against violence to bear upon whatever transient emotional release they experienced.

Also at issue was a certain amount of empathy for black violence. A former paratrooper I interviewed, for instance, who was not a member of an antiwar group, bitterly condemned the violence to which the military had exposed him, admitting that "although I have strong feelings against violence, I sometimes feel myself wanting to react in a violent way." About the blacks, he added:

As much as I detest violence, I have to sympathize because violence is the only thing people can understand. I've never been hungry. . . . To be denied something that is yours by nature—they shouldn't have to go after freedom and equality—it should be there from the beginning.

What he was saying, I believe, was that his own violent double victimization—being exposed to violence, and then feeling it necessary to become violent in order to survive that exposure—sensitized him to what he perceived to be a roughly analogous double victimization of many blacks in American society on an everyday basis. But as one struggling against his own violent impulses, he (like other veterans) brought conflict and ambivalence even to the most 'justified' forms of violence.

The men had similar ambivalence about "fraggings"—attempts by GIs to kill or injure their officers or noncoms (the name comes from the "fragmentation grenades" generally used). Again they would express understanding for the impulse, and would recall not only similar impulses of their own but shared fantasies within their military units that, given a little more desperation and threat (such as an unnecessary order endangering lives) could have resulted in actual fraggings. But the general trend of the discussion would be toward better ways to express one's rage. In this way they again differed from the randomly encountered, working-class marine veterans who spoke with pride (to Charles Levy) about "fraggings" they had witnessed or participated in. The rap group ethos, if there was such a thing, was one of nonviolent quest for personal and social change. Opposition to the war, and to institutional arrangements behind it, could provide not only a focus for rage but (as in the case of guilt) a beginning vision beyond the situations that gave rise to the rage. They did not, in other words, have the need to remain inwardly dominated (and, as Levy pointed out in relationship to his group, incapacitated) by their psychic zones of rage and violence.

Nonetheless, the equilibrium around these zones could be tenuous. Opposition to the war raised new problems around violence. At one meeting the men discussed a recent surprise attack on an American base, boldly executed by NLF guerrillas, in which a number of American defenders were killed. One or two men said things like "I found myself rooting for the Vietcong."

Indeed, they were rather consistent in their admiration for the courage and staying-power of the NLF, a sentiment widespread among Vietnam veterans in general.[4] Admiration for the NLF could combine honesty and (when expressed within antiwar circles) a kind of bravado. But during that rap group meeting, the veterans were understandably uneasy about this admiration, knowing that buddies—men who differed from themselves only in still being part of the American military—were the ones the NLF were killing. That meant they had to struggle with their feelings of *themselves* as betrayers, as men who had shifted their allegiance. For that struggle they needed a certain distance from their war involvement, partly provided by time, as well as evolving images about such things as Vietnamese history and American international policy on the one hand, and larger principles of individual responsibility on the other, within which to revise their self-judgments about loyalty and integrity.*

These first two themes—the habit of violence and the sense of having been betrayed—harken back to the past, even if mostly the immediate past. But there is a third, more forward-looking theme of rage and potential violence that seemed to dwarf the other two in intensity—or, more accurately, to combine with the other two themes to give the rage a more immediate focus. I refer to the rage associated with a man's telling his story of what he had experienced in Vietnam—to a considerable extent laying himself bare—and then being rebuffed. This rage was directed not so much toward war supporters or political opponents but toward those who "don't give a damn."

One of the most vivid memories I have of the rap groups is the former Army sergeant's description of his experience in being invited to address and show a slide film he had made of Vietnam to a chapter of the Veterans of Foreign Wars. That organization, generally right-wing, pro-military, and made up of

---

* By the time of the North Vietnamese offensive of the spring of 1972, a few of the same men were able to express much more easily their hope that the offensive would succeed.

older veterans, almost disinvited him when they learned of his antiwar views, and many left early without hearing much of what he had to say. But among the few who did stay until the end were some who seemed convinced by his claim that the war consisted largely of atrocities and generally brutal treatment of Vietnamese. Just as he began to feel pleased at having made this little bit of progress, however, one of the men in the audience spoke up and said (as the younger veteran remembered):

What you say seems to be true. But I just don't care. I am a white, red-headed Irishman, and I care most about other white, red-headed Irishmen like myself. I can't worry too much about blacks or gooks.

The response of the speaker, as he expressed it in the rap group was: "I was destroyed." He was also overcome with rage, and though generally mild-mannered and nonviolent in his radicalism, he remembered "screaming something about the revolution and how they would get him" at his tormentor, and that "for the first time I felt I could really imagine myself resorting to bombs —placing a bomb right there in that VFW building." Even in reconstructing the experience for the rap group, his rage returned, but he joined in the group's general exploration of the incident. He went on to explain that such an experience

reverts you—throws you back. It threatens everything I've devoted my life to . . . everything I had initiated in myself. The reversion is back to that same attitude . . . I had to go back to violence—blowing things up.

He felt, in other words, revictimized, thrust back into an "atrocity-producing situation" in which he again became a "violent monster." Once more, he is passively acted upon: the active agent is the "it," the encounter with Americans who defend their right to remain numbed even after learning the truth—"it" being a rejection of his survivor mission and a threat to his overall personal transformation:

It makes me think that maybe we can't really change. Maybe we'll just have to have more wars—because of things inside of us.

Over the course of the discussion, however, he could modify that judgment and look more critically at his own reaction:

I was getting too self-righteous about all that I was doing. I had simplified things to the point at which *I* would start a war. I wasn't satisfied with planting a seed—I wanted it to grow right away.

Here he was more or less conceding that the problem he encountered, that of the willfully blunted moral imagination, was too fundamental to be swept away easily, and that honest self-evaluation had to include recognition of his own personal limitations. But the crux of this reaction lies in the veteran's perceived negation of his survivor mission and formulation, which in turn undermines his sense of change and throws him back—"reverts" him to the most static form of his own guilt. Rebuffed in his attempts to animate that guilt, he becomes again enmeshed in it, 'deadened' by it.

For when the antiwar veterans hold their public hearings in various parts of the country and reveal details of brutality, murder, and atrocity, they are by no means simply beating their breasts to insist upon their own everlasting guilt. Rather, they are angrily exposing the atrocity-producing situation within which these acts were committed. Even the handful of veterans who "turned themselves in" to legal authorities at the time of the trial of Lieutenant Calley were saying something like: "Look, you bastards who are passing judgment—*I* did these things *too* —*everyone* did them." And when they flamboyantly cast away their medals near the capital building, they did so with the rage of 'survivor-heroes' not only rejecting tainted awards but literally throwing them in the face of those who bestowed them. To be sure, there is guilt behind their actions. But there is also the bitter rage of men who have been betrayed, the angry insistence that the guilt be shared, and, above all, that the nature of the atrocity-producing situation be recognized. When they make this effort and are rebuffed, the antiwar veterans are left, so to speak, alone with their static guilt and impotent rage.

Again the categories are not always distinct. Being rebuffed when making painful revelations, having one's quest for life beyond atrocity negated, becomes a perpetuation of society's earlier betrayal (the second category) in sending one on the overall false mission of the Vietnam War. And in the case quoted above we could observe a quick recurrence of the "habit of violence" (the first category)—the veteran's impulse was to "revert" to that habit when he felt himself "destroyed," newly threatened with psychic extinction.

There are also lesser explosions of rage toward one another. During a rap group a generally edgy veteran blurted out angry denunciations of two of the other group members—accusing one of them (who was unique in that he worked as a junior executive and was quite "straight" in manner) of being a "fat cat" who had become intolerant of those in more difficult circumstances, and the other for his continuing fascination with guns ("I thought we were supposed to get away from that stuff!"). What emerged in the discussion was the fear (on the part of both the accuser and others) that the two veterans in question were violating shared principles of transformation—from elitism to egalitarianism, and from gun-toting violence to nonviolent alternatives. And during a later session about four or five veterans joined in an angry condemnation of a former group member (with whom they still had active contact in the organization) for his authoritarian manner to the point of "still being a first sergeant." When I suggested that the man in question must set off something painful in them, one of them answered: "It's bad enough trying to convince guys outside—but when you have a guy like that *inside* the organization, it all seems impossible." And another put the matter even more clearly: "Those of us who have gone through the war like to feel we've come out with a certain truth—and he doesn't show that." In all these cases, the target of rage was a man from among them who held tenaciously to an identity element they had pointedly rejected, causing them to doubt their own capacity to rid themselves of that element and undergo genuine change.

These mixed sources of rage call forth special forms of struggle *against* violence. During one rap group, for example, a politically active veteran told of a "bad trip" he had just had on "acid." He had seen a very bright light, around the edges of which were the faces of friends—and his own face too—all being horribly cut to pieces. Soon after that he became aware of a desire to kill his father, and of a similar impulse toward two friends he was riding with on the subways and also toward another member of the rap group with whom he usually got on well. Yet even in the midst of the bad trip, he recognized his behavior as "irrational" and "paranoid." He was, therefore, able to take steps not only to restrain himself but also to call off a political action (a form of civil disobedience at a recruiting center) he was scheduled to lead, because "I didn't want to involve others in my trip."

In his associations to the experience, two themes predominated: his disturbing memories of the deaths he had witnessed in Vietnam; and a series of betrayals he had experienced over the course of his life. On the theme of betrayal, he told of friends he had worked closely with in a right-wing political organization prior to the war "turning on me" when they learned of his antiwar position, making him suspicious that the antiwar veterans might also turn out to be false friends, merely friends through politics. Contained in this theme of betrayal is profound suspicion of counterfeit nurturance[5]—the victim's feeling of being in special need and yet resenting help or love because he perceives it as a reminder of weakness. Since the conflict centers around dependency, it is likely to involve those closest to him— in this case his father and current antiwar friends—who, in turn, become targets of rage and imagined violence. Significantly, his LSD vision included his own physical disintegration as well as that of friends. In this and other ways he expressed not only

residual death anxiety, but his guilty fear that he too might
be a "betrayer": of the dead in having survived them, and now
of his friends (in failing to distinguish which were true and which
false) and of himself (in failing to live up to his strongest
convictions).

But what the group found impressive, and discussed with him
at length, was his actual *refusal* to betray his antiwar "brothers"—by exerting control over his violent impulses, and by
further protecting them in calling off the political action he
had been scheduled to lead. These interpretations were accompanied by expressions of appreciation and affection. The veteran,
thus supported, was enabled to explore further some of his disturbing fears about killing and being killed, and to distinguish
between image and act. All of the men seemed to understand
that, as survivors of a false mission, they were bound to be
plagued by psychological struggles around betrayal; what mat-
tered was the extent to which they could, in the rap group and in
their lives, transcend that category in the direction of integrity
and trust.

Struggles around violence can, for some, become almost
chronic. Another veteran with a right-wing background, who had
turned toward what he had called revolutionary politics, constantly insisted to the group upon the need for violent actions
"to turn the country around." He would qualify his judgment
only to the extent of saying that it would be all right to wait a
few months and see, and then if things didn't improve there
would be no recourse *but* to violence. The group, though agreeing with much of his analysis of American society, kept pointing
out to him his pattern of reverting to very general "violent talk"
as a way of evading difficult immediate personal issues under
discussion. One day he came in very anxious and quickly related
three dreams. In the first, he found himself in a "tremendous
earthquake," feared that the large building near which he was
standing "would come down on me," ducked into a large hole

nearby and "wanted to run out" but "was terrified." In the second dream he was in a prison where "people were waiting to be put to death" and "I was glad I was not one of the people waiting to be killed." In the third dream he was in a baseball stadium, where a shot suddenly rang out, and, although aimed at a policeman, hit instead a little girl. The two men who fired the shots were found and apparently killed—"I saw all three bodies, the little girl and the two men—but I was not sure whose bodies these were."

Then, three weeks later, in a very distraught tone of both self-condemnation and rage, he told of hearing that a girl he had been close to in the past had committed suicide, jumping out of a London hotel window. What impressed him most was the violent nature of her death, which, despite his fragmentary information, he envisioned in lurid and painful detail. Nor was he sure that it was a genuine suicide, suspecting that some group or other might have had political motivation for killing the girl, as she had been active in the past in protest activities and factional struggles. In the tense discussion that followed, I referred to his long-standing struggle with violence and to the three earlier dreams. He immediately responded by saying (in reference to the three bodies in the third dream) "Yes, I couldn't tell whether *I* was one of those bodies."

He was a man inundated by imagery of violence that related not only to all the patterns we have discussed, but to his deadened inner state—his static guilt and fear of disintegration. He sought to come alive via these violent images and via a survivor mission that would enable him to cope not only with his Vietnam experience but his many levels of 'personal holocaust.' Yet in his dreams and his reaction to the girl's death, there was also a warning against violence. The warning was that, should he resort to violence, he might be its victim, whether in a direct bodily way or in a more indirect psychic form involving guilt and retribution. All this occurred at a time he was making a significant shift in his life away from advocacy of violence and toward other forms of experimentation with the self (including drugs, Yippie politics, travel to various parts of the country, and various sexual liaisons). But he remained burdened by war-linked death guilt. He tried valiantly to animate this guilt in various ways: in connection with the dead girl, for instance, he insisted his guilt was "legitimate" and said that his failure to "do more" for her and offer the kind of love that might have prevented the act reflected a "gap" or deficiency in him. He remained troubled, confused, restless, unable to sustain relationships, and continued his probing in all directions.

There were also images of cosmic violence or world-destruction of a kind I encountered among Hiroshima survivors. Sometimes the world being destroyed was specific to Vietnam, as in the case of a veteran who, when in Saigon, was impressed by the glow of the artillery fire on the outskirts of the city and had a dream in which "that glow was an atomic bomb that went off and blew up everything." Hating Saigon and all of Vietnam, he remembers thinking at the time that it was "a great dream."

Another veteran told of spending his time aimlessly thumbing through magazines, "looking for something I won't find," and when asked what it was he was looking for, said that he really did not know but the words which came immediately to mind were "the ultimate weapon." He went on to say how, when studying karate in the past, "I imagined chopping up the world bit by bit." As in Hiroshima (where it reflected more directly the nature of the weapon used) this kind of imagery expresses the survivor's impulse toward cosmic vengeance for the symbolic destruction of his own moral and psychological universe. The Hiroshima survivors' underground theme of cosmic retaliation, only occasionally expressed, took forms such as "I wish atomic bombs would fall all over the world."[6] Among Vietnam veterans an equivalent underground theme is probably much more widespread than realized, and, from the expressions of it I have heard, tends to take a more general form of imagining (or wishing) everything blown up or destroyed. That kind of imagery is an amorphous psychological extension of the principle of letting the punishment fit the crime. To remain preoccupied in this way with world destruction is to remain entrapped in fixed rage, and in the death anxiety and static guilt beneath the rage.

Some such entrapment generally accompanies the impulse toward violence, and can involve an immediate inability to feel alive as well as a longer-range sense of severed social continuity or impaired symbolic immortality. The entrapment amounts to an actual or imminent 'death of the self' that one seeks to escape from or ward off. The rap groups were a way of overcoming that kind of psychic state, of finding nonviolent alternatives to it. Where entrapment persists, however, veterans are likely either to withdraw from human relationships, or else to approach them only as betrayed victims. In the latter case their rage and potential violence is directed not at an appropriate (because responsible) external target, but at someone or something that can be effectively blamed. We are then in the realm of the scapegoating formulation, in which the survivor ceases being a victim by making one of another. The ultimate result can be a vicious circle of imagined or actual violence and continuing entrapment.

The presupposition in this discussion, and in the rap groups in general, is that violence (physical harm due to other human beings) is undesirable and is to be negatively evaluated. But rage, in contrast, is valued. Large segments of rap sessions have been devoted to exploring and eliciting rage and seeking to connect it to appropriate external targets while examining its relationship to internal experience. On one occasion, for example, a veteran spoke with some pride about his "quiet rage" in various situations over the course of his life—toward schoolmates who saw him only as "a Jew," toward military superiors who humiliated him, and, more recently, toward another man in the rap group he and the others couldn't seem to get through to precisely on questions of violence. In the way of confirming what he was saying, another man in the group reminded him of an example of precisely that "quiet rage" he had encountered in the first veteran's room: an American flag decal attached to the wall over which a swastika had been drawn. The first veteran then told how it got there. He received the decal in the mail from a right-wing group asking him to support their drive to free prisoners of war, became enraged and decided to write them a nasty letter in which he told them to "go fuck themselves." Eventually he decided against sending the letter, and settled on the decal-swastika arrangement instead.

He went on to explain that (like Herzog, Saul Bellow's novelistic character) he had vented his rage by starting many such angry letters that were never completed or mailed. They were mostly to people in government, the military, universities, or veterans' groups, all of which he considered to have two things in common: their dishonorable relationship to the war, and their having had, at one time or another, some form of hold over him. He was struggling to evaluate his rage, often doubting its appropriateness: "Sometimes it seems like I'm a nasty kid who's just getting into adolescence and telling everyone to go fuck themselves." But mostly he respected it and wanted to mobilize it further "to send out shock waves" to the rest of the country. He sought to get in touch with his rage—to cease to suppress it and instead bring it forth in a way that was revitalizing to him and possibly to others as well. During rap groups and individual interviews he frequently referred to his rage, or expressed it directly, as if to establish and get used to a new, adult version of it. And indeed, over a period of eighteen months or so, one could observe at least two trends in his rage: the conversion of much of it to more manageable anger; and an increasing capacity to focus, control, and combine that which remained with a variety of political, social, and psychological energies.*

* While I accept the conventional idea of rage as a more intense, less controllable, more potentially violent emotion than anger, I question the existence of a qualitative difference between the two. No one can live, psychologically speaking, on rage alone, but that does not mean that its *complete* conversion into the milder stuff of anger—or the still milder stuff of acceptance or resignation—is necessarily the path to psychological health.

I realize, in retrospect, that the process was enhanced by the willingness of professionals, or at least some of us, to give expression to our own anger and rage directed toward groups or individuals actively responsible for the war. In that way we conveyed, much more directly than we could through interpreting others' emotions, our living convictions about the appropriateness of rage, at least under certain conditions, in the allegedly mature adult.

Rage could remain encapsulated, though, for long periods of time. I asked one veteran what helped him to deal with the extreme rage and impulses toward violence which he felt suffocated by, and he answered: "Going to war films or reading 'monster books.' " He seemed to have to immerse himself in simulated violence, not so much to "relive the trauma" as traditional theory of "traumatic neurosis" has it, as to experience and come to terms with images of violence and murder—and the underlying terror of being killed—still haunting him. Others in the group chided him about these interests, making such comments as "Didn't you have enough of that?" And for a long time his approach seemed to meet with little success as his complaints continued, and on two occasions he erupted right in the group: once tensely exclaiming "I feel hysterical. I have to scream!"; and once exploding at another member of the group who at a tense moment remained silent, and screaming, "Say something!" On the first occasion, an early meeting, the group was confused but remained calm and accepting; when the second outburst occurred, months later, he was immediately comforted by one of the other men who walked over and put his arm around him reassuringly. Over a year's time he brought much of this rage and violence under control, freeing himself sufficiently to be sensitive and helpful in detecting these tendencies in others and making constructive interpretations around them. He had a number of lapses, however, and gave one the impression that he would continue to experience apocalyptic images giving rise to uncontrollable rage, but that he was struggling (with some success) to transmute these images and impulses both into forms of creative self-expression (in the drawing and painting he did, for instance) and empathy for others.

Another example of creative transmutation of rage was the construction of the slide sequence mentioned earlier. The veteran responsible described pouring his rage into the effort, seeking to communicate to the various student, community, church, and veteran audiences

some small portion of the depth of feeling, the hurt I felt. . . . To communicate to them some of the disgust I feel for America in having perverted itself from the principles that it stood for, that I believed in.

Those sentiments also influenced background rock music he chose, ending the sequence with Jimi Hendrix' celebrated version of "The Star Spangled Banner," to convey the musician's mockery, as (in the veteran's words)

he makes his guitar sound like rockets, air strikes, artillery firing, tank firing [as he comes to] those last phrases [the words of which are] "the land of the free, the home of the brave."

In general these veterans tended to move from violent imagery to rage, from incapacitating rage to more focused mixtures of rage and anger. Indeed, for many the ability to contain violence depended upon maintaining this manageable mixture—rather than in any sense eliminating rage and anger. The difficulty of their struggle gave one pause about the reservoir of potential violence that must exist in the millions of Vietnam veterans who have no such opportunity for (as the Chinese folk phrase has it) "vomiting bitter water"—for examining, channeling, and transmuting their rage. We have referred to the very real danger of greater amounts of overt violence in this group of veterans than in veterans from previous wars. Equally grave, however, are the psychological costs of living with the absurd violence one has known and the equally absurd potential violence one fears in oneself. Virtually every kind of post-Vietnam behavior—restlessness to the point of perpetual motion, psychological freezing or numbing to the point of near-stasis, profound depression, psychosomatic complaints, recurrent nightmares, every kind of anxiety, and perhaps suicide and psychosis as well—all these can result in large part from the desperate struggle to ward off rage and violence.

Nor is war-related rage the exclusive province of Vietnam veterans. Their anger has been cast into the larger 'sea of rage' which envelops so much of American society. Within that sea one may identify the same three patterns we have observed in the veterans themselves.

Concerning the habit of violence, one must ask what ten years of the world's first televised war has done to the home audience. There is no doubt that it has contributed to massive additional numbing on the part of society, in relationship to the already existing numbed violence of those pursuing the war. The brutal but distanced game of war became a vast spectacle, removed from appropriate emotional impact both by the television medium and by the regularization of the performance. No doubt the television audience sensed some of the absurdity and evil of that spectacle, but the combination of media distortions (both technological and ideological) and official rationalizations prevented, at least for some time, much of that absurdity from becoming conscious. We can thus speak of a new dimension of habituation to violence, which in turn probably had a great deal to do with the "don't-give-a-damn" attitude that so enraged antiwar veterans.

It must also be said that television and other mass media have been a factor in the country's gradual revulsion toward the war. Once a person forms a fundamentally critical 'model' or image of the war, the distancing and rationalizing mechanisms lose their effect, and every war-linked picture and sound reveals more to him of the overall absurdity and evil. We still have much to learn about the way in which the media, television in particular, promulgate this particular violence-centered dialectic of habituation and revelation.

The more general American habit of violence, as many are beginning to discover or rediscover, runs long and deep, not only in victimization of Indians and blacks but in the extraordinary symbolic standing of the gun throughout American social history. We distort and confuse by claiming that America is the *only* country with these violent inclinations (or the only country that has known evil). But there is nonetheless much more to be learned about this specifically American habit of violence, or the American versions of the universal potential for violence. Antiwar veterans provide us with at least a beginning understanding of what it takes for individuals and groups to extricate themselves from American patterns of violence, of the continuing struggle against habits of violence in the extrication process itself.

Concerning the second principle mentioned earlier in the chapter, Americans in general feel betrayed—put upon and badly used, if not "fucked over" by the war. For in matters of war and of national destiny, Americans have always felt themselves to be a "blessed" or "chosen people." The immortalizing continuity that all people seek—what I have elsewhere spoken of as the "immortal cultural substance"—has become associated in American minds with a special kind of omnipotence. We are not supposed to lose wars, have our virtue tainted, our glory questioned. Add to this the special post-World War II situation of extraordinary American technological and military hegemony, and our failure to win a dirty little war with a third-rate military power becomes a double betrayal. At the same time there is the gnawing sense, also widespread among Americans, that what has been betrayed most of all in this particular war is our humane image of ourselves. This latter feeling is most characteristic of those opposing the war, while the other forms of betrayal are strongest among those who, at least initially, have supported it—but the point to be made is that this is a war around which all Americans feel betrayed.

There is also considerable rage, much of it beneath the surface, toward Vietnam veterans. They are resented both for not winning the war and thereby being agents of humiliation, and also for the "dirty" things they have done. Moreover, they are deeply feared by a society that sense their potential violence and is all too quick to label them as "drug addicts" or "killers" —and this kind of fear can be quickly converted into rage.

Finally, there are large elements of American society enraged at—because deeply threatened by—the antiwar veterans' transformation. For that transformation depends directly upon exposing the filth beneath the warrior's claim to purity of mission, upon subverting much that is fundamental to American warrior mythology. Americans profoundly involved with that mythology may experience considerable rage toward these bearers of bad news, whom they may then blame for the news itself—for the decline of the old virtues. Underneath that rage are the profound doubts of everyone, even those who would most like to remain true believers in all aspects of American glory. And there is nothing more dangerous than the rage men feel in response to their own loss of faith.

Doubt and confusion about war and killing brings about a larger entrapment in death anxiety and death guilt, encompassing much of our society. To be sure, the entrapment is less intense than in those who actually fought the war, but it contains the same troubling questions, however distantly perceived, about whom one should kill and how one should die. There are no questions more disturbing than these. The beginning answers provided by antiwar veterans suggest a way out of this entrapment, but a way sufficiently painful to arouse new rage and violence—unless means are found to discover new glory in the rejection of killing.

CHAPTER 6

The Counterfeit Universe

They gave me a Bronze Star . . . and they put me up for a Silver Star.
But I said you can shove it up your ass. . . . I threw all the others away.
The only thing I kept was the Purple Heart because I still think I was
wounded.

—Vietnam veteran

Your blessing, priest, make haste!
For we have no time to waste:
We must be dying, dying, dying,
Our Emperor's greatness glorifying!

—Bertolt Brecht
(from Mother Courage)

WITHIN THEIR DIFFUSE ANGER, the men reserve a very special tone—best described as ironic rage—for two categories of people they encountered in Vietnam: chaplains and "shrinks."

The very mention of a military chaplain quickly brought forth smirks, jibes, and the kind of uneasy laughter suggested by the half-conscious witticism, "Those chaplains—oh my God!" With bitter enthusiasm, they gave endless examples of chaplains blessing the troops, their mission, their guns, their killing. As one of the men put it, "Whatever we were doing . . . murder . . . atrocities . . . God was *always* on our side."

Or as a Catholic veteran explained:

Yes, I would go to confession and say, "Sure, I'm smoking dope again. I guess I blew my state of grace again." But I didn't say anything about killing.

Whatever his actual words to his confessor, he was referring to religious arrangements that held one spiritually accountable only for a meaningless transgression and not for the ultimate one. The chaplain presided over this hypocritical ritualization of Evil, and then sanctioned—even blessed—the routine, unritualized, and genuinely malignant evil. This ostensibly religious transaction became a form of "stomach talk," whose informal message was: Stay within our moral clichés as a way of draining off excess guilt, and then feel free to plunge into the business at hand.

The men also pointed to the chaplain's even more direct role of promoting false witness. One man spoke especially bitterly of "chaplains' bullshit." He went on to illustrate what he meant by recalling the death of a close buddy, followed by a combined funeral ceremony-pep talk—like that at My Lai but this time conducted by a chaplain—at which the men were urged to "kill more of them." Similarly, the veteran who had carried the corpse of his closest buddy on his back after his company had been annihilated told of "the bullshit ceremony" that followed, at which the chaplain spoke of "the noble sacrifice for the sake of their country" made by the dead. The same veteran told of having become so enraged at the time that he went back to the chaplain's tent later and almost assaulted him. Overwhelmed with death anxiety and death guilt, and desperately in need of an authentic formulation of survival, the chaplain's plea for false witness threw him into a state of rage and near-psychotic dissociation.

References to "shrinks" were in the same tone. The men told a number of stories in which either they or others had asked to see a psychiatrist because of some form of psychological suffering associated with the war, only to be in one way or another 'reassured' by him and 'helped' to return to combat. One veteran told of two men he knew of who had served as marine undertakers, which meant they had to prepare bodies for shipment and place them in body bags. After a period of time both men sought out a psychiatrist to tell him that they simply could not do the work anymore—but in both cases were urged (in effect, required) to "accept" and adapt to their assignment. Both did, only to be faced with overwhelming conflicts much later on.

The deserter quoted earlier also told of going to see a military psychiatrist because of severe insomnia and disturbing feelings of guilt related to the rape-murder he and others had committed. Fearful of revealing the details of the actual incident to the psychiatrist, he instead spoke of being "upset about the way the war was being run." During the interview he was tearful and "very emotional," for which he remembers being rebuked by the psychiatrist: "You're a specialist in the United States Army and you're sitting there with a red face and your eyes look like scrambled eggs. Man, you ain't no GI." This, as he recalls, made him still more upset, and he answered:

Oh, maybe if I was to prove myself by going and raping and killing some more girls for you. Is that what you want me to do, Major?

Those two sentences starkly reveal his depth of confusion about the two dimensions of authority he perceived in the psychiatrist having bearing on his own transgression. He was appealing mainly to the psychiatrist as a psychological and spiritual authority —as a man with whom one could discuss the nature and inner significance of one's transgression. But his reluctance to reveal the actual transgression—or at least to do so right away—suggested that he also saw the psychiatrist as a military authority, an arm or ally of "command," who could initiate severe military-legal punishment for that transgression. His perception of the psychiatrist's response was almost entirely as the latter: "He reacted in a very military way. Just like a field-grade officer." But he also knew he had put the psychiatrist in an impossible position, which made him still more confused and guilty: "I was angry at myself because I was trying to keep the incident a secret while at the same time make this man know how I felt." And he expressed his frustration at the whole situation by asking, in effect: What kind of sin do I have to commit—how far along the path of evil that you (the representative of the military) are leading me do I have to go—before I can get you (the psychological-spiritual counselor) to listen to me and help me?

For the psychiatrist's two forms of authority had become hopelessly confused:

. . . I felt more secure going to him . . . seeing that it was going to be a major [rather than a lower-ranking medical officer]—you know . . . there's a father image there I suppose with higher-ranking officers. . . . [But] I was very vague. You see I was scared to death I might be punished. . . . I was really afraid that: "Boy, if I tell . . . what happened, I'll end up in Fort Leavenworth busting rocks . . . or maybe even hung, or shot at firing squad." I was afraid of that because . . . I had murdered somebody. . . . Ridiculous things . . . and sickening things [were] happening . . . [and] there were a lot of other things on my mind that had crystallized to one central concept —"I want out of here—there's something wrong here," and I couldn't tell them tangibly without hanging myself.

In the end one could say that the officer-psychiatrist and GI-patient were caught in hopeless, indeed grotesque contradictions in role. Not surprisingly, they fled one another. Yet the psychiatrist inadvertently started his patient on the path to desertion by suggesting he see a chaplain. He was apparently able to tell the chaplain more of the story; and the latter, who must have himself felt contradictory moral pressures, called forth sufficient compassion to treat him in a "very fatherly" way and place him in a pew in a makeshift chapel, and suggest that "I . . . find the answer myself," which, of course, he eventually did.[1]

Nor does the problem end with the military itself. Another veteran told of his anger during a parallel encounter with a psychologist conducting a group session at a Veterans Administration clinic. During a general discussion of anger, the veteran described the extent of his own rage, only to be told by the therapist: "But don't you see how all of it is in your head?" The strong implication, at least as the veteran understood it, was that his rage was a personal "problem" for which he should seek a "cure."

Allowing for a certain amount of retrospective coloring or distortion in these stories, and for the individually humane chaplains and psychiatrists encountered, there is something much more fundamental at issue here. Chaplains and psychiatrists are not only spiritual counselors: Americans also perceive them, rightly or wrongly, as guardians of the spirit, as guides to right thinking and proper behavior (in this way psychiatrists resemble chaplains more than they do other physicians). The veterans were trying to say that the only thing worse than being ordered by military authorities to participate in absurd evil is to have that evil rationalized and justified by guardians of the spirit. Chap-

lains and psychiatrists thus fulfill the function of helping men
adjust to committing war crimes, while lending their spiritual
authority to the overall project.

The men sought out chaplains and shrinks because of a spiritual-psychological crisis growing out of what they perceived to
be irreconcilable demands in their situation. They sought either
escape from absurd evil, or, at the very least, a measure of inner
separation from it. Instead, spiritual-psychological authority was
employed to seal off any such inner alternative. Chaplains and
psychiatrists then formed unholy alliances not only with military
command, but with the more corruptible elements of the soldier's
individual psyche. We may then speak of the existence of a
counterfeit universe, in which all-pervasive, spiritually-reinforced
inner corruption becomes the price of survival. In such an inverted moral universe, whatever residual ethical sensitivity im-
pels the individual against adjusting to evil is under constant
external *and internal* assault.

This "double agent" problem[2] arises even in wars that are
more psychologically defensible (such as World War II), where
the alliance between spiritual-psychological authority (chaplains
and shrinks) on the one hand, and the soldier's inner acceptance
of killing on the other, is buttressed by at least a degree of belief
in the authenticity (or necessity) of the overall enterprise. Even
then, ethical-psychological conflict occurs in everyone concerned
—there is the "Catch 22" described by Heller, according to
which one's very sanity in seeking escape from the environment via a psychiatric judgment of craziness renders one eligible
for the continuing madness of killing and dying. But in Vietnam,
that alliance takes on a grotesquery extraordinary even for war,
as priest and healer, in the name of their spiritual-psychological
function, undermine the last vestiges of authenticity, wholeness,
and humanity in those to whom they minister.

Within the rap groups, I had to assume that some of the anger
expressed toward shrinks in particular was aimed at me and the
other psychological professionals there. We did, after all, belong

to that now dishonored category; and it is commonplace in psychological work for anger felt toward a 'healer' to be expressed in this indirect way. Moreover, there was a sense in which the men could still see themselves as being manipulated (even corrupted) by spiritual authorities (the professionals in the group), as being required by us to remain preoccupied with the filth of their war. To be sure, they had originally called us in because this was their preoccupation, and their entire organization was committed to examining and exposing the war. But each of the men inevitably felt a certain amount of ambivalence about dealing with the war's painful psychological involvements. Their "turning from the war stories to themselves," which we spoke of earlier as a deepening of personal exploration, could also at certain times represent an avoidance of unpleasant war-linked associations.

Just after the meeting at which the men announced they had made this shift, one of them, referring to my special concern with the war and its effects on people, asked me if I still planned to come regularly to the group.

He was asking whether the veterans had to keep dredging up the filth of their war in order to hold my (and perhaps other professionals') interest. But the steady concern of the entire group for each of its individual members, whether or not the war was immediately at issue, tended to dispel that suspicion. Indeed the spirit of integrity and openness that prevailed, and the kinds of human bonds we formed, created something in the way of an 'authentic universe' that provided sharp contrast to, and to some extent helped men to overcome, the counterfeit one they had known.

Aside from chaplains and shrinks, the men described experiencing *themselves* as counterfeit. They spoke as having been "like boys playing soldiers"—of having the feeling upon entering combat: "God, this is right out of a movie!" One said simply, "Nothing was real." We recognize here the play element in war referred to earlier, as stressed especially by Huizinga. The play element is inseparable from the idea of "contest" or "joust," from the principle of the "ordeal," that would-be hero's "trial by battle," and the religious idea of the outcome being a "judgment of God" and "decision of Holy validity."* But Vietnam veterans spoke very little of any such ennobling idea; their focus was on the element of make-believe, of "only pretending." The game of war, they seemed to be saying, was there, but reduced to childish deception and self-deception. The play element was isolated and disconnected, never a part of a believable ritual or contest. They were counterfeit warriors engaging in counterfeit play.

Precisely this sense is conveyed by a former noncommissioned officer in naval intelligence, whose job was "running spies" into Cambodia:

I knew I was doing shit. They [superior officers and associates] knew I was doing shit. And I would make fun of my spies, when they would come back, to the other guys. One of them would say, "What did he bring back?" I said, "More dirty pictures from Pnom Penh. What do you expect?". . . We used to go to briefings . . . special top secret . . . so well sealed and soundproofed and bugproofed. . . . We used to go in there and talk about our operation. Nobody knew anything. They didn't know where the VC were. They didn't know what the VC were doing. They didn't know who led them . . . where they got their supplies from. . . . You know, it was . . . laughable.

Also counterfeit in his own eyes were his reasons for staying on the job:

As my . . . team chief used to say, "It keeps us off the rock pile." And I had a safe site and I also had in mind that there was no cap-

---

* Unlike some scholars, Huizinga believes that the Greek *agon* or contest,[3] which gave rise to the Olympics, is inseparable from the idea of play, and he thus uses the term "agonistic play." Then, speaking of war, he says that "The agonistic element . . . becomes operative when the war-making parties regard themselves and each other as *antagonists* contending for something to which they feel they have a right." In that situation, there is room for the idea of glory, and "The test of the will of the gods is victory or defeat." There was agony aplenty in Vietnam, but no genuine *agon*.

tain that I knew of who lived as well as I did—my own car, my own apartment, my spies met when I decided to meet them, the reports were written when I wrote them, enough time to do a bit of sketch‑ ing, friends around Saigon, people I met with. I was pretty well distracted, or so I thought.

Only occasional reminders that the game, however absurd, was for keeps—that "my spies . . . could be imprisoned or killed"— interfered with this adjustment. He would then become uneasily aware "that there were a lot of things I wasn't thinking about." While few enlisted men had the opportunity for that level of perceived corruption, everyone had a predominant inner need to come to terms with—make one's peace with, so to speak—the counterfeit universe that defined one's existence.

The former Army sergeant described the kind of protracted struggle that could take place between commitment to immediate military tasks and ever more insistent awareness of the counter‑ feit nature of the larger project. He had doubts about the war before going to Vietnam, together with a vague but persistent patriotism, so that he tended initially to look upon much of what he encountered as "doing it all wrong" rather than ask why his country was doing it at all. He immersed himself in his highly technical radar work with the intensity and pleasure of a mechan‑ ically inclined American boy:

Nobody took the time and effort that I did to, you know, play with [the radar]. It was like tinkering with a car . . . I got along very well with my radar set. I used to play with it very well.

That "tinkering," moreover, by locating enemy emplacements, saved American lives:

They'd stop and call up, "Thanks . . . man, we only lost three.". . . They'd come back from the field . . . come in and shake your hand and cry and say, "Wow! Thanks a lot,". . . because they knew.

Conscientious, effective, and increasingly recognized, he was also sustained by ambition and pride: "I was into the [military] game. I was starting to catch on to how you played it." Over a period of time, though, his powerful sense of duty and responsibility "eroded" and "it reached me"—"it" being an amorphous sense that the war, the military, everything around him was counterfeit.

Smoking pot helped him come to this realization. He had already begun to feel that a lot that Americans were doing was "ridiculous," but would then insist to himself that "there must be a reason . . . a purpose, even though it seems ridiculous to me." Only when he and a few other enlisted men would retire to a quiet place without their weapons and light up would everything become clear:

When I was smoking, then I would say, "It's just a bunch of bullshit, it really is . . . it really *is* ridiculous . . . really stupid."

He would have such additional thoughts as, "Somebody back there in Washington and somebody in Hanoi . . . is programming both of us and we're just being tools of it." He became especially aware of the absurdity and ultimate impotence of the military-technical arrangements in which he was enveloped:

Back there they were playing silly games and we had to be somehow involved in their silly games. . . . I realized the absurdity of all this electronic warfare . . . this giant technological element that we had that was rendered entirely impotent by a few little Vietnamese running around and throwing land mines here and there.

The large amphibious tractors (or "amtracs") sent in and out of his gun station every day, containing weapons, parts, and elaborate electronic equipment, came to symbolize the absurdity of our technology.

While smoking, the men began to develop an elaborate collective fantasy about a different kind of amphibious tractor—one decked out in psychedelic colors—"all swirls and everything"—and "filled up with dope." That happy vehicle was driven by "Alice," a fortyish, apparently American woman, "kind of dumpy and matronly," whom everyone was delighted to have around:

She was . . . very much into what we were doing, and she liked to smoke dope and she had good stuff. She would come around, smoke with the men, pass out her dope to them free of charge.

Alice had the power to turn men off war and on to pot and booze. On one occasion, so the tale went, the men were ordered to sweep through a village on a combat mission, but then instead

Alice was going to come . . . [and] there wasn't going to be any fighting. . . . Instead of . . . sweeping through the village we were going to . . . say hello to the [Vietnamese] girls [who actually did sell marijuana to the men] and sit around and drink a little Vietnamese beer . . . and smoke dope.

Sometimes Alice would come along on a patrol, which would mean that "what we were going to do was go in and smoke dope with the villagers." As for the "enemy":

If there were any [Vietcong] they would have just sat down and smoked with us because they were, you know, on our side. Maybe it was absurd for them too.

Sometimes the fantasy carried Alice herself into wildly absurd situations of slapstick adventures and misadventures, a situation not unrelated to their own but now depicted in comic inversion.

Well we would just get on a kick like it was a Wild West rodeo or something. And here comes Alice . . . out there waddling around, because she wouldn't move very fast. And she was out there trying to rope a steer or something and the steer was coming after her and Alice was wobbling around, you know, and we'd go through the whole involved thing and Alice was trying to jump on the walls . . .

and get away. . . . I guess they'd gotten into a bullfight too because there was a bull chasing her and she was trying to jump on the wall and she was just too fat and big to do it, you know. So the bull had gored her in the ass, I guess. And, you know, this was very funny— poor Alice, you know. But then we all ran over and helped her. . . . You throw in some little extras . . . like . . . now somebody would pick it up and say, "Oh ya," and now here comes this thing and they'd go on for a minute and then someone else would jump in and so it was a communal type thing.

Alice even applied herself to military inequities, as in another scenario when she "left her 'trac' for repairs" and drove up instead in a smaller vehicle, the very jeep that had been illegally taken from a nearby Air Force unit and absorbed into the Army car pool (here the fantasy partly paralleled an actual incident). As the veteran explained:

They [the Air Force] had so much anyway with their PXs and everything and we had been sacrificing all this time. . . . Alice was a friend of ours so she was simply redistributing the wealth, I think. That's what she was doing.

In Alice, the men were creating something of a latter-day Mother Courage, a Mother Earth figure who gaily distributes her wares in the midst of war, and carries on no matter what.

Brecht's Mother Courage is a cynical if admirable opportunist ("There isn't a war every day in the week, we must get to work"[4]), an ironic survivor-prophet who sells not only food but soldiers' boots, belts, and guns, and predicts (accurately, it turns out) the deaths of soldiers she meets and of her own two sons as well. But Alice is a more simple and loving nurturer-buffoon whose mission in life is to replace war with pleasure. The message of Mother Courage, for whom business always comes first, might be paraphrased as "buy and die"—while that of Alice, for whom pleasure is all, is closer to "take, smoke, and live." One wonders, though, how much of Mother Courage as harbinger of death—as death itself—there is even in Alice. Her creation, at the very least, is an attempt to 'play with' and mock death anxiety; and it is possible that pursuing the fantasy further would show Alice to have more direct connections with violence and death (perhaps suggested in the "Wild West" sequence). In any case, both figures ultimately serve to reveal the counterfeit nature of war—Mother Courage by means of survival in corruption, Alice by means of her absolute reversal of the war environment.

The name Alice, of course, came from the song, "Alice's Restaurant," which the men had heard (they had not yet had a chance to see the film). The whole Alice fantasy was their way of turning the war over on its head (or, should one say, to its "heads"), finding expression for its absurdity, and replacing its grotesque death with marvelously charmed life. Even violence could be noted and tamed, in a sense domesticated, through the mildly black-humor rodeo-Western sequence, in which Alice's mishaps could provide not only imagery of violent buffoonery but still another reversal of nurturing which the men could actively help, indeed save *her*.

Above all the fantasy was a group venture, a "communal-type thing" both in creation and content. It provided a sustained counter-scenario right in the midst of actual combat. Similarly, pot-smoking in general became the center of a counter-environment in the midst of the atrocity-producing situation. Thus, the same army technician describes how, as a non-com with considerable authority over the men working under him as well as responsibility for complex technical equipment,

Pot smoking . . . was in conflict with the role that I was playing in the military . . . with the rest of the image of what I was doing. . . . People . . . in my category, that had been dedicated, and [then] started smoking . . . say, three months after they had gone over there [he began after about four months] . . . You know, they got kind of . . . they didn't care about the war. . . . They just weren't as ambitious or dedicated.

That was exactly what happened to him, as he began to smoke more and more regularly—about twice a week with the "Alice group" of enlisted men, and about once a week with a group of young officers.

Though he took a certain pride in being able to engage in the rite with both of these groups, smoking with "my men" took precedence, because "I wanted to shock them into the realization that I was a human being too. . . . I was beginning to shed the [military-authority] image . . . and become whole." The pot-centered antienvironment, in other words, could return one to a sense of integrity. For that to happen, there had to be at least a partial breakout from psychic numbing. For instance, the men "never, ever, took our weapons" to the bunker when they smoked, but they would sometimes focus on larger weapons—artillery pieces, tanks, etcetera,—with a changed awareness:

We would say, "Wow, look at this, look at the sweep of that gun barrel going out there . . . against the sunset or against the stars" . . . and look at it from just a new aspect.

That "new aspect" was a reopening of, first, one's aesthetic pores, and then one's entire world view.

It could be argued that this aesthetic-psychological outlet enabled some men to make a better adjustment to combat. But more basically, the widespread and virtually open pot smoking (in 1969, for instance, the time referred to here) constituted an act of rebellion against the immediate military environment. More than that, it provided a form of transcendence, however periodic and transitory, that enabled the men to look beyond the situation they were locked into toward a very different state of being.*

* Tragically, heroin was later embraced by GIs to serve similar psychological functions—partly because the army initiated efficient measures for making pot unavailable while very cheap and very high-grade heroin was accessible to anyone, and partly because the counterfeit quality of the environment wore on and became even more intolerable as the amount of active fighting involving Americans diminished and boredom set in.[5]

The drug-centered message of this 'antienvironment subculture' was spread by means of nothing other than the Armed Forces Radio Network. The technique was the use of double-entendres so blunt that they would escape only field-grade officers: an announcer describing air traffic reports would describe himself as "Parker Lane, the flying traffic cop" (rolled marijuana cigarettes were sold under the name of "Park Lanes"). Or a disc jockey, between rock numbers, would say things like "The pigs are running in the streets" (meaning: The CID was around looking for drugs), or "They had an inspection over at X barracks today. You should have seen the roaches come out of the walls" (meaning: Better hide your dope). A basic division took shape within the overall military culture, so that, as one man put it during a workshop (when discussing racial antagonisms): "With us it wasn't so much blacks and whites as heads and non-heads."

This expanding collective experience, as the former sergeant explains, could help tilt

the balance between the overwhelming mission and the little absurdities that had been building up and that I had been kicking away somewhere. . . . Suddenly the absurdities . . . evolved to become more important. . . . What we were blowing up or pumping over here to be our mission or something was in actuality the absurdity. . . .

And then "the absurdity of all this electronic warfare" extended still further until

I guess I started to see the whole technological society that way. That it really didn't feel—though we had improved medicine and . . . improved transportation and housing, really we still weren't dealing with the basic problems of humanity. . . . Gradually . . . little things would tick off and add up, you know, somewhere to be filled in a memory bank, and to form an image that somewhere back there the whole technological element was doing the same thing . . . in the States.

With that image one could say that his vision came full circle. The sense he gropes toward—his insight accelerated though not created by pot smoking—is that of a counterfeit universe made up of murderous technology gone berserk and equally "deadly" institutional arrangements (military, theological, psychological) for denying brutal truths, reinforcing false witness, and corrupting everyone in the process.

Many men made similar equations of combat environment, the military in general, and American society. During the rap groups there was a great deal of talk about the corporate inhumanity and stupidity of the military institution. These sentiments are hardly new or unique to this war, but they become particularly unacceptable when associated with so counterfeit a combat situation. In such a situation, the ordinary military experience of being "programmed to kill" becomes inseparable from the psychological experience of being programmed to murder. The men complained not so much that the military was too authoritarian but rather that it lacked what could be called genuine moral authority. The My Lai survivor, for instance, remembered the Catholic brothers who ran the military school he had attended in his teens as being "much more demanding and much more critical" than anyone he encountered in the army. The latter, in fact, seemed to him to be "not easier but . . . slack." He was trying to say that the military lacked, for him as for many others, the ritual power of a more viable and more genuine order of warriors.

Even—especially—when one displayed courage bordering on the heroic, there was a strong sense of being in a counterfeit game. The veteran who had carried out the corpse of his buddy on his back retrospectively mocked his own behavior: "It was time for me to play John Wayne." He also recalled an interview with a correspondent from a New York newspaper soon afterwards, in which he tried to convey some of the horror he and the other men had experienced as their company was being decimated—only to have all this ignored and the eventual article consist, as he put it, of "some shit about a Bronx boy who was a hero." It was he who then said:

They gave me a Bronze Star and they put me up for a Silver Star. But I said you can shove it up your ass. I threw all of the others away. The only thing I kept was the Purple Heart, because I still think I was wounded.

He had actually sustained a minor physical wound, but was conveying a sense of his spiritual wounds as well. Above all he was saying that, in a counterfeit universe, awards for heroism must in themselves be counterfeit.*

Indeed, the public casting away of medals by antiwar veterans has had such mythic power because it represents a symbolic rejection of this entire counterfeit universe—a rejection of being rewarded for participating in absurd evil and of the personal corrupton associated with any such recognition. Animating guilt was clearly in evidence as, in the act of throwing the medals away, men shouted such things as: "This is for Corporal William B. Jones, killed outside of Hue, for no fuckin' reason at all." They, in effect, dedicated their act to dead buddies, thereby renouncing previous false witness in favor of a more authentic survivor mission of combatting the war itself.

The men reenter civilian society sensitized to American expressions of the counterfeit, and view much of what they experience within that category. Hence, many are likely to avoid regular jobs or commitments for prolonged periods of time and to keep physically or psychologically on the move as though nothing were sufficiently authentic to hold them. Here one can say that their survivor conflicts come together with a more gen-

---

* This relationship was epitomized by the admission of a recent Medal of Honor winner that he had been able to carry out his heroic exploits in Vietnam only because he was "stoned on pot" at the time.

eralized Protean style widespread among the young,* but in a way that renders that style painful and suspicious in the extreme. Those who do take regular jobs sometimes complain that in them they experience even less freedom than they did in Vietnam. There, as one budding young executive explained, if you were asked to do something you didn't like, you could curse, show your displeasure, at times even assert yourself to the point of getting something changed. But here, when asked by a superior to do what he considered a very demeaning task, "All I could say was, 'Okay' or 'Yes, sir.'" He spoke often of the hypocritical requirements of his job, and told how, on one occasion, upon entering a movie theater and being shown to his seat, the feeling came over him that

I would like to be an usher—just taking people to their seats, at least helping them to get somewhere they want to be.

* I have elsewhere[6] described the Protean style of self-process as an interminable series of experiments and explorations, some shallow, some profound, each of which can be readily abandoned in favor of still new psychological quests; and emphasized that, while risking various forms of diffusion, it is by no means pathological as such, and may in fact be one of the functional patterns necessary to life in our times. Other characteristics of the Protean style are a symbolic fatherlessness which, whatever its pain, permits one "an image of repeated, autonomously willed death and rebirth of the self"; forms of guilt, anxiety, and rage that tend to be free-floating and relatively unformed and unrelated to clear origins; a strong ideological hunger together with distrust of comprehensive and formed ideologies and a preference for ideological fragments; a profound inner sense of absurdity which finds expression in a tone of mockery; pervading suspicion of counterfeit nurturance; various forms of polarized ambivalence toward science and technology; and a tendency toward exploring and creating new rituals of transition —*rites de passage*—within the life cycle, with a strong preference for those which encourage various forms of experiential transcendence. I stressed the prevalence of the Protean style in recent literature, art, film, political and social innovation, and virtually every form of contemporary culture—to the point of stimulating a reactive opposite, a "constricted style," emphasizing closure and an image of restoring a perfectly harmonious past that never was. Finally, the Protean style itself can best be understood as a radically experimental quest for new combinations of immortalizing modes—for a sense of immortality that permits and requires sustained flux.

He went on to equate Vietnam and post-Vietnam experiences in
the pointlessness of what he did, where he was being led, and
where he led others. He did not last too long at the job.

These comparisons between experience in Vietnam and in
civilian society preoccupied the men during many rap groups.
They recognized the military's deeper, life-and-death control
over one. But they associated a number of counterfeit patterns
they were now experiencing back home—perpetuating the war
in the name of peace, subsuming human considerations to profit-
making—with the moral inversions they had experienced in Vietnam. Any authority remained suspect, and they were very touchy
about taking orders. One man, when asked why he left a particular job, gave a typical reply: "I couldn't take the 'Do this.
Do that.'" Only on one occasion was there a suggestion of
literally "bringing the war back home," and then in a kind of
Yippie-like declaration on the part of the former marine infantryman (whose rhetoric had been previously noted as the source of
critical evaluation on the part of the group): "1984 is here!
Vietnam is in this country! I'm a Vietcong!" Mostly, the men
tried to balance their overall sense of American duplicity with
that of critical self-examination; and to estimate, with varying
degrees of hope and despair, personal and collective possibilities
for change in the direction of authentic experience.

A powerful indicator of the counterfeit universe was the recurrent image of garbage—as in the following dream reported
by the same former marine:

I was alone in a garbage dump. There was nothing but garbage all
around me. I made a fire by burning *Life* magazines and things like
that. I was wearing just a bathrobe, with nothing underneath. Then
a girl turned up, driving a truck, to dump her garbage. My interest
in the girl was, I wanted to lay her. I got into the truck with her,
and we tried right there . . . but we couldn't do anything because
there was still garbage all around. We decided to drive to her home,
but when we got there we found that people were there—her

brothers. We had to eat dinner—and I had to explain about being just in a bathrobe—with people I didn't even know.

Over the course of the greater part of a rap group meeting, the dreamer's associations and the sensitive probing of the other veterans brought out a number of predominant themes. Being "alone in a garbage dump" and "burning *Life*" conveyed the sense of being cast out with the refuse, beyond the pale of proper society, living a half-life in the filth. This sense was related to the actual life the dreamer led—casting about aimlessly among people and places, living "from hand to mouth" mostly out of the beneficence of friends and strangers. There was terror and rage underneath: he associated to a "bad trip" on mescaline* in' the midst of which he began to "tear apart every bit of technology I could lay my hands on" in the apartment where he was staying—appliances, TV sets, etcetera— equating that technology with what he and his country did in Vietnam, and with the corruption (or "garbage") of American society.

In another associative sequence he spoke of the hypocrisy behind a ten-year suspended sentence he had received in the past for possession of a small amount of marijuana, the real reason for the absurd sentence being his antiwar militancy. He went on to describe a later occasion on which he was handcuffed when taken into custody following another demonstration. Anticipating a long jail sentence on the basis of the previous conviction, he recalled a "tremendous calm" coming over him as he imagined a quiet life in jail, possibly a job in the prison library, and a chance to read and think and prepare for more effective service to the Movement.

Further associations and discussion made clear that the idea of quietude, and being taken care of, appealed to him because he felt himself to be "burning" ("burning out," destroying, causing to disintegrate) his *own* "life," living with wild intensity while

---

* The drug might well have been LSD, which is often thought to be mescaline.

actually feeling empty and deadened. "Burning *Life*," in the capitalized magazine form (standing for a respectable American institution), expressed his need for violent political imagery of destruction and re-creation, his repeated idea of "destroying society in order to build a new society—and if that society doesn't work out, then destroying it too." In that sense he felt all of American society to be a garbage dump, but one in which he was painfully mired. For him the counterfeit universe of Vietnam existed equally in civilian life, including not only the world around him but his own profound inner fear of disintegration associated with his death anxiety.

Another major theme concerned his impaired capacity for intimacy and trust. All levels of sexual realization—pleasure, union with another, love—were interfered with by the 'world of garbage' (which included early attitudes, now unacceptable, of women as objects of male domination). The "brothers" in the dream, whom he spoke of with considerable anger, were associated with the band of brothers formed by the antiwar veterans. Particularly involved were those in the rap group, whom he looked upon in one sense as intimate comrades but in another as meddlesome strangers to whom he had always to "explain" himself.

Finally, there was the theme of his own nakedness—his various forms of exposure before others—his self-exposure in the rap groups and on public occasions of inquiry and protest. Nakedness had to do with vulnerability, with a form of shame and guilt in which he felt entrapped, with victimization and defenselessness. The erotic component of the dream, both in his nakedness and in the attempted intercourse, also expressed his ever-stifled quest for pleasure and vitality, for love and connectedness.

The dream suggested the extent to which he felt his entire life to be enveloped in filth and waste. His immersion in the counterfeit universe of garbage was epitomized by his Vietnam experience, but extended prior to and beyond it as well. Central to the dream also was his perpetual and perpetually frustrated search for something in and outside of himself that might be real, actual, authentic, alive.

On other occasions veterans brought forth imagery of garbage directly associated with Vietnam, often as their image of ultimate horror—garbage piles and dumps, or garbage loaded on trucks or other vehicles. In these images the Vietnamese are recalled as immersing themselves in the garbage, scrounging about for something to eat or use in their struggle for survival. One account described how they would clamor up on the garbage truck just before it was to be emptied in the dump—"The Vietnamese won't wait until we get the garbage off because they, you know, they want to get first choice at it because they're living on this"—and how GIs would throw them off the truck and strike them with rifle butts, because they weren't supposed to be on it. The memories embody a special form of death guilt, having to do with degradation and abuse of other human beings. Inevitably, the veterans come to feel *themselves* to be inseparable from the garbage. They too feel inundated by it. Or worse, they feel themselves to *be* that garbage. In a counterfeit universe, the garbage is everywhere and everyone.

The ultimate "garbage" is the accumulation of the dead, is death itself—not just any death but grotesque, premature, and unacceptable death. Garbage is truth, the antidote to any romantic claim to nobility or "victory," as a poem by a Vietnam veteran bearing that title suggests:

> The Holy Army trampled
> In the sun of Christmas Day,
> But when they passed, the garbagemen
> Took all the dead away.
>
> "Onward Christian Soldiers
> Is our battlecry," they said,
> But the guts of houses rotted
> With the bodies of the dead.

"Someone sound the trumpet,
We have never known defeat,"
And they proudly marched by all
Who lay moaning at their feet.

"We have seen and we have conquered
Every outlaw and windmill,"
And the army looked in every place
For other men to kill.[7]

Each stanza contrasts a counterfeit Don Quixote-like claim with
a deadly truth: the Holy Army and the garbagemen, Christian
Soldiers and houses rotted with corpses, victorious trumpet calls
and the "moaning" of the dying, and finally the claim of noble
conquest and the renewed quest for victims (who seem to have
run out).

A major theme in all of this garbage imagery—in the dream,
the Vietnam recollections, and the poem—is that of the American
warrior rummaging about in his own spiritual refuse.

We are not surprised, then, that the men have sensitive antennae for the inauthentic. I remember being struck by precisely
those antennae when, just before one of our early rap group
meetings, a VVAW leader, himself black, asked another (lighter-
skinned) black to join a group appearing on a television program, making it clear that he was being selected because he had
a bit of blackness. The answer came back, quickly and curtly:
"No thanks. I don't want to be the token black around here."
Throughout one could detect a strong current of what we referred
to earlier as "suspicion of counterfeit nurturance." Vietnam
veterans are particularly sensitive to help with strings attached,
to being used or manipulated, to being drawn back into a counterfeit realm.

The VVAW, particularly in its early stages, has had special
importance in the quest for authenticity. In it one could call
forth some of the intimacy and solidarity that existed in military

combat, and do so for other than counterfeit purposes. As one veteran put the matter at a New Haven rap group meeting, "It was great to join the guys in something where we weren't going to kill anybody." Yet the inevitable personal and political differences, or simply the repetition of political litanies within the antiwar organization, ultimately caused a number of veterans to experience much of the counterfeit there as well.

In the rap groups there were extensive discussions about the kinds of personal compromise that might be necessary for VVAW to achieve its political aims and about the way in which the organization's sudden burst into the national limelight threatened individual and group authenticity.

Just before the highly successful Washington, D.C., actions of April, 1971 (demonstrations, "search-and-destroy missions," casting-away of medals, appearances before Congressional and Senatorial groups), several of the men expressed conflict over going, over having one's autonomy snuffed out by any organization, whatever its purposes. As one man put it, "I'm not sure I care about the state of the world. At times I just want to be a hermit—not part of any group." Such sensitivities were always discussed in relationship to the total destruction of autonomy in the counterfeit universe of Vietnam.

Most of the veterans in the rap group took part, nonetheless, in the Washington action, though they had mixed responses to its brilliant success and unexpected mass media prominence. The majority felt in some degree fulfilled, though not without nagging doubts about questions of authenticity. A few bitterly resented the publicity given one or two "superstars," seeing in this "star system" exactly the kind of élitism (the "stars" were usually former officers) they so condemned in the military and in society in general. One of the men became enraged whenever the Washington action was mentioned in the group, because he strongly resented the disparity between the public (media) image of success and what he considered to be the real failure—the inability to get senators or congressmen to commit themselves firmly, or take political risks of any kind, to end the war. It was the same sort of rage mentioned earlier in response to general attitudes of "not giving a damn," with the veteran feeling stymied in his quest for individual and collective change and for an animating relationship to guilt.

There would sometimes be more general expressions of the unreality of ordinary existence. One member of the rap group described to me, during a talk we had, what he called a "crisis of faith"—mentioned in connection with individual psychotherapy he was undergoing elsewhere, but extending far beyond that:

It seemed like why? why him? why there? And what was this doing? . . . Why don't we all go back to the country and chop wood? Or get quill pens and write by candlelight and just forget all this shit? War, where's the war? Where's the peace? Where's the bomb? Where's, you know, there's nothing. . . . What's the sense of Vietnam Vets Against the War? . . .

And about rap groups, after one particularly gripping session:

We come together out of the blue and then that happens within a three hour period, and you march off. . . . There were people I had nothing to do with other than meet those needs. Sometimes it strikes me as completely absurd.

He was asking himself, as were others, whether in any endeavor it was possible to be other than counterfeit. Over the course of time virtually all of the men found areas of authenticity, in ways we shall soon discuss, but the concern remains strong for most of them. It is, in fact, at the center of their survivor struggle.

Nor is the question always answerable throughout the rest of American society. Vietnam veterans are by no means the only ones asking: "Where does Vietnam end and America—the America one used to believe in—begin?" It would be too much to suggest that the whole of America had become a "counterfeit universe." But one can say that, with the Vietnam War, a vast, previously hidden American potential for the counterfeit has become manifest. From the atrocity-producing situation in Vietnam; to the military-political arrangements responsible for it; to the system of law confronted by militant opponents of the war; to the preexisting but war-exacerbated antagonisms around race, class, ethnicity, and age; to the war-linked economic recession; to collusion in the war's corruption by virtually all of the professions and occupations—what is there left that we can call authentic?

To ask the question is to assume that there *is* something left. But that something has to be sought out and re-created. Correspondingly, the expanding contours of the counterfeit universe have to be identified. The model suggested by military chaplains and psychiatrists is that of a counterfeit situation in which the price for survival includes not only external compliance but internal corruption furthered by spiritual authorities serving the prevailing power structure. Something of this kind of counterfeit universe is probably inherent in any system of social authority. And we shall return to the question of the professions—especially the psychiatric profession—at the end of this study. But we may say here that the Vietnam War had revealed and intensified counterfeit dimensions throughout American society. And once one has begun to grasp the principle of the counterfeit universe, can one continue to ignore the malignancy of related constellations around and within oneself?

Philip Kingry has put the matter this way:

The war isn't just an excuse. *It* was *everything.* I am a lie. What I have to say is a lie. But it is the most true lie you will ever hear about a war.

If the counterfeit universe is not to remain *everything,* one must explore its manifestations everywhere, even if the counterfeit manifestations seem to render those very explorations "a lie." War veterans and commentators alike can at least begin with such "true lies" as a way of initiating the difficult climb out of the abyss.

CHAPTER 7

Gooks and Men

gook. n. 1. Dirt, grime, sludge, sediment. . . . 2. Any viscous, semiliquid sauce or dressing. 3. [derog.] Generically, a native of the Pacific Islands, Africa, Japan, China, Korea, or any European country except England; usu. a brown-skinned or Oriental non-Christian . . . adj. Foreign; made in any country except the U.S.A. [Perhaps from Scottish *gowk*, simpleton, from Middle English *gowke*, cuckoo, from Old Norse *gaukr*, from Common Germanic *gaukaz* (unattested).]

—*Pocket Dictionary of American Slang*
and *American Heritage Dictionary*

[The soldier boasting of a high body count] was sort of saying how much . . . I hate the gooks—in terms that you can actually understand. I hate them a whole lot. I hate them even more than a whole lot . . . so, wow!, I killed 121 of them. That means I hate them worse than anybody does. . . . And of course the only way you could determine who hated them the most was how many times you beat them or killed them or raped them or something like that.

—My Lai survivor

Every time you'd start to feel human, you'd get screwed.

—Former GI

ONE SATURDAY AFTERNOON I arrived at the VVAW office for a rap session but found the room already in use. A man I had not yet met was showing a color-slide sequence of Vietnam to a very intense audience of fellow veterans. He had just begun what turned out to be a forty-minute presentation of several hundred slides, with a well-coordinated rock-music background consisting largely of Woodstock songs. First we see many scenes of ordinary Vietnamese people in exquisite physical settings—rice fields, mountains, ocean—going about everyday tasks in apparently effortless rhythms. Then the American military appears, more machines than men, the awesome technology and its GI-attendants abruptly taking over the landscape. There are a few indications of battle, thunderous noises from the great machines, but nothing of massive death or atrocity. Rather, when the noise subsides we see a slide of just one dead Vietnamese, impaled on barbed wire.

Toward the end of the sequence, we see a rugged-looking GI, short and stocky, with close-cropped dark hair—strong, impassive, tough, and very American. The slide is held for a "triple take" (three times as long as the others) to the accompaniment of Donovan's soft rendering of "The Universal Soldier":

> He's five foot two and he's six foot four
> He fights with missiles and with spears
> He's all of thirty-one and he's only seventeen
> He's been a soldier for a thousand years. . . .
> And he knows he shouldn't kill and he knows he always will. . . .
> And without him all this killing can't go on. . . .

A little later we learn that the GI is none other than the veteran showing us the slide sequence, now unrecognizable as the same person—not only because of his long hair and military-remnants-youth-culture style of dress but also because of something different about his facial expression, its mixture of vitality, curiosity, softness, and agitation. He had inserted himself in that way, he explained, as "my form of penance for what I did in Vietnam."

I have since been able to observe the powerful impact of this slide sequence on a number of different audiences, but there is no doubt that its greatest effect is on Vietnam veterans themselves. For it confronts them in the most vivid way with the Vietnamese as human beings—indeed as people whose humanity, juxtaposed against the malignant American technological intrusion, seems to leap out at the audience from the projection screen.

The confrontation is painful. One of the men watching it that day ran from the room in the middle of the showing, and explained later: "I sleep better if I don't see that shit." The "shit" he referred to (as he went on to make clear) included combat, killing in general, and, above all, what he and his buddies did to the Vietnamese. Most of the other veterans seemed transfixed by what they saw and had no words for what they felt. Their emotion was not too different from that of another veteran who told me that the slide sequence (which he saw in a different city) "blew my mind and changed my life"—immediately after viewing it he decided to devote himself full time to VVAW activities.

The same day, at the rap group, the veterans talked around rather than about the slides they had just seen. A discussion developed about how hardened one became to corpses in Vietnam —how Vietnamese corpses in particular became no more than "potato sacks."* Only gradually could they begin to examine

---

* On other occasions I heard men make strong emotional distinctions between Vietnamese and American corpses. As one veteran put it: "There was a hell of a difference between Vietnamese and American bodies. With Vietnamese bodies you just didn't feel a thing. But with American bodies—well, that was different."

their feelings (or lack of feelings) at the time toward the Vietnamese. Yet when someone used the word "dehumanization" to describe that state, several of the men vehemently objected because dehumanization sounded absolute and permanent, while the state being described was partial and temporary. They preferred "desensitization." They stressed that only a portion of one's mind was affected, and that behind this desensitization (often accompanied by rage and easy violence toward virtually any Vietnamese) lay great fear and a desperate struggle to survive.

The veteran who showed the slide sequence spoke of having himself lived on two levels in Vietnam: the one, of marked desensitization or numbing in which he, like everyone else, killed without feeling; but the other, of awareness of the humanity of the Vietnamese, attested to by the sensitive photographs he took during trips about the country. Everyone else in the group quickly affirmed this double level of psychic existence. But they also emphasized that everything in Vietnam worked psychologically against the second level, against maintaining an awareness of Vietnamese humanity.

Now they had come to realize that only by recovering that awareness and experiencing it fully could each of them carry through the process they spoke of as "becoming a human being again." Their survivor formulation and mission demanded nothing less. The slide show's striking aesthetic quality and content evoked a mixture of self-condemnation and bitter (sometimes bittersweet) nostalgia, all of which contributed to animating guilt enhancing the humanizing process. The transformation involved is from gooks to men: from the gooks they had created to the Vietnamese men and women they were beginning to experience, and from the gook in themselves (the numbed and brutalized portions of their psyches) responsible for this victimization to the men they were struggling to become.

The process was extremely difficult, partly because that victimization was so central to the American psychological experience within the counterfeit universe of Vietnam. Consider Dr. Ronald Glasser's rendering of an extraordinary dialogue between a medic and a twenty-year-old GI whose burns covering eighty percent of his body were to be eventually fatal but who was then having dead skin cut away (debrided) in a whirlpool bath:

Medic (kneeling down beside the tub . . . picking off . . . pieces [of skin] that was still attached but had been loosened) : "How long have you been in Nam, David?"

"Five . . . five months," David said, watching the corpsman pick up a chunk of skin off his chest. He had to tug to get it off. David grimaced, barely suppressing a groan.

"How do you like the Vietnamese women?" the medic asked.

"Don't know," David said, painfully engrossed in watching the corpsman go after another piece of his skin. "Didn't meet any gooks."

"How come?" the medic asked, scooping a piece of skin out of the water.

"We killed 'em all."

Suddenly David let out a scream. . . . Blood began oozing from the new patch of raw skin on his chest . . . the tears rolling down his burned cheeks.[1]

We get a sense of the mixture of fear, death, suffering, and confusion that enters into the American need for "gooks."

Nonmurderous encounter between Americans and Vietnamese were also characterized by hopeless contradictions and deceptions: Vietnamese seeming to be, as one man put it, "nothing but whores and thieves." The encounters recalled included kids a GI befriended stealing from him as soon as his back was turned; villages cooperating alternately with American and NLF forces; innocent-looking peasant women carrying grenades in their baskets, a perennial image but one that for most men was related less to specific incidents than to an overall sense of the environment as totally hostile and unpredictable; and, above all, allies (ARVN forces) who refused risks and fought little and badly, while Americans sent to help them did the fighting and dying, this last image combining much actual experience and a larger perception of the South Vietnamese in general as being uninvolved in their own (actually American-assigned) cause.

Feelings were also influenced by Vietnamese fratricide and the general inhumanity of a civil war, here described by a former grunt:

The NVA, when they came through, and when the South Vietnamese Army goes through, they're entirely insensitive to their own countrymen. . . . Ideology and . . . politics come first and anybody in the way—[who has] been tinged by the other side—is going to have to be executed. You know, they're going to have to be ripped off, exterminated. . . . I said, "It's all ridiculous."

Though this fratricide was part of the undifferentiated sea of atrocity in which the GI was immersed, my impression was that he often sensed, however inchoately, that the American presence had a lot to do with it. Yet even if he should try to explain or justify the behavior of Vietnamese on the basis of their desperate situation, he would still be bound by demeaning imagery of them. One veteran, for instance, spoke critically of certain officers who had condemned the Vietnamese for stealing, dishonesty, and fighting with one another for garbage scraps, "as if we should be amazed that [in a] barnyard of starving chickens, [when you] throw in a few kernels of corn, the chickens fight over them." The scene he describes is, of course, one of counterfeit nurturance in literal extreme, and his way of describing it suggests the vicious circle in which the demeaned victim, showing himself to be demeaned, must be further victimized.

Another image of the Vietnamese was suggested by a number of veterans in the form of a precaution that GIs in Vietnam urged one another to take: "When you buy soda pop from a gook you have to check out the bottom of the bottle for pieces of broken glass they might put in it." None of the veterans I spoke to have ever found any glass there. But the image, again, suggested the American sense of entrapment among ungrateful and viciously sly people out to do in the very GIs who come to help them while, at the same time, squeezing out the Yankee dollar. The image suggests a reverse victimization—that of Americans by Vietnamese—though there is also the sense of the revenge of the downtrodden, the already victimized Vietnamese striking back.

Jeff Needle's pamphlet conveys a sense of the setting in which Vietnamese become gooks:

There is a large gap of feeling and understanding between the American soldier and the Vietnamese. Most fighting men don't trust them because of the way they live and the language they speak. They don't respect the South Vietnamese soldier because they don't trust him while fighting alongside of him. They don't respect the Vietnamese people because they do our laundry, clean our buildings, fill our sandbags, polish our boots, wash our dishes, and women sacrifice their bodies, all for the Almighty American Dollar. Vietnamese people are commonly referred to as Dinks or Gooks by the large majority of American personnel. Would you lay down your life for the freedom of a Gook?

The people whose freedom we're fighting for have become our servants.[2]

Vietnamese become resentful servant-victims. In addition, they are perceived by GIs as cowardly or "chicken." Add to that perception such elements as the physical delicacy of Vietnamese men, Vietnamese cultural customs of men walking hand-in-hand, the anxious American stress on supermasculinity (further exaggerated in the military), and the GI's sense of being himself rendered helplessly passive and his need for compensatory feelings of victimizing others—and we have the image of the ARVN (or Vietnamese men in general) as "faggots" or homosexuals.[3] In contrast there is the widespread feeling that the VC, the alleged enemy, "have a lot of balls."[4] Glasser similarly quotes a trooper:

They're tough. In the Delta we killed NVA who had walked six months just to get there, and every day of that trip they had to take gunships, air strikes, and B-52 raids. Every day, man, every fucken day.[5]

The expression of respect was characteristic but the use of the terms "NVA" and "NLF," the most dignified names for the "enemy" (because their true names), was not. GIs more frequently referred to them either simply as "gooks" or as "VC" (Vietcong, meaning Vietnamese Communists), for them a relatively neutral term standing between the other two* Men would be perfectly capable of expressing this kind of respect for the enemy while still using the word gook—the more or less generic usage demonstrating how deeply the American "gook syndrome" penetrates. But, ironically, the assigned enemy, viewed in this way with respect bordering on awe (even when including elements of hatred), is the only kind of Vietnamese the GI encounters whom he does not see as a victim—and who does not therefore enter directly into the American "gook syndrome."

All this provides the basis for a sustained victimizer-victim relationship. In their struggles wth the atrocity-producing situation, GIs develop a hunger not only for an enemy but for a psychological victim. Themselves under constant threat of grotesque death, they must find, in a real sense create, a group more death-tainted than themselves, against whom they can reassert their own continuity of life. They become involved in the prin-

---

* Actually "Vietcong" is also demeaning. It is a fabricated name, apparently created by the Diem regime in order to imply that the entire movement was Communist (which it was not), and that the revolution it espoused was artificial and external (inferred from "Cong," which has Chinese roots, a word which Ho Chi Minh had rejected in favor of terms with indigenous roots that linked the revolution with sacred communal traditions).[7] But those associations were not present in the GI use of "VC," which, simply in replacing "gook," implied some respect or at least a distinction between assigned enemies and inhuman victims.

ciple of "addiction to survival," or "survivor paranoia," a pathological potential of the survivor ethos in which one requires
constant and repeated death immersions—survivals of deaths
one may witness or cause—in order to reaffirm the sense of being
alive.[6] The process then broadens into a need on the part of
GIs to make a whole people into a death-tainted group, against
which one can contrast the continuing life of one's own.

While a potential for victimization is universal, the impulse
is activated most readily by the kind of situation the American
victimizers encounter in Vietnam: a perceived threat to the life
of one's own group in the absence of an ennobling or in any way
viable mode of immortality. The South Vietnamese qualify as
victims on several counts: their inferior economic status, rendering them 'servants' or 'slaves' to Americans; their race, different
and nonwhite; their softer male cultural patterns; their low level
of technology*; and, above all, their moral and psychic disorganization. These last two factors taken together are crucial—overwhelming American superiority in the technology of destruction
gives GIs immediate and total power over the life and death of a
group (South Vietnamese who are not affiliated with the NLF)
lacking the kind of organizing (or immortalizing) vision that
would otherwise enable them to resist the role of passive victim.

Thus peasant-allies are converted into something more than
even enemies—they become *psychologically functional victims*.
The process is self-perpetuating: once seen as symbolically death-
tainted, the victims can be more readily killed, which makes them
still more death-tainted. They are cast out of history, denied the
status of a people with cultural continuity. Since they are historically and psychologically already dead, one may kill them
arbitrarily, without the feeling one is taking a life.

The pattern goes back at least as far as the ancient Egyptians:
in the Pyramid Texts, the pharaoh's eternal life is repeatedly ac-

---

* We shall discuss further in Chapter 12 this principle of victimization around
technological inferiority—as an addition to already existing racial, class, economic, and religious categories.

claimed, and (as Breasted puts it), "the word death never occurs
. . . except in the negative or applied to a foe."[8] The immortality
of the pharaoh, later of the king or noblemen, and finally of any
dominant (or potentially dominant) group has always been
contrasted with the death-tainted status of the enemy-victim.
Victimizing others can thus be understood as an aberrant form
of immortalization. Hence the phenomenon of outcast groups in
various cultures ("untouchables" in India, Eta or Burakumin in
Japan, blacks in the United States) who are associated with
images of pollution and defilement, and who tend to be relegated
to occupations associated with blood, death, and dirt—such as
slaughtering or butchering of animals, leather work or fur
processing, actual handling of corpses, cleaning of excrement,
or other forms of more or less equivalent menial labor.

Once the qualifying outcast-victim has been found, the dominant group comes to depend upon a vicious circle of victimization similar to that we described for Vietnam: because he is an
inferior outcast, he must do the polluted and defiled work of
society; because he does that work, he is death-tainted and contemptible; because he is contemptible, he must be forced to
accept his degraded condition and may be brutalized or murdered at will. There is always a scapegoating element in victimization: the idea that the victim is in some way responsible for
troubles befalling the larger community, is the bearer of the
community's burden of guilt, and must be continually brutalized
and punished lest guilt and retaliation he unleashed on the dominant group. Because men are prone to guilt and to anxiety about
individual, group, or cultural death—that is, anxiety about their
symbolic immortality—the foul breeze of victimization is ever
ready to stir.

In Vietnam the scapegoat-victim necessary to the belea-
guered American soldier-survivor is not the North Vietnamese,
nor the NLF guerrilla, not even, for that matter, the South Vietnamese civilian or soldier, but rather the "gook." The word goes
back at least to World War II and was again used actively during

the Korean War. Most commonly applied to "a brown-skinned
or Oriental non-Christian," it can encompass "a native of the
Pacific Islands, Africa . . . or any European country except
England"; and, as an adjective, any people who are "foreign,"
and any objects "made in any country except the U.S.A."[9] While
the etymology of the word is unclear (it may be from Scottish-
Middle English-Old Norse-Common Germanic roots—respectively *gowk* [simpleton], *gowke* [cuckoo], *gaukr*, and *gaukaz*),[10]
there is no doubt about its common slang usage to connote
sludge, dirt, or slime, thereby suggesting polluted liquid filth.*
Gook thus serves the psychological function of image-replace-

---

* When this discussion of the origins of "gook" appeared in an excerpt of
the book published in the *Saturday Review, The Society* ("The 'Gook Syndrome'
and 'Numbed Warfare,'" December 1972, pp. 66–72), a number of people wrote
to me questioning, or expanding on, various aspects of it. Several correspondents were certain that the word comes directly from the Korean language. They
pointed out that "Gook" is the Korean suffix denoting nationality, and that
"Han Gook" means Korean and "Me Gook" means American. One suspected
that the GIs' use of the word might have come from imitating Korean children
or soldiers who would shout "Me Gook" when they saw GIs to demonstrate
their sympathy for or identification with Americans. And it was further pointed
out that the pronunciation of that word—its long u, rhyming with "luke," is
very different from that employed when referring to liquid slime, where gook
rhymes with "look," which was cited as further evidence of the lack of relationships between them. All that sounded very convincing, until I received
two additional letters. One recalled hearing the word back in 1932 used frequently by United States sailors for Filipino mess attendants who would either
be called gooks or "goo-goo pantry boys." And the other directed me to an
article that appeared on July 10, 1920 in *The Nation* in which Herbert J.
Seligmann, then a staff member of the National Association for the Advance-
ment of Colored People, spoke caustically, after a visit, on "The Conquest of
Haiti": "The Haitians in whose service the United States Marines are supposedly in Haiti are nicknamed 'Gooks' and have been treated with every variety
of contempt, insult and brutality. I have heard officers wearing the United
States uniform in the interior of Haiti talk of 'bumping off' (i.e. killing)
'Gooks' as if it were a variety of sport like duck hunting." (For that last reference I am indebted to Harold C. Bakken, a historian at Lowell State College
in Massachusetts.) All of this confirms the continuity of victimization and its
relationship to color and race, but leaves the origin of gook as obscure as ever.
I suspect that it has several independent origins which have overlapped and
reinforced one another.

ment; through its use a human being becomes liquid slime. Some such dehumanizing term is always necessary to the numbing of widespread killing—it is much easier to annihilate "Huns" or "communists" or "imperialists" than it is men or women or children. But gook goes unusually far in implicitly imposing a death-taint in the form of inert liquid slime. The consequences are grotesque not only for Vietnamese victims but for American victimizers caught in the psychic slime of the gook syndrome.

That syndrome, for instance, was a stimulus to statistical competition around the body count (as the My Lai survivor explains):

[The soldier boasting of a high body count] was sort of saying how much . . . I hate the gooks—in terms that you can actually understand. I hate them a whole lot. I hate them even more than a whole lot . . . so, wow!, I killed 121 of them. That means I hate them worse than anybody does . . . And of course the only way you could determine who hated them the most was how many times you beat them or killed them or raped them or something like that.

One feels impelled, that is, to demonstrate one's commitment not to the mission of the war but to the gook syndrome.

The syndrome draws upon, but in a basic way violates, Biblical imagery of the scapegoat. The sin (the war) is there, but it is not confronted by the (American) community, as the Biblical ritualization of atonement prescribes. Instead the scapegoat—or gook-victim—is made to bear the *unacknowledged guilt* of the victimizing community: the human sacrifice is instead performed to appease appetites for killing (those of GIs, company commanders, generals, the Pentagon, the White House and, as perceived, of possibly still higher powers), these appetites sometimes partly acknowledged (as above) but without convincing inner justification. The gook syndrome thus requires that one kill or otherwise brutalize the scapegoat-victim, but prevents the atonement at the very center of the original scapegoat ritual. Indeed, the compulsive killing of "gooks" can reflect an aberrant substitute for that atonement—a perverse and continuous struggle toward a 'cleansing ritual' that leads only to more blood guilt and still more compulsive killing.

We recall how Company C's first death, just prior to My Lai, brought about a change in its lieutenant ("he got to be a savage too"). The My Lai survivor provides a further explanation of the company commander's behavior in shooting and "finishing off" a wounded Vietnamese woman in the midst of the slaughter:

It could be . . . that he wanted to commit himself and go along with the others because that was the way he felt. He was the leader and he had to do it too. Like an initiation.

What he had to commit himself to was not only the illusion of battle (described in Chapter 2) but the gook syndrome, and to *active* (victimizing) participation in it.

While in Vietnam, avoiding the gook syndrome was almost impossible. The former Army sergeant (whose struggles with guilt we discussed earlier around a "forgotten atrocity" makes this clear in telling of the pervasiveness of the syndrome and his own conflicts about opposing it:

I really felt sick at myself for not . . . confronting them. And yet I . . . just tired of confronting them because it wouldn't make any difference. I could tell my troops till they were blue in the face, punish them when I caught them doing it [calling the Vietnamese gooks or otherwise brutalizing them], and yet the whole military establishment was contrary to what I was doing . . . supporting the [idea] that it was gooks. The colonels called them gooks, the captain called them gooks, the staff all called them gooks. They were dinks, you know, subhuman. They used to deal with them in this way, so they took the cue from that and they considered me some kind of weird freak.

Just trying to avoid the gook syndrome made one "abnormal" in that environment, and in the end (as both the above statement

and the following one by the same man suggest), one was inevitably drawn into it:

The ARVNs were famous for stealing anything they could get their
hands on. . . . But like . . . when an ARVN would come over looking
for me or something, and one of the Americans would just toss him
over the barbed wire fence in a heap, you know . . . I just didn't want
to deal with it because it didn't matter whether I reported it because
they just didn't care. They were ARVNs, they were subhuman. . . .
If somebody had done that, an American . . . to another American,
we might do something about it, get a court-martial or something.
But they weren't going to back me anyway, so I had no authority. I
said, "What could I do?" I couldn't, as a human being, deal with
that all the time on that level of being human to them, because I
would have gone insane. So I just had to . . . sort of find a dead
space and put it all there.

Maintaining that "dead space" of psychic numbing meant ceas-
ing to feel the humanity of the Vietnamese and, at some level,
cooperating in their victimization. Moreover, he found that
breaking out of the gook syndrome and forming genuine friendships with Vietnamese—as in a caring relationship he developed
with a middle-aged Vietnamese woman and her daughter—ended
badly for everyone:

. . . they had an attack on the village where she lived, and one morning they came in and said "Mama-san is gone. The VC got her last
night because she associated with the Americans.". . . I found myself
thinking, why the hell don't you just leave well enough alone and just
function as a military idiot like you're supposed to, and you wouldn't
be getting into trouble. But you're going against the system. So it
just ends up getting people in trouble. I said, why try to make these
people responsive to Americans, or see that Americans are good. . . .
They're caught in the middle and [you're] helping them get caught
in the middle. . . . They're just going to get crushed by the whole
thing. It's better to leave them alone.

The gook syndrome then was part of the *collective* American psychological adaptation to the counterfeit universe in Vietnam. To rebel against it was to risk severe psychic or physical repercussions and possibly to endanger one's own life and the lives of others, Vietnamese or Americans. As one man summed the situation up during a rap group: "Everytime you'd start to feel human, you'd get screwed."

And beyond the situation in Vietnam, the syndrome had deep roots in American society, and especially in our popular culture —as strongly suggested by an Air Force medic stationed in Japan:

The most widely read literature among the guys that return from Vietnam, it's comics. Comic books and adventure stories. You know, *Male:* you see the picture of some guy killing somebody and the bare-breasted, Vietnamese-type Asian-looking woman. . . . These guys are just living in a dream world. They're young, easily influenced . . . Cartoons! It's the good against the bad. It's always gooks. In every war we've ever fought, we haven't killed *people.* Even when we killed whites of the same religion and they looked like us, they were Krauts. . . . There's tremendous racism. I took one guy up to eat and we were having rice and he said, "Oh, my God! Gook food!" I wonder who we're fighting for if everyone's a gook."[11]

While Americans are hardly unique in their capacity for a gook syndrome, or for related forms of dehumanizing wartime enemies, the syndrome does connect with specific American historical experience. Even the slogan so often heard in Vietnam, "The only good gook is a dead gook," has literal historical antecedents in which gook is replaced by "nigger" or by Indian (or "Injun"). The fact that black or Indian GIs (or GIs of Japanese, Chinese, or Hawaiian extraction) joined in the gook syndrome is itself somehow American: the melting-pot myth of leaving one's cultural-racial past behind and becoming totally an "American," which in this case meant joining in the collective American need, in that atrocity-producing situation, to victimize "non-Americans."*

The My Lai survivor remembered certain confusions about terminology:

Koreans they equated with gooks. . . . Koreans and Vietnamese, as far as they were concerned, there wasn't very much of a line. . . . They called them gooks over there. A gook is supposed to be a Korean. The Vietnamese is supposed to be a dink.† But that shows you how isolated we were. We didn't even have that right, you know.

Despite everything, more humane feelings toward Vietnamese did persist. They could be kept alive by involvements with families or by various encounters with the suffering of individual Vietnamese. Training in Vietnamese language could also be a factor, as it tended to lessen numbing and the impulse toward

* The recent wave of literature debunking the melting-pot myth correctly counters the notion that such "melting" of roots and identity really occurred. But it overlooks the power of that myth both in certain immediate situations in which one feels compelled to be intensely "American," and in long-range cultural-mainstream aspirations that can live side-by-side with continuing ethnic identity. That ethnic identity, much more powerful than earlier melting-pot literature allowed, not only persists but can be periodically intensified by waves of cultural and social imagery, as occurred in America, first with blacks and then with all ethnic sub-groups, during the 1960s. And such waves of reinforced racial-cultural identity, as I suggest toward the end of the chapter, has already begun to give particular shape to the revulsion of nonwhite former GIs. Again these patterns are by no means limited to the United States—many parallels could, in fact, be drawn with the classical imperialistic use of "colonials" to fight under European banners—the difference being that no melting-pot myth with its promise of merging and sameness was ever held out to those European-manipulated "colonials."

† "Dink" and "slope" are the other two derogatory words used for Vietnamese. "Dink" may be derived from "dinky," meaning of small size or consequence, though this is far from certain. "Slope" unquestionably derives from "slope-eyes" or "slant-eyes," derogatory reference to the relatively narrow (compared to Western) eye openings of Asians. As far as I could tell there was little systematic distinction of the kind suggested by the My Lai survivor (Koreans as "gooks" and Vietnamese as "dinks"); the words were more or less interchangeable, with "gook" used most widely, not only for Vietnamese but Asians in general.

victimization by enabling one to enter into cultural thought processes and feelings, and also to have some meaningful exchange with educated Vietnamese who served as teachers and inevitably reflected some of the pain of their people. Moreover, the relatively few who gravitated toward a military language program probably possessed greater than average capacity for empathy. But precisely those sensitive GIs were likely to experience strong, guilt-centered inner conflict between their inclination toward empathy and compassion on the one hand and the demands of the gook syndrome on the other.

As in all war and holocaust, children could play a particularly great part in resensitizing experiences. Veterans talked of having been shocked by the deaths of children—and described with retrospective horror scenes of American vehicles barreling through villages and running over children who happened to be in the way. The latter image was one of ultimate transgression and mismatch—the helpless young, whom adults are supposed to nurture and protect, cruelly destroyed by all-powerful but totally unfeeling American machines.

The excruciating duality of these perceptions was expressed by the My Lai survivor in describing a scene right after the slaughter. A few small Vietnamese children that "they still had left" were running about, and the same men who had just done the shooting "were giving the kids food—you know, just like nothing ever happened." He went on to explain that, unlike most of the men,

I could connect the kids with the people in the village. I could even . . . actually wonder . . . if it was his mother and father or something like that, his sister or brother that were killed in the village. And I don't think it ever—well maybe it did—I don't think it ever popped into anybody else's mind.

That scene epitomized both the absurd contradictions and the malignancy of the gook syndrome. In thus evoking parental-nurturing impulses in the men, a child was less of a gook than an adult. But that sympathy only emerged after the distinction, under duress, had temporarily disappeared during the killing.

Sexual encounters, by illuminating the gook syndrome, could contribute to overcoming it. A former navy NCO, who had been based in Saigon, spoke to me at length during individual interviews about a sequence of affairs and the way in which they came to define for him his relationship to Vietnam and the Vietnamese. Doubtful about the war and concerned about the Vietnamese, he was, from the beginning, critical of sexual exploitation on the part of American military and civilian officials, of their "whoring it up, having themselves a ball." But in vowing to himself, "I'm not going to touch any of these women over here. . . . I'm not going to be a whoring imperialist," he was also responding to his own sexual excitement. Struck by the beauty of Vietnamese women, and having considerable freedom in his assignment, he quickly broke the first part of his vow but tried to live up to the second by cultivating relationships with mutual sensitivity and consideration. The effort was defeated by deceptions emerging from the counterfeit environment. When a woman he particularly cared about ended their relationship, leaving a note for him in which "she intimated that her seeing me made her a prostitute in the eyes of her country, and that . . . [it had been] a great sacrifice," he concluded that authenticity was simply impossible.

A trip to Bangkok intensified both his attraction to what he perceived as exotic sexual possibilities and his condemnation of the overall American project. Taken by a taxi driver to a bar where one made direct arrangements with attractive prostitutes on display, he enjoyed his night of sex but was subsequently troubled by evidence he encountered everywhere of sexual exploitation:

I mean I saw it in Saigon and that was bad enough, but that was the war zone. I knew everything was shitty back there. . . . But there it was in Bangkok. Son of a bitch. There was a white man's world and it was—it got to me. I came back and they said, "How was Bangkok?" I said, "It's a fucking colony."

The dual meaning of his phrase, "fucking colony," depending upon which of the two words is given emphasis, accurately reflected his own special dilemma. He remained strongly aware of "something very exciting about someone from another race." But he was equally strongly appalled by the clear relationship he saw between sexual and racial exploitation—all the more so when he was told by a socially prominent French woman that "if I would stay long enough I would become a racist like her."

He resolved his dilemma by attending "massage parlors," where he found that relationships had a certain simplicity and integrity:

I'd pay my money and I'd get the steam bath, the massage, the blow job or whatever, and that would be it. And what happened was open. The kind of exchange it was—was *that* exchange—and it was called what it was, and there's something very refreshing about it. . . . It began to seem to me as if that was the only kind of sex I could have in Vietnam . . . because that was the only honest thing I did. . . .

He would, in fact, win favor with the prostitute-attendants by treating them with gentleness and concern for their pleasure, resulting in what he called "successful sex."

That solution—open, unvarnished sex, unencumbered by any other kind of relationship or commitment—was neither original nor ideal. Nor did it fully exculpate him, either objectively or in his own eyes, from sexual exploitation. But it did have two significant psychological values for him. First, its very directness and simplicity shed light on the convoluted deceptions that characterized the rest of his existence. As "the only honest thing I did," it helped him retain a small core of bodily and psychic integrity. Second, it enabled him to preserve, through sex, an island of sensitivity that contributed to his responsiveness to Vietnamese suffering. (One must quickly add, however, that both "values" were tainted by their being considerably less available to the girls involved, however he sought to equalize matters by his considerate treatment of them.) He saw no combat, but one can say that his kind of erotic intensity enabled him to focus on a form of transcendence that was life-enhancing and did not depend upon killing. It played a part in his capacity to look out from his Saigon rooftop at the random American artillery fire on the outskirts of the city and express to a friend his rage and his awareness that "There are *people* out there." The cry was impotent, just as the sex was tainted and incomplete: both were, after all, engulfed by the murderous deceptions of the gook syndrome. Yet the very struggle to relate his erotic impulses to human concerns gave him something of fundamental importance to build upon in emerging from the residue of the gook syndrome later on.

Most GIs, while in Vietnam, were themselves much more affected than he by the gook syndrome, in sexual as well as in other encounters. Even among those who came to the rap groups, veterans most actively concerned with issues of integrity, the syndrome had often taken hold in some depth. They found it difficult to examine specific psychic participation in it, and the whole subject was flooded with guilt. So much so that the men often resorted to idealized descriptions of the Vietnamese that stopped short of evoking the emotional complexity of collusion and mutual corruption. Nor was it easy for them to evaluate the pleasure and sense of absurd humor associated with a situation that could now be described only as exploitative. The men in the rap group could chuckle together in recalling such signs in small Vietnamese outposts as "Car Wash and Get Screwed," but they had difficulty sorting out the conflicting tones and attitudes in their own responses then and now. Overall, they did succeed in combining guilt-linked exploration of their involvement in the gook syndrome with humorous appreciation of some of the absurdities associated with it. Indeed, expressing their sense of absurdity, mockery, and self-mockery was crucial to their struggle to develop an animating relationship to the guilt specifically associated with that syndrome.

The men reached back for images around which they could come to terms with the Vietnamese and themselves in this process of simultaneous rehumanization. Sometimes a seemingly unremarkable memory could reflect many levels of abuse around the gook syndrome. One man, for instance, spoke with gentle bitterness about

... the atrocity that was there in daily life. . . . [American vehicles] going through the village at forty miles an hour, kicking up a cloud of dust when the mama-san just got through sweeping off the front porch.

Compared to other American transgressions, this one seemed highly innocuous. But the image persisted for the teller because it stood for the overall abuse of weak and helpless Vietnamese by blindly rampaging and numbed American power and technology, and for the brutal intrusion that destroyed orderly existence and spread only filth. It is also possible that the image represents a "screen memory," symbolizing a much more painful event—say, of a child run over by one of the speeding American trucks—a memory that can neither be consciously faced nor dispelled from the unconscious mind. In standard psychoanalytic practice, a screen memory inevitably derives from childhood, but the principle of a relatively innocuous image symbolizing and substituting for a very painful one can apply to adult memories (as this one of course would be) as well.

Significantly, the rehumanizing process seemed considerably easier in relationship to former enemies. We have noted GIs' divergent images of NLF and North Vietnamese soldiers as anything from gentle deer to bestial killers, but converging around respect for them as courageous and determined fighters, men who "have a lot of balls." Hence, although they too were indiscriminately referred to as gooks, veterans did not seem to have to perform, around images of them, the psychological work of extricating themselves from the gook syndrome.

In the rap groups, with their continuous focus on meaning, much was made about the fact that the NLF and North Vietnamese were "fighting for something." And even during combat, according to the My Lai survivor, doubts about one's own participation in the war could be accompanied by sympathetic curiosity toward one's assigned enemies:

I always had the feeling that when I . . . was in a situation . . . a straight combat situation where there were enemy soldiers and everything . . . you know, like who says we've got to be . . . who says we've got to do this anyway? I don't even know the guy. I might have gotten along with him. Somebody told us that we're supposed to have it out and it doesn't seem quite right, you know.

Such ideas probably occurred more during lulls than during the combat struggle to survive, but they were nonetheless important indicators of disbelief in the assigned friend-enemy dichotomy. Moreover, I heard many recollections, sometimes with retrospective uneasiness, of pleasant contact with people thought to be connected with the NLF—here described by a former marine:

Many of the people that . . . I used to talk to came through the wires . . . from the other side. They're actually . . . you see . . . I still felt that they were friends even though . . . the truth is that . . . circumstances were causing them to be shooting at me, and causing me to shoot back. And we could still, if you could get away from this, we could still be friends.

Still more revealing was a frequently told tale, one I heard in many versions, always based upon hearsay and rumor, going something like this:

A group of GIs wandered into a small bar in a village where they obtained pot and began to smoke. A friendly group of young Vietnamese came in and did the same. Americans and Vietnamese smoked together in an atmosphere of warmth, pleasure, and conviviality. The two groups then went their separate ways, each knowing it had been smoking with its designated enemy, since the Vietnamese had been "VC."

More than any actual occurrence, the image suggests a myth of communal reconciliation among young people previously coerced (by the counterfeit manipulations of their elders) into killing one another, now choosing instead to enjoy together their generation's rites of celebration.

GIs had to leave Vietnam to be able to begin to perceive the degree to which the very structure of the American presence there is built upon the gook syndrome.* And even when subsequently examined and cast off, it can recur under duress in unexpected, and for antiwar veterans, painfully illuminating ways. The syndrome can of course simply persist, mostly by making contact with the vast reservoir of the victimizing imagery available in American society. It can then enter into various inner forms that serve such defensive psychological functions as justifying the killing one has done and avoiding a sense of guilt. Such

---

* To me, one of the most uncomfortable lessons concerning the gook syndrome came from reading Ronald J. Glasser's *365 Days*. A profound and honest book by an unusually compassionate physician, it nonetheless contains such phrases as "the gooks were in the groves in front of them, behind them, and to their flanks," or "a gook moved out of the grove on the right," or, in commenting on the extraordinary courage of American medics in consistently endangering their own lives to help the wounded: "And so it goes, and the gooks know it. They will drop the point [lead man in a patrol], trying not to kill him but to wound him, to get him screaming so they can get the medic too. He'll come. They know he will." Deeply moved by the suffering of GIs—"These kids were so brave, they endured so much, were so uncomplaining, you couldn't help but feel proud of them"—the author gets sufficiently 'inside their heads' to see the world, in his sketches about them, as they would. The last quotation, however, is strictly his own observation. Paradoxically, his very compassion and empathy for suffering Americans assigned to his care at an evacuation hospital in Japan propelled him toward the gook syndrome—at least in terminology and at certain moments. The extraordinary sensitivity of the book—I believe it to be a kind of classic—makes one realize that such was the pervasiveness of the gook syndrome that one could not 'feel with' Americans fighting the war without entering into it.

is the case with hawkish veterans mentioned earlier who insist that "We should have killed all the gooks." There, an added psychological function is that of keeping the gook syndrome operative rather than confronting it. For the process of breaking out of the syndrome could be a strongly resisted source of fundamental insight into one's personal war experience and much else.

We have observed the relationship of "gook" and "nigger" syndromes, and the Vietnamese experience helps us to focus upon the more general connection between victimization and death imagery.* We have seen the extent to which the victimizing process is itself stimulated by death anxiety on the part of a dominant group, whether the death threatened is physical or social. By victimizing another group and establishing it as death-tainted, one's own collective existence or symbolic immortality can seem to be affirmed.

But that affirmation is uneasy: immortality purchased at the expense of blacks or Vietnamese (or Jews or communists or whatever) becomes tainted with death guilt. The victimizer (or former victimizer in the case of the Vietnam veteran) must cope with the survivor conflicts of the death immersion to which he himself has so actively contributed. He is likely to find himself, over years or even generations, on a perverse treadmill of guilt, rage, and numbing—or else (in more extreme cases) of false witness and even a further need, periodic or sustained, to resume victimizing others. He can get off this treadmill only by altering his relationship to symbolic immortality, by discovering (or renewing) a viable sense of historical continuity that does not depend upon denying the same to another group.

* This death-centered view of victimization is part of the general paradigm of my theoretical work, that of death and the continuity of life. While it by no means invalidates other theories of "prejudice" or "discrimination," which stress various forms of "projection" or repressed sexuality, I believe that it provides a more fundamental framework for a pattern always perceived in ultimate life-and-death images. The evidence, in the form of various kinds of death imagery, is extensive, and I present a great deal of it in *The Broken Connection.*

But there are hundreds of thousands of Vietnam veterans for whom the issue is, at best, in doubt—who, unable to find viable modes of human connection, are at least tempted to seek that connection by creating new (or re-creating old) victims.

Equally important to the outcome is the victim's (or potential victim's) rejection of that state, the refusal to be a "gook" or "nigger." By casting aside his own earlier adaptation to victimization, by instead insisting upon—living out—collective forms of protest and transformation, he initiates renewed historical connection and lays claim to modes of symbolic immortality that prevent him from being viewed or treated as a "death-tainted victim." This is precisely what has happened among Vietnamese: by becoming national revolutionaries, whether through joining the North or the NLF, men and women ceased to qualify (in the eyes of first the French and then the Americans) as "death-tainted gooks" or their equivalents. In contrast, millions of Vietnamese more or less under the control of the American-sponsored regimes of the South have remained locked in the counterfeit universe and thereby condemned to the fate of gook-victims. For the arbitrary American-Vietnamese power arrangements, lacking national or ethical legitimacy, deny Vietnamese caught in them the kind of larger connectedness that would enable them to reject that state. In this fundamental psychohistorical way, the Vietnam War epitomizes a world-wide struggle (mostly on the part of nonwhite peoples) against victimization (in the past by European imperialism and now by the Pax Americana replacing and in ways perpetuating that imperialism)—a struggle whose psychological as well as political success seems to depend upon a revolutionary mode of immortality.* The antiwar veterans thus ally themselves with a significant, late-twentieth-century pattern of defections from the ranks of former victimizers and representa-

---

* There are parallels here with ideas of Frantz Fanon, but where he lays emphasis upon the former victim's therapeutic need for violence as such, my own stress is upon the renewed modes symbolic of immortality made possible by rebellion and revolution. I elaborate these views in *Revolutionary Immortality*.

tives of the privileged in favor of some form of struggle *against* victimization. But here, too, the great majority of Vietnam veterans remain in limbo.

The antiwar veterans also make direct psychological contact with the American version of this "Third World" process: the rejection of the "nigger-gook syndrome" first by blacks and then by all groups in any way victimized within the society. Indeed that general process undoubtedly influenced the veterans' movement against their own war and has had something to do with the evolving American consensus of rejection of the gook syndrome in Vietnam.

Nor have we heard the end of anti-victimization crusades on the part of survivors of Vietnam. While visiting the University of Hawaii in January, 1972, I met and appeared on a panel with a young leader of the new Hawaiian nationalist movement. Talking with him later I was surprised to learn that he had fought in Vietnam. "Like all the GIs I just killed everyone—they were all gooks to us," he told me. "But when I came back and looked at all the faces in the shopping center [with their mixed Japanese-Chinese-Hawaiian-Filipino racial features] they looked just like all the people I killed. I felt very strange and very bad." His guilt, in other words, was related both to killing and to having in the process entered into the gook syndrome, even as a nonwhite. He then began to ask himself how he had come to fight in Vietnam, what his own relationship to America was, what America had been doing with and to nonwhites like himself. He also began to study the Black Panthers and other protest movements, and very quickly emerged as a prominent young militant. Returning to the subject of Vietnam, he added: "Wait till Japanese-Americans and Chinese-Americans really wake up—some of them who fought in Vietnam are the angriest guys I know." He was suggesting the possibility of a vast revulsion against the gook syndrome initiated by Vietnam veterans who were racially closest to the gook-victims.

Considering these potentially explosive reactions (initiated by

Americans of nonwhite extraction but sweeping up many white Americans as well), and the equally explosive counterreactions that could occur (in which veterans with a need to remain victimizers could also be in the lead), the Vietnam War could do a great deal more than it already has toward tearing American society apart. What we can say about the antiwar veterans, much to their credit, is that they have at least suggested a model for casting off the most malignant of syndromes.

CHAPTER 8

Transformation I: From John Wayne to Country Joe and the Fish

"Forward, the light Brigade!"
Was there a man dismayed?
Not tho' the soldiers knew
  Someone had blundered:
Theirs not to make reply,
Theirs not to reason why,
Theirs but to do and die:
Into the valley of Death
  Rode the six hundred.

> —Alfred Tennyson,
> "Charge of the Light Brigade" (1855)

And it's 1, 2, 3, what are we fighting for?
Don't ask me I don't give a damn
Next stop is Vietnam
And it's 5, 6, 7, open up the Pearly Gates
Well there ain't no time to wonder why
Whoopee we're all gonna die

> —Country Joe MacDonald, "I-Feel-
> Like-I'm-Fixin'-to-Die Rag" (1968)

When can their glory fade?
Oh, the wild charge they made!
  All the world wondered.
Honor the charge they made!
Honor the Light Brigade,
  Noble Six Hundred!

> —Tennyson, "Light Brigade"
> (last stanza)

Well come on mothers throughout the land
Pack your boys off to Vietnam
Come on fathers don't hesitate
Send him out before it's too late
Be the first one on your block
To have your boy come home in a box

> —Country Joe, "Fixin'-to-Die Rag"
> (last stanza)

WE HAVE BEEN TALKING about men acquiring insight. Their struggles around animating guilt, channeled rage, and reversals of the counterfeit universe and gook syndrome propelled them toward nothing less than personal transformation. That kind of transformation has been a preoccupation of antiwar veterans and a major focus of the rap groups. It is also a matter of considerable importance to psychology in general. Rarely does a clinician or anyone else have the privilege of observing and contributing to this kind of flow and action of change and growth.

The men repeatedly made clear that everything began with, and reverted back to, one fundamental insight: the absurdity of dying in Vietnam. That insight is at the center of the whimsically serious theme of this chapter—the shift from "the John Wayne thing" to the spirit of Country Joe and the Fish.

We have seen the John Wayne thing to be many things, including quiet courage, unquestioning loyalty, the idea of noble contest, and a certain kind of male mystique we shall examine in a moment. But its combat version, as far as the men in the rap group were concerned, meant military pride, lust for battle, fearless exposure to danger, and prowess in killing. I was impressed by the extent to which the men had been initially involved in this constellation, and by the persistence of elements of it even in the face of the chaos and absurdity of the Vietnam environment. For the John Wayne thing is related to honor; and it would seem that men at war hunger for honor no less than they do for an enemy—that indeed the two feed the same hunger.

One former marine from Texas brought to Vietnam what he considered a heritage of honor transmitted over the generations and going all the way back to the Alamo:

I remembered the stories my grandfather used to tell me about it. . . . So I thought that . . . like the Alamo was a special moment for people way back and World War II was my father's moment, Vietnam was my moment. . . . When I got there I kissed the earth because I considered it sacred ground.

Another former marine, with retrospective self-mockery, emphasized the elements of skill and play that went into what he called his "John Wayne image":

I was very anxious to get into a bayonet fight because I really enjoyed playing with the . . . sticks in boot camp . . . and beating up on other people, and so I was anxious to get in a bayonet fight with a North Vietnamese or someone else so that I could demonstrate how good I was at it.

No doubt marines were most prone to John Wayne imagery, but it was hardly limited to them. All men in battle require elements of that imagery, having to do with courage and male group loyalty or bonding, in order to cope with their fear of death, the concern with manhood, and the quest for higher purpose.

Not Country Joe and the Fish, however. They are not only unimpressed with John Wayne imagery; as expressed in Vietnam, they, in fact, think it mad. The frenzied mockery of their celebrated "I-Feel-Like-I'm-Fixin-to-Die Rag" propels a listener to the far reaches of the absurd and the grotesque. What is absurd is fighting there:

> And it's 1, 2, 3, what are we fighting for?
> Don't ask me I don't give a damn
> Next stop is Vietnam

What is grotesque is being killed there:

> And it's 5, 6, 7, open up the Pearly Gates
> Well there ain't no time to wonder why
> Whoopee we're all gonna die

But the ultimate obscenity is enthusiasm about—belief in—the project:

> Well come on mothers throughout the land
> Pack your boys off to Vietnam
> . . . Be the first one on your block
> To have your boy come home in a box

Ever since Woodstock (1968), the "I-Feel-Like-I'm-Fixin'-to-Die-Rag" has been one of the most popular of all songs among Americans in Vietnam. But, as one veteran told me, "You l:sten to it all the time, but it takes you a while to *hear* what it is saying."

When you do, you are (can be) suddenly flooded with truth, your own suppressed truth. Such was the case with a former grunt:

It gave me . . . the ultimate vent to all those feelings of idiocy and lunacy about the whole war. . . . Here was some way that I could release it all. . . . Because I found . . . I was forcing myself [while fighting] to be "reasonable" about [the war]—you know, to find the middle course and say, "Okay you people didn't say you wanted [the war] so [we might as well do our best] . . ." But I was really feeling that it was crazy and idiotic and I wouldn't allow myself to express that. I guess when I heard the "Fixin'-to-Die Rag" I really just let it all hang out and say that it was really crazy. . . . Everytime I hear it now I just get a good feeling inside of me. . . . "Wow, this is really where it is. It's really what I feel." I don't have to . . . make any compromises about it or anything. It's just "whoopee, we're all gonna die"—and God, how stupid of me. . . .

Nothing else, he is telling us, connects so well with the extremity of his own sense of inner absurdity about fighting and dying in Vietnam—a sense that begins to form in every GI soon after his arrival and, however suppressed, always stands ready to be released.

Even more specifically, the issue of how one might have died in Vietnam continued to preoccupy veterans during the rap groups. One man recalled his feelings while there:

I wanted to die clean. It didn't matter if I died—but I just didn't want to die with mud on my boots, all filthy. Death wasn't so bad if you were clean.

Another man strongly agreed, and told of a repetitive dream he used to have in Vietnam, always with the same terrifying conclusion:

I would end up shot, lying along the side of the road, dying in the mud.

The intense associations (of the dreamer, other veterans, and professionals) and the interpretive discussion that followed revealed that dying "clean" meant dying with a measure of dignity, for a reason or ennobling purpose—that is, dying in a more or less acceptable or dignified fashion. "Dying in the mud" meant dying in filth or evil, without reason or purpose—without nobility or dignity of any kind.*

At that point a man who had said virtually nothing in the rap group for several weeks spoke up and everyone else became silent, listening with fixed attention as he blurted out a story:

I heard of one helicopter pilot in Nam who was carrying a shit-house [portable toilet] on his helicopter. He crashed and was killed, and

---

* Michael Casey expresses a similar sentiment in a poem, "On Death," from his collection, appropriately entitled *Obscenities:*[1]

. . .
Flies all over
It like made of wax
No jaw
Intestines poured
Out of the stomach
The penis in the air
It won't matter then to me but now
I don't want in death to be a
Public obscenity like this

was buried under the whole shit-house and all the shit. I thought that if I was going to die in Vietnam, that's the way I would like to die. I didn't want to die a heroic death. That was the way to die in Vietnam.

Only excrement, ultimate filth, could provide the appropriate burial ground in Vietnam—the appropriate symbolism for dying. I heard no more telling evocation of the war's absurd evil. The story quickly evoked in others a series of memories of horrible deaths witnessed in Vietnam. The men began to contrast the bodily mutilations and especially the bleeding with the "clean" deaths portrayed by American mass media. As one veteran put it, "In Flash Gordon no one ever bleeds." The men were groping toward the kind of insight that could both relate the John Wayne thing to a romantic, superficial, media-sponsored image of cleaned-up death (or nondeath), and, at the same time shame that image out of existence by means of filthy truth.

A man's first exposure to the actuality of death severely threatens the playful romance of the John Wayne image. That experience could at times precede combat, as in the case of a veteran who described meeting, while in transit, a former buddy from basic training who told him he was being sent to accompany the body of another GI they had both known well. What the veteran mainly remembered of his reaction upon hearing this news was the disturbing idea taking hold in his mind, "It really happens!" That idea in turn undoubtedly influenced his subsequent reaction to witnessing the bodily disintegration of an NLF guerrilla he himself shot from about thirty feet when in combat. "I was surprised by how much damage my weapon did," was what he said to me, his pained tone conveying his horror and awe of *being* (as well as *firing*) an instrument of such sudden and grotesque annihilation. For him those two incidents were the beginning of his questioning *everything*.

Precisely that process is eloquently described by Jeff Needle.

His unit's first death brought about "a silence, and . . . a quiet dread thought that the games were over, that there was death lurking in this country . . ." Then, after other deaths quickly following upon the first, came the search for meaning:

. . . one of those enemy bullets traveled through space and stopped in a man's body and he was dead. And his one-month-old marriage died and the guys said, "If he had stayed lower that wouldn't have happened," and that was a good excuse because no one had any other reason why he was dead. But he was. So they decided to stay lower; that was the answer. It turned out that wasn't the answer. It turned out there was no answer.

First I wondered why he died, why him and not someone else . . . Maybe because of his background, maybe because it was his turn to go. There could have been any number of reasons. . . . But then after a short while men were dying and being wounded and being maimed and there was no common factor. They were short and tall and black and white from all parts of the country.

And when I finally gave up looking for a reason why one became a victim while another didn't, when I finally had to admit to myself that there was no answer, no easy way to go through the rest of the day, no way of saying to yourself "I know why Miller lost his leg today.". . . [or] how an old-timer who made it through the Korean War didn't make it through this one.

Then I started to wonder why *anyone* [my emphasis] was dying, why we were in Vietnam, and I slowly began to realize that the reasons we had been told back in the States, the reasons we grew up with were not true. I had been told we were fighting to help the South Vietnamese, to give them a government of their own choosing, to give them a chance to grow as a free people, to protect their rights as free people. . . . But what I actually saw in Nam was not even close to the ideals I had heard about. We brought men and weapons into Vietnam to protect Vietnamese freedom, and I found out we were taking away their freedom. . . . Most of the men in the field were not . . . fighting for idealistic purposes . . . [or] long-range goals, they were taking each day and trying to get through it alive and in one piece.[2]

The actuality of death is the test by which prior claims of the war's nobility or necessity are judged. In Vietnam that test could not be passed. One could make no inwardly convincing association between death and a higher principle. Individual survival, always the predominant preoccupation in war, became in this war the *only* purpose or cause one could call forth to justify one's actions. Nor could the attempt at logical explanation of why one person died and not another, so characteristic of death immersion in general, ward off the sense of total absurdity. Subsequent deaths one witnesses are no more acceptable, though more effectively managed by numbing—but one never really recovers from that first survival.

A former Marine grunt also told of the search for a mechanical explanation.

Like a guy would get hit in the chest—if he had buttoned his flak jacket, he wouldn't have gotten it, you know. If he had stayed in the stupid bunker where he belonged, he wouldn't have gotten killed. . . . We were always dealing with it on that level. . . . Which was the same thing they programmed into us from Boot Camp.

But the mechanistic explanation, encouraged by the military itself, could not hold for him—precisely because it made no contact with larger issues of connectedness:

You know the only times I really thought about death . . . only . . . for a couple of minutes because . . . it was too overpowering . . . was when nothing was happening, when it was quiet. Then I would think, My God, I wonder what it's like. . . . This is at the point where it was very traumatic for me because . . . when I first went into Boot Camp and we were filling out our dog tags and you had to put down what your religion was—I had been hassling with this for a long time and . . . had rejected Catholicism. But . . . I had to come to a decision. Had I rejected it or . . . what was I going to put on my dog tags? Was I going to admit that I had no religion . . . or was I going to hope that there was a God in case I got killed . . . [so that] I would be rewarded for what I had done, and I put,

"No preference." But . . . when I got to Vietnam . . . I had misgivings. . . . Do I really want to do this? . . . Am I really chucking away my chance for eternity . . . or heaven or something? . . . I think more traumatic than worrying about dying was worrying about . . . whether there was an afterlife or something. . . . I was seeing at the time that life . . . could go so easily, that it was so fragile that there wasn't really all that much to hold onto.

Unconvinced by the literal idea of an afterlife, he had been unable to replace that idea with a more symbolic mode of immortality that could absorb his exposure to the fragility of existence, to the death he witnessed and feared. There was no higher cause around which to activate a sense of connection, integrity, and movement that could sustain one in the face of death. Whether or not one articulated religious concerns, one tended to be left defenseless before death. No wonder why the statement about death veterans seem to find most convincing was the one quoted earlier: the 'excremental vision' of literally "dying in shit."

Everything that happens subsequently—whatever the veteran rejects, espouses, and becomes—stems from his rejection of death in Vietnam. Groups such as the VVAW make this rejection an explicit part of their credo, thereby providing at least the beginning of a collective formulation of American survival of the Vietnam War. Public inquiries and accusations around Vietnamese and American deaths extend this formulation while giving expression to a vigorous sense of survivor mission. Having rejected a particular kind of death, the anti-war warrior can—must—explore new ways to live.

Such men are much in need of a psychological place to land. They find that place in the amorphous but significant set of forms we call "youth culture." For some a turning point was Woodstock and its proliferation of imagery around music and ways of living. Whatever the subsequent disillusionment with that Woodstock imagery, it had a very special meaning for young Americans who fought in Vietnam.

We have observed some of the impact of Woodstock in the slide sequence discussed in Chapter 7. The former Army sergeant who prepared that sequence had heard much of the Woodstock music in Vietnam, and went to see the film twice upon his return. The impact he experienced was not only from the music but from personal examples of ways of living and feeling on the part of people making the music that were directly antithetical to his own military experience:

I was really moved by Richie Havens singing "Freedom". . . and Joan Baez singing about Joe Hill and [by] her commitment and by how I saw her life had been changed by David Harris . . . and his commitment.

Commitment meant evolving a sense of self enabling one to live out one's antiwar convictions: David Harris, then Joan Baez's husband, was a noted draft resister imprisoned for refusing to serve. Not only did the "Fixin'-to-Die Rag" reverberate continuously in the veteran's head and become something of a musical totem ("I like to sing the song as much as I can . . . [because it says] what I have to say"), but other tones and images from Woodstock music gradually deepened their hold upon him. He pondered over his own relationship to certain additional lines from "The Universal Soldier":

And he's fighting for democracy, he's fighting for the Reds
He says it's for the peace of all.
He's the one who must decide who's to live and who's to die,
And he never sees the writing on the wall. . . .
He's the one who gives his body as a weapon of the war,
And without him all this killing can't go on.
He's the universal soldier and he really is to blame.
His orders come from far away no more,
They come from here and there, and you and me, and brothers can't
   you see,
This is not the way we put an end to war.

For those words made him recall the sequence of his own rationalized collusion in war:

When I was in Hawaii [prior to going to Vietnam] I heard Buffy
Sainte-Marie sing "The Universal Soldier." And it bothered me for
a while but then, you know, I kept busy or pushed it out of my mind
somehow and didn't really deal with it to the extent of how I was
involved in it. . . . I built up some rationalization and said well, you
know, that's really nice to think about but we've got to deal with tne
realities of the world. . . . Yet in the back of my mind I always
know that I was rationalizing about it and . . . didn't want very
much to deal with the fact that she was telling what I might consider the truth.

Simon and Garfunkel, whose soft tones he had already associated for us with pot smoking in Vietnam, conveyed to him not
only the absurdity of war but

. . . the absurdity of the cities, neon lights. . . . [and being] imprisoned in the military . . . [and the alternative possibilties of] the
sounds of silence . . . and . . . animals at the zoo . . . describing
some kind of philosophic value [for] each of the animals.

An album by George Harrison, although "in many ways superficial," evoked additional personal associations:

It touched upon a lot of things that struck me and then drove me
thinking in a lot of ways . . . the idea of talking about "My Sweet
Lord". . . and the Christ image . . . [and] Hindu image and I think
sixteen different ways he addresses it. And it very much struck me
that this is the essence of what I wanted to get out of religion . . .
this essential thing, the spirit of humanity or the common bond that
unites us all. . . . Which is, you know, what many of the religions
. . . were trying to get at in different ways . . . bearing witness, and
all these ideas were crystallized . . . in this album.

The album thus enabled him to recover and build upon his own
early religious imagery, to the point of suggesting (in the terms

we have been using) a spiritualized mode of symbolic immortality. Inspired by those feelings at the time of hearing the album, he decided to use his entire unemployment check (he was then out of work) to buy seventy dollars worth of Christmas turkeys for people he knew could not afford them. And to those for whom he had intended to buy gifts with that money he sent notes instead explaining that "In your name a Christmas dinner has been given to someone who will appreciate it." That same week, after seeing the film *Woodstock* for the second time, he got the idea of combining his Vietnam slides with a rock musical accompaniment. This represented a change in an earlier plan to prepare a tape with his own narration, a change he decided upon because he found that the songs more accurately conveyed what he wanted to say than could any of his own words.

We may thus say that the word-music images of Woodstock and youth culture provided the strongest and truest expression he could find for giving form, new form, to his personal survival, his personal witness. More than that, these images furthered his sense that he could not extricate himself from the war without undergoing broader and deeper personal change:

Those people [producing the music] were criticizing parts of society or saying that love was an interaction between human beings and more important than money . . . that you couldn't attain peace by, you know, negotiating a settlement—that wasn't really peace—that peace was a way of life and it . . . got reflected into everything else you did.

Others derived similar meanings from youth culture, if more indirectly. The veteran quoted earlier about his rape-killing in Vietnam, for instance, remained preoccupied with issues of violence ("Any kind of violence is really stupid as far as I am concerned . . . a waste of energy"), and with spiritual alternatives to violence: "It seems to me, for instance, that this man Jesus was—was possibly a very ancient Bob Dylan, maybe."[3] Those youth-culture alternatives to Vietnam and a militarized society were, more often than not, absorbed gradually, on a day-to-day basis, through the psychological pores.

Over the long years of this longest American war, segments of the Vietnam environment itself have been infused with patterns loosely associated with youth culture—including language, music (rock), hair-style (long or Afro to the extent permitted), drugs (mostly pot), peace medallions, antiwar literature, and occasionally vigils or other expressions of protest. These have been rallying symbols for an enlarging number of draftees and younger officers, that is, from groups largely responsible for the ground fighting during the late sixties and early seventies. In opposition stands a "straight," conventional, and authoritarian military ethos exemplified by the "lifers" (regular army personnel—the term most frequently used for noncommissioned officers with many years of service), crew cuts, alcohol, old-style country music (or else Lawrence Welk ballroom style), and a direct line (from the rear rather than the field [of combat]) to command. Youth-culture style and attitudes, in other words, become a focus for the military underdog's rebellion against the military establishment.

I heard many stories of draftees* being harassed by lifers around petty questions of military rules and discipline. But the mythic sequence—based partly on actual experiences—was that of a draftee-grunt returning to the rear for a brief respite from battle, lighting up a joint to relax with buddies doing the same, and being pounced upon gleefully and punished by a lifer-vigilante. Though such myths oversimplify, there is no doubt that many lifers became obsessed with pot-smoking as exemplifying evil new influences undermining the fabric of the old army they had known and, if not loved, at least felt at home in; or that their vigilante methods could at times parallel the worst kind of police

---

* I use the word "draftee" to include all who view their stint in the military as temporary, whether they were actually drafted or enlisted, as opposed to those who joined the "regular" (or permanent) army.

practices back home, even to the point of planting fake evidence.

One of the men I interviewed said that the petty, vicious practices of the lifers made the situation so tense that "the war between us and them was just as great or greater than the war between us and the Vietnamese." He went on to say that he and his buddies had often discussed their impulse to turn their guns around and annihilate their "real enemy." The frequency of these stories and the intensity of the emotions expressed gave me the impression that Vietnam's particular version of the late 1960s-early 1970s "war between the generations" had a lot to do with the actual violence of "fragging" incidents.

In this and many other ways, Vietnam becomes a malignant crucible of the conflicts of American society. But the feelings of the "young freak" toward the "old square"—alienated mixtures of rage, contempt, fear, pity, and (at least now and then) love—are fueled by his war-linked death anxiety, death guilt, and conflicted survivor struggle. To the draftee the lifer comes to embody not only the counterfeit universe of the immediate environment and the larger military establishment, but also the misguided older generation responsible for sending him to fight the war, and indeed for the war itself.

His difficulty is that he can never inwardly sustain the simple mythic polarities of the "beautiful life-loving young draftee" versus the "evil death-dealing old square." For the war's death encounters make him profoundly dependent upon such qualities as military knowledge and skill, staying power, courage, and overall physical and psychological strength—qualities possessed by the best of the lifers and much more closely related to militarized John Wayne imagery than to Protean-style youth culture. How, for instance, is he to feel about a "nasty, chicken-shit lifer" whose know-how and experience save one's own life? Or toward a "sweet fellow-freak," admirable in his concern for the Vietnamese but inept militarily to the point of lessening everyone's chance for survival? Or for that matter, toward the self-proclaimed "freak" who is not only brave and skillful in combat but a bit too enthusiastic about killing? The GI, in other words, must cut through thorny psychic thickets of love and hate that defy pure categories. Yet the indelible image of the absurdity of dying in Vietnam, to which he repeatedly returns, counters some of these confusions and contributes ever again to the movement away from John Wayne and toward Country Joe.

Nor have responses of military authority been simple or consistent. As with society at large, these have varied from restorationist* counterattack, in the form of persecutory discipline directed against those who show glimmerings of youth-culture influence; to attempted absorption (what the young call co-optation)—whether by mouthing youth-culture language, adopting a veneer of hip attitudes, or by turning the other cheek in regard to such things as the use of pot (frequently the attitude of NCO's and officers who were at all close to their men); or by vacillations between the one and the other that create for both sides a mixture of some leeway and much confusion.

As in the larger society, it is difficult to evaluate the outcome of this dialectic of absorption (with muting of impact) and change (on the part of the military itself). But there was a widespread impression, over the course of war, that the lifers were losing the capacity to control their men—or even perhaps to believe fully in their own old-fashioned principles. We shall discuss in a later chapter the extent to which this represents an overall erosion of the warrior ethos. What we may say here is that youth culture posed, right in the heart of the military operation, a threat to the world-view of lifers (and regular officers too) as socialized warriors. The latter were bound to view the freak draftees as degenerate subverters of the military way of life who must be taught a lesson and put in their place. And they could call upon not only their military authority but also the resent-

* Elsewhere I have referred to American restorationism as "an urge, often violent, to recover a past that never was, a golden age of perfect harmony during which all lived in loving simplicity and beauty, an age when backward people were backward and superior people superior."[4]

ments of the large numbers of antiyouth-culture young among enlisted men.

Yet youth-culture rebellion in the military is rendered formidable, at least in psychological influence, both by the struggle throughout American society and the world at large to create what I have called a "New History"—and the extent to which the very grotesqueness of the Vietnam War lends emotional power and a certain amount of credibility to any sustained cultural-political forms that suggest fundamental alternatives. For all these reasons we may say that Vietnam provides an intense immersion into youth culture for large numbers of young men who would not otherwise be as broadly or intensely exposed to its various manifestations.* And although there are difficulties and conflicts at every point, this kind of youth-culture-linked personal change takes on particular inner significance precisely because the experiences initiating it are so concrete and extreme —because these frail beginnings of transformation are so tied in with tainted killing and equally tainted survival.

When the men return to the United States and continue their immersion into youth culture, they do so as old youths—old not in years but in what they have seen and learned. They are likely to be ambivalent about their own new brothers and sisters, and particularly touchy about everybody's relationship to the war. The former Marine grunt suggests the mutuality of that ambivalence:

[From] *Stars and Stripes* [the military newspaper] and the control they have over information, you get . . . a distorted view of what the peace movement is doing back in the United States, and you would think that they were going down and trashing the buildings in Washington and everything, and it wouldn't enlist a lot of sym-

* I include the class issue here. "Youth culture" originated among the relatively affluent, and while it has spread to a considerable extent among lower-middle-class and working-class young, I am suggesting that the military has done much to accelerate this diffusion.

pathy in me. Where I might have sympathy for the idea that they were opposed to the war as I was. I was getting the impression that they were against me too. . . . If anyone had met me, they would not have spoken to me and tried to persuade me, which would have been very easy, but rather they would have . . . had to confront me and demand that I change, which would have been hostile. So this was, in turn, keeping me in the military frame of mind. . . .

Although actually moving steadily away from "the military frame of mind" he had to rescue whatever dignity and meaning he could find in his three-year military affiliation. And that always required a certain degree of lingering identification with the very institution one renounced. Others' blanket accusations intensified the conflict by mobilizing static guilt and diffuse rage. One had to envision and inwardly experience alternatives to that identification in order to free oneself from it.

His solution, like that of many others soon after discharge, was to live out a dual identification. He became a part-time student, and gravitated strongly toward tastes and images of youth culture available at his university and elsewhere. But at the same time he sought work as a carpenter, and with jobs scarce found that it helped to tell a builder, "I just got out of the Marine Corps three months ago and I'm just getting back into things." He felt that self-presentation to be quite convincing, partly because his hair was still quite short from his marine cut:

It was getting longer and curlier on the edges, but it wasn't very long —so I could still pass as a carpenter—you know, a good American carpenter.

Most other "good American carpenters" along with their employers had seen some kind of military service, and showed particular respect for his marine background. So he felt it best to say nothing of his antiwar feelings. Later he felt guilty about trading on what he himself viewed as a John Wayne marine image, but also came to realize that at the time he had by no means been free of that image within himself.

An incident at a local basketball game revealed this continuing involvement with military symbolism. He encountered a high school boy wearing a marine dress blue jacket over a pair of Levi's, and became enraged:

I felt I'd really like to get up and deck that guy. He's got a lot of nerve . . . wearing that uniform. Even though I had those [antiwar] feelings, I felt very strongly . . . that there was still very much [to] everything that I had done. That uniform represented a lot, and I didn't want . . . [just] anyone wearing it.

He had a similar experience of feeling "really irritated" when his own younger brother wore the jacket of an Air Force uniform as an overcoat:

I didn't mind if he wore a field jacket or something, but something about wearing that uniform as an overcoat just really bothered me. . . . Because if he hadn't gone through the experiences—not necessarily earned it—but he hadn't gone through the experience and a lot of people had done great things, you know, in that uniform or for it . . . even though what we're doing now isn't.

The rhythms of his phrases suggest his conflict over who has earned what in wearing the uniform, and how whatever that might be connects with immortalizing American glory.

At the same time he gladly put away his own uniform. But when he proudly put on the sport coats and suits he had purchased in Vietnam from visiting Hong Kong tailors, he found himself in the uniform of an earlier student generation. With everyone else in jeans, his own studiedly casual dress stood out so alarmingly that a number of other students asked him if he was a "narc" (a narcotics agent, presumably sent to spy on the students). He felt "like. . . . the hostile element at the party or something," and before long replaced the jackets and suits with sweaters, old shirts, and comfortable bits of military field wear.

Having partly internalized prevailing clichés (emphasized in the military) about "dirty hippies" and "crazy protesters," his clothing problem symbolized the mixture of suspiciousness, eager embrace, guilt, and fear of rejection with which he approached student members of the youth-university subculture. For he was also looking back, again with some guilt, toward the marines and himself as a marine:

I wondered whether I was being fair to them . . . I still had some obligation to the Marine Corps and what they stood for and I wanted to be very reasonable and not to lash out at them . . . [and] externalize all the blame and guilt and put it on them.

Still, his antiwar position and survivor mission propelled him inexorably toward protest. But joining in with young protesters had its vicissitudes—as he discovered a few months later when driving his Volkswagen to Washington, D.C. (to attend the mass rally protesting the Cambodian invasion) with a peace flag flying from the car's antenna and a "strike" placard attached to its side. Not only did a few drivers in bigger cars give him "menacing grins" or "the finger" (obscene gestures), but a large truck with Tennessee plates slowly edged over to his side of the road, coming very close to causing a dangerous accident on very unequal terms. The veteran felt "washed over," and thought: "I'm back in Vietnam again. . . . Oh, my God, it's going to be a *war*." And in that war he felt (and still feels) himself in many ways more vulnerable than he had in Vietnam.

I don't have . . . the institution to rely on, the Marines. . . . There was a camaraderie about it . . . and now . . . there aren't that many people who care. . . . Many of the people I rely on now . . . would not be able to help me because of the fact that they'd have to protect their own position. . . . There are people getting very upset with what we're doing. . . . It's almost a war thing. . . . But it's a different kind of feeling. . . . There are no medals for this thing, you know.

He was learning, painfully and profoundly, the difference between taking part in a struggle while backed up by a society's power and reward system, and doing so in direct opposition to that power and reward system. The experience had much to do with what we may speak of as the radicalization of his survivor mission—in a psychological and cultural, no less than political, sense. Youth culture, in the richness of its confusions, provided much of the imagery, models, and collective support he drew upon.

Antiwar veterans manifested this combination of youth culture and grotesque survival in a variety of ways. In the VVAW office one encountered mostly former enlisted men of a temporary category, but also on occasion men who had been lifers or officers or lifer/officers, all of them dressed in mixtures of jeans and bits of military field uniform; lots of long hair, beards, and mustaches —occasional cut or shaved for personal or occupational reasons —now and then someone with "clean-cut" minimal-hair demeanor. It does not take very long for an observer to realize that they are, as one veteran put it, "different from other freaks." He was not certain what that difference was, but it had to do, he thought, with some kind of demonic obsession—whether with a piece of clothing or a particular motor bike, or with the shallowness and phoniness of American culture, or with the military and the war. To me the men seemed both more wise and more desperate than other young people, possessed with imagery of playing for keeps in a game they had learned much about, felt bitterly toward, and still did not quite understand.

Indeed their early antiwar demonstrations produced a great deal of puzzlement all around: the sight of "long-haired veterans" a shocking contradiction in terms to some policemen and older veterans of other wars; the antiwar veterans themselves at first uneasy (in their new role as protesters), then resentful of the taunts, but eventually throwing themselves into the mocking of military glory contained in the image (and their self-image) of "long-haired veterans." Their sense of proceeding from mockery (in which one is bound to the entity or institution one mimics and undermines) to irony (in which one takes on autonomy and self-definition) is suggested by a comment on these matters by one of the men during a rap group:

When they give me flak I tell them, "I was in Vietnam. I fought your dirty little war there. Now don't tell me to cut my hair."

Later of course, after police and long-haired veterans had become more used to one another and some of the encounters between them had become more nasty (mock-military assaults on the part of veterans met with severe beatings administered by the police and prosecutions by judicial authorities), the description would be more likely to contain a string of obscenities.

For these men brought a special edge of bitterness and experiential insight into youth culture's more general suspicion of authority and critique of the way people in American society lived. The quest of the young for new forms of self-process took on, in them, the compulsions of the survivor mission.

Always the men came back to the John Wayne thing, sensing that it had to do with psychological matters at the core of their struggle. Around that phrase they could explore a whole constellation of masculine attitudes, encouraged or even nurtured by American culture, and contributing to war-making: being tough (even brutal), tight-lipped, fists ready (or quick on the draw), physically powerful, hard, ruthlessly competitive, anti-artistic; a no-nonsense sexual conqueror for whom women were either inferior, inscrutable, or at best weaker creatures; and, above all, unquestioningly loyal to one's immediate (often all-male) group or one's nation to the point of being ever willing and ready to kill or die for it. They grappled with alternative modes of maleness put forth by youth culture: being gentle, open, non-competitive, 'soft' (to the point of being able to cry), aesthetically sensitive, physically graceful rather than overpowering, associative and questing, responsive to the needs and struggles of individual women—and skeptical and questioning toward all established groups and causes, especially those which call upon one to kill or die.

Veterans did not necessarily use these terms, nor did anyone fully spell out, or live out in pure form, either of these polar tendencies (or ideal types). But they did examine all of these components in highly personal terms—sometimes in reference to immediate relationships, at other times to what most disturbed them about their own involvement in Vietnam: their embrace of a form of super-maleness that lent itself to extreme numbing, to internalization of the prevailing military ethos (including the gook syndrome), and to easy (even indiscriminate) violence. They would sometimes probe premilitary sources of the John Wayne image in themselves, but that task was never easy, the results always problematic.

When they explored early childhood experience for the origins of these traits, some of the men (from the South and Southwest particularly) remembered being instilled with versions of knight-like male valor, while others (often from big cities) remembered street-corner, chip-on-the-shoulder toughness. But they found that, whatever one's childhood version of maleness, a crucial factor was the super-masculinity promoted within the military. They examined, sometimes quite ruthlessly, their own collusion in that part of the military ethos, and recalled with shame and guilt the appeal it had held for them. And they went on to examine, particularly in individual interviews, the transmission of the warrior ethos over generations and their own individual struggles to stem, if not reverse, that long-standing pattern.

The former Army sergeant, for instance, came to associate very early teachings (from family and school) "that America had a proud heritage [which] he had to protect" with his father's exploits as a pilot in World War II: the feeling that

My father had been awarded several Air Medals and Silver Stars or something for doing heroic deeds . . . and perhaps . . . I had to [also].

Significantly, his father had otherwise been a weak man, prone to heavy drinking, unable to support his family with any regularity, and on one occasion abandoning it temporarily after committing an act of petty embezzlement. As the son put it: "Other than the fact that he was a war hero . . . he never asserts himself . . ." He could respect and identify with little in his father other than the pilot-hero.

He recalled gatherings at which uncles and family friends exchanged war experiences with his father, and had the impression that these men seemed to fall into two distinct categories:

The people that were very assertive, self-assured and everything had been the people that went to World War II and went overseas. They'd seen actual combat and they had gotten medals. And the people that tended to be very quiet were the people who had been rejected by the draft [or] people that had been, say, in the Navy but had served all of their time back in the States . . . [so] that this had been reflected in their whole lives.

He held to that impression, despite what one could view as evidence to the contrary in his father, and concluded that "If this was the way you proved your manhood, I was certainly not going to be one of the wallflowers. I was going to be one of the assertive ones." He also recalled Memorial Day ceremonies, one in particular, at which the sons of a grammar school teacher took part soon after their return from World War II combat:

I [was] very stirred, patriotically [and thought] that I someday was going to have to, might have to, do this . . . That I would get my chance. . . . I remember questioning myself . . . saying this can all be a pile of crap . . . this stuff about patriotism, and yet because of this indecision . . . the confusion within myself, I said . . . I don't think I'll ever be able to live with myself unless I confront this, unless I find out, because if I [do not] I'll always wonder whether I was afraid to do it. . . . I had the whole question of whether I was a man or not . . . whether I was a coward.

Doubts were there, in other words, but could be suppressed by the all-powerful need to prove oneself a man, to become a manly warrior in specific relationship to immortalizing national principles, to grasp one's opportunity to merge with and defend the immortal substance of the nation-state.

The whole pattern was reinforced at his early jobs, where most of the others were older and "had been veterans or . . . were in the National Guard or something—they had served." Should he express misgivings to them about the military or the Vietnam War, they would say:

How can you question it? You haven't been there. You haven't been in the military, you don't know what it's like. Why don't you [t́ry it]?

Joining up, the message went, was something one was expected to do, a necessary experience. So he did, disdaining his eligibility for medical deferral on the basis of a minor ailment, and seeking out demanding and potentially dangerous assignments.

Similar patriotic messages throughout childhood inspired the enlistment of the former marine grunt, and his choice of the marines. At boot camp a number of the men who, like himself, had some college background, became aware of the manipulative nature of the extreme physical and psychological pressures they were subjected to, but always stopped short of resisting them:

We used to discuss how they always got us just to the point where . . . about one more thing and we would have snapped and fought back . . . but we always rationalized it and said, they're doing this for a reason. They want to discipline us . . . strip our individuality [so that we can] function in the context of a war.

This was so despite having been "unmercifully beaten" for virtually no reason. Whatever his intention of remaining an individual and making a critical estimate of the military, he ended up

internalizing much of the ethos of super-masculinity, and even
now places some value on the boot-camp experience:

I can see how subtle and how insidious . . . the changes are. Because
as determined as we were not to change, we certainly were changed.
. . . Unless you had this pressure on you . . . somebody beating you
. . . well, it was good in a way [in that] you found you were capable
of doing much more than you've ever anticipated you could do. . . .
So, you know, this was a valuable thing. . . . [And it] carried through
into when we were functioning later on . . . in Vietnam.

After all, super-masculinity prepares one for war—and helped
him to survive, just as his instructors during marine basic training had promised him.

Moreover, the military's constellation of super-maleness could
be readily internalized by him and others because elements of
it were familiar from related images existing throughout American life. The desymbolization of basic training—or "assault on
identity"[5]—applies only to those prior personal standards in-
compatible with the John Wayne image. The "resymbolized" or
newly reconstructed self, as the instructors make clear throughout
this coercive death-and-rebirth process, must take on the overall
values of the environment: extreme physical strength and endurance; channeled brutality and violence which one was expected first to take and later dish out; blind obedience to absolute
authority and to the immortalizing entity of the Marines; and the
ability to draw upon that obedient identification (whatever one's
awareness of weakness) to sustain a connection with and a feeling of hyperaggressive, numbed, omnipotent maleness.

As a number of former marines emphasized (and the same
principle applies, if somewhat less extremely, in the basic training of the other services), confirmation as a Marine and a man
were one and the same; one became both *only* upon successfully
completing the training. Until then one was a "snuffy," "pussy,"
or "woman"—terms which, in that environment, had the con-
notation of homosexual, coward, female genitalia, or some un-

defined non-human female creature. This debased sexual imagery served the psychological purpose of providing an intolerable alternative, one which each man felt to exist within himself and feared all the more, to the fragile-brutal male-marine ideal. Thus the Marine Corps was referred to as "the crotch," while other branches of the military were called "the sister services"[6]: any woman mentioned was likely to be named "Susie Rottencrotch"; and there were stories of women marines coming to Parris Island and being told, "There's six miles of cock on this island and you're not going to get an inch of it while you're there." The former Marine grunt emphasized this general psychosexual victimization of women and its bearing on behavior in Vietnam:

Women marines were always something less than human just as the Vietnamese women became later—something less than human. They were a lower element. We were men. And so . . . everything as it went on [in boot camp] . . . is pointed to the day when you're going to graduate and you're going to get to wear your uniform.

That is, to graduate from contemptible unmanliness—to be confirmed as a Man-Marine sharing the power of the immortal group —one had to absorb an image of women as a lower element. And that image fits in readily with (and is further magnified by) the male-female dimension of the gook syndrome in Vietnam.

Moreover, internalization of this sexual imagery, inseparable in its presentation from physical courage and combat skill, was also perceived as a matter of life and death. When drill instructors lay down the law—"You guys better pay attention and do it right because the guys that don't do it right are going to be coming home next month in steel boxes!"—"it" refers almost interchangeably to proper technique in firing a weapon* and holding the "proper" images of manhood (and womanhood) for sustaining the group's collective John Wayne self-image.

A conscientious recruit (like the former grunt) was likely to

---

* Which, of course, lends itself to easy double entendre.

respond to the situation "by being more, doing everything better than everyone else"—that is, by becoming the best marine around. With the admonition of the drill instructor ringing in his ears—"I felt that if I was going to go into a war, I had to do everything right because the people who didn't were going to come back in steel boxes"—he not only did "everything right" but carved out an unusually distinguished military career. Excelling at a number of training assignments, he could probably have taken advantage of his skills to remain in the continental United States but did not do so because

My purpose in going into the Marine Corps was not to avoid Vietnam but to go there, because I wanted very much to find out about it and what we're doing. . . . I had to confront the issue. I had to confront Vietnam.

The whole sequence suggests the extent to which not just basic training but war itself—and for this generation of Americans, Vietnam—becomes a *rite de passage* through which a male youth earns a place in his society's immortal chain of manhood. To refuse that *rite* is to be relegated, once and for all, to a purgatory of unmanliness and failure, to an inferior (symbolically death-linked) status outside of that immortal chain. As each generation of young men responds to the call, each produces its survivors who justify and formulate their experience by recasting their war in terms of heroic service to the external principles of group or nation. That formulation is passed along from father to son (or uncle to nephew, teacher to student, older to younger friend) in a continuous reinforcement of a society's version of the manliness of its socialized warriors (wearing the mantle of warrior-heroes). For each man the immortalizing claim is that of having contributed to the survival of one's group, of having stood fast against a threat to the life of one's people. Claim and call must, as part of the survivor mission, be passed along to the next generation, until there takes shape a continuous demand that collective immortality be achieved by means of killing.[7]

The principle is primarily male—male obligation and male

glory—but women are crucial to it nonetheless. They may provide chivalric inspiration or less noble models of debased creatures whose at least partial victimization is required to sustain the brutalized super-manhood cultivated among certain groups of socialized warriors. Above all, women are called upon in a variety of ways to offer their crucial confirmation of the manhood of men in the service of war-linked collective glory.

What we have called the John Wayne image, then, includes both chivalric and brutalizing images of manhood, and becomes associated with a principle of honor formed around a survivor mission of either avenging old defeats, or else perpetuating old victories and their related codes of behavior. The young man can be true to this legacy, repay the "debt of honor" he owes his father and his nation, and take responsibility for his portion of the unending survivor mission, only by answering his call to his war.

But with Vietnam something went wrong for that young man. *This* war at *this* time did not, psychologically speaking, work for him. If it occasionally afforded him a glimpse of himself as a warrior-hero, he much more often felt himself a confused monster or a "blind (or helpless) giant." The nature of the war and a more general historical questioning of warrior ethos combined to break (or at least put a strain upon) the psychological chain linking war to war.

The former Marine grunt suggested, in simple personal terms, something of this interruption of glory and debunking of John Wayne imagery:

Even people that . . . come on with a big facade of being . . . military heroes or something, they were really, when it came down to the fact that somebody was shooting at them, or the rockets were coming where we were sitting in a rice paddy, we were both scared shitless, you know—it didn't matter.

There are other ways in which war can hold out the appeal of a particularly demanding challenge—as suggested by the military experience of the former naval intelligence NCO. His sense of

cultural-generational legacy had less to do with fighting heroically
for America than with a Jew standing up and being counted.

Not long before his enlistment he was deeply affected by reading Sartre's essay, "Anti-Semite and Jew," especially by issues
it raised about Jewish integrity. One side of him knew the American intervention in Vietnam to be absurd, and yet he responded
to the war with imagery of Jewish courage:

I'm a Jew. I would have gone to fight Hitler twenty-five or thirty
years ago.

Only in retrospect could he realize:

That was an irrelevant conclusion. I wasn't capable of saying, "Well,
that's another age," because I was living in the past . . . [and] that's
what I saw.

The "past" that so dominated his idiosyncratic response both to
Sartre's essay and the war itself had to do with collective Jewish
experience of victimization and survival, as well as a more
personal struggle to be steadfast:

I knew I couldn't turn my back on this. . . . I remembered about how
men would falter at a point, at an extremely crucial point in their
lives, and always have to live it down, always be living under a
heavy burden. I didn't want that. I would stand up. . . . I won't die.
They can kill me but I won't die.

He angrily disdained suggestions by family and friends to help
him stay out of the Vietnam War for he came to see the war as
a challenge not only to manhood but to his capacity to act and
be relevant to his times:

I wanted to go. I didn't want to be cheated. . . . I wanted to go to
Vietnam. I wanted to see it. I wanted to be able to come back and
say, "Look, I've seen this shit and you can't tell me anything.". . .
It was kind of like a gauntlet thrown at my feet. Somebody had

thrown it down. I didn't know who and I didn't know why. But I was not going to be one of those tortured characters who refused to pick it up.

Again drawing upon dubious historical analogies, he thought of a man he knew who had been a member of the French Resistance during World War II and had managed not to break under extreme torture:

He . . . stood . . . just on the strength of something in him the Nazis couldn't reach. And when I thought of torture, I thought of somebody trying to make me say something I didn't believe. . . . I didn't know whether it was the Army or the Vietcong who were going to do that. . . . But I knew I wanted to stand.

Once in boot camp, the "Nazis" he was determined to stand up to appeared in the form of NCOs and officers who tormented him. Tall but unimposingly thin, and until then out of shape, he embarked on a policy of "beating them at their own game," and threw himself fanatically into the physical requirements until he could march longer, do more push-ups, have more general endurance, than anyone else. He even began to like some of it.

When [a demanding black noncom] . . . dropped me for fifty push-ups, I did them. I got up, stood erect at attention, proud. And when we had marching drills he'd say, "Miller, get your gum-chewing ass out there and show the rest of these lily-white trainees how it ought to be done. Miller, get out there and march." I'd get out there and I'd march. It sort of felt good in a way.

His pleasure came not only from a form of masochistic submission, but also from that special male pride of the realized (at least at this training phase) warrior, whose disciplined stamina permits him to merge with and share the amorphous omnipotence of the overall military institution. Underneath everything was his struggle for assertive survival in the face of threatening forces: "I didn't want the Nazis to get me no matter *who* they were."

The Nazis thus remained his model for these threatening forces
—within which the American military and the Vietcong were
virtually interchangeable.

Possessor of an Ivy League degree, he was told that his learning could be best made use of in naval intelligence "where the
cream went." But when exposed to the poor quality of intelligence training and trainees, his image of absurdity was strengthened, more or less at the expense of his particular version of the
John Wayne image:

I was thinking, are you trying to put this group of asses through spy
school? You've got to be out of your nut . . . this is a wild joke. Then
they handed out material for study and explained what the course
was going to be. I just couldn't believe it. No. This is some kind of
absurd play. This is a black comedy. . . . What's up?

His focus then shifted from "meeting the challenge" to "playing
the game"—well enough to be safe from *all* Nazis. Although relieved to be sent to Vietnam—that was what he sought and expected—once there he effectively maneuvered himself out of
being assigned to a dangerous post that had been previously
overrun:

I didn't dig that at all. If I could stay out of it, I would. It was one
thing to want to go to Vietnam and tell my mother the hell with
phony strings. It was another when it got to the difference of going
out in the field and staying in Saigon. And now that I think of it,
that's quite peculiar. But at the time I thought it was logical.

He seemed to have made an inner pact with himself that he
would go just so far in proving himself via the immortalizing role
of the warrior-hero, the limiting factors being his urge to stay
alive and his quest for personal comfort and sensual pleasure,
the latter sometimes an island of sensitivity within the prevailing
atmosphere of numbing (as discussed in Chapter 7) but at
other times an important ingredient of the John Wayne image.

The cultural-generational legacy worked in many ways. One could, for instance, feel compelled to compensate for the fact that one's father had *not* been able to respond to his generation's war—as in the case of the My Lai survivor:

Even if I could slip out of it I would try not to. Because . . . I would have felt guilty about it if there was a war going on and there were some guys involved in it—as a matter of fact most guys were involved in it—and I wasn't. I never held it against my father that he wasn't in World War II. He had a heart murmur. He was . . . 4F. He was crushed, you know.

His father provided him with a negative model—a model of what you should not let happen to yourself when your war comes along. The son, in fact, took on the mission, as a survivor of lost family honor, of regaining that honor by wiping away the stain the father had left upon it. The passage also suggests that, until enlisting, he felt himself to be a guilty survivor of friends who had put their life at risk by going to war—and when one of these friends was killed in Vietnam, his guilt was exacerbated ("I felt like a heel . . . like a real slob") and his survivor mission became more concrete, giving significance to that death by going to war himself and furthering his dead friend's military project and much more compelling.

   These elements of mission, together with a need for order and authority ("I wanted someone to run my life. . . . I wanted to join the Army because there, it's more or less laid out for you") converged in him to produce an unusually energetic relationship to the military ethos. He thrived on both basic training and advanced programs and became what he himself called "a super-soldier," much to his father's pride (and, one suspects, vicarious compensatory satisfaction). Genuinely proud of the uniform, and seriously considering making the military his career, he volunteered for Vietnam for reasons not too different from the two men quoted earlier:

If I wanted to say something about the war . . . I could [only] actually do it if I've been there.

Overall, his John Wayne image was built around what was then a highly functional combination of order, discipline, structured authority, and an ideal of service to a 'higher cause' (one's country) and the honor of the warrior.

We know that his disenchantment, even revulsion, toward the war in Vietnam and the military in general—and his refusal to fire at My Lai—stemmed from his sense that his idealistic image of the warrior was being violated, rather than from a rejection of that image in itself. One of his conclusions about the massacre, in fact, was that, had the men been more carefully trained and better disciplined there would have been much less killing.

But after being in Vietnam for a while, his warrior ethos, significantly, did erode, indeed collapsed. Like many others, he became desperate for an excuse for evacuation: "I just couldn't seem to get sick, to get wounded, to get a piece of shrapnel, nothing." He did try, however, and would drink the local water (medically forbidden), and intentionally skip his malaria pills, all to no avail. Eventually he developed rather severe immersion foot in both extremities (his state of mind could have been a factor) and more or less bypassed command authority (which wanted to keep him in combat despite his genuinely incapacitated state) in arranging evacuation, virtually sneaking out by jumping on a helicopter and flashing an evacuation tag given him by a medic just before takeoff. He had just one more week to go in the combat area, a time when men get most jumpy about taking chances or being there at all.

We may suspect that his subsequent guilt had to do not only with failing to stop the slaughter at My Lai but also with a sense of tainted honor over this collapse of the warrior ethos within him. No wonder he expressed to me the sad wish that these moral dilemmas could be reduced to the physical prowess and honor of a brave knight slaying a "big dragon":

I mean I'd like to be able to think that there's a way out of this thing. That you can just somehow or other fight your way out of it. . . . It would be great if this thing . . . you know, the war, the state of things in the world—I wish it were one big dragon. . . . If it were one big dragon I'd just do what I could do. You know, if it ate me up well okay . . . it's a simple solution . . . sort of a do or die thing. But it's never that way.

What he longed for was a code of honor both believable and simple, a contemporary chivalry to live by, a John Wayne image in the service of humane goals—a way to live out the *genuine* myth of the warrior-hero.

We can see that the John Wayne image neither thrives nor disappears, but tends to attach itself to *a current of profound ambivalence.*

A former army grunt of working-class background had a brief contact with youth culture at a community college prior to his induction. He was wary of the military, careful to stay in line ("because I was afraid of . . . military justice"), but viewed it as an essentially alien monolith with full power over him. Yet during the course of our interview he mentioned, quite casually, that he had nonetheless volunteered for jump school. When I asked him why, he told me it was the special prestige—"You know, the glory and the excitement"—of being a paratrooper. The negative component of his ambivalence again emerged when he was offered a chance to attend a school for additional advanced training as a noncommissioned officer. He abruptly resigned when he learned that the course would have some resemblance to basic training, which for him had been less a test of manliness than a form of degradation, and "I didn't want to go through that again." Once in Vietnam, he fought with minimal

ardor, horrified at buddies who enjoyed killing and, by implication, at any such tendencies in himself. He was glad to come
home and sever his relationship with the military—though one
suspects there may be a lingering nostalgia for at least some
moments in it.

For one's relationship to John Wayne imagery was characterized not only by ambivalence but by considerable flux. It would
seem that virtually any man is capable of forming close bonds
with a male group around immortalizing principles of unquestioned loyalty and even killing on behalf of the collectivity that
claims one's allegiance—and equally capable of mocking rejection of that constellation in favor of live-and-let-live experiments
in mixtures of wider identity, more immediate loyalties, pleasure,
growth, and change. The ambivalence is old, but the flux may be
relatively new. That is, the relative accessibility of even polar
positions, each of which can be and is collectively codified, has
to do with the contemporary Protean style. And that style, though
not itself totally new, is a product of the threat and possibility
emerging from the combination of dislocation, holocaust, and
flooding of imagery (mostly over mass media) that characterizes
our historical moment.[8]

Consider again the quotation at the beginning of this chapter.
Tennyson poses a question and then supplies a quick and definite
answer:

> "Forward, the Light Brigade!"
> Was there a man dismayed?
> Not tho' the soldiers knew
>   Some one had blundered:
> Theirs not to make reply,
> Theirs not to reason why,
> Theirs but to do and die:
> Into the valley of Death
>   Rode the six hundred.

But in fact if one reads accounts of that actual charge, one finds
that many (after their survival or even prior to their death) were

not only "dismayed" but appalled and enraged at the orders for the charge, which surely ranks high among the great "blunders" —meaning tactical stupidities—of military history.[9]

But the social ethos expressed by the poem—the heroic-romantic vision of the socialized warrior—was still sufficiently strong for Tennyson to write those words. Even then, however, he was seeking, as part of his duty as Poet Laureate of England, to cover over national resentments surrounding the Crimean War and reinforce an already threatened image of the loyal warrior dying without question for his country.

Country Joe MacDonald asks the very question that, for the soldiers in Tennyson's poem, is unaskable ("Theirs not to reason why,/Theirs but to do and die"). Again there is no direct answer, not out of silent loyalty but mocking contempt:

> And it's 1, 2, 3, what are we fighting for?
> Don't ask me I don't give a damn
> Next stop is Vietnam
> And it's 5, 6, 7, open up the Pearly Gates
> Well there ain't no time to wonder why
> Whoopee we're all gonna die!

MacDonald's answer—following upon all the history that has taken place between Tennyson's time and his own (World War I, holocausts of World War II, breakdown of traditional-national symbols, endless years in Vietnam) is that there is *no* answer. Or if there is one, that answer can only be that the cause we are fighting for is madness and grotesque death.

One is tempted to say that the overwhelming response to Country Joe's wild and bitter mockery subverts the John Wayne image once and for all. But that is hardly the case. What one can say is that during the century or so between the Crimean War and the present counterinsurgency action that concerns us in this book, a skepticism toward romantic killing has sufficiently permeated collective human consciousness to raise questions at every reappearance of the deadly romance of war, and to impel large numbers of men and women toward a continuing search for symbolic alternatives. The issue becomes a little clearer if we examine once more the last stanzas of the same two works. Tennyson's rings of confidence in eternal glory and in the eternal hegemony of the modes of immortality formed around the warrior ethos:

> When can their glory fade?
> Oh, the wild charge they made!
>   All the world wondered.
> Honor the charge they made!
> Honor the Light Brigade,
>   Noble Six Hundred!

While Country Joe converts glory to murder:

> Well come on mothers, throughout the land,
> Pack your boys off to Vietnam.
> Come on fathers don't hesitate,
> Send him out before it's too late
> Be the first one in your block
> To have your boy come home in a box.

A direct image of death, empty and naked, is put before those—the mothers and fathers "throughout the land"—who might otherwise be tempted to respond to a new call to military glory. MacDonald, in effect, transforms that call into an insane competition to be the first mother-father team to kill (have slaughtered for false glory) its own son.

Tennyson, as a Poet Laureate, was supposed to be a kind of official glorifier. Country Joe, something of an anti-poet and certainly an anti-Laureate, probably qualifies as the unofficial musician-Poet Laureate of the rock-Vietnam generation. If MacDonald did not sound the death knell of the heroic-romantic warrior vision, we can at least say it will never be the same again.

The VVAW provided the men with a special post-Vietnam sub-culture and collective forum for subverting super-male John Wayne imagery. That imagery could be explored in its various individual and social connections even as the men were living out alternatives to it.

The discovery of this subculture and forum could be liberating, as the former Marine tells us:

You know, talking on the phone, Vietnam Veterans Against the War —[they had] a professional poster and an ad and everything—I thought I was going to walk in [and find] guys in business suits and everything. And then I walk into the office and . . . I said, What is this? . . . They're freaks just like I am. . . . So I . . . felt kind of like at home. And [I thought] well maybe they're just guys that were in Vietnam and they're just a bunch of idiots like me.

"Freaks" and "idiots" meant comrades—not only in antiwar commitment but in youth-culture centered anti-John Wayne life-style. Within the framework of youth's collective mockery of prevailing arrangements, to be "freaks" and "idiots" was to be odd and mad—which meant partial (and partially intentional) internalization of straight society's view of this group of the young along with youth's sense that one had to become odd and mad in order to subvert destructive 'normality.'

In the rap groups the men talked constantly about their changing attitudes toward maleness. They spoke often of becoming more tender and vulnerable, though this 'softening,' as we saw, could also be a kind of toughening. One veteran told of his girl-friend's reaction upon seeing him cry. "How did you get so soft?" she asked him. To which he answered: "It took a war to do that." That 'softness' had been an aspect of his reintegration, following a post-Vietnam period of profound confusion and partial immobilization.

The men noted tendencies in some to retain the John Wayne style—violence-prone super-maleness—in antiwar activities. They chided a particularly militant veteran for having become "a marine of the Left." After some months, however, one of them noted that he had "softened his tone and no longer needed so much personal bravado." There was something particularly poignant about this group of men—with their field jackets and beards, mustaches and combat boots, still a bit military in their antimilitarism, a touch of male bravado in their subversion of the John Wayne image—earnestly tracking down evidence of male chauvinism in one another.

I remember one veteran describing with some excitement a new sense of personal authenticity made possible by a relationship with a particular "chick." The group responded by simultaneously affirming that authenticity and questioning the word "chick." The veteran was a little hurt at the group's failure to concentrate only on the authenticity, insisting that "chick" had no special significance but was "just the word I always use." But the others insisted upon connecting this usage with the struggle for authenticity, one of them gently asking: "Is it possible to love a 'chick'?"

There were occasional discussions of homosexual feelings. Once a veteran asked, with some anxiety, whether having erotic thoughts about other men was "normal." Others were moved to bring out similar feelings they had experienced, reassuring him that they were hardly unusual. One of the women professionals then spoke sensitively about the value of opening oneself up to one's own feelings, and I referred to contemporary psychological inclinations toward doing just that in the sexual area (whether or not acting upon homoerotic feelings) and to the changing climate in the psychological professions in evaluating these explorations. The men could then go on to examine individual sexual conflicts in a receptive spirit that was itself in part an expression of youth-culture ethos.

They did so with the restraint of men who had witnessed too much rock-bottom behavior to risk overall pronouncements or easy enthusiasms, whether these came from youth culture or anyone else, and whether sexual or otherwise. What seemed to characterize them in their relationship to male sexuality, at least at their best, was a combination of resilience and openness, a sympathy for residual (or even predominant) John Wayne elements as well as for the "softening" process; they were, after all, men familiar with both, and with all of the in-betweens. But this does not mean that they were free of severe conflicts around maleness and male sexuality, and how to combine and make cohere the changing images of maleness in each of them. Nor were they always inclined to probe these conflicts fully. But in providing an atmosphere that detoxified the male terror of homosexuality so widespread in American society, the rap groups helped the men to move beyond anxiously narrow imagery of maleness and to live somewhat more freely with and beyond their conflicts.

It often helped to be able to claim possession of the John Wayne image prior to renouncing it. The former Marine grunt, for instance, upon learning that marine recruiters were coming to his university, decided to constitute himself what he called a "one-man countergroup" by setting up a stand directly across from them where he, also in full marine regalia, distributed VVAW antiwar literature. His approach clearly was to 'out-marine the marines':

I put on my uniform for the first time [since being discharged] . . . and I had to do everything perfectly—shine my brass, my shoes better shined than any recruiters there, my uniform . . . immaculate, . . . everything . . . perfect. . . . You know, there was a certain pride on my part that I had all these medals . . . four rows of medals . . . and they [the recruiters] only had two rows. None of them had anything to compare with me. . . .

He gauged the recruiters' reactions by imagining what his own would have been earlier:

I know how when I was in the service, somebody that did this with my hair and beard . . . you know, how pissed I would have been. And that's exactly why I did it.

His confidence, and much of his motivation, stemmed from possessing superior marine credentials:

They would have to deal with me—the fact that I did rate the right to wear that uniform, that I had earned it in their eyes, and they couldn't dispute that. And that would really drive them up the wall —especially since most of them were on the recruiting team and hadn't spent as much time in Vietnam and didn't have . . . all these medals. . . . So they were overwhelmed by this, and I knew that would irritate them.

His initial fear that the recruiters might become enraged to the point of violence was probably also based upon recollections of his own earlier attitudes (and perhaps upon his present inclinations toward rage as well). But he was able to approach the recruiters, have coffee with them, and explain his antiwar position to them. He was pleased by their willingness to hear him out, especially by the request of a marine captain (the highest officer there) to be put on the VVAW mailing list ("just to see what we were doing—he didn't want to join"). He seemed particularly gratified by the feeling that "I knew that I was right, that I had the answers, that I could ask [the captain] questions that would make him think." And at the end of the day he went over to the captain, took off his medals and handed them to him, saying, "They don't mean anything. . . . [Because of] what we're doing it's not worth wearing these." He said little to me about the effect of his antirecruiting 'countergroup' on any students who came around; to a considerable degree the episode was a personal test of his ability to combat the going version of the warrior ethos by simultaneously staking and renouncing his claim to that ethos.

But something happened soon afterward that cast doubt upon his having completely passed the test. He received a hate letter which, as he remembered it, read something like:

Dear Scum . . . I guess you must have been in the Marine Corps, but you must have been a really shitty marine. You don't even wear your ribbons or your uniform properly. And if you were in Vietnam you probably spent most of your time in a psycho ward and you're not worthy of living in this country of ours.

He was upset by the letter in general, not least by its slight to his marine demeanor ("I couldn't figure out what he was talking about because I had [dressed] very meticulously"). He was sufficiently concerned to attempt to trace the authenticity of the signature by checking on whether there was a telephone listing for that person in a town where the letter had been postmarked (there was no return address). Though nothing came of his investigation, he concluded that the letter was probably sent by one of the recruiters, a Staff Sergeant who "gave me . . . kind of a feeling that I had gotten to him in some way." He was especially troubled by the idea that a fellow marine had unjustly impugned his past dedication and performance in the Corps, especially after having made such a point of displaying his superior marine credentials side-by-side with his antiwar position.

Despite everything, he still had pride in those medals because "I knew when I did it that I thought I was doing right and that we did a good job." (He also pointed out that giving the medals away was not as conclusive an act as it might appear, since he retained among his records the certificate entitling him to the decorations.) But he went on to say that "I know that I will not accept an honorable discharge from the Marine Corps." With eight months of inactive reserve status remaining, he planned to apply for conscientious objector status—

Because in good conscience I really don't feel that I can take an honorable [discharge] and say that I was honorable because I don't really consider it honorable. I think what I'm doing now is more honorable.

He was struggling hard to maintain a sense of honor—one by no means unrelated to what he had previously considered to be the finer aspects of the warrior ethos: both involved loyalty and dedication to principles beyond the self to the point of taking risks that threatened one's security and safety. His paradox lay in having to seek that sense of honor by combatting the ethos from which he had at least partly learned it. But rather than attempt to renounce totally his relationship to the marines, he had reconstituted himself as a 'soft counter-marine.' What was impressive was his capacity to explore and live out some of these inner contradictions in ways that enabled him to function as a dedicated VVAW leader and as a man deepening his insight in the midst of extensive personal change.

But for some, the John Wayne image would remain more problematic. During one rap group a veteran was taken to task for two things said in an earlier conversation at the VVAW office: first, that he was still fascinated by guns of all kinds; and second, that he "admired" the efficiency of the Nazis, though of course disapproving of what they did. He pointed out in his defense that he had always liked guns—"It's a kind of a hobby—like collecting stamps." As for the Nazis, he claimed he had been misunderstood, since he was talking only about matters of efficiency and organization, having been struck recently by the inefficiency and disorganization of most of the people he knew around VVAW, including himself. But the discussion left the men feeling uneasy, sensing as they did the complex byways of the John Wayne constellation and its continuing melancholic influence not only on the veteran in question but on all of them.

At one meeting concerns about maleness (and much else) were tested in a very special way when one veteran raised the issue—in a manner somewhere between that of a question and a proposal—of women in the rap group. The idea, it turned out, had originated with his girlfriend who, like a number of other girlfriends and wives, was a bit unhappy about the rap group and felt excluded by it. The women involved had, in fact, just initiated a rap group of their own, at which these matters had been discussed. But such was the explosiveness of the subject that, even before the men's meeting, what had been merely a suggestion became, after a day or two of rumor-spreading around the office, an imminent threat. The men could recognize in this sequence their own anxieties—"It's as if we're afraid of being castrated or something," was the way one of them put it.

Asking for calmer deliberation, he nonetheless admitted that he too had reservations about admitting women to the group because he did not wish to reveal to them the weaknesses that lay beneath the relatively confident bearing he could generally present to women. Another man opposed the idea because he saw it as a form of sexual temptation that would undermine the accomplishments of the group. He went on to criticize a third veteran who had, in conversation prior to the rap group, expressed himself as being in favor of the arrangement because it would enable him to "meet girls." Nor did that veteran's now adding that he also wished to "learn from them" make too much of an impression upon the men.

But as the discussion proceeded, one of them pointed out that it was by no means certain that the members of the women's rap group would wish to join the men's group. Indeed, the women did not seem to tell the men too much about their own discussions. What was finally decided was that, should the women wish to, they could get together with a few of the men to discuss the formation of a joint group, but that the men's rap group would continue in its existing form. The women's group, in the end, was not able to maintain itself, and the question was allowed to drop.

There was, of course, a strong argument for continuity in the identity and eligibility requirements of the group, formed as it was within an organization made up exclusively of Vietnam veterans. Underneath the logic of that argument was a form of male bonding—a group of men whose profound need for and involvement with one another had to do with carrying out a specifically male task. In this case the task was that of undoing

the male activity of war and the specifically male corruptions of
the Vietnam War.* For this psychological work, the men seemed
to require continuing male exclusiveness—but there was also a
beginning sense that a mixed group could lead to special insights
precisely around maleness, and the impression was left that such
a development would by no means be impossible sometime in
the future.

Pervading the whole discussion, however, was an anxious
vulnerability: having essentially rejected the John Wayne image
in favor of a softer and more sensitive maleness, the men had
also divested themselves of considerable psychological armor.
No longer able to hide behind male bravado, their fear of women
was more out in the open, in some men more intense than ever.
But by the same token that fear could now be faced and explored
as a central issue in personal change.

We need not dwell on the links we have already suggested
between antiwar veterans and the rest of American society
around a vision of broader social transformation initiated by
rejection of absurd death in Vietnam in favor of an alternative
ethos put forth by what we call youth culture. What is especially
valuable about the experience of antiwar veterans is their raising
these ancient questions about how to die (live) and what to die
(live) for in connection with equally central questions concerning male-female imagery—then refusing answers put forth either
by American conventional wisdom or youth-culture cliché, and

---

* We have noted occasional exceptions regarding eligibility requirements of
the rap groups—veterans who had not been to Vietnam, active duty GIs, and
for part of one rap group a girlfriend of a black veteran. What would have
tested still further these issues of male identity and exclusiveness would have
been the appearance of women Vietnam veterans in the rap group, which probably could not have been openly contested. As it turned out, another woman's
group did form much later involving women working with VVAW; and some of
the veterans joined more general "men's groups." The inclination to remain separate from each other continued, but was expressed more calmly.

insisting instead upon the excruciating human complexities involved. Indeed they illuminate, as can no other group I know of, the relationship of caricatured maleness to war and killing, and of the inseparability of revitalized maleness and femaleness for turning away from war.

CHAPTER 9

Transformation II: Learning to Feel

—Yet when we came back, late, from the hyacinth garden,
Your arms full, and your hair wet, I could not
Speak, and my eyes failed, I was neither
Living nor dead, and I knew nothing,
Looking into the heart of light, the silence. . . .
                                        —T. S. Eliot

I feel like hiding out in my own head.
                                        —Vietnam veteran

Once you were a strange, alien name. . . .
then you were a small, damp green
hostile land
where . . . I . . . nearly died

Now you are . . . a part of me
                                        —Jan Barry, "Viet Nam"

BEYOND JOHN WAYNE-ISM and maleness, the men have been deeply preoccupied with love and intimacy—ultimately, with the capacity to feel. These struggles involved all of the veterans in the rap group. They were usually immediate, often traceable back to early childhood, and always related to Vietnam.

When exploring questions of intimacy, for instance, the men talked a great deal about how much they suffered when they lost close buddies, how the knowledge that "anybody might die" would cause them to try to limit and routinize their friendships. Yet the very nature of the combat situation made such restraint impossible. As one veteran explained:

When I was cold, *everyone* was cold. We were all hungry *together*. We were *all* scared shitless. When we were out of water, we were *all* out of water.

In contrast, there was something distant and isolated about life in civilian America: "Here, everyone's doing their *own* thing."

One is reminded of a passage from *All Quiet on the Western Front*, describing two men sitting by a fire, during a lull in the fighting, preparing a stolen delicacy:

We sit opposite one another, Kat and I, two soldiers in shabby coats, cooking a goose in the middle of the night. We don't talk much, but I believe we have a more complete communion with one another than even lovers have.

We are two men, two minute sparks of life; outside is the night and the circle of death. We sit on the edge of it crouching in danger, the grease drips from our hands, in our hearts we are close to one another, and the hour is like the room: flecked over with the lights and shadows of our feelings cast by a quiet fire. What does he know of me or I of him? Formerly we should not have had a single thought in common—now we sit with a goose between us and feel in unison, and are so intimate that we do not even speak.[1]

Whatever its romantic excess, Remarque's passage captures the intensity of combat intimacy and its relationship to—I would say, source in—the "circle of death" behind and around it.

But although the World War I soldiers of Remarque's novel experience great disillusionment and elements of absurdity and guilt, one cannot detect in them the collusion in corruption we have observed in Vietnam. There, even authentic intimacy and love had to be in some degree contaminated by the counterfeit universe, had to be a little distrusted. Just as men felt that "Whenever you tried to be human you got screwed," so one of them added: "If you got close you got burned."*

Vietnam had absolutized (or totalized) the whole question of intimacy for its American survivors. Having experienced a particularly poisonous version of the "end-of-the-world" image that characterizes extreme situations, they distrusted, feared, and could not believe in, the renewed human ties they desperately craved as a psychological basis for reconstituting that world.[2] The death-dominated imagery they retained had to do with disintegration, stasis, and separation.[3] The overall sense of disintegration (physical, psychic, moral) associated with the Vietnam environment is internally maintained in approaching the environment back home. The stasis or cessation of feeling derived from extreme psychic numbing in Vietnam leaves one with an image of a world that neither lives nor moves. Vietnam's extreme element of separation—from familiar landscapes of any kind and especially from purposeful or viable images and symbols—results in an inability to find or catch hold of anything with which one can authentically connect.

---

* Other World War I writings do suggest considerable inner corruption, perhaps glossed over by Remarque's romanticism, but the circumstances of that war, murderous as they were, permitted intimacy with relatively less contamination than did Vietnam.

Toward potentially intimate relationships the men at first brought a sense that any such promise of renewed life was counterfeit. This intense suspicion of counterfeit nurturance—a form of "tainted dependency" in which love and help are equally strongly sought as a personal need and resented as a sign of weakness—also had direct origins in the counterfeit universe of Vietnam. There, as the men recalled all too readily, any form of help, nurturing, or love was equated not only with the weakness of the blind-helpless giant but with the corruption of the executioner-victim. To be sure, the men brought to Vietnam earlier imagery of a similar kind involving suspicion and doubt concerning love and nurturing they craved. But that negative imagery, present from all childhoods, ordinarily combines with alternative images of trust enabling one to respond to love and care with the mixed capacities characteristic of all adult life. In Vietnam, however, the negative inclination—the image of the counterfeit —is likely to be aggravated to the point of dominating one's entire psychic life—which is why we can speak of the totalizing of conflicts around intimacy, love, and nurturing.

The men revealed their sense of the importance of these issues in their energetic criticism of one another for maneuvers of any kind that seemed to be flights from intimacy—whether these took the form of shifting the discussion toward safely distant matters, telling shallow war stories, or suddenly shifting into revolutionary diatribes or leaden silences. Adept as they were at exposing these maneuvers, none was free of profound individual conflict concerning intimacy.

Associating Vietnam as they did with their parents' generation, ultimately with the whole of American society, their shared sense was something like, "After Vietnam, what could you trust of anything?" Or as one of them actually said:

You found out that your country—your parents, and the people you believed—told you a whole pack of lies.

A man with unusually profound difficulties with intimacy (exceeding but touching upon those of the others), he seemed to lapse into puzzling understatement when he went on to conclude: "People aren't perfect" and "People are fallible." But what he really meant, as his subsequent behavior revealed, was that unless people (and all relationships with them) *were* "perfect" they were threatening, untrustworthy betrayers.

An engaging person with a certain talent for human relationships, his pattern of keeping people at a considerable emotional distance was interrupted by his falling in love with an attractive young married woman. He enthusiastically described to the group their plans to save money in order to buy a Volkswagen bus and drive around the country together. But at subsequent meetings he seemed much less certain and talked of going south alone for a couple of months in order to earn the money for the trip. He said also that he wanted to "test the relationship" in various ways in order to find out "whether two people can really get along when they are with each other twenty-four hours a day."

It was he who had the garbage-dump dream, and in it he was expressing (in addition to the themes already described) his fearful sense that all claim to love and intimacy was counterfeit, filthy, "garbage." Others in the rap group pointed out that he was being hopelessly absolute about the relationship, that *nobody* could stand *anybody* for twenty-four hours a day, that he was "manipulating" arrangements with the girl, "preparing a time bomb" and "setting things up for a break." He denied none of this, and was even willing to explore sources of his distrust, but nonetheless insisted upon doing things his way. He went further and said, "If I can't love her, then I don't think I'll be able to love anyone." And when one of the men gently commented, "Most of us are afraid to love," he answered with a poignant question, "How do you tell when you feel love?"

He was soon to prove the men right: before long the relationship dissolved. But he went on insisting upon "complete independence—being able to get along without needing anybody." His all-or-nothing approach to relationships—the totalism we

spoke of before—was discussed extensively both in connection
with the Vietnam experience and his own psychological development. He did not, during the six months or so I knew him, overcome either this totalism or his profound and generalized sense
of distrust. But he did open himself a bit to his own feelings and
to glimmerings of insight; and the rest of the group seemed to
benefit greatly from what they learned about themselves through
him.

Falling in love, or feeling oneself close to that state, could be
especially excruciating—an exciting glimpse of a world beyond
withdrawal and numbing, but also a terrifying prospect. A typical
feeling, when growing fond of a girl was "You're getting close—
watch out!" The most extreme emotion of this kind expressed
was:

If I'm fucking, and a girl says I love you, then I want to kill her . . .
[because] if you get close . . . you get hurt.

Love or intimacy, in other words, posed the threat of still another
form of corruption and disillusionment, of still another 'death.' *
It was much easier to avoid that risk and stay numb (remain in
an evenly deadened state)—"I feel like hiding out in my own
head," was the way the same man expressed it.

But the men did of course fall in love. When that happened,
especially if soon after returning from Vietnam, they would find
themselves breaking off relationships because "I couldn't go
through with it" or "I didn't want to be tied down to anything."
What they meant was that their psychological work as survivors
was so demanding as to preclude, at least for a certain period of
time, sustained intimacy or long-range personal commitment.

* It is possible that he and many others continue to associate the nakedness
of sex with Vietnam images of grotesque bodily disintegration—as did Guy Sajer,
with memories from the German Army experience of World War II: "As soon as
I saw naked flesh [in a beginning sexual encounter] I braced myself for a torrent
of entrails, remembering countless wartime scenes, with smoking, stinking corpses
pouring out their vitals."4

That state was well described by the former naval NCO in response to pressures toward marriage coming from a girl he became close to soon after his return:

I'd say, I can't make a decision—not for the rest of my life—in the shape I'm in now . . . [after] what I've gone through. . . . I said I'm going to need—this was a very prophetic thing I kept saying last year—I'm going to need a year just to dry out after all this. I somehow had the sense of just how much torment was going on even though I didn't seem to acknowledge it.

"Drying out" meant getting over one's habituation (if not addiction) to the disintegration, numbing, and separation of the Vietnam environment—including, by implication, the attractions, or at least escape elements, of that environment. Again his erotic impulses propelled him toward feeling. While still in Vietnam he had been drawn to a woman there temporarily in a way that permitted him

to talk . . . and put down this spy business. Then I began to feel better—not only because I had a friend and woman and we liked each other very much and spent a great deal of time together but . . . because I was invested in something, somewhere, and there was something new about that.

Upon returning to the United States he became involved in a series of sexual relationships, in which he groped toward a clearer idea of authenticity and love. Throughout, the idea of sustained commitment, and especially marriage, remained a threatening source of conflict. Yet each time he took steps to limit or end a relationship, he would experience a profound sense of loss, which on one occasion left him close to an emotional breakdown.

The general dilemma of these veterans had to do with the extraordinary intensity of both their need for and difficulty with sustained intimacy. Breaking off relationships was as painful as it was necessary. On many occasions entire rap groups were devoted to such closely related themes as: the general problem of fidelity, notably sexual fidelity*; the hunger for love and nurturing and the sense of being chained by sustained intimacy in a relationship; and the powerful influence of Vietnam corruptions —with their residual fear and guilt of great magnitude—extending backward and forward into old and anticipated corruptions that touch virtually all aspects of existence. This entire pattern of holding on and breaking off contained a continuing dialectic between persistent death imagery and imagery of life renewed. But the men came to realize that the equation was never simple: holding on could take the form either of revitalizing intimacy (life renewed) or of numbed distance in proximity (a new death), and breaking off could be a pathetic need to reject the intimacy one craved (a self-inflicted death) or a liberating opening out to deeper experience and greater self-knowledge (renewed life). Over the course of time most of the men increased their capacity for intimacy, but that dialectic would simply not go away.

These conflicts gave poignant intensity to expressions of intimacy within the group itself. During one meeting, after a veteran had spoken at length in pained tones of his inability to feel close to anyone and his fear of any kind of intimacy, another man responded by saying that he himself felt very close to the veteran and had wanted to touch him to show him that he did, but had not quite been able to do so. Then, as if to say, "Why not?" he walked across the room and embraced him. The two met in a bear-hug that was both manly and childlike. Both became tearful, and several others were on the verge of tears. As the first veteran went on describing how his closest friend in Vietnam had been

---

* I use the term fidelity here to suggest more than loyalty, though loyalty itself was of great importance. Also involved was authenticity—in sexual matters, for instance, the genuineness of an impulse to find a new partner at precisely the time that an existing relationship showed promise of deepening intimacy. Fidelity thus involved being true to, having faith in, the animating principle of the new self being formed. It included overcoming fears that one's residual destructiveness and death taint would not harm or contaminate others.[5]

"shot full of holes," another man put his arm around him and the whole group moved, almost imperceptibly, into a tighter, protective circle. I had the impression that the men had never felt closer to one another, and rarely to anyone, than at that moment.

At a later meeting, the first veteran remembered experiencing a certain amount of discomfort in the incident because of its homosexual undertones. He had also clearly been pleased by it, and afterward seemed much more at home in the group—to the point of becoming, for a bit, one of the coordinators of the rap group program. Overall, the men came to value this form of hard-won intimacy, whatever its erotic overtones. Their capacity for it had much to do with the softening we have described in their subversion of the John Wayne warrior ethos, as well as with the pervasive spirit of youth culture. But to men who felt themselves to have returned from the land of the dead, that kind of simple expression of intimacy toward one another could be experienced as a significant breakthrough on the way to rebirth.

During that same earlier session, another veteran who rarely opened himself to the group (though he was an articulate and regular member) also spoke of his difficulty in establishing intimacy or, for that matter, experiencing any kind of genuine feeling. Another man then referred sympathetically to the *struggle* to feel:

That's being *alive*, man! Much better than being the robot I used to be.

This encouraged the first veteran to speak further of his shortcomings, including a tendency to be dishonest—"I lie a lot"—to tell stories around the office, often about the war, that simply were not true. But he also spoke of having recently met a girl he felt so drawn to that "I had to tell her things about myself I never told anyone before." When he told her of this tendency to lie, she answered very simply that she preferred him the way he is now rather than the way he used to be. To which he added, this time to the group:

I'm getting to be the kind of person I want to be—the kind of person I like. I didn't like the kind of person I was.

When he went on to express doubts about whether the relationship could last, the men did nothing to dispel these doubts; instead they pointed out to him how much he had grown in his capacity for authentic emotion, and emphasized that this personal growth would continue, whether in this or in other relationships. It was the reassurance he sought, fearful as he was that this new capacity depended entirely upon another person. As the discussion continued, he became tearful, apparently overwhelmed by his own revelations—and one of the other men embraced him and kept his arm around his shoulders as the two sat down. Toward the end of the meeting he became more calm, told how relieved he felt, and added that he wished the other two professionals (who had had to leave a few moments before) had been there to see (and by implication share in) what had happened.

On many other occasions men moved their chairs closer to someone they saw to be suffering. Both nonverbally and with words, they tried to express their intimacy, sometimes to the point of speaking openly of their love for one another. These physical and verbal manifestations of love and intimacy would have been unremarkable had they occurred during Esalen-style encounter groups, where they tend to be explicitly encouraged. But the rap group had no such tradition (even if one can say that it was affected by these experiential currents in American culture in general). Our group was both more conservative and in a way more experimental, and such expressions of intimacy came as one of the many surprises of our trial-and-error method. They meant all the more for that, and for the expression of shared pain and glimpse beyond that pain that they represented. But these high moments were few; for some intimacy remained beyond grasp; in none did distrust fully disappear.

Struggles with intimacy were part of a more general process of learning (or relearning) to feel. We observed the painful efforts these men made toward experiencing their own guilt. They had to make similar efforts in connection with virtually every other kind of feeling as well. On the most basic levels they raised questions about what emotions they actually experienced, did not experience, or should experience—about when one should laugh, when one could cry.

One veteran, who had experienced a severe breakdown and had been recently discharged from a VA hospital, complained on several occasions that "I can't cry. I would like to cry." Some time later he announced triumphantly that, when moved by a friend's description of having been greatly helped by an experimental psychiatric program (which he himself was considering entering), "I cried for the first time in four years." Crying for him was linked with hope, with the possibility of renewal.

The men also talked of their need to scream, to find ways to be alone to give expression to that need. Or of their own and others' inability to laugh—the tendency (as one man commented about someone else in the group) to "cackle" instead. They pressed toward nothing less than a reeducation of the emotions —as suggested by the question that had been asked: "How do you tell when you feel love?"

They were alert to the dodges they all used to hide their feelings, or hide the fact that they couldn't feel. Thus, one told how

I became a freak—because when I am a freak, I don't have to say what I feel.

They spoke of various forms of dissembling—feigning indifference when actually they were deeply upset, or pretending to feel what one did not; in either case, they were unable to make appropriate (in their own eyes) connections between event and feeling, and between feeling and expression.

The most politically and ethically conscientious among them would raise questions about their right to pleasure. One, for instance, criticized his own tendency to be so totally absorbed at rock concerts—so lost in ecstatic response to the music—that all thought about the war or responsibility of any kind dissolved. Yet on the whole one could not describe them as an unusually ascetic group. They could be lively and humorous, and quite capable of enjoying their whiskey or dope. But their survivor struggles with guilt and numbing prevented them from accepting fully the pleasure they pursued.

All this could lead to much confusion about feelings. For instance, the veteran-coordinator of the rap groups was much appreciated for his sensitive help to others (whether introducing them to the group or referring them for individual therapy), but was sometimes criticized for avoiding his own feelings in the process. One of the men put it in the form of a challenge: "You helped me—now I'd like to see you help yourself." After some sharply-worded interpretations both by professionals and veterans, he began to feel unappreciated and unjustly attacked. He asked angrily:

Christ, do I have to throw a fuckin' fit for people to think I'm human?

Later he said he had felt himself goaded into anger, and that the group more or less required and demanded anger from him— which in a way some of its members had in their effort to jar him out of his intellectual armor. The group then heatedly debated whether this tendency in him should be viewed as a significant problem for him to overcome, or whether it was simply (as one of the men put it) "George's style." Undoubtedly both views were true, and (again the mediator) I said so. I also emphasized, and others readily took up, the theme of emotional complexity: that focusing on other's feelings could be in part a way of avoiding, in part a path toward, one's own; and that combining that focus with sensitive and needed help was an ethical act that contributed to the emotional capacities of all concerned.

Some of the men seek a double liberation from the related entrapments of the warrior ethos and suppressed sexuality. One veteran, for instance, described in an interview a sustained relationship with a girl soon after his return from Vietnam, in which both discovered their bodies and explored ways of living that might free them of oppressive conventions. But the relationship collapsed under the pressure of her fear of pregnancy and the effective opposition of her mother—leaving the veteran much more capable of intimacy than he had been and generally wiser, but also puzzled about his inaccurate perceptions of both the girl's and her mother's feelings. He came to recognize the connection between sensitive response to others' emotions and getting in closer touch with his own.

Months later, his exposure to the rap group seemed to release emotions of every kind:

That first session when I went down there, I almost couldn't drive back to New Jersey. Every song that came on the radio, you know, now I feel it. . . . If I hear . . . about something beautiful, I just want to cry . . . because [I] get so sensitized that I can't even function. . . .

He was describing the lifting of psychic numbing: the uneven process of gaining access to previously blocked feelings around loss, death, and the possibility of joyous life. This formulative struggle of the survivor—in this case a struggle for feeling related to form—has many parallels with what Freud called the "work of mourning." But it is a more generalized process of resymbolization, involving the entire psyche and the inner images and forms built up (and broken down) over a lifetime.

The same veteran went on to tell how he would sometimes recall pleasant childhood memories ("Howdy Doody and kids and things"), only to be caught up short: "I [would] remember . . . what we've done [in Vietnam]." As he explained further:

So it's very difficult to deal with . . . and yet . . . I feel a lot better about it. . . . I'm looking inside myself. I'm able to get deeper inside myself and deal with it, which is ultimately what I want to do. . . .

The process of getting "deeper inside" oneself meant achieving not only the capacity to feel but the right to feel as well. It had to include the kind of animating confrontation with guilt we have previously described. The process also required a vision of experiences worth feeling. Hence the same veteran (like many others) placed great stress upon involving himself with groups (the rap group, VVAW, youth culture) in which

people [are] not pressuring me or saying, "You're a war criminal," but just saying "Life is really great when we treat each other as human beings."

But his words seem to have double meaning: his need for freedom from pressures toward self-lacerating guilt; but also his retained guilt ("You're a war criminal" may be partly his own inner judgment) along with his ambivalence about pursuing questions around guilt and the war in general.

Overcoming psychic numbing meant transforming a 'dead self' into one infused with life. Until they can begin to do that they find themselves in that survivor state of death in life that is not quite the one or the other—a state movingly described by T. S. Eliot:

> —Yet when we came back, late, from the hyacinth garden,
> Your arms full, and your hair wet, I could not
> Speak, and my eyes filled, I was neither
> Living nor dead, and I knew nothing,
> Looking into the heart of light, the silence.[6]. . .

If Eliot spoke for an entire epoch, as we have come to believe, then we know that this group of men has had to struggle not only with the numbing of Vietnam but with the everyday absence of feeling that, midst our large and small dislocations, forms the basis for so many lives. That is, to overcome their war-linked numbing, the antiwar veterans have had to go far in transcending the ordinary kind as well.

CHAPTER 10

Transformation III: Self and World

What I'm describing are different seeds that were
placed and I'm not quite sure myself what happened,
what clicked—the one that set the process going.
And it is a process.
It wasn't a [sudden] change. It's a process.

        —Vietnam veteran

There are so many things to do—so many things
to be—why should I limit myself to one thing?
Well, I'll probably have to to survive.

        —Vietnam veteran

You cannot step twice into the same river, for other waters are continually flowing.

        —Heraclitus

OVER THE COURSE of the rap group experience the men did not merely look inward; they also looked outward. Their transformation depended upon extrospection as well as introspection, and changes in the self required an altered relationship to the external world. This extrospective aspect of personal change is always important—in experimental institutions like the rap groups, in psychotherapy, and in living—but it tends to be denied or ignored because of the implicit assumption that psychological experience, being internal, is totally self-contained.

But this group of men had been too exposed to historical forces to fall into that false assumption. In looking back at Vietnam and the military they automatically examined questions of situational and institutional destructiveness and evil, as well as their own internal collusion in that destructiveness and evil. And we also explored whatever growth they experienced in that environment. Both the difficulty and necessity of this combined intro-extrospection was reflected in the pained question one of the men asked:

What do you do with a year of your life spent in Vietnam—or three or four years in the military?

Once they did begin to deal with these complexities, they were able to bring out various psychological achievements in the military—a situation where, in different ways and to different degrees, many of them had thrived. Some recalled a gradual growth of judgment about themselves and their environment. For others, growth was epitomized by a single act. The former naval intelligence NCO, for instance, proudly told the group how, when asked to provide a code name for himself he quickly suggested "Peter Cohen." Having tried to hide the fact that he was a Jew throughout most of his childhood, and later having struggled to shape himself to an Anglo-Saxon Ivy League model, his pride lay in the proclamation of his Jewishness.

Their combination of psychological and political perspective allowed the men to make incisive judgments about self and world. They could, for instance, reexamine their love of the combat community and relate it to a tendency (particularly strong in one of them) to try to revive the Vietnam combination of communal love and easy violence now under the name of political revolution. Similarly, the former Marine grunt who judged the war and military system to be counterfeit while still trying to rescue as valuable the dedication he had brought to it, could go on to examine general questions of relationship between conscientiousness and larger ethical purpose. His plan to seek a conscientious objector's discharge from the Marine Reserve was a way of living up to that principle. On the basis of these explorations, the men could begin to discuss an ideal of "inner revolution," not as a psychological substitute for but rather as an essential part of a social-political one.

But the actuality was always far from the ideal, and in everyday lives even the way toward that ideal was often far from clear. Most of the men exemplified what I have called the Protean style—quick and frequent shifts in identification and belief, in interests and immersions of all kinds, with a ready capacity to reject each one (or portions of it) in favor of another. A product of general psychohistorical dislocation as well as the mass media revolution, this psychological style inhabits us all, but is particularly intense in the young. Protean man in general is a survivor with a keen sense (and suspicion of) the counterfeit, a survivor of twentieth-century holocaust and of lost ways of life.[1] In this sense the powerful survivor emotions of Vietnam veterans join in with a general contemporary psychohistorical pattern; in them the Protean style takes on a life-and-death quality, along with a particularly strong and guilt-ridden suspicion of the counterfeit, which cause them even greater difficulty than the rest of the young in holding onto images or evolving enduring inner forms in the midst of change.

One of the men, for instance, backed away slightly from a tense confrontation with problematic elements in himself by saying:

There are so many things to do—so many things to be—why should I limit myself to one thing? Well, I'll probably have to to survive.

He was more convincing in his commitment to flux than to anything enduring. His way of polarizing the question (wanting to be "so many things" versus having to be "one thing" to survive) precluded steady experimentation and growth. Though he had gained insight from the rap groups, I was not surprised when, shortly afterwards, I heard that he had taken off on a cross-country jaunt of unspecified destination and duration.

Another of the men carried the Protean theme to a greater psychological extreme when he said that at times he wished he had no bodily restrictions so that he could be "free to just move anywhere and feel everything."

The veterans' relationship to the Protean style was both intense and problematic. Their survivor mission committed them to deep personal and social transformation. But their disintegrative experience in Vietnam left them particularly vulnerable to the diffusion that the more extreme forms of shape shifting could produce. The depression mentioned earlier in the former naval NCO, for instance, represented a survivor's inability to create viable inner forms either in relationship to the war he had fought or the world* he had reentered. We have said that the depression was

---

* Significantly, "the world" was the term used in Vietnam for anywhere else: there was "Nam" where one was and "the world" outside—conveying the sense that Vietnam was a special 'nonworld' with characteristics unto itself, to be distinguished from the more 'normal' but also threatening (once one had made one's adjustment to the nonworld of Vietnam) world one was eventually to return to.

precipitated by the breakup of an intense love relationship, but its deeper sources were revealed in two simple sentences:

I didn't know what to do. I didn't know what I could become.

His recovery—finding out what to do and become—depended upon confronting what he *had* done and been (in the war and before), and gradually evolving a new world view that gave prospective impetus to his survivor emotions and his self-process. As he explained in retrospect:

If the [war is] bad . . . I want to remember it and know what's bad about it. . . . And the more I came to grips with that sort of thing, the more I refused to forget, and the more I refused *not* to deal with the issue, the stronger I felt.

The forms the men evolved had to be personal and idiosyncratic but also drew upon various collective imagery, old and new. The former Marine grunt, for instance, in organizing a political action in which a church was to be used as a sanctuary for deserters, was calling upon and revitalizing religious imagery from his Catholic boyhood. Though that plan was not completely realized, his involvement in it was part of his struggle to integrate certain enduring psycho-ethical essentials while continuously reconstituting himself: from loyal Marine, to humane Marine critic from within, to vaguely liberal antiwar veteran, to youth-culture convert, to radical nonviolent veteran-activist. In that way he could feel sufficiently rooted (though by no means without anxiety) to alter meaningfully, over the course of the progression, his overall sense of self and world—his modes of symbolic immortality.

From this standpoint the importance for him and others of VVAW (especially when combined with rap group experience) lay in the collective base it provided for thought and action that could be not only psycho-ethical but psycho-political and (over all) intro-extrospective. Whatever the confusions, this group of men, more than any other I know, kept insisting—either concretely or by strong implication—upon the unity of these categories. They gave the lie to the distorting shibboleths that politics, being external, must be distinct from personal growth and well-being; and that psychology, being internal, has nothing to do with institutional and historical process. Indeed for antiwar veterans a believable critique of society lived out in some form of political protest, became crucial to psychological health—just as authentic psychological experience became crucial to political judgment.

I was struck by the emphasis of the men, in thus reconstituting themselves, placed upon responsibility and volition. While freely critical of military and political leaders, and of institutions promoting militarism and war, they inevitably came back to the self-judgment that they had, themselves, entered willingly into these processes. They stressed that they had done so—enlisted in the military or had gone along with it in one way or another—for the most foolish of reasons. But their implication was that they had chosen the military and the war, rather than the military and the war choosing them. Nor was that self-judgment totally attributable to residual guilt: rather, it was part of a struggle to deepen and stretch the reach of the self toward the far limits of autonomy.

All relationships and, above all, all work experience, tended to be examined in terms of volition and autonomy. For instance, a rap group participant from a conservative background, unique in holding a junior executive position in a business firm, described little humiliations he was forced to undergo and a basic feeling at work of being "like a machine—not like a person." In addition, he told how he would, when at work, "suppress my political opinions a little and my war experiences too because nobody wants to hear about them." He contrasted those restraints with the more authentic sense he had when at VVAW ("I feel better here")—but that very contrast had its problems:

It's okay [at work] until I come here [weekends] and become a big ole radical again—but what happens when I go back on Monday morning?

Most of the veterans could recognize something of themselves in that problem. Some reacted sympathetically: "I'm just one step on the other [VVAW] side of the line—I understand everything Jim says." But others reacted more sharply around issues of volition and self-betrayal, one commenting: "It sounds like Nazi Germany." The discussion came to include related issues of authenticity involving blacks and whites, and the veteran in question mentioned the term "Oreo cookie" (black on the outside, white on the inside) to describe "token blacks" in the firm. The veteran also revealed that his position in the firm was somewhat strengthened by the fact that his father held a higher executive position in it—causing his critic to comment angrily:

You *could* say what you want. You *choose* not to. *You* are an Oreo cookie.

After that the veteran returned infrequently to the group. He was eventually let go from his job because of economic cutbacks, apparently with a mixture of concern and relief. But the group went on with a focus upon volition, self-betrayal, and autonomy —the struggles within each of the men rendering the subject especially delicate and touchy.

Yet there were surprises. Once when a few men were griping about constant questions asked them concerning what they did in Vietnam, and about the fact that people "always harp on those things," one of them blurted out:

Well we bring it on ourselves by telling them we're Vietnam veterans. Next time someone asks me where I was I'll say I spent three years in Arkansas.

The others, predictably, came down hard on him. They saw that kind of evasion as a direct violation of their struggle—so crucial to survivor integrity—to confront what they had been and done. But the vehemence of their response reflected their uneasiness: the suggestion had voiced a temptation, probably present in all of them, to turn their backs on their self-created survivor mission and take the seemingly easier path of dissembling and evasion. As in many psychological matters, overcoming that kind of temptation energized the struggle toward heightened awareness—so long as they could engage in it collectively as part of an integrity-seeking group.

Inevitably, the group returned to the subject of death, treating it very differently from the way it had at the beginning. In one tense session at which the men offered warm support to a new-comer who had recently attempted suicide, a long discussion ensued about killing and dying. Four of the veterans described suicidal inclinations of their own. One of them told how the realization, in Vietnam, that "what we were doing was murder" led him to thoughts of killing himself there. He rejected the idea partly because "I wanted to tell the world what it [Vietnam] was like in the loudest voice possible"—which is what he has been do..ig ever since. While much else entered into his first considering, and then rejecting, the idea of suicide, his reconstruction revealed something of the power of the survivor mission ("tell[ing] the world what it was like in the loudest voice possible") for integrating death with life. In the end the discussion was less about suicide per se than about some of the questions of meaning surrounding this ultimate form of personal integrity.

Both the difficulties and possibilities in this survivor struggle for integrity are revealed in the experiences of the former naval NCO. Having lived in Europe prior to enlisting, he planned to go back there after being discharged—in order to "do some painting, go to Vienna, Germany, Eastern Europe, you know" while holding a job with an international business firm "to earn bread." But when that time came, there were inner impediments:

I wasn't very happy. I was sad, very sad. I asked myself, "Why are you going away?"

The plan had to change because he had changed:

I was getting less and less the Ivy League guy others couldn't approach and a little bit more somebody who went through the same shit. And [I thought] the day I got out of the army, I want to work with other vets. I want to work with people. . . . I'm in that right now. I can't go away. . . . How am I going to be working for some company in Europe supposedly trying to get the inside view so I could come back and write something about companies. Holy shit. I haven't finished with this war yet.

His psychological work had in fact just begun. Authenticity for him meant remaining in this country and throwing himself into VVAW activities. His self-examination along the way was much enhanced by Erik Erikson's writings on questions of identity and integrity. Erikson's book, *Insight and Responsibility*,[2] which had lain untouched on his shelf for a long time, could become a source of wisdom because he had reached the point at which

I was in a position of recognizing when something that had very much to do with *me* was under scrutiny. It wasn't 'out there.' I wasn't reading an intellectual essay. . . . The complete investment of myself . . . in a vision of the romantic wandering Jew in Europe or whatever it was . . . was no longer feasible at the time I read that.

He has continued ever since to search out what can be most authentic in himself. While by no means even now "finished with this war," he has been able to examine his role in it in a way that includes unrelenting self-scrutiny and critical sociopolitical views that are increasingly informed.

This does not mean he has been free of doubts. Aware of the

"huge change in my life" over the span of just about a year, he wondered about a girlfriend's concern that he might "snap right back and go from a hippie to a nice business man." Like many, he has been confused about how best to protest the war—and confused also by the sudden prominence he and a number of other antiwar veterans have received in the media. Aware of having previously been attracted to hypocritical, aggressive, and grandiose elements in American culture, his efforts to cast these off led to a somewhat romantic vision of a withdrawn private existence as a humble practitioner of a healing profession, serving a few clients without fee. But he was jarred out of that stance by a new kind of awareness of the very larger questions he had sought to escape and by the demands being made on him by others who came to recognize his talents.

As we examined all these questions together during interviews, we could both observe his growth and his perpetual inner reordering:

What I'm describing are different seeds that were planted and I'm not quite sure myself what happened, what clicked—the one that set the process going. And it is a process. It wasn't a [sudden] change. It's a process.

What "set the process going" was the war. Over time he realized that his continuous confrontation with the war and his part in it was a source of strength and an impetus to the kind of transformation he sought. We recall his contrasting another man's claim of having "completely forgotten" about the year in Vietnam with his own realization that strength lay in remembering it ("the more I refused to forget, the more I refused *not* to deal with the issue, the stronger I felt"). He was drawing upon his increasingly animating relationship to his death encounter and his guilt. In saying on one occasion, "I resent in a way the fact that we're almost heroes now," he was expressing his concern lest these energies be blunted by the temptations and problematic moral issues associated with public renown. He wanted to keep his self-process inseparable from more general explorations of (in his words) "how much evil we do others and how they do evil on us." More than most he was aware, to put the matter in theological language, that his demons were necessary to his salvation. That salvation—his continuing transformation—meant combining inner authenticity with the connection and flow of larger principles, of a viable mode of symbolic immortality around one's works.

A survivor-veteran's sense of integrity can come in a great change-stimulating surge—as in the case of the deserter when reaching the point of condemning his military experience and deciding to flee:

I began to wonder where you get this little red book by Chairman Mao. . . . For the first time I found myself sincerely believing in the black cause. I saw what they were saying. I began to understand some of their feelings of alienation—of not being part of the established ruling order.[3]

In fits and starts, he came to a broader condemnation of all war:

I began to realize that [what I had done] wasn't that big a thing . . . just a war incident . . . happens in all wars. And then I realized that if that's true, then there's something wrong with war. How the hell do you justify that, man? No way. I don't care . . . what kind of labels or flags you can live in splendor of, there ain't no war worth it. And . . . I really started to believe a lot of things I'd been saying about . . . the murderous genocidal procedure that causes these things to happen over there.

He was struggling to integrate his sense of overwhelming transgression (or guilt) into a more or less coherent self-process and world view. As it turned out he lacked the psychological strength to do so without periods of immobilization and breakdown, but it is still likely that the struggle has brought him considerable psychological and ethical gain.

In others that movement toward integrity could be more grad-ual and steady. The former infantryman we quoted earlier con-cerning the empathy for blacks he developed while in service (around anger at "having been denied something that is yours by nature") continued after his discharge to explore questions of justice. These included what he considered justice to himself, his feeling "more confident in demanding things myself" because of having "done the maximum for society," and having "fulfilled my obligation." Though far from having resolved issues of guilt and personal corruption in Vietnam, he was aware of them, approached them cautiously, and recognized that "I need more time to get myself together." Over a period of five months he was able to come to a fundamental criticism of the war and of a number of forces in American society responsible for it, but was still troubled by the extent to which these views violated so much he had previously believed. This conflict made him reluctant to belong to any veterans' organization—as did his fear of being duped once more and his wish to be certain this time "not to join a movement for the wrong reasons."

Many of the men expressed similar fear. Having been drawn into a false survivor mission (what we have called false witness) in Vietnam, they became wary of being deceived by *any* mission laid before them. During one of the later rap groups, a veteran told at length how he had been deceived by the romance of war, how he had rallied enthusiastically behind his country's cause— and how, having now become an active member of VVAW, he could not help feeling suspicious about the possibility of being deceived in turn by the excitement and romance of *its* cause. This kind of suspiciousness and anticipation of still another betrayal is undoubtedly very widespread among large numbers of veterans who share much of VVAW's condemnation of the war but remain wary of any collective mission on the premise that it might well turn out to be still another counterfeit enter-prise.

Such suspicion of the counterfeit is a classical survivor pattern

and is bound to be extremely strong in survivors of the counterfeit universe of Vietnam. What is remarkable is not the extent to
which it immobilizes so many veterans—or even to which it contributes to the widespread personal and political conflicts that
have plagued VVAW—but the fact that a sizable minority of veterans can overcome that suspicion sufficiently to join together in
various combinations of antiwar activism and personal quest.

The men in the rap group were equally suspicious toward
potentially counterfeit forms of transformation, such as those
depending mainly on drugs. Here one must distinguish sharply
between their attitude toward pot and toward other drugs. We
have seen that pot smoking in Vietnam could contribute importantly to the early stages of transformation; its continued
use by many in the group was sufficiently casual to require no
special comment. Smoking pot was important to those men not
only because they derived pleasure from it but because it was a
social ritual that confirmed their membership in the subculture
of the young. But in none of them did the quest for personal
change depend upon pot or any other drug.

Hard drugs such as heroin were not a personal issue for any of
the men in the rap group, having mostly been discharged prior to
the development of the "heroin plague." * A number of the men
did speak of using LSD and mescaline. One described the clarity

---

* Heroin was, however, very much a general issue for antiwar veterans. While
heroin users did not tend to enter the rap groups (probably because of the informal but accurate word to the effect that we were not equipped to handle
drug problems), many had contact of one kind or another with individual addicts or drug programs. I talked to several veterans involved with heroin in
varying degrees, who were disinclined to attempt any available therapy. I also
heard of a few deaths among veterans close to men I knew related to drug over-
dose or to automobile accidents while under heavy drug influence. In addition,
a number of VVAW leaders were knowledgeable critics of existing military drug
programs, linking the false promises of these programs with the rest of the
war's deceptions. In the case of a few of the men, this role contributed greatly
to an inner balance of feeling oneself both healer and healed, as well as to the
satisfaction of acting on behalf of one's own group, for the benefit of veteran-
"brothers" rather than just oneself.

he felt when using these drugs ("You can really tell what people are really feeling") and suggested something close to a death-and-rebirth experience: "Things get very beautiful—and then later you feel yourself more together." But most of the tone was negative. In addition to the "bad trips" already mentioned in connection with LSD and mescaline, the men tended to see sustained involvement with these drugs as another tainted enterprise with false promise; as counterfeit nurturance in an almost literal form. There was some ambivalence because a number of the men valued the kind of psychic intensity (or experiential transcendence) the drugs could afford. But what they feared was a new passivity and dependency, another situation in which they would be trapped and acted upon, and in some cases a drug-induced numbing on the order of what they remembered from Vietnam ("That year in Vietnam I wasn't really alive" or "I was really a robot then"). For them to thrive on any experience now, drug or otherwise, they had to be able to associate that experience with a contrasting vitality and life-affirming vision that they could connect with the new self-world relationships they were carving out.

Significant change required one to explore what one was changing from, to examine social and family roots. The men did not focus continuously on these roots as a matter of course, as one would, for instance, in a personal psychoanalysis. Rather they approached them in connection with immediate psychological and political struggles. Nor could they separate these roots from immediate conflicts they were experiencing with their parents often having to do with their opposing political views.

Above all, the men had the impression that their parents did not want to hear or know about the extent of horror, absurdity, and corruption they had experienced in Vietnam. Many felt that their parents had been much more comfortable with them when they put on the uniform than when they threw it off—prouder of their conventional patriotism (or at least its outward mani-

festations) than their unconventional opposition to their war and
their country's leaders. The ex-Marine from Texas put this impression in rather extreme terms:

When I got home my parents had a welcome-home party and they
introduced me as "This is our son, Jim. He just got back from Vietnam." And that has been two and a half years now, and when I go
home and my parents introduce me, they say, "This is our son, Jim.
He just got back from Vietnam." They used to say, "This is our son
Jim, a college student" or "This is our son Jim, the Marine"—but
they don't want to say, "This is our son Jim. He's doing his goddamn
best to overthrow this government."[4]

While few of the others in the rap group saw themselves in that
kind of classical revolutionary stance, the passage reflects the
veterans' strong sense of their parents' self-deceptions. As the
same man added:

So I let them have their little fantasy, even though it looks kinda
weird having a son who just came back from Vietnam with long hair.

The "little fantasy" the men perceived in their parents was
that everything was all right, nothing much had changed, the
American nation and its people still possessed special virtue and
were living out a noble destiny. Not that parents necessarily
favored the war—a large number had apparently soured on it—
but rather, as one of the men put it, "They just didn't want me
to do anything to rock the boat." The "boat" they didn't want
rocked was the whole set of institutional arrangements and conventional cultural images and forms, within which one is expected to sit quietly over the course of a life's voyage. But that
was precisely the boat the men had to rock to be true to their
experience in Vietnam and to their quest for transformation
afterward.

Some parental attitudes were said to have changed when
VVAW received extensive TV and newspaper coverage, much

of it sympathetic, on its early public actions. This media attention seemed to legitimize for those parents what their sons were
up to and evoke a certain amount of a parental pride at their
sons' (and their son's group's) sudden prominence.

Even where family communication was minimal, some of the
men remained dependent upon their parents—whether for
money, board, or that tenaciously ambivalent, mutual nurturing
hold Saul Bellow once called "potato love." To be sure, these
conflicts and contradictions are widespread throughout their
(and every other) generation. But with Vietnam veterans they
are accompanied by a uniquely intense image of generational
interruption: the sense that their holocaust had thrown into question everything previously transmitted from parents to children.
They, in fact, felt their psyches so ripped apart by that holocaust
that, without any special thought, they tended to relate their
responses to the war to every other significant emotional area,
including especially parent-child conflicts—rather than making
conventional (and misleading) separations between such internal
(individual-familial) and external (social-historical) dimensions.
Hence it was with considerable *personal* emotion that a man on
one occasion said: "I realized for the first time that my parents
are part of middle America." That realization, precisely by being both psychological and social-historical, provided a basic
self-world orientation concerning where he had come from and
where (in his continuing struggle toward autonomy) he was
going.

Conflicts of this kind emerged vividly in the gamut of emotions
described by the former Army sergeant. Always close to his
mother he tried to maintain their relationship by conveying to
her in letters from Vietnam his most private thoughts—mostly
doubts—about the war, only to find upon his return that

I was not very close to my family because things that I knew now,
the person that I was, was entirely foreign to them. And [despite]
what we had shared before . . . there was still a vast gulf there.

He was preoccupied with the gulf between himself and, not only his parents, but his brothers, who tended to take more conventional paths:

I was just wondering how all of us are so different—we come from the same background . . . but we're not really, any of us, close to one another, like my best friends.

The gulf had much to do with a war which his brothers, unlike him, refused to question—but whatever the cause, his reaction was one of sad recognition of loss:

I can see that . . . I'll never, ever have a deep conversation with my brothers again because we're different . . . we think different, our lives are going in different ways . . . our values are different and so I guess now that we've established that pattern we're not going to . . . find many places where we can meet.

In the course of these family-centered psychological associations, he described a moving and highly illuminating father-son impasse around the warrior ethos. His father (a pilot-hero in World War II but an otherwise ineffectual man) had expressed interest in his slide show of Vietnam. He described his sense of what they both felt as he showed it to him:

I was almost sorry that I had done it because I knew that many things struck him about what I was saying about war, and reflected on what he said about [it]. In a song . . . The Great Mandala . . . Peter, Paul, and Mary . . . talk about, "Why don't you do your job like a man?" He [the antiwar voice in the song] thinks he's better than his brother who died. What's he doing to his father [the song asks] who brought him up right? . . . And I knew, when I looked over, what was happening to my father, that he felt in some way responsible for having put us in this situation by giving us the thinking. . . . That was probably the closest that I've ever felt to him in a long time because I knew what he was going through, and I very much didn't want to do that to him—yet I felt . . . he wanted to see the film and I wasn't going to shut it off then. . . . It brought up questions about what he did in World War II. And I didn't want to give him the pain of having to deal with that. . . . I wanted . . . him . . . in some way . . . to realize it without any of this pain.

The warrior ethos evokes conflict and pain in both men, and yet draws them together. Both feel guilty: the father, over having transmitted that ethos in a way that led to so much death and suffering (including the suffering of his son); the son, over the pain he caused his father by forcing upon him that recognition and thereby, perhaps, calling into question one of the father's few sources of self-esteem, his long-standing vision of personal military grandeur. The "closeness" he experienced (very likely mutual) had to do with a shared sense of loss that made possible an unusual moment of mutual empathy.

The experience gives us a hint of the extent to which the warrior ethos can bring men together around a nostalgia of pain and loss, even as they disagree fundamentally about their attitude toward that ethos. The veteran's combination of compassion for his father and desire for honesty (or meaningful impasse) between them characterized the general tone of his personal transformation—its gentleness and insistent integrity. His whole chain of emotions and associations suggests the degree to which the newly forming self requires painful reevaluation of, and often separation from, family roots bound up with conventional imagery around the warrior ethos.

We know of inner doubts in these men concerning the possibility of genuine change in themselves or in anyone. They felt highly vulnerable to negative forces around them undermining their claim to change, as well as to the absence of clear psychological models or social charts for their rather unprecedented collective journey. Through these difficulties, however, they conveyed a strong sense that they were indeed changing and had already changed, that they were involved in a process that was real if fragile.

Their very doubts, together with their survivor guilt, could press them to impossible demands upon themselves and others—demands for what might be called 'instant transformation.' They were also capable of looking critically at this pattern. At one rap group a veteran spoke feelingly about "the American hangup of having to change everything and convert everyone"—a hangup he believed was operative in getting us into Vietnam and which he now feared could be present in veterans who had turned against the war. He referred particularly to the illusion of bringing virtue and truth to the unenlightened and of making them over in one's own image.

Mostly the men knew that they were in the midst of a demanding, long-term effort full of limitations. They developed a considerable tolerance for complexity and at one meeting responded very positively to a professional's emphasis upon "the need to live with ambiguity." More difficult to cope with was the problem raised by an especially thoughtful veteran:

If they ever took the government or the structures away we really couldn't deal with it because we're programming ourselves to be always against something—struggling to build something new but in conflict with something that's already established. And if they took that away we'd be lost because we have to have that in order to function in our role. We're . . . accepting our identity . . . as in opposition to the established one.

The self-accusation may have been somewhat overdrawn—one can speak of genuine innovation in quests shared by some of the men, whether these were psychological (toward openness, aesthetic sensibility, and altered states of consciousness) or political (new forms of protest, altered authority relationships, and beginning visions of a different kind of society). Yet what he said rang true nonetheless. For however interwoven these political and psychological forms, the men felt entrapped within and ultimately defined by the tenacious institutional arrangements of the larger society. Some would achieve significant psychological change only to feel paralyzed in the face of continuing war and political irresponsibility, which would in turn pose some threat to that psychological change. Others related themselves to dramatic political breakthroughs, as in the case of VVAW demonstrations in Washington, D.C., in April, 1971 (including the celebrated casting away of medals), only to question their efficacy a little later and to become wary of mere experiential gratification within new forms of protest. Overall, the men felt themselves part of innovative efforts, but always unevenly, in questionable balance, and with uncertain outcome.

More concretely problematic was the nagging question, both psychological and political, of how long one was to remain primarily an antiwar veteran, or veteran at all—as opposed to moving beyond that identity into a *post*war and *post*-veteran relationship to American society. The issue was never fully absent from a rap group meeting, but it particularly dominated one that took place about six months after the program began. After a number of critical remarks about staying a "professional veteran," one of the men, planning to move shortly to another city to attend law school, complained that the war was still "too much with me." But another strongly disagreed with him, insisting that he found newly presented war experiences (often by someone coming to the rap group for the first time) to be refreshing in that they brought everyone back to where they had been and what they had done, which they might otherwise be in danger of forgetting. What he feared was leaving the war too soon, going on to other things without having come to terms with it.

The first veteran countered by going back over his own earlier obsession with the war. That obsession was so strong when he first returned that he would, while riding on his motorcycle, buzz cars with prowar or right-wing stickers and scream obscenities at people in them. He came to recognize this behavior as "crazy" and self-destructive, abandoning it in favor of organized VVAW-sponsored antiwar activities. But he had wearied of these and especially of VVAW rhetoric. Even now he sometimes felt the impulse to resort to his old "crazy" behavior, which he recognized as evidence that he had by no means completely overcome his obsession with the war. But he felt it necessary to move actively on to other things. Another man pointed out that total focus on the war could result in its own form of desensitization (or numbing), in which one lost the sense of the human issues involved in stopping it and instead lashed out blindly in all directions.

The conflict between the two positions had much to do with the psychology of guilt, with the capacity to animate one's guilt rather than being held in static relationship to it. But beyond questions of guilt alone was the more general survivor issue of how much to cling to one's holocaust—an issue I found to be excruciating for the people of Hiroshima. Nor can the question be answered by fiat or by simple rational choice. And men varied enormously in the psychological and political combinations they were able to maintain, depending upon such things as their satisfactions in immediate relationships and in working in veterans' programs, inclinations within the self-process toward experimentation as opposed to strong needs for structure, and capacity for an animating relationship to guilt.

But after four or five months of rap group meetings, one could detect considerable restlessness in the men concerning their relationship to the war and an increasing need to move beyond that relationship. Generally speaking, there were two ways of doing that, and the men struggled, if not always successfully, to differentiate them. They could enter into a denial-numbing pattern, relegating the war to what they themselves called "a dead space" in their minds, doing their best to avoid—wish away—its thorny ethical and psychological ramifications (a pattern undoubtedly very widespread among the unaffiliated majority of Vietnam veterans). Or they could maintain what we considered to be a healthier pattern of both confronting and transcending the war: making use of a continuing examination of involvements in it as a source of the illumination that propels one beyond it—in personal relationships, work, and life in general. The overall problem was that of the survivor not only formulating his death immersion but doing so in a way that gave rise to *new forms*, rather than either avoiding any confrontation with it or clinging statically and literally to *its* forms. Extending over months and years, this was the essence of the struggle for transformation— a struggle still very much in process. While we never applied clinical criteria—on the whole the men did not join the rap groups to relieve symptoms—my impression was that almost all who took part in the rap groups for at least five meetings had significant psychological experiences in the direction of transformation. The degree and nature of the experience varied enormously among individual men, from a minimal increase in self-understanding without much visible alteration otherwise, to remarkable achievement of insight and sensitivity to others along with impressive expansion of overall personal and socio-political capacities.*

No transformation is possible without play. An incident at one of the rap groups illustrates the importance of what can be best described as a spirit of playful trust. It was a particularly despairing meeting, at which men presented problem after problem, all of them seemingly insoluble. They were tired of being veterans, tired of the war; they couldn't combine antiwar activities with the needs of relationships with wives and girlfriends, couldn't sustain these relationships anyhow. The night wore on and the men seemed unable either to resolve anything or cease their expressions of helplessness. The only professional present, I suggested some of the issues that I thought lay beneath their depair, notably a recent escalation of the war and its restimulation of all

---

* There was, of course, great self-selection. Men sought out rap groups out of a beginning commitment toward confronting the war or its residual effects and in the process undergoing change. Their transformation, at least in some cases, was well underway before they came to their first meeting. Similarly, those with less inclination toward confrontation and self-questioning, even if they came to one or two rap groups, tended to drop out prior to dealing with basic issues.

of their survivor conflicts. I also tried to make my response more personal by saying something about my own similar difficulties in balancing intimate relationships with political and professional activities.

But the flow of despair continued, and only after about four hours when it was close to midnight did it gradually subside out of sheer fatigue. As we began to make preliminary motions of leaving I found myself, without quite knowing why, saying: "Well, for whatever it's worth—and maybe it has to do with laziness or tolerance or whatever—my wife and I, in a couple of days, will be having drinks on our twentieth wedding anniversary." Very quickly, almost as though he had been waiting for the remark, a veteran who had been particularly depressed all evening looked at me with a twinkle in his eye that lit up his whole hirsute face and said, "Well, there's one freak in every group."

The message I think I was trying to convey was something like: "Yes, I know how difficult things really are for you. In fact it's hard for anyone to bring together these often conflicting elements into a coherent way of living, as I too have had occasion to learn. Still, certain things are possible—relationships and commitments can prevail—one can somehow find one's way." The veteran's return message was: "Your situation is just about unimaginable to us. But since everything is absurd—who is to say which of us is a 'freak'?—and since we can trust one another, why not play a bit with the absurdity of things as a way out of despair?"

Vietnam veterans embark upon their undertaking in an age of transformation. The idea of radical psychological and social upheaval is in the air everywhere, even if it is slow to influence arrangements that prevail on the ground. The special importance of Vietnam in all this was suggested in a comment by Gyorgy Lukacs shortly before his death, in answer to the simple question, "What about America?":

You will recall that the Lisbon earthquake of 1755 had shocked the civilized world more than any other event since the fall of Rome in the 5th century. But it did more than that. The optimism of the first half of the 18th century did not long survive the disaster. It inspired Voltaire to write his famous poem against the *tout est bien* philosophy of Leibniz and Pope, which was in turn attacked by Rousseau, and there was *Candide* with its important scene in Lisbon. In Portugal it was widely felt that a sinful Lisbon, this modern Babylon, had been punished by God and should perhaps have been completely wiped out like Sodom and Gomorrah. Penitential processions were organized. The people were told that the awesome destruction of the wealthiest and best-known city of its time was God's way of shocking not only the affluent and sybaritic Portuguese but the whole of Christendom into penitence.

It seems to me that Viet Nam is fast becoming America's Lisbon disaster, and American society is reading the signs of *its* earthquake in a similar spirit.[5]

Lukacs implies what we have already suggested: all Americans are survivors of the Vietnam holocaust, and are faced with the task of recognizing and bringing significance to their death immersion. In this man-made—essentially American-made—holocaust, the secular equivalent to divine punishment may be found in the shocking emergence of the sins of our national past, long hidden under a cloak of unadulterated virtue, to the point of threatening the entire American historical experiment.

To be sure, Americans (and others throughout the world) are surviving much more than Vietnam. Our unprecedented historical velocity and our holocausts (actual or potential) merge into a confusing but compelling survivor ethos, with Vietnam at the malignant cutting edge. Lukacs' claim that America is reading the signs of "*its* earthquake in a similar spirit" is perhaps best rephrased as a question: Can a significant number of Americans muster enough survivor wisdom to create the kind of forms that would be ethically adequate to the filth of the holocaust—and psychohistorically adequate to the unprecedented needs of our social moment? That is, can we respond to the constructive model of transformation suggested by certain veterans, whatever its imperfections and fragility? To answer that kind of question— even to begin to ask it seriously—we must turn to what can best be called the prophetic function of these antiwar warriors.

CHAPTER 11

Truth and Prophecy

✻

Now if you don't believe what you read in the newspapers or magazines, what you see on television on the news, or what you see in the movies, or what you hear from other people, what do you believe? What you see yourself. And, ah, can you believe that?

—My Lai survivor

I was there to be sought by a people who did not ask,
    to be found by men who did not seek me.
I said, "here am I, here am I,"
    to a nation that did not invoke me by name.
I spread out my hands all day
    appealing to an unruly people
who went their evil way,
    following their own devices,
a people who provoked me
    continually to my face. . . .

—The Book of the Prophet Isaiah

ONE'S IMPRESSION of antiwar veterans can shift quite abruptly. At moments they appear to be ordinary young men with more than their share of confusion, as they discuss everyday irritations at job or school, and raise such questions as whether or not to marry "a nice Jewish girl." At other times they manifest the excruciating intensity of men who view virtually all issues as matters of life and death and who seek contact with the mythic or formative zone of existence in which basic psychological images and transformations take shape. They themselves seem to move readily from one stance to another, and to various stances in between—with sudden manifestations of that mythic intensity that can surprise even those of us who know it to be in them.

In general, men who have killed take on, for others in society, a quality of being a little more (and perhaps a little less) than human. They are felt to have entered into a forbidden realm of control over life and death, which separates them psychologically from the rest of us. Society cannot treat them casually. Where they have been given no sanction to kill, they are cast out and severely punished (sometimes killed in return). But where that sanction has been given, as in war, they are honored as heroes; what would ordinarily be taboo and a form of transgression is celebrated for its boldness. From this standpoint Vietnam veterans are in a strange position: they have been given that sanction to kill, but neither those who gave it nor the veterans themselves can accept the killing as legitimate. They emerge more stigmatized than heroic, but can still lay some claim to the rights and prerogatives of the warrior-hero. Then, in the case of antiwar veterans, they use those prerogatives to do something heroes are not supposed to do: reveal the hidden secrets of the place into which they have trespassed and tell of the truth they have touched at its source.

What is that truth? Partly, the simple, unflinching rendition of grotesque, empty suffering—as suggested by an Air Force medic talking about his work:

I don't like them . . . the stump dressings and the amputations—they smell. And I've not gotten used to people's bodies looking like that. I'm not callous . . . I get over it, but I think about it. A lot. I can do it. I can joke with the guy about it. But it's just I can't help thinking, "Why the hell's this guy lost his legs?" It's unreal. . . .[1]

Partly that truth is the widely felt admiration for our Vietnamese enemies, as contrasted with bitter contempt for our allies:

I'm gonna find the VC that got [wounded] me, I'm gonna shake his hand, 'cause that was a smart mother fucker, no question about that. . . . Don't call him [the NLF] Charley, call him Mr. Charles. . . . The ARVN doesn't fight at night, the ARVN steals things, the ARVN is lazy. . . .[2]

Partly what amounts to the most terrible realization of all (here expressed by the My Lai survivor):

Ah, what a waste. . . . It wasn't worth even just one guy [killed]— just him, it wasn't worth.

The ultimate truth at the source has to do with the ease with which a man can become (the American GI became) both victim and executioner; with the malignancy of the romantic and ideological deceptions about the war; and with the further source of these deceptions and victimizations in the deep recesses of America and Americans. When exposed to those levels of "subversive" truth, the response of society can be at best ambivalent.

Nor can the men themselves be free of ambivalence, as they (in Wilfred Owen's metaphor) return "starkly" to tell the starkest of truths—to "stare upon the ash of all I burned." That truth can be frightening, even blinding. And we have seen how the survivor's divided loyalties, his fear that, precisely by telling the truth, he may do harm to those who remain in the center of the holocaust—to his buddies who are still dependent upon deceptions. "You'll be helping them but they will think that you're hurting them," was the way the My Lai survivor put it.

The same man told how this knowledge of truth at the source makes one reject others' simplistic categories. He was disdainful, for instance, of the trial of Lieutenant Calley and the attempt to "bring him to justice," because

It wasn't that way. . . . I couldn't see him really as a mass murderer. . . .

When called before an official inquiry about My Lai, he had expected something on the order of a fundamental investigation that could get at the overall military (atrocity-producing) situation in Vietnam and the way in which the men were locked into that situation. Instead he encountered a formal, narrowly based military procedure seeking out individual culprits:

Actually all it was . . . was a criminal thing. They were just investigating these "criminals" and they called on me.

What he was saying was that nobody really wanted to hear truth at the source.

Which led him in turn to wonder just what had blocked for so long his own and others' access to this truth:

All the while that I was over there I was thinking, well, what are my sources of information? Whatever made me believe the war was the way I thought it was? . . . My source of information, of course . . . you know, war tales, movies, something else, newspapers. Why didn't newspapers ever say the war was like this? Why didn't they say there were so many civilians killed today instead of so many

troops? And I was wondering just how far the press has been taken
in by this [false] feeling? Or was it all just a big military cover-up?
And if it was a big military cover-up, how did they do it? How did
they do it? They must have been fantastic.

Going still further in his questioning, he "began to doubt everything that I knew because I read it in a newspaper or magazine."
This skeptical stance, however, did not necessarily make truth
more accessible:

Now if you don't believe what you read in the newspapers or magazines, what you see on television on the news, or what you see in the
movies, or what you hear from other people, what do you believe?
What you see yourself. And, ah, can you believe *that?*

"That"—what he himself had seen and felt—was at least a beginning. Yet even personal or "organic knowledge" of that kind was
far from immutable:

It didn't look to me when I was over there at all the way it looked
to me when I was back home talking about it.

When many others in the United States began "talking about
it [My Lai]" as well, he had been hopeful that truth would
emerge—

I thought there was going to be some kind of turnover in the system
in the upper levels . . . [that] they were going to . . . start to find
out what's going on in Vietnam. . . . I thought maybe we were going to find out the truth now.

—only to discover all too quickly that "it wasn't coming out that
way."
    Men who turned against the war knew something of the force
of this resistance to truth from having experienced it within themselves. In his illuminating pamphlet, Jeff Needle drew sharply
what many others had expressed more vaguely and with only

partial awareness. He had been working in supply at Base Camp, and began to hear disturbing tales from the men returning from the field:

And when they came out of My Lai, I heard the stories they came back with. I didn't know whether they were true because I wasn't there. If they were true, it meant my company had murdered people, it meant I had helped by making sure the weapons worked, it meant my friends were in serious trouble because they had been taught their job too well. It meant speaking out against something I was told was right, but deep within me, I knew wasn't right, it meant because of lies I had been told I was sitting in the middle of a useless war, it meant if I died in Vietnam my life would have been used and wasted, it meant that each day as I did my assigned job, I was contributing my small share to keep the war going, it meant the men who already died and the men who were going to die were throwing their lives away, it meant I was helping to continue something I felt was wrong. It meant if I decided not to do my job anymore I would be sent to jail and court-martialed. It meant a lot of people would think I was a traitor to my country because I didn't believe in the war anymore, it meant some of the people in the company and outside the Army would hate me because they wouldn't understand why I had changed my mind, it meant I would get a dishonorable discharge, it meant I would find it hard to get a job, it meant losing the privileges of the G.I. Bill for schools and hospital care, it meant hardships on my parents. It meant a lot of bad things I didn't want to think about, based on stories I wasn't sure were true. So I decided to forget about it.[3]

He went on to explain that only the courage of the former GI who spoke out publicly on My Lai gave him "the strength not to forget."

Conveying truth at the source is the essence of the antiwar veteran's survivor mission, and the basis for his personal transformation. We have observed the difficulties of that mission at various levels—getting people to believe the truth, being able to convey it, and having an inner sense that one knows it. Such are the external and internal barriers and resistances that the anti-war veterans may well come to doubt whether truth at the source is possible—for others, for himself, or as an entity at all. Yet whatever his doubts, he feels compelled to continue to carry out his mission of at least approaching that truth. VVAW was once spoken of as "a spiritual home for a lot of lost souls"—by the same man whom we quoted earlier as saying "Those of us who have gone through the war like to feel we have come out with a certain truth." The spiritual home in question, then, is in effect a home for the truth—but given the state of society and of one's post-holocaust self, one must pay a high psychic rent if one is to live in that home.

The urgency felt by men who embark upon this kind of truth-telling mission and its high psychological stakes for themselves, can lead to an intolerant righteousness that one of the men called "our sanctimoniousness." That sanctimoniousness, which can itself take many forms, is related to a survivor potential to claim an elite status of men who, having crossed over to the other side and returned, now claim an exclusive knowledge of all matters related to death and holocaust.[4]

Another component of this claim to higher wisdom can be angry disillusionment at discovering that they are quite as capable as anyone else of pettiness, nastiness, and emotional cruelty —often in ways related to that sanctimoniousness, and to other war-linked conflicts.

The pattern was painfully illustrated by an incident that occurred in the VVAW office at the same time that our rap group was meeting in a different room. All during our session we could hear loud noises of celebration, and it was quite obvious that a party of some magnitude was going on. But late in the evening, after much of the gaiety had subsided, we began to hear the quieter tones of something that sounded very much like sobbing. We went on with our session, more or less assuming that the sounds were in some way connected with the celebration, which we knew to be a last bachelor party for a member of the organization who was to be married the next day. When the sobs persisted and became more uncontrolled (to the point where we were jarred out of our own numbness), one of the veterans rushed from the room to see what was going on, and then ran back to call me out because, as he hurriedly explained, there was a girl who seemed to be passing out and having trouble breathing. When I saw her, however, she appeared to have no physical difficulty other than uncontrollable weeping, possibly on top of some drinking. After she had calmed down a bit, and was attended by a girlfriend who said she would take her home for the night, I returned to the group and we discussed what had happened. One of the men explained that she was the girl who was to marry the other veteran, but that a few of the organizers of the party had their specific goal of preventing the wedding, convinced as they were that it would be a terrible mistake for their VVAW "brother." They had apparently succeeded, probably through some revelations about the girl's sexual involvements.

Veterans and professionals discussed the incident in terms of its being an unusually cruel bit of manipulation. Then one of the men, who described himself as merely "visiting" the group, shouted angrily that it was just that sort of nasty, unfeeling behavior that had caused him to quit VVAW some time before: "They may have revolutionary politics but they are vicious in the way they can treat each other," was the way he put it. The whole incident seemed to reflect not only the veteran-survivor's impulse toward sanctimoniousness—his claim to the kind of ethical purity that gives him the right to ordain and manipulate the behavior of others—but also perhaps a sense of threat experienced by some members of a closely bonded male group at the prospect of losing one of their band of brothers.*

On the whole the men were capable of being self-critical about

* These two factors hardly exhaust what was at play in this incident, about which there is much I do not know. Since a number of veterans belonging to VVAW married during that eighteen-month period, and this was the only such incident I heard of, we must assume that there were additional issues involved.

such tendencies as well. They generally understand that one never quite gets to 'the truth,' and that the struggle to approximate it is unending. At the end of an intense series of interviews with the My Lai survivor, for instance, he told me that he had learned a great deal

just by talking about it because . . . it's something that I never talked about before. So I don't think I could have ever made sense of it . . . even to myself if I hadn't actually said it.

What he was saying (here and elsewhere in the interview) was that our talks, in comparison to those with journalists and military investigators, had brought him closer to his own experience, to his most authentic version of truth at the source. He had still not achieved anything like comfortable mastery of this truth, as we know from his residual guilt, self-doubt, and confusion. But he had touched a certain level of truth, an interface of personal experience (self) and larger forces (world), around which he could build and grow.

That level of truth became inseparable from personal integrity and wholeness, as suggested in the description by another veteran of his behavior on two public occasions:

I keep wondering about the difference between the first time I ever got up in front of a group of people and told them anything about myself which was January 31, 1971. The Winter Soldier [Investigation], and I'm shaking and half in tears. And barely two months later, with nothing in between except the group raps, in Washington [at a professional meeting he and other veterans addressed], when I felt—I was moved by that conference and I felt as if I was being something other than just an objective commentator. It seemed to just flow off my tongue and I felt very at home. . . . It seemed the most natural thing. And I take that as . . . part of the feeling of being put all together and having a much greater proximity among those various levels and experiences.

The former Army sergeant derived similar satisfaction from composing his slide sequence and observing its effects upon audiences. Having previously had mixed success in talking about Vietnam to anybody who would listen to him, and beginning to conclude that "people just weren't interested in Vietnam," he prepared the sequence in response to a student's casual question, "Hey, do you have slides or something?" We have said that his combination of slides and rock music constituted his artistic re-creation—or survivor formulation—of his death immersion. We can also say that the slides were a way of conveying to others truth at the source while he himself was reexperiencing it. He came to realize, as he put it, that "the slides say it all."

But once gaining access to that kind of truth, the problem he and others faced was holding on to it. They sensed that in each retelling—in each public presentation or performance—there was inevitable movement away from the source, away from truth.* The problem was magnified by political compromises they felt called upon to make as their group entered more actively into public life. The former naval intelligence NCO, referring to a political meeting he had just attended, conveyed something of this break-up of truth and return to deception:

Suddenly this feeling came on me again, the compromise that the advocate faces—all the feelings and thoughts that came on me when I was supposed to be schooled in espionage. I came [then] to appreciate and discern double, triple, quadruple faces of an individual and see the different voices speaking at different times, never quite being sure which one was which and struggling to perceive that because it's so crucial—then resolving after that that I wanted to speak with one voice, but finding out that sometimes in situations there is pressure to divide it up again.

* The creator of the slide sequence, for instance, eventually had to give up showing it because he found himself merely going through the motions, which he felt to be unauthentic. Yet he was slow to follow through on a suggestion that the slide sequence be made into a film, which could then have a certain autonomy and be shown without his being present. He might well have felt, however unconsciously, that making the slide sequence into a separate entity, in that way would be another step away from truth at the (his personal) source.

One could say that his psychological association to Vietnam
deceptions was a way of returning to "the source" in order to
rediscover where truth lay. He was thus carrying out his survivor
mission, both in reconfronting his "death immersion" and in
struggling toward maximum truth in his post-Vietnam formulation of self and world.

The kind of truth-mission suggests a prophetic element. I use
the term "prophecy" in the classical sense of an inspired message
that "extends the margin of the moral and religious present into
a future which is its immediate consequence, and is morally con-
ditioned."[5] In all such prophecy, prediction is less important than
insight in the service of spiritual regeneration. The antiwar veterans take their place among a special contemporary group of
"prophetic survivors" whose "inspiration" derives, not from the
Divinity, but from the holocausts they have survived. Also included in this category are those among the Hiroshima victims[6]
and also among the scientists responsible for the Hiroshima
weapon,[7] who have managed to emerge from their holocaust with
similarly regenerative insight. For these prophetic survivors, who
are never more than a minority of those who have shared their
death immersion, the holocaust takes on an ultimate (virtually
sacred) quality that carries them into a realm of death-linked
experience never before known or comprehended by man. Their
experience parallels that of priests and shaman, the predecessors
of biblical prophets, who ventured into the "land of death" and
then "returned" to bring to their people deepened knowledge of
the mysteries of death and life. The majority of Vietnam veterans, as we have indicated, cannot be viewed as prophetic. And
even those antiwar veterans to whom I am now applying the
term would probably either reject it out of hand or subject it
(and themselves) to leavening mockery. But one could nonetheless feel in the rap group, at least on the subject of the war and
its consequences, a special force and tone that combined hard-
won wisdom, crusading energy, and "the spiritual vitality and

permanent worth of . . . work and message"[8] said to characterize prophetic inspiration.

The men used such terms as the "message" they felt impelled to spread or, on occasion, the "revelation" they had experienced as a little more than casual metaphor. Their holocaust had become sacred in that it served as an absolute reference point for ultimate meaning—all the more so because they perceived themselves in it as both destroyers and victims. Holocaust always becomes sacred to survivors in some of these ways, but the particular false witness of Vietnam with its legacy of guilt and betrayal, and the historical moment at which it occurs, provide survivors able to confront this land of death with a particularly compelling mission and a special potential for prophecy.*

That very intensity led to fears, in the words of one veteran, "that I'll be caught up in something beyond my control." Or, as the former naval NCO mused concerning his personal dialectic between withdrawal and energetic social involvement:

I'm touched by the irony of what's happening. . . . In struggling for what I thought was a more . . . humble and modest but primarily a more tenable, basic view of life . . . I was imagining that what I was really striving for was a point where I would be a humble practitioner someplace and I'd be treating addicts and troubled people. I would not make a lot of money, but I would have a wife and some kids and some kind of tangible happiness. And Princeton and Europe

---

* While this study is limited to American survivors, we will do well to look among Vietnamese for prophetic survivors with equally important messages. The obvious and outstanding Vietnamese prophetic survivor is Ho Chi Minh, whose life included a series of holocausts, culminating in the American-induced one, from which he constantly brought insights. But there are others emerging with messages that have to do with the capacity of men and women committed to an immortalizing vision to prevail against extraordinary forms of technological destruction, and perhaps with aspects of heroism and of new civilian-military combinations of the warrior ethos. This latter message is both moving and not without eventual pitfalls. I have heard several Americans, either after visits to North Vietnam or close study of the full horror of Vietnamese victimization by American ground and air assaults, compare that people to early Christians in their suffering and ultimate significance for mankind.

and a vision of world order and world integration that in a way inspired me [in the past]—I would put that away as a childish thing.
And the irony is that through the ethics that come attached to something that I believed in strongly, was more rooted in and more earth-
bound, I ended up getting involved in a very historic thing, a mo-
mentous thing, and I feel it's extraordinary, and that I'm part of it,
willingly a part of it, and with some integrity. But there's still that
irony there.

When I asked him what that "extraordinary thing" was, he responded:

Saying it makes me frightened. It's that simple little office with those
people struggling with four telephone lines and a mimeograph machine in the back, with some fund-raising dinners . . . [making
appearances] on the House floor—the Senate floor—lots of TV programs. And those are the people that think I'm a focal point for a
special kind of interest [involving] thousands and millions of people.

Typically, the prophet in him coexisted with the forlorn voice of
the 'nobody,' and therefore had to be constantly questioned:

Maybe one day I'll wake up . . . and look back on what I'm doing
now and say, "What a ballsy little snot nose you were. The whole
idea of entertaining such thoughts—what presumption!"

Another time he expressed similar ambivalence toward his own
intensity, especially concerning the war, simultaneously affirming
that intensity and mocking it by telling of the discomfort it
caused in a relative he was visiting:

Finally, he just said to me: "Don't be so good. Why don't you just
look at television like everybody else?"

In the long run this kind of mockery, however self-deflating,
lived side-by-side with his survivor passion. Indeed such is the
contemporary need for mockery that it is called upon for many

levels of expression and can generate (as it frequently did with him and with other veterans) a passion of its own.[9]

The men sensed that whatever recognition they had as prophets was time-limited. They knew that the identity of the antiwar veteran could not serve them forever. We recall the comment, "Our life is being against the war. When the war ends then *we* end as people." Not only did they fear that they would be left without an identity but that, should their prophetic message fail to be heard soon, it would be too late. Then both the prophecy and the individual psychological struggles within that prophecy would have failed. The prophetic effort is collective: no single antiwar veteran has emerged as *the* prophet. Rather, a group of men have come together to stir up the beginnings of prophecy. And around their collective power will the prophecy succeed or fail—or, more likely, succeed *and* fail.

In their prophetic stance, the men have an agonizing relationship to their own national-cultural roots. They know they are very much creatures of American society—of its institutions and styles of upbringing no less than its wars, and of its possibilities for future realization or disaster. Even as they condemn so much of their society they sense, as their audiences do, that they originate from its cultural, socio-economic, and ideological center— which is why so many Americans can more readily identify with them than, say, with student radicals or long-standing pacifists. Indeed their journey into the land of death was, so to speak, the killing (and dying) edge of the contemporary American agony over Vietnam and related dislocations and breakdowns in our society.

While there is no doubt about their conflict with and alienation from much of the society, their fundamental relationship to it can contribute to the message of restoration* that is always part

---

* The "mode of restoration" (footnote, p. 232), together with the "mode of transformation" and "mode of accommodation" are image-patterns called upon in relationship to the threat of possibility of social change. They are categories involving self and world, a way of talking about the "psychohistorical inter-

of social prophecy. Such restorative imagery was often implicit, but it can also be consciously explored, as in one contemplative veteran's examination of some of the old virtues, national and personal:

I [thought of] going . . . to Canada or something [but] . . . I sort of feel a responsibility to change things because there are many things . . . the Declaration of Independence and things like that . . . that I still feel are valid and that I want to preserve. . . . The sense of responsibility that my parents had in bringing us up . . . the idea of being concerned for other people . . . the feeling of being responsible . . . [so that] when you're doing a job to do it well. These kinds of things I do very much value.

He admitted that "conflicts come up" around the difficult matter of "keeping . . . what is essential and discarding that which gets in the way." And he asked, rhetorically but worriedly: "Are we going to end up destroying something instead?"

The same man went on to grope with still more fundamental images of man and civilization:

Something struck me about two weeks ago that I haven't been able to get rid of. The overwhelming thing that being with the veterans has given me—this feeling of independence or looseness—can in many ways be a very dangerous thing—because so many people have gone through it and . . . we don't really have a great attachment to all the buildings and the civilization. If everything were to go, I wouldn't be all that upset. I'd go out into the woods and I know how to make myself comfortable. I'd know how to clothe myself, to build a shelter, to hunt and trap. . . . In some ways the Army and my Boy Scout training gave me that, and I can see that among a lot of vet-

---

face." From this standpoint my impression is that prophets make use of all three modes: they set forth a vision of *transformation*, of making all (social and individual) things new; at the same time they stress the *restoration* of an exquisitely harmonious (and mythic) "golden age" of the past containing the immortalizing origins and substance of one's people; and even advocate a certain amount of selective *accommodation* to the extent necessary for realizing the more fundamental prophetic vision.[10]

erans . . . that they're not all that committed to ["the buildings and the civilization"] . . . [the] dangerous thing [would be] . . . if someone wanted to go out and . . . fight in the streets or something because . . . they'd be perfectly capable of doing it [tearing things down, and thinking] "Ya, we'll accept that, keep the Yale Medical School. [But] it really isn't all that important. We could still survive as a race without all this stuff.". . . I'm willing to get rid of all the superhighways. I'm willing to sacrifice my car . . . my . . . travel. . . . I can function with myself out in the woods. I can raise a family out in the Berkshires somewhere providing we haven't polluted it. . . .

He attributed this "change in my whole outlook" not only to military and Boy Scout training, but to having been in Vietnam

and seeing . . . that life boils down to just—whether you're alive today or tomorrow—[being] in the right place at the right time, just a combination of circumstances. And all the advances of medicine and technology and everything don't mean a blasted thing when you're dealing with a rocket. And I guess having been, you know, those couple of times when I knew I was dead, and death not being all that frightening. Or not having the things that I wanted . . . food . . . going without it, being cold and [other] things, you're able to put up with it. . . . Seeing so many things go wrong . . . in addition to seeing that they weren't necessary for me to survive, the combination seemed to give me independence.

The death immersion in Vietnam, that is, provides the basis for the prophetic position, the sense that much of our environment and our way of living in it is superfluous and can (must?) be jettisoned in order to uncover fundamental, energizing truth. But the prophet is uneasy with his prophecy: having witnessed too much of violence, he is wary of any new holocaust in the name of purification and renewal. Valuing his American roots, he is wary of jettisoning what might turn out to be essential to his or his country's continuing identity. And as a contemporary man he is aware (in a way that 'practical prophets' must be) that even basic forms of 'return' (in this case, to nature) are not free of the threat of impurity ("I can raise a family out in the Berkshires somewhere providing we haven't polluted it").

There were many hints among antiwar veterans of reaching in this way for truths beyond the arrangements of society or even of existing civilization. But most were less clear about relating their survivor mission to these larger questions. One had the sense that their prophetic impulse was strong; they could be brilliantly articulate about it and, at other moments, almost inchoate. What remained unclear was the meaning and power of this collective impulse, the extent to which it can be given the voice and form necessary to genuine prophecy. That in turn depends greatly upon the way in which this potentially prophetic group is received by American society.

We are hardly surprised that Americans respond to their antiwar Vietnam veterans with hopelessly mixed feelings—not just ordinary ambivalence but love and hate on a grand scale. We have pointed to distinctions in their eyes between these veterans and other militant peace protesters. Campus radicals can convey an aura of forbidding intellect and privileged disdain for common-sense ways of thinking and acting and for conventional compliance with national authority—all of which can render them, as a group, alien and suspect. But when antiwar veterans, emerging from the less privileged socioeconomic heart of American society and from its central assumptions and self-evident truths as well—when such a group goes to war for these assumptions and truths, then turn against the whole package (against the war, the assumptions, and the truths), Americans are bound to be profoundly moved, equally profoundly enraged, or both.

We know the antiwar veterans to be messengers of bad tidings, of nasty, unacceptable news. They must inevitably meet from many Americans, who cannot psychologically afford to have national-personal truth questioned, the rage aimed at rejected prophets. Those who would convey truth are then denounced as "betrayers" of the nation and (in a biblical and perhaps more-than-biblical sense) of "the king." (Again we note how *everyone* feels betrayed by the Vietnam War.)

This process of denying the prophets is rendered all the more intense by already existing doubts in many about old images of American virtue. Having lost considerable faith and trust in what had been considered their national essence, Americans bring desperate, sometimes violent energy to attacking those who challenge that which they already doubt, and to holding onto at least the psychic frames and appearances that might pass for the essence.

But antiwar veterans can also be perceived as envoys from the center or source of a nation, bearing their own form of good news. For accompanying their apocalyptic tales from the land of death is a dim, flickering suggestion of illumination. While few Americans would say this, many perceive it and respond to antiwar veterans as a very special group of men not to be easily dismissed.

In the end, one either accepts the truth of the prophecy with its message of guilt, and joins with the antiwar veterans in the difficult struggle to render that guilt animating—or one angrily denies both prophecy and guilt and separates oneself from them by casting them out as alien betrayers "unworthy of wearing the American uniform." There are, of course, in-between responses, but they too are likely to contain some of this passionate imagery. American society cannot avoid being haunted by these men.

It is haunted by the specter of a new kind of hero-prophet who turns his fleshly knowledge of violence into a rejection of that violence. His claim to having entered the myth of the hero stems from his confrontation of death and mutilation as the source of his insight. He therefore enters the category of "hero as warrior" —having transmuted his killing (and death witness) into "not . . . things become but . . . things becoming" and having chosen as his enemy not the one designated but "the keeper of the past . . . [who] in the seat of power . . . turns to his own advantage the authority of his position." His "hero-deed" is not what he did in war but his rejection of that war in favor of "a continuous shattering of the crystallizations of the moment." Like all heroes he has performed what Erikson called "the dirty work"—and what we may now call the "death work"—of his generation. He emerges from that "death work" with an image, however tenuous, of transformation of the human spirit.

In struggling toward prophecy, the antiwar veteran parts company with the socialized warrior who, having also known death and mutilation, chooses (as his way of dealing with survivor conflicts) to remain enmeshed in his corrupting relationship with them. This corruption of the socialized warrior—of the entire American military—has been one of the most striking consequences of the war in Vietnam. The process is exemplified by the celebrated case of Colonel Anthony B. Herbert. The most decorated soldier of the Korean War and a hero in Vietnam as well, Herbert insisted upon reporting atrocities his superiors did not want reported. Though all evidence pointed to the accuracy of his accusations, he was rewarded by humiliating harassments (lessons in saluting, meaningless jobs, etc.), illegal disciplinary procedures (personal silencing and refusal of proper military legal defense), until he was literally hounded out of the Army. As in the case of the My Lai survivor, his attempt to live up to the more noble traditions of the socialized warrior—not only those of chivalry but also that of truthfulness—could not be tolerated in *this* war. The man of truth and honor—the would-be prophet—is thus doubly victimized.

This new kind of hero-prophet, while rejecting the romance of war and exposing the filth beneath, in a certain sense retains some of that romance in the service of the new mission. (We shall later contrast the cool, technocratic warrior who is the low-profile rival for society's approval of the men we are describing.) The antiwar veterans have held on to and in some degree transformed the mutual love and dependency of combat, its self-abnegation and group dedication, now rechanneled into an antiwar direction. In rejecting the roles of executioner and victim, they demand neither pity nor glory so much as an end to the war and fundamental change in the society that produced it.

To be sure, their prophetic style poses many difficulties for their countrymen, including the simple matter of prophetic passion. Such ethical passion in itself, especially when sustained, makes many Americans uncomfortable. In addition there is the culture's continuous demand for novelty, for "new stories" and images that can catch the attention of, and be re-created by, the mass media. Thus six months or so after the first wave of media response to the antiwar veterans, one broadcaster, when asked about them, expressed his own lack of interest by saying, "Their story has now been told." But has it? Can these fragile and fallible prophets continue to make use of their death immersion on behalf of renewed life, their passion on behalf of reason? And can they be heard?

CHAPTER 12

On War and Warriors

✣

You have lied to us too long. You have burned too many babies. You may have taken our bodies, but you haven't taken our minds.

> —Ron Kovic, former Marine sergeant,
> speaking from wheelchair at VVAW
> protest rally held at Republican
> National Convention, August, 1972

The name of the game is air.

> —American pilot involved in
> bombing of Laos

We are easy riders to the fields of grace,
A bomb shell in the gut.

> —Richard Eberhart

THE STORY OF ANTIWAR VETERANS has not yet been told, has in fact hardly begun to unfold. But some of that story began to be heard as the American project of Vietnam fell into increasing dishonor. Unfortunately, the first result was a substitution of one counterfeit universe for another.

The official claim of winding down the war (1971-72) could be more accurately described as a further "grinding down" of American integrity. As the last of our ground-combat troops left, our airplanes expanded the radius of killing and destroying. The haunting phrases of an early VVAW leader—"How do you ask a man to be the last man to die in Vietnam? How do you ask a man to be the last man to die for a mistake?"[1]—reverberated throughout American consciousness . . . but not to the extent of being applied to the Vietnamese.

The message, coming as it did from many sources, had already been received by the American ground troops in Vietnam. A correspondent who went out on patrols with grunts in late 1971, spoke of the war as "not so much a test of strength under pressure, as it often was a few years ago, as a daily hassle to avoid patrols, avoid the enemy, avoid contact—keep out of trouble and not be 'the last American killed in Vietnam.' "[2] The policy of "search and destroy" had become "search and evade," and the prevailing slogan of the men: "CYA (cover your ass) and get home." Above all, the "notorious past" of the Americal Division inspired in its men something less than pride:

First there was exposure of the massacres at My Lai . . . followed by the case of a former brigade commander charged with mowing down civilians from his helicopter and . . . revelation of the use of chemical defoliant capable of inducing cancer. Then . . . the commanding general was relieved in the aftermath of an attack on a firebase in which thirty-three GIs were killed. "I'm afraid to tell anyone back in the world I'm with the Americal," says one of the lieutenants, laughing sardonically. "No one has much pride in the division. That's one reason morale is so bad."

The winding-down policy increased rather than lessened the men's sense of the counterfeit in Vietnam and was reflected in two patterns of resistance: refusal to follow combat orders, and "fragging" (killing or wounding) officers judged too enthusiastic about exposing men to danger.

The first pattern was symbolized by "Fire Base Pace," an advance area where a number of GIs announced, to newsmen as well as to their officers, that they would not go out on dangerous patrols. The famous *New York Daily News* headline, "Sir, my men refuse to go," epitomized a widespread resistance to fighting (often passive but sometimes direct) that spread among American ground troops throughout Vietnam and the helplessness of their officers (themselves often in conflict) in the face of it. One man explained his reasons for refusing—

Besides being short [having little time left in Vietnam], I didn't have any knowledge of the area. It wasn't worth maybe getting shot.[3]

—conveying the inglorious sense of futility with which the men came to view their project.

"Fragging" was a form of violent resistance. Only the name is new: violence by soldiers toward their superiors has occurred in all wars, often in response to having been abused and humiliated by them. But fragging incidents were unprecedentedly widespread in Vietnam, where they were frequently associated with resentment of officers' risking men's lives in aggressive pursuit of the war.* Equally significant has been the extent of what could

* Fraggings of racial origin were also rather widespread, especially in Vietnam but elsewhere as well, and are related to the broader black rejection

be called fragging imagery among enlisted men who took no such
action but shared with each other such ideas, and for the same
reasons. The correspondent described a gung-ho officer, full of
plans for daring patrols and ambushes, pleading with his bat-
talion commander to give him "a few more days to work the area
by the stream," while his men "curse[d] him silently." And, as
it turned out, not so silently: "God dammit," one of them says,
"if no one was looking, I'd frag the sonuvabitch."

The counting of time—of the "three hundred and sixty-five
days"—always an extreme preoccupation of men in this war of
rotation, became (in a literal sense) a morbid obsession. To be
time-bound, as a poem by Larry Rottmann suggests, was to be
locked into absurd death:

> Before it hit me
> that I was to be here
> a *whole year!*
> 365 days
> 8,760 hours
> 525,600 minutes
> 31,536,000 seconds
> in which to die.[4]

Resentment over fighting a limited war increased. "We was
fightin' to win, that'd be one thing, but we're just wastin' time,"
was the way one man put it—a feeling which contributed to the
deepening sense of meaninglessness. Donald Kirk attributes these
attitudes to men finding themselves "at the butt end of a bad
war"[5] or (I would say) the dead end of a counterfeit project.

---

throughout American society of anything perceived as victimization. Any individual fragging is likely to result from several of these factors, as well as from
individual-psychological issues around fear, resentment, and violence. But I
would emphasize the overall importance of a violence-dominated environment
in which the moral authority of those in charge has disintegrated—that is, of
the counterfeit universe.

The heroin plague, which we discussed earlier as symbolic of the evil and taint of the war, is the social expression of its counterfeit dead end. For not only were the victims of the plague American (soldiers turned addicts), but it was created and perpetuated by a variety of American practices: legal/criminal definitions of drug use and collusion in the Southeast Asian drug trade by American officials.[6] It was also considerably stimulated, according to Zinberg, by a misplaced military crusade, that of stamping out the "evil" of the marijuana trade, which caused man to turn to readily available high-grade heroin. As Zinberg[7] and others have suggested, evolving social pressure or custom contributed greatly first to smoking and then injecting heroin. So did the pervasive boredom and feelings of meaninglessness among the troops. The rates were often highest among those in the rear. While it would be wrong to suggest a specific single cause of the heroin epidemic, the uniquely high rate in Vietnam (even as opposed to nearby Thai American bases where the drug was also readily available) suggests the overall influence of the counterfeit environment of Vietnam.* More than that, Vietnam and heroin, for both literal and symbolic reasons, became inseparable in American imagery in ways that reached deeply into the national military ethos—as I had occasion to observe during several public confrontations.

The first two of these confrontations took place during evening seminars at Yale (in late 1971) run by the Drug Dependency unit there, under contract with the military, for groups of military psychiatrists, administrative officers, and chaplains who were in one way or another involved in dealing with the "drug problem." I participated, not as a representative of Yale, but rather at the request of a group of antiwar veterans invited by the Yale organizers to form a panel at which they, including among them

---

* There have been mainly Air Force personnel in Thailand, which could be an important factor in the lower rate of heroin use there. But I believe that my general argument holds.

several former drug addicts, could present their views. Two of the veterans involved had actively participated with me in the New York rap group and felt that my presence on the panel would add professional legitimacy to a general view they knew that I shared.

On both occasions the veterans did most of the talking, warming to this opportunity to 'speak truth to power,' particularly to the power that had been the source of their pain. With considerable passion they told of deception after deception they or their friends had experienced in the military. And they went on to denounce, rightly I thought, the official insistence upon seeing the whole drug question as a problem calling for a technical solution, rather than examining the true causes, which lay in the military's own structure and the war it was waging. Again with the authority of their own experience, they could point out to those who made up their audience that they (the doctors, administrators, or chaplains) were there only because ordered to be there, and because, as middle level officers, they were caught between the needs and sufferings of the addicts on the one hand and the unrealistic orders from above for effective programs. These proliferated as educational programs consisting of lectures to the men on the evils of drugs, medical programs that contradicted one another, and obscure special programs with newly created positions, etcetera.

When my turn came I discussed the conflicts of the atrocity-producing situation, the relationship of the widespread heroin addiction to the shared sense of being trapped in this meaningless, tainted environment; and the process by which the war corrupted (or further corrupted) the military itself. I then questioned whether any effective treatment program could be mounted within the military, at least while the war continued to be fought, considering the taint of the military in the eyes of those it wished to help or cure and the degree of trust necessary for any such therapy.

Not surprisingly, many of the officers in the audience responded with a passion of their own, but a very ambivalent passion. Towards the veterans they sometimes shouted back and reaffirmed principles of military discipline, but equally often expressed sympathy and sought some middle ground of partial concession and reconciliation. Towards me they were at moments respectful, even referring to principles they had learned from my earlier work (one of them raised my Hiroshima study, for instance), and at other moments bitterly resentful, accusing me of asking them to "cop out" on their responsibilities and on the whole problem. But at no time could they really counter our arguments, and we heard a few days later that in further sessions within their continuing seminar almost half of them tended to accept our general thesis, the other half warning their colleagues not to be influenced by this dangerous effort to undermine morale, and a number talking of resigning from the military.

Equally interesting were talks I had with chaplains and psychiatrists in small groups (the larger seminar consisted of from thirty-five to forty military officers, and would later be subdivided into four or five discussion groups). A psychiatrist in the regular army, after hearing me out silently on my claim that, at least in this war, he and his colleagues were in the position of helping men to adjust to committing atrocities, approached me later and told me that "It's funny but almost everybody we saw in Vietnam [among American GIs] acted like a victim." And a chaplain, after a similar discussion concerning the conflicts between ministering to one's flock on the one hand and offering spiritual strength to go on murdering civilians on the other, came up to me as I was leaving and said: "I guess it's a little like the way it was for chaplains in Nazi Germany." Probably most of these officers (chaplains, psychiatrists, and administrators alike) found psychological ways to reaffirm their credo and go on with their military lives, but one could not help but be struck by the profound conflicts Vietnam had induced at least among the more sensitive among them, and the extent to which they were vulnerable to the kinds of messages the veterans and I brought to them.*

The other exchange occurred at a panel on Vietnam veterans held in Dallas at a May 1972 convention of the American Psychiatric Association. The panel not only included psychological professionals with various military and veterans-administration associations, but also Dr. Jerome Jaffe, President Nixon's special advisor on drugs and the man designated to "solve" the heroin epidemic. Dr. Jaffe's talk consisted of elaborate visual aids— slides and statistics ostensibly demonstrating that, though there had been widespread heroin addiction, the military programs had been effective in treating men, returning them to duty, and generally handling the problem. Another psychiatrist on the panel, who had resigned his medical commission because of objections to the military infringement upon civil rights in its drug program, questioned the accuracy of these statistics, as did I in both my talk and later comments. Our position was that the military generally discharged addicts while claiming to cure them, lacked (indeed avoided) follow-up studies that might invalidate their claims of cure, and had repeatedly broken promises of amnesty for drug-users; and that under the title of "medi-

---

* This brief summary, of course, leaves out complicated variations in attitude and tone among all of us. The veterans expressed considerable rage, but most of them tended to settle down to a relatively systematic presentation of their position and to a certain amount of empathy for military officers. In my own case the small group discussions could gradually become rather gentle and open. I would grant moral complexity around issues of "duty" for the doctor or chaplain whose task was to offer some form of healing to men in battle, though I would insist that they weigh that against the evil of the larger project they were thereby serving, and would also raise questions about whether a psychiatrist or chaplain could carry out his true therapeutic-spiritual function while under administrative control of the military. They in turn, or at least a few of them, could gradually reveal the depth of their own horror at the war and the extent to which it had raised questions about their work and their lives. At one point, in the midst of a friendly exchange with a military psychiatrist I encountered in a pizza parlor after the seminar, I began to caution myself against letting individual compassion for men caught in these dilemmas in any way interfere with clear expression of the larger issues.

cal program" (replacing "military discipline"), it continued to abuse them, and to avoid fundamental examination of its own practices.

But all this was rather low-key and relatively inconclusive until Dr. Jaffe got up to leave. At that point an angrily articulate questioner arose from the audience, identified himself as both a psychiatrist and a Vietnam veteran, and suggested to Dr. Jaffe in compelling tones that he "sit down for a few minutes and listen to what I have to say" (which Jaffe did). The questioner had pursued the drug question on his own, and recounted first-hand observations made both in Vietnam and the United States that pointed up the deceptions in the military program and rendered Dr. Jaffe's statistics on improvement or cure absurd. He concluded: "Official statistics about drugs are just like the body count—all lies." Admitting that there were *some* accurate claims in Dr. Jaffe's presentation, my own view is that his critic's equation of drug statistics and body count was profoundly true—in their inaccuracy, their use to distract everyone from the absurd evil of the war, and their ultimate epitomization of that very evil.*

---

* The audience critic, to whom I am grateful, is Dr. Gordon Livingston of Johns Hopkins University. My quarrel with Dr. Jaffe is not over his psychiatric competence as such, but rather the apologist-technicist trap into which he has fallen. Nor do I mean this to be anything in the nature of a detailed discussion of the drug question, in the military or elsewhere. I wish only to suggest some of the ways in which the heroin question is related both to our counterfeit project in Vietnam and its related social and professional corruptions. In effect, the military created the drug problem, set forth a grand principle of treating all drug users prior to release from service, but ended up discharging most of them either without treatment or with minimal effect on their drug habit, relieved to be rid of them. Authoritative criticisms of a similar kind has been made by A. Carl Siegel, the psychiatrist who had resigned from the military. Dr. Siegel later provided me with extensive documentation containing firsthand evidence of primitive attitudes, profound confusion and continuing victimization of GIs—as summed up in a comment by a former colleague of his in the program: "I find it most repulsive that the army can trap a man on questionable evidence, stop him from going home, cancel his leave and extension, lock him in a cage for six to eight days, hold him beyond his ETS, strap him to a litter and ship home as an 'addict,' confine in a hospital at home without

As the counterfeit scenario of the American ground war played itself out through 1972, the My Lai atrocity trials did the same back home—and with equal disparity between the public claim of honor maintained and the depth of actual dishonor. After the initial national excitement and multiple confusions of the Calley trial, interest waned as Captain Ernest L. Medina and Colonel Oran K. Henderson were tried and acquitted. In the end twenty-five enlisted men and officers were charged with various offenses related to My Lai, five stood trial, and only Lieutenant Calley was found guilty. Two generals—Samuel W. Koster and George H. Young, Jr., received no more than mild reprimands and were never brought to trial. All this despite the emergence of increasingly detailed documention of the extraordinary web of lies and deceptions around the military cover-up.[9] Few Americans seemed to care—partly because they remained numbed to their country's atrocities, partly because the air war had rendered these events on the ground mildly anachronistic, and partly perhaps because at least some of them sensed that the trials could not deal with the disturbing moral issues raised—with depths of evil and deception that neither conviction nor acquittal could adequately respond to or make go away.

Midst these many-layered corruptions, something palpable was happening to the American military. Without arguing the extent to which the Vietnam War built upon preexisting military corruption, we can turn to an interesting account by a retired Marine

---

leave, kick him out of the army possibly with a bad discharge, disrupt or destroy his family relations, ruin his career, severely limit his prospects for employment, and cast him out into the world branded as some kind of 'fiend'—all under the disguise of a non-punitive, medical type action."

Prior to the panel and subsequent to it as well, I have had much confirmation from people working in military drug programs of the disparity between their essential ineffectiveness and at times virtually total breakdown on the one hand and their public claim of "meeting the problem." In addition, several psychiatrists knowledgeable about the question (including Dr. Zinberg) have privately expressed agreement with my (and Dr. Livingston's) contention that statistics put out by the military on drug issues are decepive and misleading.[8]

Corps Colonel and historian-advocate of the military, Robert D. Heinl, Jr., for a description of the intra-military situation in mid-1971. Entitled "The Collapse of the Armed Forces,"[10] its thesis is set forth in starkest terms:

The morale, discipline and battleworthiness of the U.S. Armed Forces are, with a few salient exceptions, lower and worse than at any time in this century and possibly in the history of the United States.

Heinl goes on to explain:

By every conceivable indicator, our army that now remains in Vietnam is in a state approaching collapse, with individual units avoiding or having refused combat, murdering their officers and noncommissioned officers, drug-ridden, and dispirited where not near-mutinous. . . .

Intolerably clobbered and buffeted from without and within by social turbulence, pandemic drug addiction, race war, sedition, civilian scapegoatise, draftee recalcitrance, malevolence, barracks theft and common crime, unsupported in their travail by the general government, in Congress as well as the executive branch, distrusted, disliked, and often reviled by the public, the uniformed services today are places of agony for the loyal, silent professionals who doggedly hang on and try to keep the ship afloat. . . .

. . . Nowhere . . . in the history of the Armed Forces have comparable past troubles presented themselves in such general magnitude, acuteness, or a concentrated focus as today.

Above all, the military has been *betrayed* by the Vietnam project:

To understand the military consequences of what is happening in the U.S. Armed Forces, Vietnam is a good place to start. It is in Vietnam that the rear guard of a five hundred thousand-man army, in its day (and in the observation of the writer) the best army the United States ever put into the field, is numbly extricating itself from a nightmare war the Armed Forces feel they had foisted on them by bright civilians who are now back on campus writing books about the folly of it all.

For Heinl, what is most outrageous is not so much resistance to fighting but the widespread casualness of that resistance ("It is no big thing to refuse to go") and the helplessness of the Army before it; not so much the widespread fragging but the enthusiasm behind that fragging ("Word of the deaths of officers will bring cheers at troop movies or in bivouacs of certain units"); not so much the antiwar demonstrations within the military, the fasts, and flaunting of peace symbols, as the "booing and cursing of officers and even of hapless entertainers such as Bob Hope"; not so much the fact that 10 to 15 percent of American troops in Vietnam were estimated to be using high-grade heroin but that an Air Force major who was command pilot for Ambassador Bunker was apprehended with eight million dollars' worth of heroin in his aircraft and that "an Air Force regular colonel was court-martialed and cashiered for leading his squadron in pot parties."

Heinl goes on to proclaim his own

. . . awful litany of sedition, dissatisfaction, desertion, race, drugs, breakdowns of authority, abandonment of discipline, and, as a cumulative result, the lowest state of military morale in the history of the country.

He lists the impressive burgeoning of underground GI newspapers, GI dissent organizations, the "nation-wide campus-radical offensive against ROTC," the "antiwar show-biz front organized by Jane Fonda, Dick Gregory and Dalton Trumbo," the sponsorship by Congressman Ronald V. Dellums of Ad Hoc Hearings on "Alleged" American War Crimes in Vietnam—and, worst of all:

. . . the fact that five West Point graduates willingly testified for Dellums suggests the extent to which officer solidarity and traditions against politics have been shattered in today's armed forces.

Heinl is intent upon frightening his military colleagues about how far things have gone, and it is possible that his lurid litany exaggerates here and there. It is also possible that he understates the depth of the military dilemma. What is at stake is not so much the collapse of the American Army in Vietnam, or even the immediate problems of the American Armed Forces in general, but the widespread breakdown of the prevailing American version of the cult of the warrior. Heinl seems to sense that something on this basic level is taking place—hence his reference to West Pointers, men from the heart of the American warrior ethos, who "willingly testify" about the crimes of American warriors. The disturbing truth Heinl avoids facing, however, is the extent to which the American military, literally from top to bottom, has been corrupted by the Vietnam War, and the extent to which that corruption has been perceived, dimly or clearly, by Americans.

Not that Heinl is entirely wrong about the military having had an unpopular war thrust upon it by belligerent irresponsible civilians. But whatever the initial tactical reservations military leaders had about involving the United States in another (post-Korean) war on the Asian mainland, many of these same generals and colonels responded enthusiastically to the mystique of counter-insurgency warfare, have welcomed a chance to "experiment" with new weapons* and have issued constant calls for more troops, more bombings, and expanded war.

Still more corrupting have been the malignant deceptions around military policies—the body count, the free-fire zone, the military targets of the air war. And men whose loyalty to the military, or at least to an honorable version of it, impelled them to reveal these corruptions—such as Colonel Herbert, and in a related way the My Lai survivor—were rejected and ultimately viewed as enemies of the military. Complaining about a bad war

---

* Arthur Fink, of New England Action Research, on the military-industrial complex, for instance, reports attending a meeting of the American Ordnance Association, at which representatives of the military and of industry (essentially the same people) emphasized the value of Vietnam in terms of what we are learning there about weapons. The "experimental" aspects of our use of weaponry there are openly discussed in military and ordnance writings.[11]

while demanding the wherewithal to make it a worse one, the military has presided not only over its own ethical disintegration but over considerable American loss of faith in war and warriors. That is why Heinl's article, originally published in the *Armed Forces Journal,* was most widely circulated by none other than the Peace Education Committee of the American Friends Service Committee, that is, by a peace group.

I could observe some of the workings of this process during a visit (in May, 1971) to the Virginia Military Institute. I had experienced some trepidation at speaking at an institution not only military in nature but with close traditional ties to the Marine Corps and the Southern Confederacy. But I was greeted warmly by two cadets who, after their stiff salute, assured me, almost as stiffly: "Sir! You will find an audience of mostly doves here."

His prediction turned out to be correct. I found many students and faculty there to be not only antiwar but antimilitary as well. Over the next two days the cadets seemed to respond affirmatively, even enthusiastically, to my references to the atrocity-producing situation and other counterfeit features of the war, and also to my general discussion of patterns of transformation taking shape in American society. In contrast, they seemed to have little sympathy for W. W. Rostow, the other keynote speaker, or with either his defense of the war he had contributed so much to or his technological projections for the future. The cadets arranged for a public debate between us, and while I was walking to the building where it was to be held, one of the cadets came running up to me, snapped to attention, and announced breathlessly:

Sir! A number of us have been talking in the barracks, and we wanted to tell you that we hope you'll annihilate him, sir!

To be sure, such a statement has more than a little of the warrior in it, but essentially the antiwar warrior. And before I left, I was informed that only about 10 or 15 percent of the cadet student body planned to stay in the regular military (an unusually small percentage, they said), the rest merely intent upon doing their time before returning to civilian life. Yet most had come to the institution with considerable military enthusiasm, or at the very least some degree of family commitment to the military, only to be profoundly disillusioned by the war and by what they had seen of the military in association with the war. Of course one must be careful about generalizing from the experience: we know that attitudes about war are notoriously labile, and that the military-warrior ethos runs deep. But considering the place and its traditions, we can say that the experience offered evidence of serious questioning from within of at least one American version of the warrior ethos.*

In the article mentioned above, Heinl points out that the troubles he describes in the military "mirror the agonizing divisions and social traumas of American society." The statement is undoubtedly true, but what is not acknowledged is that a major source of these "agonizing divisions" lies in contemporary American war-making, or resistance to that war-making, and to related technicizing and bureaucratizing of the society. Men like Heinl prefer instead to speak of "a crisis of soul and backbone," and to attack permissiveness" not only of society at large, but in the Army and Navy in seeking to "seduce recruits." Their answer is just one word: "discipline." Heinl recalls for us the discipline George Washington imposed to quell outbreaks within the Continental Army "by disarming the Jersey mutineers and having their leaders shot in Hollow Square"; and by the U.S. Navy in 1842 when a mutiny aboard the U.S.S. *Somers* "was quelled when the captain hanged the mutineers from the yardarm while still at sea." It is Heinl who calls forth the wry words of Pogo ("We have met the enemy, and they are us"). But what he identifies as "the enemy" and "us" is what I would call the frail beginning of a new struggle to replace deadly contemporary versions

---

* I have been told of similar manifestations occurring at West Point, though I have no direct knowledge of these.

of the warrior ethos with alternative paths to immortalizing honor and glory. In that sense Vietnam resembles other holocausts in at least holding out the possibility of new visions emerging from the wisdom of survivors.

Consider, for instance, the sequence from, first, Le Jouvencel, based on the memories of a man who fought under the banner of Joan of Arc in the fifteenth century:

It is a joyous thing, is war. . . . you love your comrades so in war. When you see that your quarrel is just and your blood is fighting well, tears rise to your eyes. A great sweet feeling of loyalty and of pity fills your heart. . . .

To Alfred de Vigny's early-nineteenth-century cry of disillusionment with service under Bonaparte, even if that cry turns out to be somewhat ambivalent:*

O dreams of command and slavery! O corrupting thought of power, fit only to deceive children! False enthusiasms! Subtle poisons, who will ever succeed in finding an antidote for you!

To, finally, the lines from a song written and sung by Len Chandler, Jr., in performances at military bases in the United States and abroad as part of the Jane Fonda FTA (Free the Army is the polite version) troupe that so horrified Colonel Heinl:

> First they draft your ass . . .
> Then they drill your ass . . .
> Then they shoot your ass.
> Well they can kiss my ass.
> My ass is mine.
> That's why I'm smiling all the time
> Even when my ass is on the line.
> Because I know they know I know
> My ass is mine.[13]

---

* De Vigny ends up with an expression of admiration bordering on worship for the soldier's uncomplaining "abnegation" and his continuing "honor" in the face of disillusionment and suffering.[12]

While only a small minority of servicemen responded actively to the GI movement with which Chandler and the Fonda troupe have been associated, his words made contact with a vast, free-floating sentiment growing largely out of rebellion against the counterfeit demands of Vietnam. For in Vietnam GIs did indeed begin to insist that "This ass is mine!"—which posed a considerable problem for the military. This problem, however, had a solution.

That solution lay in what is best called numbed warfare. Or as the principle has been well expressed, "Replace men who won't fight with machines that will."[14] Hence the shift in Vietnam from the filth of counterinsurgency warfare on the ground to clean forms of technological warfare conducted mostly from the air, or by means of highly automated air-ground combinations. This timing—the appearance of automated arrangements just when resistance to the human ones became significant*—is undoubtedly considered fortunate by American military authorities but must be viewed as ominous for mankind. In this development the action shifted from Vietnam back to Laos. Fred Branfman, who spent four years in Laos and interviewed both Laotian victims and American pilots, put the matter in perspective:

If Khe Sanh and My Lai were the symbols of American ground intervention during the 1960s, the Plain [of Jars, an area of Laos bombed so heavily that an entire small-scale civilization was destroyed] is the symbol of the automated war of the 1970s.[15]

Those who bomb need not experience the searing inner conflicts of ground troops. With their targets in Laos chosen for them by none other than the American ambassador and the CIA, and their victims totally beyond their vision, theirs was strictly

* This resistance to human arrangements included the increasing disfavor with which the American public came to view the ground war and the various political expressions of that disfavor, even if the resistance has often been all too slow, half-hearted, mixed with numbing.

a 'from-here-to-there' technical job. That is what one of them meant when he told Branfman, "Look, we're just bus drivers." Similarly, Branfman tells of a technician involved in bomb preparation who later came to oppose the war but, when accused of having been a war criminal, answered simply:

I don't *feel* like a war criminal. What I was doing is just like screwing fuses into sockets.

As for guilt, so crucial for ground-war veterans, Branfman explains:

Men are freed from the hatred, doubts, greed or rationalizations that killing usually entails. The issue of guilt becomes meaningless. Conscience and morality are irrelevant. One does not set out to kill and therefore, psychologically, one does not.[16]

Here is the essence of numbed warfare: killing with a near-total separation of act from idea. And in numbed warfare we encounter the most malignant expression of our more general socio-cultural gap between technology and feeling. But is it true that "The issue of guilt becomes meaningless?" I believe it more accurate to say that avoidance of guilt is built into the technology. To call forth guilt, and to achieve an animating relationship to it, requires at least an opportunity and sometimes a concerted effort to reconnect the act and idea of killing.

Precisely that reconnection was made by Jon Floyd, a former Marine Corps pilot, in his testimony at the Winter Soldier Investigation of early 1971:

Anywhere in Vietnam basically is a free drop zone. There were no forbidden targets. If you didn't find any particular targets that you wanted to hit, then normally you'd go ahead and just drop your bombs wherever you want to. . . . This war, from the pilot's standpoint, is a very impersonal war. You go over there and whether or not you believe the goals that the government prescribes for us to fight for or whatever, most of the pilots just go along and figure, well, it's a job. And that's the way we all looked at it. You fly. You see flak at night. That's about as close to war as we get. Sometimes you get shot down, but you don't see any of the explosions. You can look back and see 'em, but you don't see any of the blood or any of the flesh. It's a very clean and impersonal war.

You go out, fly your mission, you come back to your air-conditioned hootch and drink beer or whatever. You're not in contact with it. You don't realize at the time, I don't think, what you're doing. It dawned on me, I think, when we got reports of thirteen-year-old NVA soldiers coming across and being captured; that most probably they had young girls driving most of these trucks that we were destroying up north. And as far as the damage reports that were put out by the pilots, it was a kind of a standard joke . . . among the officers . . . this was just a place to advance your career. They tried to give everyone a command of some sort. They made sure everyone pretty well got a medal. . . . In my unit . . . it was a Distinguished Flying Cross.[17]

The numbed or "impersonal" war does protect participants from guilt. But the war could become "personal"—numbing could give way to animating guilt—by the breakthrough of images of one's victims as sympathetic human beings (in this case dedicated young women and thirteen-year-old-boys) and by accompanying images of the counterfeit nature of one's project (hypocritical use of medals, etcetera). Accessibility to these breakthrough images is, in turn, made possible by the emergence of a collectivity of veterans dedicated to pooling such imagery and giving it shape within a new formulation of their war and their survival.

Always working against that recognition of guilt is the pilot's preoccupation with technical skill and performance. In him the professional's insistence upon 'staying in shape' is intensified by an at least partial awareness of death being the price for failing to do so. As an Air Force officer explained:

When you go down in Laos you don't face a very bright future. So you need motivation to bomb a place like Laos—this turns out to be

mainly professional pride. . . . You become a part of the machine
as you really do it. Guys who fly keep their professionality. That's
why as we phase down here the Air Force will want to bomb. . . . I
haven't bombed now for three months and I really feel out of shape.
The key is to be able to bomb without really thinking about it, automatically, to take evasive action . . . instinctively—to be able to do
this you have to be flying every day.[18]

Branfman found a striking correlation between altitude and
the potential for guilt: B-52 pilots and crews bombing at high
altitudes saw nothing of their victims and spoke exclusively of
professional skill and performance; those on fighter-bomber
missions had glimpses of people below and tended to have an
inclination to explain or rationalize what they did; those who
flew helicopter gunships saw everything and experienced the
kinds of emotions we have described in ground personnel, along
with added passions and conflicts having to do with their special
kind of work.

An example of one sort of justification, by an F-4 pilot in the
second category, was the comment

My way of killing is better than their way. The Pathet [Lao] and
North Vietnamese are a plague. We have to eliminate them. They
have no regard for human life.[19]

Whatever the grotesquely unconscious irony in the statement,
it does connect his own bombing with killing people. And since
imagery associating the two eventually becomes in one way or
another available to all pilots, we may suspect that all of them
possess at least a measure of potential, over time, for experiencing animating guilt.

That potential, however, is always muted by the numbed warrior's technologically induced obliviousness towards his victims:

American atrocities in Laos are . . . not so much inhuman as ahuman.
The people of Na Nga and Nong Saa were not the object of anyone's
passion. They simply weren't considered. What is most striking

about American bombing in Laos is the lack of animosity felt by the killers to their victims. Most of the Americans involved have little if any knowledge of Laos or its people. Those who do rather like them. . . . That American policy-makers have been capable of such destruction is due less to baseness of motive than vastness of resources. It is not the men who have changed, but rather their technology.[20]

Numbed warfare, then, is conducted within a self-enclosed system: one's only psychological contacts are with military cohorts and with one's equipment. Lacking emotional relationship with his victims, the numbed warrior receives from them very little of the kind of feedback that could permit at least one layer of his mind to perceive them as human. He does not, therefore, require a dehumanizing gook syndrome since, psychologically speaking, no one is there to render into a gook.

Number warfare follows its own self-enclosed imperatives. One of these we have already seen as that of professionality, maintaining high standards of skilled performance function. Another has to do with what Ralph Lapp has called the "technological imperative": the strongly felt impulse to make active use of any technology that is available. Thus Branfman points out that systematic destruction of Laotian villages dates from the November 1968 bombing halt over North Vietnam, which freed hundreds of bombers for Laos. There was no special activity of Pathet Lao forces or any other strategic reason for a bombing escalation, but, as the American Ambassador told Branfman:

You gotta understand, Fred—we had all those planes coming in to Laos. What could we do? We had to bomb villages.[21]

Another self-enclosed imperative of numbed warfare is intra-service competition for "program funds." This competition encourages falsifications in the truck count, the air version of the body count, which purports to record the number of enemy vehicles destroyed. And there is the related imperative, again parallel to the ground situation, of atrocity stimulating further atrocity—of a circle of atrocity in which escalating one's bombing can strengthen the illusion of appropriate (even ennobling) warfare, and thereby help one avoid recognition that one is mainly victimizing civilians and that the project is ineffectual since enemy supplies are still getting through.

As a result, in a small, technically backward country in which there have been no American ground forces to support and extremely few industrial or military targets of any significance, over two million tons of bombs (by conservative estimate) were dropped on the one million people of the Pathet Lao zones—as much tonnage as was absorbed by several hundred million people throughout both Europe and the entire Pacific theater during all of World War II.[22] Nor was any substantial popular support for that bombing and the prior (and later) bombing of North Vietnam sought on the home front:

Information about the air war is as ethereal as the atmosphere itself. . . . since there are no tales of atrocities and few pictures of the bombing, domestic reaction to its more questionable moral aspects is muted.[23]

Concerning the bombing of Laos, most senators and congressmen remained in ignorance while the Plain of Jars, where fifty thousand people formerly thrived, was destroyed: "An entire society has been wiped off the face of the earth and no one in this country knew about it."[24]

One begins to understand the extent of the numbed warrior's dissociation from events outside of his self-enclosed system by contrasting the desensitized pronouncement of one of them*—

Sure, some of the villages get bombed, there's no other way to fight a war out here, for God's sake. . . .

---

* Significantly, he was not a pilot but the USAID Refugee Relief Chief of Vientiane, capital of Cambodia. Numbed warriors can also, of course, be officials or bureaucrats, whether back home or in the field.

All refugees talk about the bombing. They don't like [it]. But even if you found an example in which it was proven conclusively that houses were bombed, so what?[25]

with two Laotian refugees-survivors' direct descriptions, and reactions to, what actually happened:

This village woman was a person of good character. . . . Why did she have to die so pitifully? She died in the middle of the forest beside the cow she tended . . . in misfortune with unsurpassed sadness. . . . The airplanes truly killed the people at a time when we knew nothing about what was going on. They came to do this, why? When you see this, how do you feel about your own brothers and sisters and relatives? Would you not be angry and concerned? Compare our hearts to yours. And what are we to do?

In the year 1967, my village built small shelters in the forest and we had holes in the bamboo thicket on top of the hill. It was a place to which we could flee. But there were two brothers who went out to cut wood in the forest. The airplanes shot them and both brothers died. Their mother and father had just these two sons and were both in the same hole with me. I think with much pity about this old father and mother who were like crazy people because their children had died.[26]

Laos has also been the site, as has South Vietnam, of the advanced electronic air-ground constellation known as the "Automated Battlefield." While as yet far from perfected and often erratic in performance, the Automated Battlefield has enormous significance for the changing psychology of war. The principle is that of an all-embracing system of electronic circuitry, which renders the area of fighting "a manless, foolproof, giant lethal pinball machine out of which no living thing could ever escape."[27]

On the Ho Chi Minh Trail in Laos, for instance, there has been a project known as "Igloo White," in which acoustic and seismic sensors—devices highly sensitive to sound and vibrations—have been placed in long spears flung from high-speed aircraft and

stuck into the ground in series. The radio-connected micro-
phones, dropped near the spears by parachute, record information from the sensors and transmit it to a surveillance plane
flying in the area which, in turn, relays the signals to a ground
control station. After being fed into a computer, the information
is evaluated by "skilled target analysts" who decide whether it
suggests enemy forces, friendly troops, trucks, animals, or whatever. If the decision is enemy troops, an air strike is set in
motion. "War has gone electronic. Laos has been bugged," is
one commentator's summary of the arrangement.

The only awareness of "the enemy" comes from electronic
feedback in the form of "blips" on a screen. One cannot even
speak of the process of victimization described earlier in connection with the gook syndrome, since that process requires the
psychological work of turning a human enemy into an ahuman
victim. Here, from the beginning, they are nothing but blips,
and, in the words of the same commentator, "A blip is worse than
a gook." Moreover, such a battlefield, with its amorphous electronic structure as well as its association with the full repertoire
of American military-industrial technology, can extend indefinitely over geographical and temporal boundaries, so that "no
one exactly knows where the battlefield begins or ends."[28]

The various names chosen for the systems and component
devices—Sensors, Gravel, Grasshopper, Walleye, Black Crow,
Comfy Bee, Puff the Magic Dragon—serve to domesticate them
by means of an aberrant mixture of humor and play. They lend
an Orwellian character of words meaning their opposites (war
is peace), since "Generally, the more innocuous the code name,
the more deadly the weapon."[29] By thus eliminating as completely as possible the human element, not only the battlefield
but the psychological relationship to it—numbing itself—is
"automated."

The Lieutenant Calleys of war will be left home—if a drone helicopter is ordered by a computer to strike at a sensor post being
passed by children and water buffaloes, it means there has been *an*

error in information, not in law or conscience—a court martial cannot try a manless helicopter, nor can a chain of command be easily recognized in a more modern form of organization where only machines can be held responsible for their own actions.[30]

Such an event would certainly be slaughter, but it would not be called an atrocity. It would not even in fact be referred to as a "false alarm" since that phrase, as a military spokesman made clear when testifying before a Senate Committee, "has been stricken from the vocabulary."[31] Rather, it would be a "nontargetable activation." There would be no blood or death for anybody—except the people caught in or "picked up by" the circuitry. Everyone else, warriors included, would "watch war on television." Whatever lingering sense war permits of cause-and-effect, of connection between victimizer and victim, now disappears.

Nobody will be able to tell what or who has been killed, or why the computer ordered the bombs dropped on a specific piece of real estate.[32]

We arrive at an ultimate expression of what Masao Maruyama has called "the system of nonresponsibility."*

To be sure, there is still room for the gung-ho pilot who, in defying death and gravity, re-creates the image of the World War II-style immortal pilot-hero. There is also room for the playful American-boy tinkerer, joyously and lovingly blending with his machines and dials, which he finds much more manageable and knowable than either the rest of himself or other people. And there is room for the ideological purist, for whom the sensor-

---

* Maruyama attributed this process to certain psychological and institutional patterns in Japanese society, involving a "sharing of responsibility" to the point of dissolving all individual relationship to responsibility.[33] But here the "sharing" and "dissolving" are built into the technology: it, the machine—or simply the circuitry—is "responsible." Numbed warfare ultimately depends upon both technological and institutional arrangements to maintain its separation of human actions and human consequences.

airplane-computer constellation is a means of disinfecting the
environment, eliminating the communist "plague." But the psychological type most sought by this new form of numbed warfare
is that of the technicist-perfectionist, the man (or woman) who
can be depended upon to perform consistently and with precision
the required tasks, confine himself completely to the self-enclosed
electronic world around him, and embrace his electronic technology to the exclusion of any potentially disrupting ethical questions. While technical-intellectual challenges undoubtedly exist
for those engaged in this form of automated warfare, it requires
of them, most fundamentally, a sustained stance of selective,
professional numbing, that is achieved merely by blending
smoothly with technological and institutional arrangements.

How much further, psychologically speaking, can one travel
from the image of the warrior-hero who, with his superhuman
skill, strength, and courage in battle conquers death and immor-
talizes himself and his people? Consider the following complaint
of an F-4 pilot stationed in Da Nang in South Vietnam and flying
regular missions over Laos:

One day we went in over a North Vietnamese military camp [in
Laos] on top of a mountain. It was right out in the open, so we
could see it and everything. We plastered the place, napalm, five
hundred-pounders, the works. I know we had kills, you could see
people running all over the place, buildings burning. There was no
way for there to be no KIA [killed in action]. But do you know what
happened? The grunts came in and reported twenty-five enemy killed
by ground fire. All they did was shoot their M-16s into the corpses
and then claim they'd killed them. The nerve. Can you imagine. . . .
The fuckin' grunts are stealing our kills.[34]

We recognize in this grotesque complaint an inverted quest,
within the counterfeit universe of Vietnam, for honor and recognition. That quest, on the part of a man caught at a technological
half-way point (he could see enough to be reasonably certain

that he "had kills" but not well enough to make a definite count) took the form of intraproject competition over technology versus human effectiveness.

Consider also the following vision—something on the order of a military man's macabre equivalent of Martin Luther King's "I have a dream":

I see battlefields or combat areas that are under twenty-four-hour . . . surveillance of all types. I see battlefields on which we can destroy anything we can locate through instant communications and the almost instantaneous application of highly lethal fire power. . . . Hundreds of years were required to achieve the mobility of the armored division. A little over two decades later we had the air-mobile division. With cooperative effort, no more than 10 years should separate us from the Automated Battlefield.[35]

This 'dream' of General W. C. Westmoreland, the man most identified with the American military effort in Vietnam, differs from King's in being more realistic and closer to realization. We can only agree with Dickson and Rothchild that before long descriptions of battlefield victories and defeats "will be indistinguishable from those used in second-level electronics textbooks" and that "modern war stories will be confused with circuit diagrams."[36]

But who, then, will emerge as the new warrior-heroes? the designers of the circuits? the technicians who run the electronic system? the "skilled target analysts" who read the "electronic tracks"?

Or can one find an answer in the strange parable of the "people sniffers"? The latter are sensors that detect human presence by means of organic odors. But in Vietnam, where "people sniffers" have been used, the NLF has devised a counter-measure: hanging urine-filled containers in trees, thereby confounding the electronic system. In this mocking defiance of the electronic system, one would seem to find confirmation (as one has throughout the Vietnam War) of the black power-Third World slogan:

"The power of the people is stronger than the Man's technology." More precisely, though, this 'parable of piss-power' is a metaphor of the absurdity of high technology employed as a military replacement for ennobling human goals—a mocking of any claim on the part of the numbed warrior to the mantle of the warrior hero.

Yet even as the technicists reach their spiritual dead end in Vietnam, their technology continues to take on apocalyptic dimensions. The electronic battlefield turns out to be fallible, and with the withdrawal of American ground troops, less applicable, but the escalated air war becomes ever more automated. "Smart bombs," guided to targets by television or laser beams, are employed with increasing effect by psychically 'dumb' (or ethically numb) technicians; fighter-bombers, with their automatically activated fire power, destroy enemy missiles with less and less human intervention; and we hear of the first unmanned bomber planes, doubtless to appear in large numbers before too long. While all this technology may, in turn, reveal its own vulnerabilities, only the most romantic of revolutionaries can be certain that the "power of the people" will always be able to defeat it, at least in a military sense.

As autonomous technology fills the psychohistorical void left by the demise of the traditional cult of the warrior, technicists joyously welcome the shift: "Even the bravest and most skillful of old-fashioned warrior-heroes were humanly fallible," they tell us. "Our automated devices give us fewer problems, are more efficient." And, however absurdly, those who create or wield the technology of destruction offer themselves to us as new technological heroes.

With these prospects before us, a full memory of My Lai, indeed of the entire Vietnam experience, takes on crucial importance—as does the transformation of a significant minority of American survivors of Vietnam into antiwar warriors. For such memories contain human-centered images that illuminate our capacity for both murder and its renunciation—precisely the kinds of images and illumination increasingly denied us by the ahuman mechanisms of numbed warfare.

Increasing automation renders the war ever more inseparable from American society as a whole. As we hear endlessly of new or newly revealed horrors associated with our high technology— the "smart bombs" mentioned above, the mining of harbors, the bombing of dikes and dams and seeding of clouds, which could combine to produce flood disaster and starvation of enormous dimensions, and burning of forests—we are less and less able to distinguish these events and images from the society and culture responsible for them. For this malignant technicism to be put to use there must be a functional equilibrium between the Vietnam battlefield and American society, with such mutual stimulation and reinforcement that the counterfeit universe of the one begins to merge with some equivalent in the other. Then, when we speak of "truth at the source," that "source" becomes America and Americans, whether in Vietnam or the United States.

The massive psychic numbing associated with that equilibrium is no mere passive reaction to the use of military technology. Rather we must speak of insistent, indeed aggressive forms of numbing, related in turn to an all-pervading (in Daniel Ellsberg's phrase) "need not to know." Only by such a mechanism can we explain the bizarre uses of our society's high technology: giant computers, sophisticated sensors and infra-red devices tracking down peasant-farmers no less than the small trucks ostensibly sought; complex anti-personnel bombs scattering their deadly fragments into the tissues and organs of children and other by-standers in ways that render these fragments undetectable even by X-ray; laser-guided bombs and missiles dropped on buffalo and primitive huts or rice storehouses, or possibly on obscure figures most likely to be ordinary villagers.

Behind this aggressive numbing, or in various ways associated with it, we sense a new form of victimizing impulse. Technological omnipotence and collective immortality are reinforced by brutalizing technologically backward people who are seen as non-human, even death-tainted, and therefore fair game, because of their very lack of technology. What has resulted is the first example, in Laos, of a military situation consisting almost entirely of bombardment of populated areas, where there are no ground troops to support or to coordinate with in pursuit of any specific goals.

A conversation between a pilot and an Air Force information officer suggests some of the currents that feed the functional equilibrium and aggressive numbing we have been discussing:

PILOT: Our five hundred-pound nape cannisters are newer, they have a better dispersal pattern than the older one thousand-pounders.
INFORMATION OFFICER: Hey, you're not supposed to talk about the napalm.
PILOT: No shit. Why not?
INFORMATION OFFICER: Well, you know those college kids. Pretty soon they're going to get poor Dow Chemical out of business.
PILOT: It seems pretty ridiculous for people to get so emotional about how you kill people. What's so bad about nape anyway?[37]

The aggressive numbing is also promoted by Madison Avenue. Glossy advertisements feature electronic battlefields in military journals, with such slogans as "A-7 makes ground movement after dark a nightmare" or "turns night into day;" or "You can be sure if it's Westinghouse."[38] Nor should we be surprised that General Westmoreland's new military vision turns out to be, the old civilian principle of factory economy:

Today, machines and technology are permitting economy of man-power on the battlefield, as indeed they are in the factory. But the future offers even more possibilities for economy. I am confident the American people expect this country to take full advantage of its technology—to welcome and applaud the developments that will re-place wherever possible the man with the machine.[39]

We encounter here more than mere economy; we have nothing less than a military extension of salvation through technology.

No wonder this mode of winding down the war has been described (not by an antiwar activist but by a highly decorated active-duty officer) as "a public relations man's dream." The sequence of man/machine is another example of the functional equilibrium between Vietnam and America, the further merging of counterfeit universes there and here, and the re-enmeshment of the American people in the war's falsehoods, just as they had begun to show signs of extricating themselves.

Hannah Arendt, discussing official deceptions revealed in the Pentagon Papers, emphasizes the "fragility" of "factual truths," their dependence upon "testimony to be remembered and trustworthy witnesses." Where truth is painful, falsehood and deception are constant temptations "since the liar has the great advantage of knowing beforehand what the audience wishes or expects to hear."[40] But the kind of numbed warfare we have been discussing makes lying still easier: if you do not *feel* the actuality of events, you can deny it or replace it with untruths without, psychologically speaking, telling a lie. We recognize this as the same malignant paradox as when one "kills" but does "not kill," as from high altitudes. Lying and killing are coordinate—necessary to each other and both rendered painless by the broken symbolic connections of numbed warfare.

With actuality not only distanced but psychologically undernourished, lies, deceptions, and self-deceptions can readily come to feel truer than truth. The habit of deception takes on an actuality of its own. Those caught in the habit may alter or modify the deception as a means, so to speak, of protecting it—can admit that the war is not good (thereby partially abandoning the vision of immortalizing purpose) but escalate it in the name of ending it. The forms of resistance that are most bitterly contested are those that threaten to expose and break through American numbing and related "truer-than-truth" lies—such actions as Daniel Ellsberg and Anthony Russo's release of the Pentagon Papers,

Philip and Daniel Berrigan's destruction of Selective Service files, James Douglass' pouring of his own blood on secret air-war files at Hickam Field in Honolulu, and the various demonstrations of mock warfare on the part of the Vietnam Veterans Against the War. Putting aside the arguable legal issues involved in these actions, we should notice the government's panicky overreactions. There have been conspiracy trials (of mostly Catholic activists at Harrisburg, Pennsylvania, and antiwar veterans at Gainesville, Florida) contrived around government-manipulated informers, impostors, and *provocateurs*, so that the counterfeit universe of Vietnam extended directly into the courtroom; continued harassment of resisters, so that men imprisoned for homicide or armed robbery have a better chance for parole than those found guilty of raiding draft boards. Six months after the disclosure of the Pentagon Papers we learn that the Pentagon has "suppressed a study by the Rand Corporation that concluded that high ideological motivation was behind Vietcong successes" and "implied that the policy of Vietnamizing the war was futile and contradicted the thesis favored by the United States Government that terror tactics were responsible for the communist victories."*[41] The action of Douglass and his two companions of the "Hickam 3" has special significance as the first major act of civilian resistance directed specifically at the air war. They sought to dramatize and, as Americans, take responsibility for the importance of Hickam Field and Hawaii in the planning and operation of the entire American air war—contrasting it with the public image of Hawaii as a "tropical paradise."[42] Significantly, the Air Force's reluctance to reveal the contents of the bloodied files resulted in a minimal effort at prosecution and minimal sentences.

* The Pentagon acknowledged the existence of the report but, "Officials refused to comment further." The study in question was performed by Anthony Russo, whose continuing protests, including a demonstration held right at Rand Corporation, finally led to the study's release. But the way in which the release was accomplished—the report's appearance in an extremely obscure government document—was calculated to keep it in maximum obscurity.

The next counterfeit criterion for winding down the war was the increasingly small number of weekly American deaths. It received the same emphasis that the Vietnamese body count had formerly received and bears an interesting relationship to the earlier figure. The emphases were reversed. The enemy body count, at first an achievement and therefore inflated, became, in the absence of troops, played down. The large number of Americans killed had been muted and understated,* but was subsequently given great emphasis when the government could claim weekly totals of ten or less. But the later criterion, like the earlier, is an expression of malignant technicism: figures (however corrupt) would "count" as a means of justifying slaughter. In place of a grotesque preoccupation with Vietnamese dead, we find an equally grotesque loss of interest in Vietnamese being killed, since their very high numbers (particularly if one recorded dead civilians as we did so promiscuously in the ground-war body count) would directly expose the Orwellian winding down of the war. The critical point is the official insistence upon a death-centered number that lies about killing.

Can we apply the concept of integrity we have described for individuals to an entire society? Not directly, since there are too many divergent groups and subgroups, and one must be wary of equating individual and collective psychological experience. Still, there is a sense in which the integrity of a nation is constantly judged and felt, by outsiders as well as by its own people, around images parallel to those of individual psychology. These feelings and images have to do with general intactness and cohesion, relative harmony, ethical behavior of a government toward its own and other people, and emanations of decency, hope, and community, as opposed to those of destructiveness, disintegration, and hopelessness. To be sure, none of these images

---

* These distortions include not counting men who die from combat wounds soon after being evacuated from Vietnam or from various technological (or vehicular) accidents not directly part of combat but clearly a product of our Vietnam presence.

are absolute or pure; nor can we build precise psychohistorical theory around the principle of integrity alone. Yet we can note the striking suddenness with which perceptions of America, held by Americans and others, have shifted from the first category (intactness, decency, hope) to the second (destructiveness, dis-integration, hopelessness). Or when these images have not so clearly shifted, a good deal of psychic energy has been expended warding off the shift, often with loud claims to the integrity that has been lost.

Of course Vietnam is hardly the sole cause of this shift. The war is as much a product as a cause. To consider the source of some of this negative imagery, one need only examine the vast problematic pantheon of American social struggles—whether having to do with race, recession and unemployment, poverty, crime, drugs, personal services, the structure of cities, the func-tion of rural areas, morale among workers, professionals, and civil servants . . . and just about everything else. The larger crisis has to do with more fundamental psychohistorical dislo-cation, around no longer viable psychic symbols and forms in general and around technology in particular, and with the in-adequacy of our entire institutional structure as now constituted for coping with unprecedented historical forces.

Yet Vietnam is central to this breakdown of national integrity, whether as cause, effect, or, in most cases, both. I do not mean simply the war's exacerbation of ethnic or racial conflicts, or its ruinous effects on our economy, or for that matter the ways in which our form of high-technology capitalism has helped to create and maintain the war, but rather the extent to which the Indo-china War has blanketed these and related problems in an aura of negativity, ill will, corruption, and numbing, so that, in the shadow of that war, no problem can seem decently soluble.

What is generally called a "credibility gap" between American leaders (especially the two Indochina-war Presidents) and the people becomes, more fundamentally, the extension of the war's counterfeit universe to the entire national polity. Of course not everybody would put it that way, and war-linked leaders continue to exert enormous influence on the American people precisely by helping them to avoid confronting the war's unpleasant truths. But underneath that influence is the terror of disintegration—as suggested, for instance, in the remarkable finding that

forty-seven percent of the [American] people—almost one in every two *and a majority of those with an opinion*—now believe that the unrest is likely to lead to "a real breakdown in this country." [emphasis mine][43]

Whatever one's explanation of this sense of impending national breakdown—quite possibly more people would blame radicals, college students, women, or blacks, than Vietnam or domestic injustice or outmoded American institutions or unprecedented historical developments. But there is no denying Americans' widespread feeling, sometimes overt and sometimes partly underground, that their society ceases to adhere, and that the Indochina War has much to do with that process of social disintegration. The universal imagery of betrayal mentioned earlier extends itself in large numbers of people from all groups—the young, the aged, blacks, women, white ethnics, "wasps," middle Americans —into a sense of being 'torn apart,' even "unhinged." We may thus speak of a collective sense of lost honor and integrity, a radical impairment in immortalizing visions of enduring meaning and ethical substance—visions that all lasting civilizations must maintain and draw upon for their nurturing imagery.

Precisely that sense of lost honor and integrity was responsible for the national fury around Lieutenant Calley, a case that seems to haunt this book as it does American society. For whether one thought Calley a scapegoat for his military and civilian superiors (as did many Americans, whatever their views on the war itself), a guilty murderer (a position again held by divergent people, including many who also thought him a scapegoat), or a national hero (here one had to be a kind of hawk who insisted upon viewing all American killing as glorious)—however one felt about Calley, one shared with virtually all Americans the sense that the Americans' immortal national-cultural substance had in some fundamental way been compromised. This was true whether one considered the source of this compromised integrity to be the actions of Calley (and possibly of his military superiors, extending right on up to the White House), or in the prosecution of Calley (an American soldier doing his duty) rather than his glorification. Correspondingly, people who held all of these positions were bent upon reasserting standards of integrity: by condemning Calley individually for his violation of proper military-ethical standards; by exposing the atrocity-producing situation of the war in general and viewing Calley's action as epitomizing that situation (my own attempt at the time); by a combination of cynicism and rationalization that permits one to accept Calley's behavior ("war is war") without acknowledging any taint on American honor; or by a total reversal of actuality and imagery in which Calley emerges as a great American war-hero who performed noble deeds on the battlefield (for example, the song introduced at the time, "The Battle Hymn of Lieutenant Calley") and thereby enhanced American honor.

These questions of integrity are further confused by the technological distancing of numbed warfare. Calling forth principles of integrity requires acts of moral imagination about events that take place far away "out there" and "up there." And the difficulty of that psychic task is further aggravated by the strange American situation of being able to annihilate but not defeat a tiny enemy. The same President who was so skillful at the war-related public relations dream worries about America being made into a "pitiful helpless giant"—and with good reason because that is precisely the image we have of ourselves. Some years earlier I had used a related perception in describing America-in-Vietnam as a blind giant loosing his technology of destruction on a people he is unable and unwilling to see—that is, to understand or acknowledge as human beings whose psychological and historical needs and inclinations are not encompassed by our anti-communist and technicist ideology.[44] Increasing technicizing of the war makes certain that the people we kill are outside of our immediate and imaginative vision. And this overall combination of blind killing and equally blind ethical disintegration is behind the all too telling accusation, made mostly by her young critics, that America is on a "death trip."

Rather than acknowledge these manifestations of disintegration, the society seeks to cover them over by an embrace of technology, an affirmation of the technological mode of immortality around ever new forms of weaponry. We learn much by taking another look at the automated battlefield, this time as it operates not in the field of combat but inside the walls of the United States Senate. The key document here is "Investigation Into Electronic Battlefield Program," hearings before the Electronic Battlefield Subcommittee of the Preparedness Investigating Subcommittee of the Committee on Armed Forces, United States Senate, November 18, 19, and 24, 1971.[45]

The hearings featured electronic demonstrations of the latest weapons systems, but even before these began Senator Goldwater expressed his anticipatory excitement: "I personally think it has the possibility of being one of the greatest steps forward in warfare since gun powder." The actual demonstrations and explanations by military representatives evoked similar enthusiasm, as far as one can tell, among all senators present. The transcript conveys a sense of great fascination, renewed power, and pride restored: "We may be fighting a dirty, unwinnable war in Vietnam, but look what we now have—extraordinary machine-circuits that can wipe out any enemy with no American losses."

Military representatives, some of whom had used the equipment in Vietnam, employed elaborate audio-visual aids in order to illustrate their descriptions of what the new weaponry could do. One slide, for instance, portrays a Night Hawk helicopter attack during which, the transcript tells us

323 additional enemy were killed and 10 live prisoners taken. I had to move two additional bulldozers up to the area to bury the dead.

So filled with boyish enthusiasm for gadgetry and efficient machinery were the senators' responses that the taint and corruption of Vietnam seemed to give way to a kind of childlike innocence.

But the process runs deep: technology can be deified in this way because its precision and enduring stability contrast so sharply with our will-o'-the wisp human confusions, and provide an awesome mode of immortality at a time when existing modes are under question. The nostalgia we have observed for the gadgets and games of innocent childhood can be very much a part of the equation, as can a broader psychohistorical *image of restoration*,[46] in which the technology will somehow help to recover an imagined past of total harmony. This combination of deification of technology and strong restorationist imagery is consistent with some of the social attitudes of the enthusiastic senators at the hearing (notably those of Senator Goldwater), and with general principles I have been able to elaborate in other studies. What is dangerous in this alliance of restorationist and technicist imagery is the possibility it provides for romanticizing numbed warfare. Through it numbed warriors might even take on some of the innocence or even purity of the knight-in-armor of the past.

Buttressed by that alliance, war makers can mount their counterattack against people (certain ones) who bring the bad news of the breakdown of the American warrior ethos and of the ethical disintegration of American society. They are denounced not only as "effete snobs" (meaning overprivileged, bookish, weak, and unmanly) but as disruptive elements who "belittle our country and its institutions" and spread "negative attitudes" and "despair and a feeling of hopelessness about the future."[47] The enemy becomes not the war nor even the North Vietnamese or the NLF but those Americans who respond sufficiently to the actuality of the war to make negative judgments. Technicized nostalgia is invoked in the service of a national prescription of massive psychic numbing and hollow pseudo-integrity.

Yet despite all, Vietnam ghosts will not be laid. They appear in the form of thousands of veterans returning without limbs, and hundreds of thousands, or even millions, with the unresolved if not unresolvable pain, conflict, and the bitterness of the betrayed. They appear also in the form of Vietnamese survivors, whose voices are just dimly beginning to be heard by Americans,[48] bearing witness to the suffering we have caused. And they will continue to appear, above all, in memories and images concerning death and the dead, images that will not easily lend themselves either to healthy absorption or a meaningful survivor formulation.

There is in fact a genuine psychological sense in which confronting the war, at least for Americans, is a question of corpses:

. . . each body in its casket is to have, at all times, a body escort. . . . an effort has been made to find an escort whose personal involvement with the deceased or presence with the family of the deceased will be of comfort and aid. Your mission as a body escort is as follows: To make sure the body is afforded, at all times, the respect due a fallen soldier of the United States Army. Specifically it is as follows: 1) To check the tags on the caskets at every point of departure. 2) To insist, if the tags indicate the remains as non-viewable, that the relatives not view the body. Remember that non-viewable means exactly that—non-viewable. . . .[49]

These are official military instructions to "body escorts." One could say that the military is being sensitive to family survivors' feelings by insisting that they not view severely mangled corpses of sons and husbands. But the larger symbolism of these instructions lies in the general collusion—asked for by the military and acceded to by civilian society—in turning away from the actualities of war, in keeping the corpses "non-viewable." I recall a veteran's skeptical comment about the possible impact of a videotaped discussion we were about to initiate: "The only way Americans could begin to understand what this war is would be for them to have to see a few corpses right in front of them."

Perhaps no society is capable of taking more than a passing glance at its corpses, actual or metaphorical. Yet there are indications of some members of American society doing a little more than that, beginning to "view"—even *see* and *feel* those corpses —and thereby to open themselves to truth and the possibility of renewal.

That kind of constructive corpse-viewing involves taking a hard look at such questions as the operation of the warrior ethos in Vietnam and the morality of killing or dying there (in the service of one's country) as opposed to refusing to do either (in the service of conscience and what one takes to be more universal principles).* The active discussion of amnesty for exiles and convicted draft resisters, and less frequently for "self-retired veterans" (deserters) as well, suggests that some of these issues are at least being raised. Amnesty in this sense means legal forgiveness, and various kinds of partial amnesty have been granted after each of America's major wars. But the whole issue of amnesty has unique significance for *this* war—because of the unprecedented numbers of young men to whom it might apply (sometimes estimated as close to one hundred thousand), and because of the equally unprecedented intensity of moral revulsion the war has caused among significant segments of those asked to fight it. Amnesty can be viewed, of course, as a psychologically superficial matter, but it can also cut deeply into war-linked mystifications having significance far beyond Vietnam.

Politically, ethically, legally, and psychologically, amnesty is replete with paradox. We can hardly be surprised that amnesty is strongly opposed by those who have most actively pursued or supported the war, along with those who have simply never seriously questioned it. This group stresses the importance of men subsuming themselves, without question, to the laws and demands of their country (equated with its government), and

---

* Willard Gaylin, by entitling his sympathetic study of draft resisters, "In Service of Their Country,"[50] was making the point that the polarity of country versus conscience is a false one since refusing this war better served both.

"paying back their debt" for privileges enjoyed. The argument, in effect, contrasts the courage, self-sacrifice, and responsibility of warriors who fought, with the weakness, unmanliness, and selfishness of draft-dodgers and "expatriots" who, literally or figuratively, ran away from that responsibility. The argument has far-reaching echoes in conventional patriotism, as Richard Nixon well understood when, during the recent Presidential campaign, he spoke of amnesty as "the most immoral thing I can think of,"[51] and reassured the bearer of an anti-amnesty poster:* "Don't worry about that amnesty . . . never, never will we grant amnesty."[52] And an earlier statement of Vice President Agnew suggests some of the rage and indeed victimizing impulse that can accompany this anti-amnesty position:

> . . . as for these deserters, malcontents, radicals, incendiaries, the civil and the uncivil disobedients among our youth, SDS, PLP, Weathermen I and Weathermen II, the revolutionary action movement, the Black United Front, Yippies, Hippies, Yahoos, Black Panthers, Lions and Tigers alike—I would swap the whole damn zoo for a single platoon of the kind of young Americans I saw in Vietnam.[53]

Yet appearing to join the war-makers and war-supporters in opposition to amnesty is a group at the opposite end of the war-peace spectrum, which includes many of the very exiles and convicted resisters who would ostensibly be the beneficiaries of that amnesty. For them amnesty becomes no more than an extension of the American-created counterfeit universe: the war-criminals self-righteously "forgiving" those who had possessed

---

* The poster was apparently carried by the parents of a GI killed in Vietnam, suggesting the extent to which survivor significance can be sought around this kind of imagery. It must also be said that President Nixon has been far from consistent on the subject. On another occasion he said that he "would be very liberal with regard to amnesty" after all Americans have left Vietnam and the POWs have been returned, though even then he added that any such amnesty "would have to be on a basis of their paying the price . . . that anyone should pay for violating the law."

sufficient personal integrity and moral imagination to refuse the criminal venture. On most issues the two groups could not be greater antagonists, but what they have in common is a rejection of amnesty as a glossing over of issues surrounding the war, of amnesty as " 'sop' to the liberal," a phrase used by an imprisoned resister[54] but one which also could have been expressed by a war enthusiast. For the word "amnesty" carries the meaning of forgetting and even oblivion, or in a political sense, "a general overlooking or pardon of past offenses by the ruling authority"— all this suggested in its Greek roots, *amnestia* and *amnestos*, meaning "forgetfulness" and "not to remember."[55] But "remembering" is, for each of these groups, an imperative, a matter of honor. Where they differ is in just what should be remembered, and in where honor lies.

For the first group (of war-supporters and conventional patriots) honor lies in the warrior ethos itself as expressed by the American socialized warrior, in serving the nation within this ethos to the point of giving one's life, if necessary, for the stated cause. For the second group (war-resisters) honor lies in the personal risk and sacrifice one undergoes in resisting precisely that ethos and the immoral 'call' associated with it, on behalf of an alternative ethos, however dimly perceived, of peace and social justice. What both groups reject is the original psychopolitical principle around *amnestia* or "law of Oblivion," according to which "no man should be called in question nor troubled for things that were past," and the likelihood that "by mutual amnesty men avoid seeing the real drift of each other's statements."[56]

And it may well be that the amnesty favored by a growing coalition of liberals, radicals, and conservatives contains some of that forgetfulness and oblivion of the past and the war, a desire to be humane and let bygones be bygones. Yet another meaning is, or at least can be, involved. In general historical practice, amnesty has meant the granting of a pardon to rebels by the government in power. The latter, secure in its overall hegemony, welcomes those who have opposed it and its principles back to the fold. But in the present case one can say that the rebels, though politically weak, have come to possess something very close to national *moral* hegemony. That is, the resisters' claim that the war is evil, even criminal, has taken considerable hold on the country, at least to the extent of most Americans (even those who have opposed the more militant resisters) viewing it as in one way or another "wrong."* Amnesty, in this second meaning we are pursuing, could serve to recognize (and in Buber's term) "confirm" this moral hegemony—or at least recognize and confirm the profound ethical value of committed resistance to this war. If then accompanied by a significant national debate on war responsibility—a very big if, to be sure—amnesty could even serve as a point of major political-psychological breakthrough in the nation's critique of its own warrior ethos. But amnesty in that spirit could be granted only by leaders not given to blindly conventional reiterations of the warrior ethos,† or to seemingly expedient glossing over of fundamental issues— that is, by leaders who, either through their own evolving opposition to the war or (much more rarely) through genuine personal transformations not unlike those described in this book, are

---

* It is true, of course, that many among the majority that came to oppose the war did so because of the war's inconvenience, its not being worth its price, rather than because of its immorality per se. But any such either/or division of reasons for opposing the war undoubtedly oversimplifies. My sense of the matter is that, despite widespread American numbing, moral repugnance toward the war did seep through the society and, directly or indirectly, played a more important part than many commentators (and public-opinion polls) acknowledged in turning the country against the war.

† I will not try to discuss the complicated psychological issues resisters face around amnesty, though some of these—its aura of hypocrisy and corruption as opposed to its powerful attraction—have already been suggested. It is worth pointing out, however, that a resister's ultimate ability to integrate his active resistance with related moral principles in his own society, as well as his capacity to value himself for having performed that act, can be greatly affected by the manner and spirit in which amnesty is discussed, proposed, and perhaps eventually granted.

themselves capable of accepting and acting upon its impossible truths.

The antiwar veterans, and the survivor mission they have chosen, have great bearing on the amnesty issue. They bring a unique combination of historical authority and self-exploration to the fundamental question around which the amnesty debate hinges: How is one to reconcile amnesty with American sacrifices in Vietnam—the wounds, exposure to death, and above all the deaths themselves. The antiwar veterans speak to that question in the way they formulate and act upon their own survival: "We have undergone the suffering and witnessed the deaths," they in effect say, "and the only way to do justice to the dead and the maimed, to make certain that their sacrifices have not been in vain, is to tell their true story, reveal the false witness they were called upon to bear, and thereby help prevent similar pointless sacrifices of American (and other) youth in the future." Without that kind of testimony on the part of men who have been there, attempts to equate the sacrifices of resisters with those of warriors, however justified the equation, are likely to fall upon deaf American ears.

Antiwar veterans have taken strong stands for amnesty, and have done so in their own special fashion. Their attitude toward resisters often contained some ambivalence, and during rap groups one could observe their struggle to overcome resentment toward anyone who "sounded off" about the war without having been there, in favor of increasing admiration for the courage and moral imagination of those who could "see the light" about Vietnam without having to go there to find out, or having to struggle so long with stifled inner doubts about the war (as many of the antiwar veterans had).

The public position of VVAW on amnesty was stated, during the summer of 1972, as the fourth of ten "objectives"—preceded only by those of ending the war, terminating American suppression of other "people's movements" throughout the world, and obtaining full constitutional and democratic rights for active-duty servicemen:

. . . To support all military personnel refusing to serve against their consciences in wars at home and abroad. We demand that Congress enact legislation for the immediate repatriation of those brothers and sisters who are in prison or in self-exile by reason of their refusal to serve in the military. It must also involve an end to all repression and a freeing of all political prisoners.[57]

Here the veterans invoke the authority of their own military experience and go on to connect their anti-Vietnam War survivor mission to all other forms of war resistance. By using the term "repatriation" instead of amnesty—other antiwar groups speak of "self-return," and of "self-retired veterans" instead of "deserters"—and by expressing the entire principle in the form of a "demand" relating to the human rights of those affected, the veterans avoid the hypocrisy and "sop" we spoke of earlier and address the amnesty issue as an integral element of their larger project of individual and social transformation.

If Vietnam turns out to have any value at all for Americans, it will be in the form of a broad turning away from the image of war as a "joyous thing," and to a beginning grasp of war's "false enthusiasms" and "subtle poisons." But given man's dependence upon these poisons and enthusiasms, such a collective psychic turning is as difficult as it is tenuous, always prone to uncertainty and relapse. One thinks of Wallace Stevens' lines:

> How cold the vacancy
> When the phantoms are gone and the shaken realist
> First sees reality.[58]

That "cold vacancy" is already there in all of us; something in each American has become the "shaken realist" even if he has not yet seen "reality." American society may yet make use of its longest, most unpopular, and (from the standpoint of national cohesion and integrity) most dangerous war to bring about a fundamental ethical shift.

If such a shift in consciousness were to occur, one could imagine a future moment in which a son would ask his father the perennial warrior-centered question, "Daddy, what did you do in the great Vietnam War?" and the father's answer—instead of being "I fought bravely at Khe Sanh or in the Delta"—would be: "I opposed it." Or, "I took steps—or went into exile—to avoid fighting in it." Or, "I went to prison because I resisted it." Or, "I fought in it, rejected it, and then did my best to reveal the truth about it."

There are more than a few American fathers who can already begin to answer the question in that way, but a true national change would require a collective psychological shift around the image of integrity or honor—and as Huizinga suggests, a re-examination of the "life heroic":

In the beginning of civilization rivalry for first rank was undoubtedly a formative and ennobling factor. Together with a genuine naivete of mind and a lively sense of honour it produced the proud personal courage so essential to a young culture. And not only this: cultural forms will themselves develop in these ever-recurrent sacred contests, in them the structure of society will unfold. The noble life is seen as an exhilarating game of courage and honour. Unfortunately, even in archaic surroundings war with grimness and bitterness offers but scant occasion for this noble game to become a reality. Bloody violence cannot be caught to any great extent in truly noble form; hence the game can only be fully experienced and enjoyed as a social and aesthetic fiction. That is why the spirit of society ever again seeks escape in fair imaginings of the life heroic, which is played out in the ideal sphere of honour, virtue, and beauty.[59]

Never has there been a greater necessity for recognizing the power of the "social and aesthetic fiction" of war with its "fair imaginings of the life heroic," and then making a tough-minded distinction between this psychic power on the one hand and the technological actualities of "bloody violence" on the other. Translated into contemporary terms, the need is for an ever-broadening segment of society to judge Vietnam on the basis of an altered, life-enhancing image of honor and integrity. An important part of that process would be the evolution of firm principles of responsibility for technological war-making, so that men involved in automated killing—whether as low-level technicians, generals, or civilian officials—can become psychologically and ethically related to what happens at the other end of their technology. Man would then be free to explore non-lethal expressions of the "life heroic," undoubtedly drawing upon some of the kind of immortalizing imagery that, as Huizinga tells us, has been so frequently associated with war.

The paradigm of death and the continuity of life, with the related principles of transformation we have been exploring, can take on much more than mere conceptual significance. For though de Vigny spoke of the "slow recovery from the disease of military enthusiasm," we have seen in antiwar veterans that such "recovery" may not be all that "slow." Nor need any of the elements of the warrior mystique de Vigny described—"the absurd infatuation . . . for my illusions," or the "Warrior's Abnegation" or "sacrifice of self"—remain unquestioned. De Vigny was himself ultimately drawn to the very mystique he exposed, and went on to claim that repeated military holocaust ("vast convulsions and . . . perpetual ordeals") deepens and perfects the character structure ("as a film of beauty to the pearl . . . a . . . patina of translucent gold") around the ennobling principle of "humble and austere devotion to Duty."[60] But the antiwar veterans suggest for themselves and their society a very different model, one which associates honor with autonomy, so that honor requires that one question any project that demands blind devotion and unquestioning surrender of the self.

We have been speaking, then, of dislodging the individual and collective sense of honor from the warrior ethos. We have earlier discussed the altered images of maleness necessary to that shift. Also altered would be society's use of the evolutionary-biological principle of male bonding (the tendency of men in all cultures to group together to carry out tasks originally involving survival, and later challenge, competition, and virtually any aspect of social order).[61] For rather than fly in the face of biology or evolution, the transformation we are discussing could call upon a full store of manly and womanly virtue, of male bonding (and possibly female bonding as well), but around forms other than those of the warrior ethos. Such alternative areas of symbolization are described in every culture around images of strength, power, and capacity reaching out virtually beyond the mortal: *areté* for the Greeks, *mana* for the Polynesians, and (in a different but not unrelated sense) grace for Christians. Death and guilt are central to reclaiming and revitalizing these areas of experience, because only by confronting both in their inseparability can individuals or groups extricate themselves from war-linked standards of honor and open themselves to alternative visions of the continuity of life.

Clearly, honor is at stake. But nothing is more difficult than the recognition of dishonor at the very center of national authority. The quick tendency on the part of those resisting that recognition is to rally around desperately contrived images of pseudo-honor—to insist that "good men have shown fortitude" or, at worst, that "good men have made honest mistakes"—and to mobilize this amorphous imagery via the mass media on behalf of blocking precisely the moral probing and self-questioning that might initiate the kind of shift we are discussing. For such a shift would call forth an ancient principle of responsibility dating from the beginnings of Western civilization, one all too rarely upheld but never fully forgotten: namely, that mortal and fallible men of mixed virtue, at a critical moment, have taken their people down the wrong ethical path, and have had their honor—their integrity and intactness—profoundly compromised.

For increasing numbers of people to take this view would require not brutal recrimination but a return to this principle of responsibility, with its insistence that actions have consequences and that society's future depends upon recognizing and condemning, not ignoring and certainly not rewarding, disastrously immoral actions.

All this suggests that American society requires ancient principles of honor to alter equally ancient warrior imagery. Indeed one could view the whole process as a further progression of the myth of the warrior hero: from the Homeric and chivalric principles of glory and courage on behalf of unquestioned immortalizing principles; to the post-Renaissance Shakespearean ambivalence, recognizing both military glory and irony in misplaced quest for glory (as in *Henry V*); to the nineteenth-century effort to re-create, and extend *ad absurdum*, the warrior myth ("The Charge of the Light Brigade"); to the twentieth-century (notably World War I) recoil from that myth; to (ideally) the post-Vietnam War reversal of the myth, so that honor is bestowed upon the resister of a dishonorable war, and dishonor upon its perpetrators.

For that post-Vietnam turning to occur, the technicist's claim to the mantle of the warrior-hero would have to be firmly rejected in favor of a new hero who, out of courage, refuses violence, and out of knowledge of holocaust exposes and transcends that holocaust. Is this model, this survivor mission of the antiwar warriors, a total break with a two-thousand-year-old cycle of warrior mythology? We can more accurately understand it, I believe, as drawing directly upon that cycle—upon the immortalizing principles of the "hero-deed" as a "continuous shattering of the crystallizations of the moment"—for a new cultural beginning. That beginning, the new mythology of the antiwar warriors, has already entered the American consciousness. What could be more appropriate to the technologies and techno-bureaucracies of our time, or to our newly discovered sense of ourselves as a single species?

CHAPTER 13

On Change

✵

Drive your cart and your plow over the bones of the dead.
—William Blake

> The lost self changes,
> Turning toward the sea,
> A sea-shape turning around,—
> An old man with his feet before the fire,
> In robes of green, in garments of adieu.
> —Theodore Roethke

THROUGHOUT, we have been talking about change. We need now to explore general principles, individual and collective, suggested in what we have so far observed. Depth-psychological theory tends to be rather impoverished on the subject of change, so we shall have to extend that theory in order to suggest new (and old) principles having to do with death and transformation.

Veterans participating in the rap groups underwent changes that can be understood around the three sub-themes we have already emphasized as part of the larger paradigm of death and the continuity of life. In place of excruciating separation and isolation, the men sought new forms of connection—within themselves, with each other, and with viable American and worldwide subcultures of experiment and protest. In place of the disintegration of the counterfeit universe of Vietnam they sought integrity and new definitions of honor. In place of a static and numbed state, they sought movement, development, transformation. They did not, of course, at the time distinguish these three elements of their quest; rather they understood themselves to be struggling toward a new sense of wholeness and completeness that depended both on intrapsychic authenticity and principles beyond the self —they sought, that is, a new and viable sense of symbolic immortality. And not just they but we. The professionals in the group underwent something of that struggle too, if in less dramatic and much less articulated fashion.

None of the veterans succeeded fully in their quest, but virtually all realized it in some degree, a few astonishingly so. The successes and failures of the rap groups cannot be evaluated in medical or psychiatric terms. Most of the men came to the rap groups out of common survivor confusions and aspirations. Whatever symptoms they experienced—periodic anxiety or depression, or the various forms of emotional, interpersonal, and ethical conflict we have discussed—were not seen as discrete clinical conditions, but rather as a part of life struggles and common survivor conflicts. My impression was that almost everyone who came to more than one or two sessions experienced some sense of personal gain. There was not only a relief of pain but, virtually always, an expanded insight concerning self, war, and society.

The rap groups are part of a larger contemporary process of social experimentation—creating new institutions from direct need and then exploring the possibilities they open. These are often spoken of as counter-institutions or alternative institutions, to suggest their opposition to or replacement of institutions already in existence. But by using the terms counter and alternative, the newer institutions define themselves in terms of the older ones and take on a certain unwanted thralldom to them. We may instead use the term animating institutions.

Among such animating institutions (or would-be animating institutions) are work communes (in law, medicine, and other professions), rural communes, various radical institutes (in Washington, D.C., Cambridge, Mass., and San Francisco, for instance), various political and educational groups dedicated to social change, and a large number of still more informal structures and arrangements associated with almost every segment of American society, and having to do with ways of living, working, thinking, feeling, organizing, and acting upon society. They tend to resemble the rap groups in following the principles of affinity, presence, and self-generation, which seem to be necessary for new institutions (or major innovations in older ones) if they are to be truly animating.

Each draws upon its own particular cultural or intellectual tradition but mounts a fundamental critique of the tradition as well as of broader social and political arrangements. The rap groups, for instance, called upon professional traditions associated with psychological healing, and perhaps even on a few elements of military tradition, to mount critiques both upon the Vietnam War and upon a variety of emotions and social arrangements that contribute to war-making. Animating institutions thus are not only critical and innovative functions but serve a conservative function as well; they confirm and extend certain traditions which might otherwise be jettisoned by those who are profoundly disenchanted with what the traditions have come to.

To be genuinely animating, an institution must enhance individual breakout from numbing and offer the promise of individual and collective vitality. Much of the energy for this process, again as in the rap groups, can come from prior emotions of anxiety, guilt, and rage that not only find new channels of expression but join with various ideas and images to create newly viable psychic forms. For participants in all animating institutions are likely to feel themselves survivors of the dead or dying (or, at the least, numbed) institutions or structures they have known. The rap groups' close relationship to the survivor state was, in this sense, not unique but rather an extreme case of a principle applicable to animating institutions in general. All such institutions struggle toward their own survivor formulation.

Part of that struggle has to do with the apparent paradox of surviving themselves: combining long-range commitment to principles of growth and change with an awareness of their own limited institutional life span. They must counter the tendency to seek literal institutional immortality which resembles, extends or replaces the individual version. This tendency is found in old and new institutions alike. Contemporary animating institutions are notoriously short-lived, emerging as they do in a "Protean" historical situation. Like the rap groups, they are likely to be always in crisis, always in question. Absolute stability (literal immortality) is pursued at the cost of the animating principles themselves. Affinity can then become exclusivity, elitism, and a demand for sameness. Presence can turn into forms of anti-reason and suppression of individual autonomy and give rise eventually to cultism. Self-generation can fall to authoritarian control by self-appointed generators whose obsession with keeping the institution going replaces the earlier animating ethos.

The rap groups were by no means always able to fully confront this question of limited life-span. Several groups ended without their members knowing why. We have pointed to such factors as professionals' inability to surrender their conventional models of group therapy, veterans' general withdrawal and wariness toward groups of any kind, and geographical transfers of groups (from the veterans' own turf to private professional offices) that undermine the process of self-generation. But in some cases one could speak of the more or less successful completion of a particular phase of group work: men had been able to look at the war and their relationship to it in newly illuminating ways, without wishing to commit themselves to more protracted intrapsychic explorations around their character armor. Had the men been able to discuss these choices, they could have retained a clearer sense of the logic of a group's ending (whatever the accompanying sense of loss), along with a sharper awareness of accomplishments that live on within them.

Actually, the groups themselves have undergone a constant death-and-rebirth process. One that died in Manhattan was reborn in a slightly different form in Queens; and emanations from New York groups with brief life spans gave rise to others in Milwaukee, Philadelphia, and many other parts of the country. Published descriptions of our experience in New York brought responses from more than thirty places where groups were already going or were about to start. These groups have to some extent mirrored the vicissitudes of the larger antiwar organization. VVAW, initially tiny and informal, then suddenly prominent and (apparently) remarkably together, found itself before long torn by political and personal sectarian disputes, which did not prevent it from growing in numbers and in certain forms of political and symbolic influence. In that process many veterans have experienced, at times, profound despair, immobilization, and outbursts of suspiciousness bordering on paranoia.* For among all animating groups the antiwar veterans (notably the rap groups among them) take on the most fundamental, difficult, and tragic of all tasks: that of transforming the human stuff of warmaking to something else not yet quite discovered. A powerful image of that "something else" appeared on the front page of the VVAW newspaper, "The First Casualty," in October 1971, in the form of a picture of one of its leaders being embraced by a Vietnamese guide, also a veteran, in a Hanoi war museum.[1] That kind of image—of heretical reconciliation with designated enemies—has great importance for all animating institutions, and is reminiscent of the lines of W. S. Merwin:

> I know the martyrs sleeping in almonds
> I know the gloves of the hours I know Pilate the fly
> I know the enemy's brother.[2]

Depth-psychology has been living too long on the psychoanalytic claim, only half believed by its exponents, that individual character is essentially formed during the first six years of life and does not change much after that.† The claim is not only half-believed but half-true: important models do take shape in those early years, including those around connection, integrity, and movement. But when those models are directly equated with the adult character itself (which in classical psychoanalytic termi-

---

* The suspiciousness was often all too justified as VVAW has been one of the organizations most actively infiltrated by FBI agents (perhaps an indication of the government's sense of its potential impact). But some of the suspiciousness must also be attributed to the Vietnam War-related conflicts we have been discussing.

† Recent psychoanalytic work gives considerable stress to "Character Formation in Adolescence" (Peter Blos, *The Psychoanalytic Study of the Child*, Vol. XXIII, N.Y. International University Press, 1968, pp. 245-263) ; and Erikson suggests, throughout his work, the capacity for growth over the course of the entire life cycle. But there remains scant depth-psychological work on the theory of adult change.

nology becomes "oral," "anal," "phallic," or "genital"), the argument becomes circular and meaningless. The original claim is understandable in terms of the paradox that surrounds all intellectual breakthroughs. Freud's discovery of the significance of early childhood for later adult conflict probably required that other truths would be excluded. But those "other truths"—those, for instance, surrounding adult change—are far too important to be ignored further, either in theory or in healing procedures.

We have in fact been discussing in this study the kinds of changes that can take place *only* during adult life. And we have observed how certain relatively enduring elements of the psyche shaped during early childhood could enhance, rather than impede, this change. (The former Marine grunt, for example, called forth early images of integrity to initiate his personal transformation; so did the My Lai survivor when he refused to fire during the massacre and when he had earlier refused to treat the Vietnamese as inhuman.) We have also observed the central significance of issues of integrity for adult change, and the extent to which the idea of the self can be equated with process.

In speaking of self-process, then, I would suggest the image of continuous psychic re-creation.[3] But instead of setting up a false argument about the self—as either essentially fixed, or in constant flux—we may assume that continuity and change co-exist and that they are not antagonistic, but work themselves out in response to a constant flow of images and a continuous building and alteration of inner forms. Only with extreme numbing does the process stop, or rather seem to stop. For that kind of numbing blocks access to the kind of combination of death encounter (actual or symbolic) and the psychic and social possibility beyond the encounter that can bring about transformation centered on integrity.

Integrity begins with the organisms's earliest physiological struggles to remain intact, comes to signify a sense of wholeness that is bodily and psychic, and, during adult life, sustained ethical commitment or honor. A more detailed examination of the Greek principle *areté* suggests the centrality of the principle of integrity for all transformation. One of the earliest Western concepts of honor and worth, *areté* originally (in Homer) meant "heroic strength and courage," especially during war—a man's ability or "power which is peculiar to himself, which makes him a complete man,"[4] as determined by others' judgment. But gradually, over centuries of Greek experience, *areté* became associated with an "inner standard" according to which physical and intellectual excellence could "merge with ethical value so as to form a higher unity." In either case, *areté* was directly bound up with symbolic immortality—with

the aspiration of the individual toward that ideal and super-personal sphere, in which alone he can have real value. Thus it is true in some sense to say that the *areté* of the hero is completed only in his death. *Areté* exists in mortal man. *Areté* is mortal man. But it survives the mortal, and lives on in his glory, in that very deal of his *areté* which accompanied and directed him throughout his life.

The Greeks came to recognize that *areté* could be corrupted into a mere quest for fame, as the later medieval concept of honor could deteriorate into (in Huizinga's phrase) "a mixture of chivalrous caprice and political advertising."[5] We have seen precisely that kind of "political advertising" in contemporary degradations of honor associated with the Indochina War—the former American Ambassador to Saigon, Ellsworth Bunker, telling American soldiers at a division ceremony that their fight was part of "man's unending struggle for freedom and dignity"; and the devastation of much of Indochina from the air in the name of "peace with honor." Yet these very degradations attest to the universality of imagery of honor and integrity, the necessity of such imagery to the claim of leadership and the call to individual or collective action.

Where integrity is genuine and animating, it extends to principles beyond the self. In this sense integrity is always a quest rather than a completed state, a reaching out toward continuity and connection that is characterized by harmony and honor—hence, an ideal to be attained by a process (whether slow or rapid) of transformation.

For an appropriate model of transformation, I would return to the sequence of "open personal change" I delineated some years ago,[6] as an alternative to the closed, coercive form of change called forth by totalist dogma, or what I called "ideological totalism." I described "open personal change" in terms of three overlapping steps or processes: confrontation, reordering, and renewal. The entire sequence is a symbolic form of death and rebirth. My experience with antiwar veterans reaffirms the general principle as well as the stages of open personal change. But it also strongly suggests the relationship of this symbolic death-and-rebirth process to the psychology of the survivor, and to an overall paradigm of death and continuous life. We can briefly redelineate the three stages from this standpoint.

Confrontation consists of a sudden or sustained questioning of personal integration and integrity brought about by some form of death encounter. Whether or not actual physical dying is involved, the encounter includes an indelible image of personal threat. But accompanying that threat is an opening toward greater awareness of the non-viability (falseness, inadequacy, deadness) of previously unquestioned inner forms (values, assumptions, symbols), and the possibility (however dimly perceived) of alternatives. The image representing all this is indelible (though often ineffable) because it suggests the idea of death or nothingness in newly powerful fashion. It does this by bringing together, at least for a moment, adult knowledge (or perhaps "middle knowledge") of actual death with reactivated early images of disintegration (or annihilation), separation, and stasis. In this way the idea of death is newly connected with the primal images on which it is built—hence the sense both of newness and of "shock of recognition."

Confrontation thus blends external stimulus and internal readiness. Without the latter, it can be refused, in one way or another blocked out or defended against, as in the case of the large numbers of Vietnam veterans who seek to cover over their war experience and avoid being changed by it. In that sense, confrontation involves acknowledging something one dimly knew but kept oneself from consciously recognizing. But something in the external experience—a blend of its novelty, intensity, and timing —leads it to be perceived as a discovery. That discovery is related to an image of death (such as "People can die," "Death exists for *me*," "I have been living in a deadened state," or "I have been wasting my limited lifetime"). The other side of the discovery, an inseparable part of it, is a glimmering of renewed life, of the possibilities of integrity, connection, and movement.

Whether confrontation occurs in a moment or very gradually over time, in experiencing it one takes on the psychology of the survivor. Like the survivor, one can close oneself to the encounter through numbing, move away from it rather than toward or through it. But that kind of flight requires considerable psychological work, which in turn has consequences: static and self-destructive fear of the encounter and its death-linked personal insights, as well as guilt over having refused it. Even a partial opening toward the encounter and its insights can offer access to neglected psychic recesses and call into question all experience that takes place on a less authentic plane. The very confusions of confrontation, prior to any clear survivor formulation, can be liberating or at least contain the promise of liberation.

We have seen the antiwar veterans' confrontation taking place on immediately ultimate terms: the issue of dying in Vietnam. Transformation was initiated, however, only if the soldier came to recognize the fact of death, and to reject that particular form of it as absurd and unworthy. This extreme form of death encounter illuminates the more humble varieties of death—what Kurt Vonnegut calls "plain old death"—where similar principles apply. We can thus speak of confrontation in connection with surviving a person one has loved, with witnessing death of any kind, and, more broadly, with any experience that brings psychic force to bear upon one's existing symbolizations of death and continuous life—the loss of a particular status or belief, contact with a new principle or image that undermines previous assumptions, the perception of a different form of honor or integrity to which one can aspire. Once confrontation has occurred, there is a shaking of psychic foundations. With existing inner forms and symbolizations under duress, man's innate and continuous impulse to master his environment by means of movement and change is released from the relatively static compromises of ordinary existence, from their mixture of numbing and security. For so pressing is the bioligically rooted psychoformative process of perpetual symbolization that stasis is the artificial condition and change (more precisely, a balance of continuity and change) is the norm.

Confrontation of this sort cannot be conceptualized as an expression of some form of innate thrust toward death or "death instinct." Nor can it be understood as an activation of negative identifications or "bad objects" internalized in life. Rather, it is an experience of psychic shattering that is the beginning of a new accessibility to the richness of imagery and form man is capable of creating around his simultaneous relationship to anticipated death and continuing life.

To confront this kind of threat to integrity is to experience guilt, and to confront that guilt in turn is to initiate the second stage, that of *reordering*. Reordering involves alteration and re-creation of every aspect of self-process, but it revolves around the struggle to achieve an animating relationship to guilt.

We must note that guilt has become a "bad image" for contemporary man, and no wonder. For he is a survivor of a variety of life-destroying obsessions with guilt promulgated by dubious premodern expressions of the Judeo-Christian tradition; and also of Freud's exposure of man's ubiquitous unconscious guilt as a major threat to the future of civilization. There is no denying the modern significance of the critical exposure of these static forms of guilt (self-lacerating guilt and numbed guilt respectively, in the two examples given). But what has been forgotten is the potentially integrative functions of guilt as well. For the breadth of psychic experience with guilt is such that it can serve a variety of forms and symbolizations, often of polar ethical consequences. To view guilt within this kind of paradox is consistent with the psychoanalytic emphasis upon seemingly opposite functions performed by many kinds of emotion.*

My experience with antiwar veterans and other prophetic survivors (notably those on both sides of the atomic bombings) leads me to emphasize the animating possibilities of guilt—not to the exclusion of its negative consequences but rather in combination with them. For while static and animating guilt are never entirely separable, what we are calling reordering depends heavily upon the conversion of the one to the other (along lines already discussed in Chapter 4). We thus enter into a border area between guilt and responsibility.

Indeed, in the history of their usage, responsibility and guilt (or potential guilt) are inextricably bound to one another in common function. The word "responsibility" derives, via "response," from the Indo-European root, *"spend,"* (related to the Latin *spondēre* and the Greek *spondē*), meaning "to make an offering, perform a rite, hence to engage oneself by a ritual act." In present usage responsibility involves being "answerable for . . . a duty, obligation, or burden" and "personal accountability or ability to act without guidance or superior authority."[7] Thus the present image of being responsible or accountable stems from an earlier image of integrity based upon ritual engagement and the sense of wholeness derived from such engagement. An early use

* Rage, for instance, can be associated with paranoid psychosis and with murderous violence; but also with the kind of protest against injustice that enhances individual integrity and can even help to maintain life itself. Anxiety (of which the sense of guilt is one form) can be associated with almost every form of incapacitating mental disturbance; but is also a necessary indicator or signal of threats or missteps in optimal forms of psychological function. Finally, ecstasy or transcendence can occur in connection with love on the one hand, or with victimization and killing on the other.

of the word guilt (Tillotson's *Sermons*, 1735) says it is "nothing else but trouble arising in our minds, from a consciousness of having done contrary to what we are verily persuaded was our Duty."[8] That definition closely resembles Freud's description of a "sense of guilt" about 175 years later. The "trouble arising in our minds" is the anxiety of the breakdown of integrity (of ethical cohesion and the more general cohesion of symbolic forms). Guilt can thus serve as a protective indicator, a weather vane of psychic integrity. It serves as a warning to the organism that it is losing that integrity, that its ethical and even psychobiological intactness are under duress. Thus each society makes use of—requires—its reservoir of guilt to maintain the arrangements of responsibility so crucial to all psychic bonds, and the psychic images and forms behind those arrangements.

Throughout the reordering process there is a struggle to confront guilt and reclaim (or establish for the first time) a sense of integrity. Reordering can include the softening we spoke of earlier, the breaking down of some of the character armor, the long-standing defenses and maneuvers around numbed guilt, in order to release feelings appropriate to conflicts around integrity. For the person undergoing this process is struggling to bear witness to the upheaval (death encounter) he has experienced, and to do so with autonomy and authenticity. Bearing witness implies being present to share pain and wisdom, and to take on the responsibility to 'tell the story' afterward. Autonomy means self-rule, what we have called self-generation, and must be in balance (even if in seeming conflict) with accuracy and genuineness of witness (authenticity). Precisely these qualities were absent in the false witness veterans had undergone in Vietnam. That false witness, taking place in an environment that destroyed integrity and worked against true confrontation, could be understood as a form of pseudo-reordering in which attitudes and actions held out as a source of significance, and of animating guilt turn out to be destructive in the extreme—not only externally but in their further assault upon inner integrity and their reinforcement of numbed guilt.

Analogous forms of false witness can occur in a variety of situations that suggest death symbolism (broken friendships, changes of landscape, dislocations or losses of any kind), in which the survivor mission taken on—that of vengeance, withdrawal, or sustained numbing—perpetuates and aggravates the symbolic "dying" and killing. Confrontation reveals the falsity of previous witness; reordering seeks to render that witness autonomous and authentic by infusing it with the inner authority that can enable one to be the author of one's own life story.* All this in turn requires inner forms that are potentially viable or animating, and access to guilt as a warning signal of violated integrity.

Numbing is the adversary of this animating process, because the anxiety of responsibility requires, above all, a sensitive capacity to feel. I have seen men confronting their guilt and altering their relationship to it in thoughtful silence, overt rage, and (most commonly) periodic swings in and out of both. More crucial than any of these external manifestations was their consistent struggle to feel both the falsity of previous witness and at least the start of a more authentic (because more honest, loving, and actualizing) kind. Psychic numbing and static guilt exist in a vicious circle, the one maintaining and reinforcing the other, until interrupted by confrontation and reordering, by the initiation of an animating process.

Where softening and some access to feeling occur without the integrative forms that support reordering, extreme situations are experienced with only partial confrontation; there is, therefore, no real integration, and we can expect profound psychological

---

* "Authentic," "authority," and "author," have a common Latin root, *auctor*, creator, from *augére*, to create or increase, their common significance here lying in the genuineness of the source of attitude and action. This derivation is distinct from the "auto" of autonomous, which is from the Greek *autos*, or self. In these two root meanings lie the survivor's double responsibility in reordering: he must be true both to the origins of his witness (the death encounter) and to his own special relationship to it, the inner forms he brings to it (to himself).

difficulty. In the case of Vietnam veterans, it meant psychiatric casualties. The extremity of their felt transgressions, and the bizarre kinds of psychic armor they had had to call forth to avoid feeling, could create a particularly grave and malignant circle of static guilt and numbing—as we are beginning to observe in case reports making their way into psychiatric literature. There is, for example, a case (reported among "Three Psychatric Casualties from Vietnam" in the December, 1971, issue of *Archives of General Psychiatry*)[9] of a "husky eighteen-year-old Marine" who "appeared to like duty in Vietnam and told with pride of '40 confirmed Vietcong kills,' " but who, after six months of duty, experienced a "severe depressive reaction" that necessitated several months of psychiatric hospitalization. During a barbiturate-amphetamine interview* he described shooting and killing a fourteen-year-old Vietnamese girl he had befriended, on the orders of a corporal whose sexual advances the girl had rebuffed; of becoming disturbed and provoking a fight with the corporal, and then shooting him too; and then of arranging things so that the corporal would appear to have been killed by the Vietcong. His depression and hospitalization followed. After telling the full story to the interviewers he said: "How can I ever live with myself knowing what I have done?" He apparently meant the question literally. He made three failed suicide attempts until, about two months after the interview, he finally succeeded with a twenty-two-caliber shell he had been carrying around with him and a "harmless" gun he found in his girlfriend's house.

We may say that the numbing that had sustained him through the "40 confirmed Vietcong kills" broke down under the duress of his two additional killings (of the Vietnamese girl and his

* The authors explain that amobarbital sodium and methamphetamine hydrochloride are used together as a modification of the psychiatric use of barbiturate interviews, in order "to recover and abreact relatively recent suppressed and lightly repressed material." In their study of psychological reactions to World War II combat reactions, Grinker and Spiegel made extensive use of barbiturate interviews for diagnosis, treatment, and elucidation of psychological principles.[10]

corporal), which were much less psychologically manageable.*
His very troubled pre-military history contributed significantly
to the outcome, including a survival at age eight of a playmate's
death from a fall, confirming a preexisting feeling of being a
"bad influence on others"; a subsequent preoccupation with
death and dying including such bizarre efforts to master severe
death anxiety, and guilt, as sticking pins into his own arms and
drinking diluted weed and rat poison or the blood of a dead cat
"to see how much I could take." Vietnam experiences always
make psychological connection with earlier survivals, which were
in his case unusually severe. He became depressed when overwhelmed with guilt that he was unable to animate in any significant way. The interview gave him greater accessibility to actions
(killings) and feelings (guilt) he had previously known but had
distanced through becoming numb. He showed some improvement after the interview, suggesting a reordering process in the
direction of integrity, of a new integration that might include
both his guilt and his vulnerability to that guilt. But the task was
much more than he could manage, and there is reason to question
the use of this kind of uncovering interview in such cases.†

---

* The psychiatric authors of the paper, though tending to believe the description of the two additional murders, raised the possibility (in the absence of
corroborating evidence) that it may contain some elaboration of fantasy. If so,
and the murders did not actually occur, the fantasy of them would be, in large
measure, a product of guilt over things he had done in Vietnam. In earlier work
on Chinese thought reform I encountered extensive confabulation in which a
sense of guilt was a primary factor, and where it took a confessional form that
the environment expected and demanded.[11] There have been reports of atrocities among Vietnam veterans in which guilt of that kind could be extremely
important. Also involved could be the need to reaffirm, through retrospective
expressions of sadism, group-defined feelings of male toughness.

† I have heard such criticism expressed by a number of psychological professionals in direct response to reading this paper. From my experience with
Vietnam veterans I would be wary of drug interviews because of the extreme
guilt, shame, and overall degradation associated with certain memories of Vietnam's specific counterfeit universe. Those memories, generally speaking, are
best brought out when the veteran himself is ready to deal with them. In this
particular case the authors imply that there might have been a questionable
decision on the part of a physician-duty officer who, on a weekend, approved

Ideally, I believe, this kind of patient could be helped by active
involvement with a group of fellow veterans committed to conveying to him the nature of the atrocity-producing situation and
the inevitability of personal corruption and guilty acts. In this case
both the patient's psychiatric condition (he was psychotic or
near-psychotic) and his world view (pride in VC "kills") could
well have precluded such involvement with an overtly political
group like VVAW or the kind of rap groups we have described.
But if there were a similar kind of group of a less specifically
political kind that he could have responded to, one could imagine,
again speaking ideally, that it might lend collective support and
legitimacy to a reordering process that would enable even young
men as disturbed as he to achieve a more animating relationship
to guilt.

The psychiatric authors stress the centrality of guilt in their
three cases as the "core affect leading to symptom formation,"
and point out that the guilt "represented to varying degrees
realistic responses to actual situations." They conclude that all
three patients were suffering from traumatic neuroses, whose
potential is increased by the moral ambiguity of the war, so that
the official military claim of low psychiatric casualty rates is "at
least partially spurious." I would agree, and put the matter more
strongly, from the perspective of the psychology of the survivor:
Vietnam's atrocity-producing situation and counterfeit universe
created an extraordinary constellation of mutually reinforcing
guilt and numbing; which in turn blocked and undermined the
kind of meaningful survivor formulation and mission that could
animate the guilt and initiate a reordering process. The result
has been that efforts at reordering tend to be fragile and highly
vulnerable, ever endangered by explosive outbreaks of self-lacer-

---

the patient's impassioned demand to be allowed to go home on pass just before
he shot himself. Any overall judgment must take into account the complexities
of this case (for instance, the considerable possibility of a suicidal outcome
independently of the drug interview), and would have to be based upon a
careful review of the entire therapeutic program.

ating guilt that can precipitate various forms of psychiatric disturbance or, more commonly, by retreat from any form of confrontation, back one into numbing and more or less permanently static guilt.

Still, happier outcomes can occur, as in another case reported by the same authors with many parallels to the first. A twenty-six-year-old computer operator was admitted to the hospital following a suicide gesture after an argument with a girlfriend. His personal background, no less complicated than that of the other patient, included transvestite behavior, which had much to do with his enlistment in the army at the age of eighteen and his volunteering for airborne and Special Forces training and then for three tours in Vietnam with the Green Berets. All this enabled him to "feel . . . manly in his daring exploits," and gave him "a sense of stopping the communists in Asia"—at least during his first two tours. During his third tour, however, he became "horrified by the futility and cruelty of the war" and resorted to heavy use of amphetamines. One night while high on the drug he became "jumpy," and opened fire on a nearby boat, killing several Indochinese from his own unit and wounding two American advisers. Though he was never held militarily responsible for the incident (again the Vietcong were blamed), he became further agitated and self-destructive, and provoked frequent conflict with his superiors, until his military performance deteriorated sufficiently for him to be given an administrative discharge for unsuitability with the diagnosis of "character disorder."

But he was obsessed with guilt, and "felt he could only justify living by serving others." He made progress, one surmises, because he found ways to do just that. Responding well to a drug interview and forming a good working alliance with his therapist, he "participated in group and ward meetings . . . obtained a challenging job . . . and [after leaving the hospital] attempted to resume responsibility for his brother." His softening and partial confrontation of his guilt were psychologically precarious but led to a new integration based upon his own viable, if humble, survivor mission.

We may thus postulate a three-sided model of post-Vietnam psychiatric health and impairment involving reordering, survivor formulation/mission, and the access of numbing and guilt. Where there is a combination of absent or profoundly impaired survivor formulation and mission, together wth vulnerability to guilt (when numbing is no longer effective), reordering cannot take place and casualties are most likely to occur. With impaired formulation/mission and relatively intact numbing, reordering again is impossible but reactions are likely to be more indirect—subclinical patterns of suspicious withdrawal, periodic rage (sometimes bursting into violence), and impermanence of relationships with restless dissatisfaction. Where the survivor mission/formulation evolves with some force but numbing remains strong, a sustained struggle between the two may ensue, and gradual reordering is possible. Where there is a combination of active formulation/mission and equally active confrontation of (and vulnerability to) guilt, animating forms of reordering are most likely to occur. Even with this relatively ideal combination of elements, however, the process is likely to remain tenuous and subject to relapse. Previous life history is, of course, enormously important, but in much more subtle, unpredictable ways than usually assumed—and always greatly influenced by the degree to which a post-Vietnam environment (or group) encourages, gives shape to, and emotionally supports the reordering process. Nor does a veteran's reordering process merely "restore" an earlier state; rather, his animating relationship to guilt is itself newly formative and prospective.[12]

Three million Vietnam veterans carry this model to all corners of American society. I have heard of case after case—whether through direct interviews or various communications from veterans, their families, from lawyers, or from other psychological professionals—in which the sense of guilt was so overpowering that the veteran was not only immobilized but felt himself responsible for every subsequent misfortune taking place around him. In several instances the death was that of the veteran's child, infant, or fetus, suggesting Greek tragedy (Euripides: "The gods visit the sins of the fathers upon the children")—both in immediate pathos (the child representing the most innocent and vulnerable of creatures) and in specific eye-for-an-eye retaliation (for having killed children and other helpless beings in Vietnam). The ultimate transgression, at least in the mind of the veteran, comes home: the "punishment" consists of the death not only of the child (the ultimate loss for any parent) but of the veteran's mind, since the pattern is generally associated with psychosis.

But the real American casualties of the Vietnam War, at least in numbers, may well be those who see no psychiatrists and bear no psychiatric or medical labels, yet are nonetheless plagued and diminished by numbed guilt they can neither animate nor even recognize. For them reordering is out of the question, and their continuing struggle against awareness of transgression or guilt may drive them to extreme acts of destruction and self-destruction—as in the many cases already reported among Vietnam veterans of seemingly purposeless violence or mass murder, the significant but unknown number of veterans who stay on hard drugs, or who (according to the testimony of many families) continue over considerable time to live in distraught withdrawal from fellow beings because unable to risk vulnerability to guilt in that dimension. Even a society whose leaders are bent on numbing cannot hide these casualties; we shall hear of more and more of them bringing their bitter guilt and rage, which they are unable to reorder, back to a society already suffused with dislocation and bitterness.*

* That unresolved bitterness, confusion, and sense of betrayal, together with the government's recruiting policies, has led a number of them to work against their fellow veterans as impostors, double-agents, or *provocateurs* assigned to antiwar veterans groups. The best known of these is the veteran-turned-FBI

Home From the War

I am reminded here of Alexander Mitscherlich's descriptions of Germans who, after World War II, remained in various ways immobilized and static because they simply could not psychologically afford to confront or even acknowledge guilt commensurate with their actions (or inactions). Only the next generation, according to Mitscherlich, could challenge them to awaken from this numbed state.[14] But rather than be awakened in this way by their children, Vietnam veterans, in their additional resemblance to *victims* of holocaust, are more likely to pass along negative aspects of the survivor experience down through the generations.

I could observe suggestions of that process in Hiroshima survivors, and it has begun to be more systematically studied in survivors of Nazi death camps. Veterans' death anxiety and death guilt, along with their bitter rage, are bound to enter into the emotional tone of family transactions. Like concentration camp survivors they are also likely to impose compensatory burdens on their children—whether in the form of exaggerated fear and overprotection, or demand for purity and perfection.[15] Children in turn, in coping with their legacy, may identify sufficiently with the Vietnam holocaust to feel entrapped in it, or spend considerable psychological energy trying to flee from that identification— the two related patterns found in Hiroshima and concentration camp survivors. With children thus constructing their own elaborate constellations of guilt and numbing, reordering becomes an important matter for subsequent generations as well. We still have much to learn about family transmission of the survivor experience, but we may be certain that Americans will be struggling with the guilt-numbing constellation of Vietnam survival for many generations to come.

Still around reordering, there remains one final question, as

---

informer in the Gainesville, Florida case, whose drawings on the walls of his own apartment showed imagery of holocaust, of taking the world down with him, of rage toward virtually everyone, and the written graffiti: "PVS [post-Vietnam syndrome] kills."[13]

elusive as it is important: Why is it that some men can, appropriately and constructively, "feel sorry," and others, most, cannot? What enables men to confront death, take sufficient risks with their vulnerability to animate their guilt and reorder the self? I do not think there is any single answer, and the complex array of relevant influences I have observed in antiwar veterans makes me skeptical of simple explanations of any kind. I suspect that this access to animating guilt has to do with an interplay between pre-Vietnam history (and early psychological style) and post-Vietnam social exposure (to environments encouraging that kind of expression and use of guilt). There seems to be a highly delicate continuum—from partially numbed guilt to animating accessibility to guilt to vulnerability to breakdown. That animating accessibility to death and guilt was crucial, of course, to veterans, but has much broader significance as well. In soldiers' capacity to feel sorry, and in the related capacity to anticipate that feeling and avoid transgression, we recognize guilt as an emotion crucial to human survival. While static guilt endangers human life by the destructive behavior it stimulates, animating guilt protects it by relating, potentially in advance, action to consequences. This broadest of reordering processes—the understanding and nurturing of animating guilt in the individual and at every level of collectivity—becomes one of the central psychological issues of man's continuing evolution.

Renewal, the last of the three steps, is partly simultaneous with the other two. But it requires that much of the psychic work of confrontation and reordering already be done. We can speak of renewal as the self's attainment of form (structure) and style (process) in relationship to its new integrity. Form itself is fluid, which is why structure and process cannot be separated; through both, the individual develops an inner sense, persisting through continuing change, that his new integrity is part of him.

This does not mean that guilt disappears. On the contrary, the process of converting static to animating guilt is continuous and continuously important. But as an animating relationship to guilt comes to predominate, it is increasingly accompanied by play. Piaget has said that a child, in order to understand anything, must construct it himself or "re-invent it" through play. And Erikson, in a recent study of the full gamut of play, concludes that play is so widespread and fundamental a human phenomenon as to be grasped only by the word "aliveness."[16]

From early in life play is at the center of the formative process, the means by which the self, in a state of freedom, re-creates its images and forms. That freedom to create and explore—to subvert, mock, or reinforce old forms and initiate new ones—is a psychic key to play, though play is never without a structure and set of rules of its own. And play always envisions a state of unity encompassing inner and outer worlds. Significantly, the Indo-European root of play, *plegan*, means "to pledge for, stake, risk, exercise oneself," and one Germanic derivative noun, *plehti*, means "danger, peril, and plight [meaning solemn pledge]."[17] These etymological roots suggest the special relationship of play to the shaking of the foundations, its element of risk, and its association with commitment. Indeed only play, in its broadest psychic meaning, can enable one to approach the ecstasy or experiential transcendence necessary to affirm a mode of immortality or bring about a shift in modes.

Play is also the great unifier of the life cycle—its formative-symbolizing function enabling the child to build adult forms, and the adult to retain the child within. But adult play differs from that of the child in the experience that informs it. In adults we may speak of 'play after the fall,' play informed by the knowledge of death and guilt. Adult play may become tinged with sadness or tragedy, but is deepened and even liberated by awareness of mortality, or of threats to the psychic and physical organism* Play enables adults to feel their way beyond their large

---

* Under extreme duress, play is likely to take the form of "gallows humor," in which the death awaiting one is mocked, along with one's helplessness before it. For instance, a professional cremator in Hiroshima, who lived right next

and small deaths. One may speak of this adult alliance with animating guilt as regenerative play, which in turn combats many forms of adult numbing, two of which we may consider here: the numbing of holocaust, and the numbing of normality.

Antiwar veterans, in recovering from their holocaust, make extensive use of every form of play—horseplay with one another, playful mockery toward the war-makers and the good Americans who remain uninvolved, playful teasing around painful areas of love and friendship and in connection with their own mixture of toughness and softening, playful communion in pot-smoking, and the whole gamut of related playfulness (about work, authority, and sacred objects of any kind) so characteristic of youth culture. As with Hiroshima and concentration camp survivors, their play had to contend with their holocaust's legacy of massive deadness related to numbing and guilt. There were important interactions between play and guilt given little recognition in psychological theory. Painful explorations of guilt were often preceded and followed by playful exchanges that seemed to provided not only a needed shift in tone but an immediate alternative to the counterfeit universe associated with the guilt, one in which people could relate to others with a combination of spontaneity, shared skepticism, and an appreciation of pleasure. Play thus suggested and helped carry one toward a new world view or partial recovery of an old one; and supplied imagery and energy crucial to the transformation of static to animating guilt. Where static guilt persisted, either in self-lacerating or numbed form, play was impaired, and at best sporadic and half-hearted. Together, animating guilt and play—that is, regenerative play—

---

to his crematorium, told me how, at the time of the bomb, he had been very pleased at being able to make his way back to his home, despite his severe burns, because "I thought I would die soon, and it would be convenient to have the crematorium so close by." And Jean-François Steiner tells of the "professional attitude" of the corpse-carrier, in calling to another prisoner during a meal: "Hay, Moshe! Don't eat so much, you'll gain weight. Think of us who'll have to carry you!"[18]

gave access to the "formative zone," to portions of the psyche in which images can be transformed.

Holocaust, sometimes even anticipated holocaust, is a destroyer of psychological continuity, individual and collective. It brings about a sense of "world-destruction" (prominent in Hiroshima and concentration camp survivors, and, in more symbolic ways, in Vietnam veterans too), or, what I have called, "a vast breakdown of faith (or trust) in the larger human matrix supporting each individual life, and, therefore, loss of faith (or trust) in the structure of existence."[19] Play counters this ultimate loss of faith, not only in connection with the process of renewal now under discussion but also with the two earlier stages of change as well. For instance, play can provide liberating elements of absurdity, along with glimmers of shared integrity, that enable one to initiate a confrontation with death and disintegration in a way not previously possible (as in the case of the former Army sergeant and friends in their collective, pot-induced fantasies about Alice). And play can pit against the shattered forms of holocaust and post-holocaust experience a suggestion of ritual that, in its very imperfection and acknowledged limitation, serves human needs (as in the playful exchange in the rap group concerning my twentieth wedding anniversary).

Play is the essence of renewal, constantly affirming the 'new man' in a 'new place' (regarding loyalties, ideology, and personal style). Play generates trust, and is, above all, a life force—a message that "The world is back!"—that "We are alive!" In these and endless other ways play reasserts lost connection, movement, and above all, integrity, to the point where the pre-holocaust faith is almost regained—or a new faith is born to replace it.

But veterans, like their youth-culture cohorts, were also reacting to the less dramatic and more insidious deadness and numbing of ordinary existence. They come to see the "average normal person" in America as profoundly numbed to his country's killing abroad and various forms of abuse at home, to the feelings of others at his job or in his family, and to his own emotions.

They came to view adult existence in America as a locked-in, desensitized state, and sought, however inchoately, a form of adulthood with more play in it. Elsewhere I examine in greater detail questions around the necessity for numbing in adults of any culture.[20] Here we can say that the veterans had a special vantage point from which to sense the dangerous forms and degree of numbing in our society and their interference with arrangements necessary to limit destructiveness of all kinds. All this suggests, of course, that, in our present world, normal adult numbing is inseparable from the numbing of holocaust. Regenerative play suggests paths beyond their common technicist entrapment. I believe Andrei Voznesensky had something like this idea in mind when he declared: "Let the grassy generation judge our Apocalypse."[21]

Again like their cohorts in youth culture, antiwar veterans bring powerful elements of play, especially mocking play, into their political demonstrations. But in the case of veterans this play involves what they know and confront—"weapons" that fire "fried" [hot] marbles, ball bearings, "cherry" bombs, and smoke bombs; "wrist rocket slingshots" and "crossbows."* Several prosecutions of antiwar veterans have involved confusing this mock violence with the real thing—by government officials highly sensitive to the mythic power of antiwar veterans and all too willing to make the confusion. The matter can be compounded, and the prosecutions made likelier, by similar confusion in some of the veteran-militants whose personal-ideological struggles with guilt and rage take them to the border between play and violence.

In thus emphasizing play, I am suggesting that renewal itself is at no point simply accomplished. Rather, it is a process that, once established, can combine enduring forms with perpetual

---

* This list is taken from the grand jury indictment of May 27, 1972, at Gainesville, Florida, of six antiwar veterans accused of conspiracy to disrupt communications in Miami Beach, Florida, at the time of the Republican Convention, and various other felonies.[22]

re-creation based upon an ever more accessible ideal of integrity. The process can extend into diverse areas of work, human relationships, contest or competition, and teaching and learning— all of these increasingly infused with combinations of animating guilt, playfulness, and responsibility. To be sure, this overall three-stage process is itself ideal, as is the integrity to which it aspires, and always vulnerable to internal and external impediments. But the forms of individual and collective rebirth we have witnessed in Vietnam veterans, flawed but profound, suggests that the ideal model can be at least partially realized.

The veterans also make clear that young people, even when considerably confused, can take powerful steps toward new integrity: I think of the My Lai survivor, able to call forth at a crucial moment his idiosyncratically derived ethical forms (from military chivalry, Catholic principles, and the habit of autonomy) to refuse participation in that atrocity. I think of the former grunt whose company was virtually wiped out, appearing at early rap groups in a dissociated state close to breakdown, emerging as a man still highly conflicted but able to mobilize extraordinary sensitivity in furthering his and others' renewal. I think of the former Naval NCO undergoing a series of debilitating personal crises, and through them all evolving a fierce commitment to a vision of integrity new to him and yet so palpable as to provide a nurturing standard for the entire group—and later, through various kinds of writing and consulting, becoming a leading national interpreter of Vietnam veterans' aspirations and needs.

This model of change has potential significance for society at large. And we find glimmerings of the process there too. Consider Daniel Ellsberg's trajectory from zealous, war-entranced, counter-insurgency-minded "defense intellectual" to thoughtful critic and then courageous resister of the war. His (and Anthony Russo's) release of the Pentagon Papers (containing much of the suppressed history of American war-making in Vietnam) was an act of nonviolent resistance that, whatever its immediate effects on the war, extends to the very heart of questions of national integrity. To be sure, Ellsberg's zealousness and sense of destiny were involved at both ends of the trajectory—transformations are always selective and must make use of prior psychic forms and energies. But the change in Ellsberg is nonetheless profound, and includes much of what we have described (death immersion, learning to feel, new orientation of self and world) in the softening and overall psychic journey of antiwar veterans. Any such change is greatly overdetermined, never a matter of simple cause and effect. But Ellsberg tells of one particular confrontation with death and murder, involving official American attempt to cover up a killing by Green Berets of a Vietnamese double agent, which seemed to symbolize for him the murderously counterfeit nature of the entire American project in Vietnam:

. . . the specific significance of the Green Beret clipping [about the event] for me was that it focused me on the role of lying by the Executive, automatically, unreflectively, to conceal murder. It had a very strong effect. I read that and felt I cannot be a part of this system anymore. I cannot anymore be led to lie because superiors or regulations tell me to. I acted almost immediately. I decided that I would reveal the deception of the Executive Branch, the concealment of murder over the last twenty years, to the Congress.[23]

This confrontation came at a time when Ellsberg's Vietnam-centered world view had already been shaken by his Pentagon Papers research, which revealed "just one war, continuously for a quarter of a century. . . . an American war almost from its beginning. . . . after all, a foreign aggression. Our aggression."[24] He had also been influenced by American critics of the war, by statements and writings of Gandhian principles of nonviolence and civil disobedience, and by the example of young Americans he met

. . . for the first time, face to face . . . who were on their way to prison for refusing to collaborate in an unjust war . . . sober, intelligent, principled, demonstrating in fact, the dedication I had respected in many officials I had known in Vietnam, but . . . acting on different premises, which I now shared. These personal acts of "witness" gave me what reading alone could not.[25]

Much more went into Ellsberg's transformation, but we can see that it included patterns of reordering and renewal involving images and examples of new forms of integrity coming from without, and reactivation of suppressed truths from within—all made possible, we suspect, by one loving relationship that provided sufficient nurturing trust to enable him to probe these matters and come into contact with what was most authentic in himself.*

I would mention also, as exemplars of this kind of change, a number of West Pointers, including one of the founders of VVAW, who have brought old principles to a new integrity. And there are other defections throughout the society—from war-making, technicism, and brutalization of various kinds, whose trajectories are not yet clear. Indeed the whole process has barely begun, and we cannot yet know how far it may go. We can say, however, that this kind of integrity-based quest has deep psycho-biological roots; it is not something alien to man. But it must be constantly pursued and recaptured, its forms continuously created and re-created. And it can flourish only by equally continuous confrontation of the myriad images of death on behalf of commitment to continuity of life.

---

* This description of Ellsberg's change is not meant to be an exhaustive psychological (or psychohistorical) interpretation—though I hope one will be made someday—but no more than a suggestion of some of the elements involved. It is based upon his writings, speeches, and a few informal discussions I have had with him and others close to him.

CHAPTER 14

On Healing

✿

So it becomes almost inevitable that good people say: Look, it's good to be working at this job, or that job, it's good and important and in certain respects rewarding; but against the measure of what might be done, what might *be*, were things different, we can only feel driven to experiment, try different tacks, make changes in our lives.

—Daniel Berrigan

A god outgrown becomes immediately a life-destroying demon. The form has to be broken and the energies released.

—Joseph Campbell

. . . .
The self persists like a dying star, ...
Death's face rises afresh, ...

—Theodore Roethke

THE STORY GOES full circle and returns to the teller. The rap
groups involve people in risk, a stance that came more easily to
veterans than to professionals. The whole experience raised questions for me about my own profession and the professions in
general—about the extent to which everyday professional function means washing away these struggles around integrity instead
of pursuing them, the extent to which the special armor of professionals blocks free exchange between them and the people they
ostensibly serve.

Part of the excitement a number of us experienced in the rap
groups had to do with divesting ourselves of that professional
armor. The same was true for me in individual interviews—more
dialogues—in which I would at times discuss or answer for my
own views and actions concerning the Vietnam War, being a
professor at Yale, the psychoanalytic movement, marriage and
family, and just about anything else. This in no way meant a
merging of my role and the veteran's; they in fact remained
quite distinct. As an antiwar psychiatric investigator I was both
gathering information and helping with a therapeutic procedure;
the veteran told of Vietnam experiences in order to contribute
both to my investigation and to his own understanding and well-
being. This was not my initial foray into unorthodox investigation: I had done idiosyncratic research in Hong Kong and in
three cities in Japan, as well as in the United States, all of which
involved open dialogue and considerable improvisation. But I
felt on this occasion a fuller commitment to the entire process—
to what I would call my investigative advocacy—than I had in
any previous work. This was partly because all of us, veterans
and professionals alike, were more or less in the middle of the

411

problem—the war continued and we all had painful emotions about what it was doing, and what we were doing or not doing to combat it.*

But I also came to realize that, apart from the war, the work had important bearing upon a sense of long-standing crisis affecting all of us in the psychological professions and the professions in general—a crisis the war in Vietnam both accentuated and illuminated but by no means created. We professionals, in other words, came to the rap groups with our own need for a transformation in many ways parallel to that we sought to enhance in veterans. We too, sometimes with less awareness than they, were in the midst of struggles around living and working that had to do with intactness and wholeness, with what we have been calling integrity.

One source of perspective on that struggle, I found, was a return to the root idea of profession, the idea of what it means to profess. Indeed, an examination of the evolution of these two words could provide something close to a cultural history of the West. The Latin prefix *pro* means "forward," "toward the front," "forth," "out," or "into a public position." *Fess* derives from the Latin *fateri* or *fass*, meaning "to confess, own, acknowledge." To profess (or be professed) then, originally meant a personal form of out-front public acknowledgment. And that which was acknowledged or *con*fessed always (until the sixteenth century) had to do with religion: with taking the vows of a religious order or declaring one's religious faith. But as society became secularized, the word came to mean "to make claim to have knowledge of an art or science" or "to declare oneself expert or proficient in" an enterprise of any kind. The noun form, "profession," came

* In contrast, my Hiroshima work, in which I also experienced strong ethical involvement, was retrospective and in a sense prospective (there were immediate nuclear problems, of course, but we were not in the midst of nuclear holocaust); my study of Chinese thought reform dealt with matters of immediate importance but going on (in a cultural sense) far away; and my work with Japanese youth had much less to do with overwhelming threat and ethical crisis.[1]

to suggest not only the act of professing, but also the ordering, collectivization, and transmission of the whole process. The sequence was from "profession" or religious conviction (from the twelfth century) to a particular order of "professed persons," such as monks or nuns (fourteenth century) to "the occupation which one possesses to be skilled in and follow," especially "the three learned professions of divinity, law, and medicine" along with "the military profession." So quickly did the connotations of specialization and application take hold that as early as 1605 Francis Bacon could complain: "Amongst so many great foundations of colleges in Europe, I find strange that they are all dedicated to professions, and none left free to Art and Sciences at large."[2]

Thus the poles of meaning around the image of profession shifted from the proclamation of personal dedication to transcendent principles to membership in and mastery of a specialized form of socially applicable knowledge and skill. In either case the profession is immortalizing—the one through the religious mode, the other through works and social-intellectual tradition. And the principles of public proclamation and personal discipline carry over from the one meaning to the other—the former taking the shape of examination and licensing, the latter of study, training, and dedication. Overall, the change was from advocacy based on faith to technique devoid of advocacy.*

---

* One can observe this process in the modern separation of "profession" from "vocation." Vocation also has a religious origin in the sense of being "called by God" to a "particular function or station." The secular equivalent became the idea of a personal "calling" in the sense of overwhelming inclination, commitment, and even destiny. But the Latin root of vocation, *vocāre*, to call, includes among its meanings and derivatives: vocable, vocation, vouch; advocate, advocation, convoke, evoke, invoke, provoke, and revoke. Advocacy is thus built into the original root and continuing feel of the word vocation; and vocation in turn is increasingly less employed in connection with the work a man or woman does. If we do not say profession, we say "occupation," which implies seizing, holding, or simply filling in space in an area of in time; or else "job," a word of unclear origin that implies a task, activity, or assignment that is, by implication, self-limited or possibly part of a larger structure including many related jobs, but not, in essence, related to an immortalizing tradition or principle.

To be sure, contemporary professions do contain general forms of advocacy: in law, of a body of supra-personal rules applicable to everyone; in medicine, of healing; and in psychiatry, of humane principles of psychological well-being and growth. But immediate issues of value-centered advocacy and choice (involving groups and causes served and consequences thereof) are mostly ignored. In breaking out of the pre-modern trap of immortalization by personal surrender to faith, the "professional" has fallen into the modern trap of pseudo-neutrality and covert immortalization of technique. As a result, our professions are all too ready to offer their techniques to anyone and anything.

Consider once more the case of psychiatry and the military. We have observed the part played, even if inadvertently, by the military psychiatrist in Vietnam who helps men adjust to their own atrocities. Whatever his intentions, he is in collusion with the military in conveying to individual GIs an overall organizational message: "Do your indiscriminate killng with confidence that you will receive expert medical-psychological help if needed." Truly this is the psychiatry of the executioner. The psychiatrist is brought to this point by the combination of a particularly evil and counterfeit war with the advanced technicism of his own profession—the unexpressed assumption that his knowledge and skill are useful and good, no matter where applied.

That technicism is not without psychological power. What is sometimes in the military called "the new psychiatry" has three apparently sound principles, recently restated for the Vietnam War by H. Spencer Bloch: *immediacy* . . . "The man should be treated as soon as possible after he develops incapacitating symptoms"; *proximity* . . . "He should be treated as close to his own unit and comrades as possible"; and *expectancy* . . . "His treatment is undertaken and maintained with the expectation that he will respond favorably and return to duty."[3] For as early as World War I, and more systematically in World War II and the Korean War, military psychiatrists have found that soldiers treated according to these three principles tend to lose their psychiatric symptoms (even severe ones) almost overnight, and are able to return quickly to useful duty. In contrast, those with similar symptoms who are evacuated to the rear and probed intrapsychically tend to hold onto their symptoms tenaciously, require medical discharge, and retain as civilians dependent demands for compensation as well as feelings of guilt and shame over their failure and "unmanliness."

Hence, at Bloch's unit in Vietnam, "a very high level of expectation was maintained: patients were there to get well and to conduct themselves appropriately"—that is, as soldiers with pride in their unit. Treatment was always supportive—rest, sleep therapy, drugs to relieve anxiety, and a certain amount of discussion and intervention concerning interpersonal conflicts: "Our rationale was that these men had run into some difficulty in interpersonal relations in their units that caused them to be extruded from these groups." Overall, "The therapeutic endeavor . . . was to facilitate the men's integration into their own groups (units) through integration into the group of ward patients."[4]

The approach is convincing, until we recall that precisely "some difficulty in interpersonal relationships"—being in some degree "extruded from" the combat group—helped one (the My Lai survivor, for instance) to avoid committing atrocities. For where the shared adaptation is to absurd evil (the atrocity-producing situation), group integration (or reintegration) undermines personal integrity. Yet it is also true that maximum group integration or cohesiveness is of enormous importance for group survival, always a central preoccupation in combat, and an exclusive one in Vietnam. Given this fundamental conflict between integration and integrity, the psychiatrist has little ethical space in which to move. But should he be there at all occupying the space he is in?

The question raises issues about the psychiatrist's own conflict between personal integrity and (military) group integration. For when he serves in the military he becomes integrated with, and to a significant degree the advocate of, a group "the aim of which," according to Bloch, is "admittedly a very pragmatic one . . . to conserve the fighting strength." Yet the psychiatrist's long-standing personal integrity is likely to depend upon a very different form of advocacy: that of individual well-being and larger humane principles having to do with justice and realized lives, as opposed to killing, premature dying, and especially to widespread atrocity. During World War II psychiatrists experienced this integrity-integration conflict—again one thinks of Catch 22—but they could, in that war, achieve a measure of reconciliation between group integration and personal integrity through the realization that their collusion in killing and dying was in the service of combatting a force that promised killing and dying on an infinitely larger and more grotesque scale. The point is, that for the psychiatrist, as for everyone else (but in many ways even more so), there is no getting away from an evaluation of the group one is to serve and, above all, the nature and consequences of its immediate and long-range mission.

I wonder how many colleagues shared my sense of chilling illumination in picking up the October, 1971, issue of the *American Journal of Psychiatry* (the official organ of the American Psychiatric Association), and finding in it two articles by psychiatrists about Vietnam: one entitled "Organizational Consultation in a Combat Unit,"[5] and the other "Some Remarks on Slaughter."[6] The first, by Douglas R. Bey, Jr. and Walter E. Smith, lives up to its title in providing a military-managerial view of the psychiatrist's task. The authors invoke a scholarly and 'responsible' tone as they describe the three principles of combat psychiatry and trace their historical development. They then elaborate their own "workable method of organizational consultation developed and employed in a combat division in Viet Nam." The method combines these principles of military psychiatry with "an organizational case study method" recently elaborated for industry at the Menninger Foundation, and, according to the authors, has bearing on possible developments in community psychiatry. Their professional voice sounds tempered, practical, and modest as they tell of their team approach (with trained corpsmen), of interviews with commanding officers, chaplains, and influential noncoms, and acknowledge that commanders

were far better prepared to work out solutions to their problems than we, since their area of expertise was in administration and fighting whereas ours was in the area of helping them to see where their feelings might be interfering with their use of these skills.

It was enough for psychiatric consultants to serve as an "observing ego" to the particular military unit. To back up that position they quote, appropriately enough, from an article by General W. C. Westmoreland recommending that the psychiatrist assume "a personnel management consultation type role." The title of that article by General Westmoreland—"Mental Health—An Aspect of Command"—makes quite clear just whom psychiatry in the military is expected to serve.

The authors' combination of easy optimism and concern for everyone's feelings and for the group as a whole, makes one almost forget the kinds of activities the members of that group were engaged in. Reading that lead article in the official journal of the national organization of American psychiatrists gave me a disturbing sense of how far this kind of managerial technicism could take a profession, and its reasonably decent individual practitioners, into ethical corruption. What is most significant about the article is that the authors never make mention of the slightest conflict—in themselves and their psychiatric team any more than the officers and men the team deals with—between group integration and personal integrity. Either they were too numbed to be aware of such conflict, or (more likely) they did not consider it worthy of mention in a scientific paper.

William Barry Gault's article, "Some Remarks on Slaughter," was a particularly welcome antidote, even if a bit more hidden in the inside pages. As his title makes clear, Gault's tone is informed by an appropriate sense of outrage. Significantly, his vantage point was not Vietnam but Fort Knox, Kentucky, where he examined large numbers of men returning from combat. He was thus free of the requirement of integration with a combat unit, and we sense immediately a critical detachment from the atrocity-producing situation.

Gault introduces the idea of "the psychology of slaughter," combining the dictionary definition of that word ("the extensive, violent, bloody or wanton destruction of life; carnage") with a psychological emphasis upon the victim's defenselessness ("whether . . . a disarmed prisoner or an unarmed civilian"). He can "thus . . . distinguish slaughter from the mutual homicide of the actual combatants in military battle." He sets himself the interpretive task of explaining how "relatively normal men overcame and eventually neutralized their natural repugnance toward slaughter." He is rigorously professional as he ticks off six psychological themes or principles contributing to slaughter, and yet his ethical outrage is present in every word. His themes are: "The enemy is everywhere . . . [or] the universalization of the enemy"; "the enemy is not human . . . [or] the 'cartoonization' of the victim"; the "dilution" or "vertical dilution" of responsibility; "the pressure to act"; "the natural dominance of the psychopath"; and "sheer firepower . . . [so that] terrified and furious teenagers by the tens of thousands have only to twitch their index fingers, and what was a quiet village is suddenly a slaughterhouse."

Gault sensitively documents each of these themes in ways very consistent with experiences conveyed to me during rap groups and individual interviews. He ends his article with illustrative stories: of prisoners refusing to give information being thrown out of helicopters as examples to others; of a new combat commander who refused to shoot a twelve-year-old "dink" accidentally encountered by the company while setting up an ambush, and thereby deeply jeopardized himself with his own men, who in turn saw the whole company jeopardized by the survival of someone who might, even as a prisoner, convey information about the ambush. Gault admits he does not know "why similar experiences provoke so much more guilt in one man than in another," and, still professionally cautious (perhaps overly so), remains "unwilling to attempt to draw any large lessons from my observations." At the end he insists only that "in Vietnam a number of fairly ordinary young men have been psychologically ready to engage in slaughter and that moreover this readiness is by no means incomprehensible."

One senses that these stories made a profound impact upon him, that he became a survivor of Vietnam by proxy and that the article was his way of giving form to that survival as well as resolving his own integration-integrity conflict as a morally sensitive psychiatrist in the military at the time of the Vietnam War.* He was able to call forth his revulsion toward the slaughter (and, by implication, his advocacy of life-enhancing alternatives) as a stimulus to understanding and to bring to bear on the Vietnam War a valuable combination of professional insight and ethical awareness.

Even by the limited criteria of well-being and efficacy, the new psychiatry of the military might well be found wanting. Its claim of brilliant success—return-to-duty rates of 56 percent for psychosis, 85 percent for psychoneurosis, 90 percent for alcohol and drug problems, and 100 percent for combat exhaustion[7]—are impressive indeed, until one begins to look at them more closely. Ronald Glasser, in a brilliant chapter on combat psychiatry, interweaves a lecture by a psychiatric consultant (whose theme is, "Gentlemen, It Works") with two case histories in which it does "work"—the symptoms are alleviated and the men return

* This assumption that the article was an expression of Gault's own survivor formulation, which I made originally only on the basis of reading it (and, of course, on my experience, personal and professional, with the psychology of the survivor), was strongly confirmed by a brief talk he and I had when we met as members of a panel on Vietnam veterans at a psychoanalytic meeting.

to duty. "But," as the war psychiatrist depicted in the chapter observes:

the war goes on. . . . there is no medical or psychiatric follow-up on the boys after they've returned to duty. No one knows if they are the ones who die in the very next firefight, who miss the wire stretched out across the tract, or gun down unarmed civilians. Apparently, the army doesn't seem to want to find out.[8]

In other words there is neither medical-psychiatric follow-up nor concern with other forms of destructive or self-destructive behavior that might replace the original symptoms. Nor do we know enough about delayed psychiatric casualties—men who did not break down in combat but who, according to a number of former military psychiatrists (with experience at various bases receiving Vietnam returnees) I have spoken to, have appeared in very large numbers. They have also appeared at VA hospitals and in civilian settings. Add to this the amorphous and yet profound imprints of the war on Vietnam veterans, as I and others (notably Chaim Shatan) have observed,* which psychiatrists,

* The effects of the war are often categorized as the "post-Vietnam syndrome." The phrase has been attributed to me because I was one of the first to suggest that there would be psychological effects specific to the Vietnam War, in testimony I gave before a Senate subcommittee in January, 1970.[9] But I have never used the term, and it appears to have been employed rather early by Veterans Administration psychiatrists encountering men from Vietnam. One can of course delineate consistent patterns in Vietnam veterans (as we have done in this book), and the term correctly suggests something special about the psychological impact of the Vietnam War. Other than that, however, post-Vietnam syndrome is a dubious, easily-abused category, especially in its ready equation of effects of the war with a clinical condition (a "syndrome"). That has been done, for instance, in relationship to various forms of rage, guilt, and protest which, as I have suggested, are actually appropriate to the experience and can be expressed in constructive, 'healthy' ways. The implication that can often accompany the use of the term is that normal or desirable behavior (in contrast to the post-Vietnam syndrome) would be to adapt quietly to existing American social and war-making arrangements. Still, the evocative quality of the term—its availability as a catchall—makes it widely used by almost everyone.

veterans, journalists, and educators throughout the country now note with some dismay. Finally, there are the vast drug problems and the violent crimes mentioned earlier. Taking all these into account, the Army's use of ostensibly brilliant psychiatric statistics in connection with the Vietnam War is one more example of psychiatric technicism. As with statistics on drugs, it is just another "body count."[10]

Compare Bloch's optimistic statistics and case material—men who show "moderately severe combat exhaustion" or "probable marijuana-induced psychotic episode" or "anxiety reaction in a recent arrival," all returning triumphantly to duty—with the grim, and I suspect more experientially authentic, tones of Solomon's three cases: the completed suicide of the man who had been involved in a double atrocity following "forty confirmed Viet Cong killed"; the depression and suicidal gesture in the veteran who had killed and wounded several of his own men while on amphetamines; and a third case we have not yet mentioned, that of a black construction worker who disliked combat in Vietnam but did his job until a combat incident, in which a grenade he had told another soldier to throw, bounced back and killed the thrower and two others, leaving the veteran haunted by guilt and depression.

We still have a very great deal to learn about the psychological casualties of Vietnam. But we can say now that the evidence strongly suggests that even the relatively narrow sphere of "effectiveness" of treatment and "prevention" is inextricably bound up with ethical issues. Psychiatric technicism, in denying that link, falsifies the effects of the war and further corrupts the profession.

Nor do we have follow-up studies on psychiatrists and their spiritual-psychological state after service in Vietnam. I have talked to a number of them, and my impression is that they find it no easier to come to terms with their immersion in the counterfeit universe than does the average GI. They too feel themselves deeply compromised. They seem to require a year or more for them to begin to confront the inner contradictions they experienced. They too are survivors of Vietnam, and of a very special kind. I know of one or two who have embarked upon valuable survivor missions, parallel to and partly in affiliation with that of VVAW as an organization. But what is yet to emerge, though I hope it will before too long, is a detailed personal account by a psychiatrist of his struggles with group integration and individual integrity, and with the vast ramificatons of the counterfeit that this book only begins to suggest.

Large numbers of American psychiatrists, in the midst of their considerable success, are experiencing profound uneasiness bordering on despair. One feels that despair in the anxious defensiveness of the psychiatric and psychoanalytic older generation, as well as in the confused eclecticism of younger professionals. Allan Wheelis, one of the first to point out this recent wave of despair, attributed it to the mature psychoanalyst's inner division between continuing to profess publicly the truth of the elaborate conceptual scheme he inherited while privately losing faith in it and denying and violating it.[11] Leslie Farber's description of "therapeutic despair" in many who treat schizophrenic patients involves a similar division between proclamation of special "meanings" in therapeutic transactions that endow first patient and then therapist with "oracular powers"—and the actual "emptiness, meaninglessness, and lack of confirmation" in the work.[12] These legacies operate in many of the psychiatrists-in-training I regularly teach, who express in varied combinations: disbelief in most received theory (sometimes taking the form of a desperate embrace of that theory), criticism bordering on contempt for the morality (or immorality) of the profession, and a sensitive openness to a variety of currents consistent with what I have described as the Protean style. They often strike me as young men and women awaiting a transformation of their profession and of themselves, a transformation that seems always in the offing but never quite accessible.

I believe that parallel dilemmas exist throughout the professions, and are part of the broader psychohistorical dislocation mentioned earlier. I focus on my own profession both because it is my own and because its particular ethical-psychological struggles are especially well illuminated by encounters with Vietnam veterans. I believe that psychiatric stasis and despair have to do with a shared sense of breakdown in integrity and wholeness around two untenable self images: that of the master psychological scientist-technician and that of the omniscient spiritual guide. Put simply, American culture has so technicized the idea of psychiatric illness and cure that the psychiatrist or psychoanalyst is thrust into a stance of scientifically based spiritual omniscience—a stance he is likely to find much too seductive to refuse entirely. Anointed with both omniscience and objectivity, and working within a market economy, his allegedly neutral talents become available to the highest bidder. In a militarized society they are equally available to the war-makers.

The technicist model in psychiatry works something like this: A machine, the mind-body function of the patient, has broken down; another machine, more scientifically sophisticated—the psychiatrist—is called upon to "treat" the first machine; and the treatment process itself, being technical, has nothing to do with place, time, or individual idiosyncrasy. It is merely a matter of being a technical-medical antagonist of a "syndrome" or "disease." Nor is this medical-technical model limited to physicians —nonmedical psychoanalysts and psychotherapists can be significantly affected by it. And the problem is not so much the medical model as such as it is the technicism operating within that model.* The technicism in turn feeds (and is fed by) a denial of acting within and upon history.

---

* In this sense I am in sympathy with Szasz[13] and Laing[14] in their stress on the repressive uses of the medical model, but also with Humphrey Osmond's defense of the enduring, human core of the medical model, which has "stood the test of millennia,"[15] and contains still untapped resources for us. I believe that the medical model of disease and healing is still needed by psychiatrists, at least in some of our work and thought, but that it must itself be liberated from its technicist fetters.

To be sure no psychiatrist sees himself as functioning within this admittedly overdrawn model. But its lingering technicism is very much with us and can have the catastrophic results we have observed. Even psychological groups bent on breaking out of this technicism, such as some within the humanistic psychology movement (or "third force"), can be rendered dependent upon it by their very opposition, to the point of being unable to evolve an adequate body of theory and practice of their own.

An alternative perspective, in my judgment, must be not only psychohistorical (in ways suggested throughout this book), but also psychoformative. By the latter I mean a stress upon the evolution of inner forms and upon the specifically human mental process of inwardly re-creating all that is perceived or encountered.[16] As in the work of Langer and Cassirer,[17] my stress is upon what can be called a formative-symbolic *process,* upon symbolization rather than any particular symbol (in the sense of one thing standing for another). The approach connects with much in twentieth-century thought, and seeks to overcome the nineteenth-century emphasis upon mechanism, with its stress upon breakdown of elements into component parts—an emphasis inherited, at least in large part, by psycho*analysis,* as the word itself suggests.[18] Twentieth-century technicism could be described as an aberrant (and in a sense nostalgic) re-creation of nineteenth-century mechanism. In contrast, a focus upon images and forms (the latter more structured and more enduring than the former) and upon their continuous development and re-creation gives the psychiatrist a way of addressing historical forces without neglecting intrapsychic concerns.

The antiwar passions of a particular Vietnam veteran, for instance, had to be understood as a combined expression of many different psychic images and forms: the Vietnam environment and the forces shaping it; past individual history; the post-Vietnam American experience, including VVAW and the rap groups and the historical forces shaping these; and the various emanations of guilt, rage, and altered self-process that could and did take shape. Moreover, professionals, like myself, who entered into the lives of these veterans—with our own personal and professional histories, personal struggles involving the war, and much else—became very much a part of the overall image-form constellation.

Applied to more routine situations, this perspective would view people undergoing discomfort or incapacity, and the "healers" or "professionals" of any kind from whom they sought assistance, as coming together at a particular historical moment during which a culture tends to promote certain styles of disturbance (or deformation) and certain kinds of "treatment" (or resymbolization). The understanding that their approach is only one among many socio-historical possibilities could foster, among "healers" (not only psychiatrists and psychoanalysts but teachers, clergymen, and in many cases social and political activists) crucial restraints against technicism and claim to omniscience. With that knowledge also conveyed to those who seek help or change, choices are possible for everyone: "seekers" may select healers sympathetic to the forms they wish to cultivate (whether having to do with religious mysticism, political radicalism, or personal openness); and even if their quest for integrity and new integration should lead them to modify or abandon these forms, they would be active agents in those decisions rather than becoming passively entrapped in someone else's (often counterfeit) expertise. The healer, in turn, would make conscious decisions about where he wishes to apply his capacities, according to the personal and professional forms he seeks to investigate or cultivate. He would thus combine the technical knowledge and skill associated with his profession with ethical and political decisions concerning what he does, to what effect, and for whose benefit. And these decisions would involve not only people he seeks to work with but institutions and groups with whom he becomes affiliated and the overall question of the extent to which he lends his talents to perpetuating—as opposed to significantly changing—existing social and political arrangements. What I am suggesting is that the healer, no less than the seeker, functions intellectually and ethically from a particular formative place, from a particular relationship to history.

This book, then, emerges from my own formative place: as an investigator, writer, and teacher struggling to develop and convey new approaches and a new body of theory responsible to and autonomous from the psychoanalytic-psychiatric tradition in which I was trained; as a physician (however vestigial my actual medical talents) and a psychiatrist with a continuing commitment to healing; as a radical critic of American institutions with particularly intense concerns about war and nuclear weapons and equally strong involvement with issues of personal and social transformation; as a forty-six-year-old man with specific struggles toward and conflicts around wholeness and integrity—having to do with mixtures of commitment, ambition, and temptation, and involvements with family, friends, institutions, groups, money, and work. All this was at issue during every moment of encounter with antiwar veterans and every decision about what and how to report concerning these encounters.

This psychohistorical and psychoformative model permits us another look at the idea of insight, so basic to any psychological work. Derived from inner sight, the word suggests "the fact of penetrating with the eyes of the understanding into the inner character or hidden nature of things; a glimpse or view beneath the surface; the faculty or power of thus seeing."[19] In psychoanalytic psychiatry the "hidden nature of things" has to do with unconscious motivations, and the distinction is made between intellectual insight, the capacity merely to describe these motivating patterns, and emotional insight, the further capacity to feel them in operation. But we may say that every insight expressed by a healer or investigator—every use of "the eyes of the understanding"—is a function of his own formative place, of all that goes into his special relationship to history. Thus for the same experience, a Freudian would suggest insights different not only from those of a neo-Freudian or a Jungian but also to some extent from a Freudian of another generation, country, city, or institute—or from those he himself would have offered ten years before. These divergent insights can be confusing to the professional and non-professional alike, but the only alternative to such divergence is the false claim that a particular insight represents absolute, universal, and eternal truth.

To be sure one can speak of eternal principles characterizing the physical universe as well as human and other life within it (what we spoke of earlier as psychobiological universals) but our way of grasping these principles is always partial, one-sided, approximate. Nor are all insights by any means of equal value. Certain individual and group "places" allow for greater profundity, come closer than others to lasting truth—and we have witnessed, in just that one psychiatric journal, the way in which one's formative place can lead either to ethical blindness (uncritical application of the new psychiatry to Vietnam) or admirable ethical sensitivity (interpretative examination of the "psychology of slaughter"). But even though there are many intellectual and ethical distinctions to be made among competing conceptual systems—psychoanalysis, biological psychiatry, behaviorism, etcetera—none is inherently immune from the temptation to abandon genuine insight in favor of opportunistic technicism and related forms of corruption.

What all this suggests is that he who would provide insight—let us now say the psychohistorian—is inevitably present in that insight—present in the immediate situation, the traditions that inform the insight, and the ongoing historical forces that occasion it. The presence of the psychohistorian (or of any professional or would-be knower) is a dialectical one: He is *in* the situation or experience he interprets, is affected by and susceptible to it, and in turn acts upon it. At the same time he delineates—*separates*—himself from that situation in order to get "a glimpse or view beneath the surface" and express "the faculty of power of thus seeing." He can then associate what he observes with other situations, experiences, principles, in order to evolve a new (sometimes old) interpretive form or insight. But the point to be remembered is that the dialectic itself takes place in history—not in some special 'technical place' immune from history.

Thus Freud's insights about sex and neurosis had both to do with his immediate relationship to late Victorian sexual hypocrisy and repression and to the organic-neurological emphases of the traditions in which he was trained. These two patterns greatly affected his life and thought, despite his capacity to separate himself from them sufficiently to subvert them eventually with his insights. Freud's findings are neither equally true for all men and women of any time or place, nor are they specifically limited to middle-class Viennese Jews (who made up most of his patients) during the late nineteenth and early twentieth centuries. Rather, Freud was able to penetrate a particular psychohistorical situation in a way that led to profound insights applicable far beyond that situation and are valuable in knowledge they stimulate even when they require change or replacement. Similarly, what psychiatrists or psychohistorians say about death today has much to do both with immediate involvements during our death-centered historical moment and with a certain degree of separation from these involvements permitting generalizations beyond them. The power of those very generalizations depends in turn upon the authentic presence of the investigator in them.

But there is a tragic paradox here: penetration of "the inner character of hidden nature" of some things seems to require blindness toward other things. A revolutionary insight demands a form of onesidedness that must in some degree distort. That is, the formative place and the individual gifts of a thinker provide him with a selective prism through which light can be brilliantly —and exaggeratedly—reflected. And that very illumination renders all the more pale by contrast the surrounding areas of "conventional wisdom" he must inevitably retain.

A case in point is the contrast between Freud's extraordinary breakthrough concerning repressed sexuality and the unconscious origins of neurosis on the one hand, and the limitations of his writings on the subjects of women and of death on the other. Though his depiction of women was not without new insights, his general view of them and their sexuality as essentially passive, masochistic, and to be understood primarily in relationship to male comparisons (anxiety and envy over the *absence* of a penis, etcetera)—all this reflected rather directly his conventional Victorian patriarchal attitudes and perhaps his rather limited personal experience with women as well.

On the subject of death, Freud was profoundly ambivalent. He insisted upon breaking out of cultural-historical conventions encouraging the denial of death, and upon confronting both that denial and the hard fact of individual annihilation in death. Moreover, in positing a death instinct, whatever its limitations as a theory (it is actually a contradiction in terms—since instincts always serve to maintain life), he gave recognition to the all-encompassing significance of death for life. Yet, other than the death instinct (which stands alone on a metaphysical limb) he made no room for death in his theoretical structure, insisted it had no psychic representation, and viewed the fear of death as secondary to fear of castration. There is no simple answer to why Freud stopped short of achieving the kind of conceptual breakthrough on death he did achieve on repressed sexuality. But we can say that Freud responded to a historical 'call' to expose and combat truly dangerous dimensions of sexual hypocrisy and repression, and that once he had responded to that call sexuality, so to speak, became his project. He then had to cover over, at least conceptually, his own insights about death, lest these interfere with the force and consistency of his sexual (libido) theory (hence the theoretical primacy of castration over death).

Freud's relationship to death, viewed from this formative-historical standpoint, raises some interesting general questions about men and ideas. There is a good deal of evidence that, for the young Freud, death was no less an area of personal conflict than was sexuality. He transcended sexual conflicts through his

work, through a combination of personal abstinence and detailed
case studies of patients that would provide enduring generalizations.* But one cannot, so to speak, "abstain" from death, and
Freud faced his own with extraordinary courage. One can speak
of a transformation of early fear of death to impressive mastery
of that fear over his sixteen years of extremely painful and
humiliating symptoms of and treatment for throat cancer. But I
believe that once more Freud's work was very much involved:
inwardly convinced that, through his insights, he had achieved
a truly viable mode of symbolic immortality, death held considerably less terror for him than for most men. A much greater
concern for him was the fate of psychoanalysis, of his ideas and
the movement they had spawned.

The questions he asked of a disciple and patient, Maryse
Choisy—"What will they do with my theory after my death?
Will it still resemble my basic thoughts?"[21]—continued to preoccupy him. But he was clearly confident that, no matter what
others did with them, his ideas would last. He had not always
possessed that confidence, certainly not during his twenties and
thirties when his fear of death was greatest. A recently published
letter Freud wrote in 1894 at the age of thirty-eight suggests a
turning-point in his life as he reveals both that fear and its path
of resolution:

Among the gloomy thought of the past few months there is one that
is in second place, right after wife and children—namely, that I shall

---

* In his correspondence with Fleiss, Freud indicated that, at age forty-one,
"sexual stimulation is of no more use to a person like me." It is quite possible,
however, that his own combination of almost superhuman work energy and
sexual abstinence led him too quickly into what I would consider to be a misleading theory of sublimation: the concept that culture itself is the product
of rechanneled sexual energy. It is generally assumed by his biographers that
Freud overcame his sexual difficulties (those originating in the Oedipus complex, for instance) through his self-analysis. But I would put the matter the
other way around and say that both the self-analysis and the sexual conflicts
were mobilized on behalf of his work. This view is consistent with Erikson's
conclusion, at the end of a searching study of Freud's own classical "Irma
dream," that the dream was dreamt for the purpose of discovering psychoanalysis.[20]

not be able to prove the sexual thesis anymore. After all one does not want to die either immediately or completely. . . .

. . . They look upon me as pretty much of a monomaniac, while I have the distinct feeling that I have touched upon one of the great secrets of nature.[22]

When he wrote that letter he was undergoing what is now thought to be a genuine cardiac episode. In any case, his "distinct feeling" of having "touched upon one of the great secrets of nature" was beginning to enable him to face death less fearfully, if not "immediately" (he was just embarking on his opus) or "completely" (one wants something to live on).

But this contradiction between living out this quest for symbolic immortality while totally denying, in his work, the existence of any such principle, was not without its cost. Erik Erikson once commented, when responding to my presentation of some of these views on Freud in a small working group: "He went on being Freud and did not accept his mortality as affecting his concepts." While Erikson was referring specifically to the possible relationship between Freud's cancer and the elaboration of the death instinct, the point has further ramifications. Freud's rationalistic and iconoclastic dismissal of all imagery of immortality as mere denial of death negated, or at least allowed for no clear imagery of, his own extremely strong *sense* of immortality. This negation in turn might well have been an important factor in his and his later disciples' focus upon a more or less literal immortality bestowed upon both the original (and pure) psychoanalytic ideas and the psychoanalytic (group) *movement*. Lacking a sense of formative place, Freud viewed his concepts as detached scientific truths in no way beholden to time or history.

The general problem is the degree to which a great theorist, or a great man (or woman) of any kind—requires the sense of immortality or an image of living on in the eternal truths of his (or her) once-and-for-all insights or unalterable revolutionary institutions—as opposed to living on in the continuous flux and flow of these insights and institutions within the larger historical tide of human thought and action. So consistent is this difficulty even (perhaps especially) in great men—not only in Freud but in different ways in Einstein, Marx, and Mao*—that one suspects it to be the ultimate form of tragic paradox mentioned earlier: the necessary blindness of greatness.

A formative-symbolic perspective not only permits us to approach these questions but suggests something else as well. We can retrospectively recover the sense of a man's greatness less by focusing upon his concrete words (at least some of which are bound to be rendered static by time and by others' subsequent words on similar subjects) than upon the process and experience through which he came to his particular "formative place" and achieved his breakthrough—upon what the theologian John Dunne calls the "life story." In that way we can avoid, or at least recognize, the numbed literality and technicism so often called forth by intellectual and social movements on behalf of holding fast to the words of their founders.

The perspective we have been discussing throws further light on several varieties of contemporary psychiatric corruption. Consider, for instance, the use of psychiatrists for government-initiated suppression of political heretics, now scandalously rampant in the Soviet Union. The psychiatrist forced (or tempted) to falsify his diagnosis—label a truthful critic of society "insane" or "ill" for the sake of providing authorities an excuse for punitive incarceration—abdicates his authentic formative place for a counterfeit bureaucratic-repressive function. He becomes "de-professionalized, and loses any capacity for presence, since the last thing possible is an ethical interaction between the alleged patient and himself. Nor should one assume that such situations

---

* I discussed closely analogous questions involving Mao and the Chinese Cultural Revolution of the 1960s in my book *Revolutionary Immortality*.[23] This issue of literalized versus symbolized immortality has special intensity in association with greatness, but also has considerable relevance in relationship to more prosaic lives.

are limited to the Soviet Union or communist countries in general. While no such flagrantly systematic psychiatric-political repression exists in this country, there has been no lack of individual cases of coercive incarceration of people found disturbing or inconvenient to dominant groups in society. Also relevant here are various uses of psychiatry by the American military, in combat as described, and for punitive administrative purposes in dealing with recalcitrant soldiers. Both the flagrant Soviet and more indirect American examples of state manipulation of psychiatry and medicine reflect a totalistic assumption that any profession or group in society and indeed history itself are to be subsumed to the state's alleged "higher purpose."

A more widespread American corruption involves deception and self-deception around psychiatric care. The psychiatrist frequently makes the socio-historically naive assumption that he is "available to anyone who needs help." In actuality his social and institutional 'place' brings him together with a specific kind of patient or problem. If he opens a private office in a fashionable neighborhood, he attracts upper middle-class, largely professional people, who seek, on the whole, relief from conflict, greater meaning in their lives, and more effective personal function. By joining a street-corner clinic he encounters young people, often on bad trips from drugs, struggling to find their way in and out of the counterculture. When employed by an industrial firm, diagnostic and therapeutic work with executives or workers is geared to improve the company's efficiency and earnings. A university affiliation can associate him not only with teaching and transmission of knowledge but with various administrative interests pursued, at times, at the expense of faculty colleagues and students, and also in some degree with the university's economic and military connections.

In other words the psychiatrist *is* involved with historical forces and groups, whatever technicist neutrality he may proclaim. These involvements influence the goals of his work, his therapeutic or investigative style, and his generally unspoken forms of "ultimate concern"—the directions through which he seeks his own symbolic immortality. Nor does the increasing tendency of psychiatrists toward seeking more of a "mix" in their activities—combining private practice, teaching, and perhaps some community consultation—necessarily bring about insight into these unacknowledged involvements (though it does in many cases suggest their dissatisfaction with the exclusive realm of private upper-middle-class practice.) For the psychiatrist, like other professionals, becomes an advocate of his clients, though his form of advocacy can be subtle and complex. The clients, moreover, are not always who they appear to be: they may be patients or research subjects, or they may also be institutions, subcultures, or unofficial power groups with hidden pulls on his loyalty. He may in fact balance a variety of loyalties, so that in some cases he may have considerable sympathy for people he investigates or treats while being ethically opposed to their individual or group activities. But on the whole his professional place, at least as presently located, tends to be close to or in support of existing institutional arrangements.

This means that the psychiatrist very often finds himself in a cooling role. Problems arise, people get upset, and through his reasoned insight, he is expected to calm things down. For many individual and social situations, such cooling can very usefully head off destructive patterns, give people a chance to reassess their own and others' behavior, and stave off social or even military holocaust. But in the midst of present-day dislocations, cooling can also be the means by which those in power maintain their exploitation and their various forms of violence.

The antiwar veterans, as we well know, exemplify precisely that kind of situation. While they were cool, in our terms numbed, they remained in the roles of victim and executioner; only by breaking out of that numbness and becoming a bit warm (or agitated) could they actively reject those roles. We have also observed psychiatrists functioning, so to speak, on each side of the numbing. Those maintaining it include not only military psychiatrists but large numbers of civilian professionals who cool opposition to the war by therapeutic undermining of the sense of outrage toward it, or toward serving in it, or who contribute actively to the function of institutions (companies making weapons, etcetera) directly involved in the war. In a similar sense, psychiatrists contributing to the breakout from numbed victim or executioner roles were by no means limited to professionals working in antiwar rap groups but include among their numbers all practitioners who, in one way or another, conveyed antiwar values in their work—whether in their interpretive writings, their psychiatric reports on behalf of young men seeking to avoid military service,* or their sympathetic confirmation, in therapy or investigation, of the authenticity of various forms of war resistance.

Very much at issue for the psychiatrist is his view, both an ethical and a psychological matter, toward the various forms of normal numbing he encounters. Ideally one can say that the psychiatrist seeks to help people to break out of numbing and, as in the case of antiwar veterans, to learn to feel. But there are situations where patients' feelings are so self-lacerating and generally destructive that he may, again for psychological and ethical reasons, seek to reinforce numbing, perhaps on a temporary basis and sometimes with the use of drugs. Yet we have seen some of the dangers of normal numbing when that numbing is a way of adapting to a group bent on destruction or self-destruction. There are occasions, increasing in frequency I believe, on which psychiatrists must choose between enhancing individual well-being by supporting patterns of numbing that contribute to various collective forms of harm—or combatting that numbing at the risk of individual anguish. This is roughly the civilian equivalent of the dilemmas we described for military psychia-

---

* In writing these reports psychiatrists had to deal with questions of professional integrity as well, which could be resolved by taking care to be accurate and truthful but at the same time giving strong emphasis to whatever findings could contribute to a psychiatric deferment.

trists. As in our earlier discussion, the psychiatrist cannot resolve the dilemma without asking himself questions about how he got to that 'place' and whether he should be there.

Psychiatrists, like everyone else, are bound by their own numbing, and the great temptation is for them to swim with an American tide that grants considerable acceptance to depth-psychological explorations but resists, at times quite fiercely, serious attempts to alter existing social and institutional arrangements. They thus fall into a devil's bargain in which, as psychiatrists, they can stress intrapsychic insights that undermine personal numbing, so long as they leave relatively undisturbed the widespread numbing (in themselves as well as in others) toward social and historical issues.

The rationalization is always that the latter are far away, the task of sociologists or of historians, in any case of somebody else, while the former are closer to home (the psyche) and therefore in the psychiatrist's domain. But with antiwar veterans we have seen that distinction to be false: numbing had to be overcome simultaneously at intrapsychic and historical levels. To gloss over a veteran's relationship to the atrocity-producing situation and its contributing elements was to leave him with a socially induced psychic wound; any psychological function then attained might well require new forms of destructiveness to reinforce numbing and avoid insight. In that way both the veteran and his society would be denied a fuller grasp of, and a capacity to move beyond, the dubious place they had both been. As with everyone else, the psychiatrist's choices must involve compromise. But all choices would be better served were the psychiatrist to recognize his collusion in numbing toward all matters beyond the self, and his refusal to ask himself the question so many others are now raising: To what extent do my professional activities contribute to exploitation and destructiveness, as opposed to individual and social liberation?

Such questions have been raised, notably by the potential consumers, in connection with federal- and state-supported proliferation of mental health centers. How much do the programs created press participating psychiatrists into cooling-numbing roles toward social protest or potentially innovative social disorder? Without trying to give anything like a full answer to that question, we can say that the building of large centers as extensions of existing psychiatric-university complexes, rather than smaller units right on the turf of those for whom the programs were to serve, immediately raises issues concerning the three principles we have identified with animating institutions. Self-generation can hardly be encouraged in this way, nor is a process of affinity permitted to make itself felt therapeutically. And presence tends to be impaired as well, as the psychiatrist tends to be seen as a distant upper-status figure from a strange land. Without laying claim to a guaranteed solution, one could imagine some form of experimental equilibrium between drawing upon the professional centralization of existing complexes while increasing the arrangements for local self-generation. But that kind of experiment would require sensitivity to precisely the kind of immediate social and historical currents psychiatry has so determinedly resisted.[24] Yet without such experimentation, our great psychiatric institutions and the people in them come to be viewed by many as enemies not only of social change but of authentic psychological insight. As I heard a Vietnam veteran and former drug addict (who had been helped to kick his habit by a small, intense, community-based group) exclaim: "When I see a psychiatrist I think, 'There's a man who can't understand me.'"

All we have said points toward the need for a transformation of the healing professions themselves, following the general principles of change already described. The idea is worth stating at least as a model—not with any expectation of instant transformation, but with the recognition that, here and there, people are already pursuing it, and will undoubtedly continue to do so in forms we have not yet imagined.

Confrontation for psychiatrists would involve taking seriously the ancient paradigm of the death and the continuity of life. This in turn could relate living and dying to the larger historical process, and help psychiatrists to cast off their death-(and life-) denying image of themselves as technicians of human emotions —or of libido, or ego strength, or interpersonal relations, or even of being.

Such confrontation can hardly be realized merely by elevating the idea of death to the status of a concept. Doing that alone could result in psychiatrists extending their area of alleged technical expertise and becoming no less than technicians of death and dying. One can observe such a pitfall in the proliferation of groups and symposia around the hot new subjects of death, violence, and aggression. Genuine confrontation, however, would require psychiatrists to combine intellectual recognition with critical examination of our own lives and deaths. That would mean probing, not once but continuously, our own modes of immortality—the ways in which our ultimate concerns enter into our lives and our work. This in turn would call forth risk, make it conscious and legitimate, and raise fundamental questions not only about man's own mortality but the mortality of ideas, schools of thoughts, and institutions. Always at issue would be the many forms of collective psychiatric numbing that now desensitize the profession to critical ethical questions.

The line quoted from Roethke at the beginning of this chapter, "The Self persists like a dying star" is followed by: "In sleep, afraid. Death's face rises afresh." Roethke has further thoughts that express the spirit of the kind of psychiatric confrontation I suggest:

> I learned not to fear infinity,
> The far field, the windy cliffs of forever,
> The dying of time and the white light of tomorrow,
> The Wheel turning away from itself,
> The sprawl of the wave,
> The on-coming water.

And:

> I am renewed by death, thought of my death,
> The dry scent of a dying garden in September,
> The wind fanning the ash of a low fire.
> What I love is near at hand,
> Always, in earth and air.[25]

The *reordering* in psychiatric transformation would have to do with examining various forms of professional guilt, whether associated with technicist transgressions (military or civilian) or exploitative arrangements of any kind—ultimately, with a critical examination of the present ethical-historical 'place' of the profession.

As in personal transformation, the stress would not be upon static *mea culpa*, but rather upon the animating possibilities of this guilt and related shame and despair—all long-present but now rendered conscious and, so to speak, accepted. Psychiatric despair could be a particular focus, arising as it does out of a sense of lost integrity, of doubt concerning overall personal and professional life-energy or viability, and of the contradictions between what one says one is and what one feels oneself to be. Were it to be faced in its wide manifestations, psychiatric despair could be an invaluable source of illumination, fundamental to both confrontation and reordering. This continuing pursuit of integrity and wholeness, once initiated in the reordering process, could become (as it has already for many) self-energizing, in the true sense ecstatic, as one experiences a new level of harmony around being both a professional and a person. But such integrity and harmony in turn depend upon altered institutional and group arrangements in the direction of more human professional sensitivities at all levels of encounter and impact.

Renewal for psychiatry would center upon desperately needed breakout from technicism and numbing, and especially the social extension of the capacity to feel. The crucial process might well be the rediscovery of professional play. While the capacity to play is greatly affected by experiences of early childhood, it is also quite possible to create professional arrangements that encourage the emergence of the playful healer and the playful investigator. While some psychiatrists are, in personal style, more playful than others, everyone has some play in him that can be brought out under the right conditions. The difficulty is that being 'professional' has too long stood for the antithesis of being playful—thereby narrowing professional function to rules and responsibilities and eliminating the very qualities of imagination and spontaneity that would render professional work more sensitive and humane.

But neither playfulness nor the inner freedom that is a prerequisite for it can be produced by fiat, or by ideological declarations around joy, touch, or sensitivity. While movements espousing these principles in group process can help some people to regain their playfulness, this absolute experiential focus, seemingly unrelated to broader social or ethical commitments, contains a considerable potential for hidden coercion, faddism, and a false polarity between feeling (good) and intellect (bad).

Rather I refer to the joyful possibilities of the marriage of professional discipline to imaginative spontaneity, the coming together of ethic and technique to create a harmonious flow of internal form and external action. This kind of harmony and wholeness is by no means the deadly clarity of an image or landscape that neither moves nor changes*—but the playful freedom that can live with the demands of ultimate concern and the ambiguity of unpredictable change. While this personal-professional utopia is not about to arrive for any of us in full realization, I suspect that most of us, at better moments, have had glimpses of it.

When I consider these issues of change, in psychiatry and elsewhere, I think of Stanley Milgram's response to his own "Eichmann experiments" (as they came to be called). Milgram found

---

* I owe this image to John Dunne.

On Healing 441

that a surprising number of naïve research subjects were all too willing, upon instructions from an experimenter, to press buttons they were told would cause pain and injury to people (trained subjects sitting in nearby booths who would convincingly act out suffering), even, in the many cases, when told that death might result.* Milgram's troubled state over what he found, and perhaps over a certain amount of criticism he met concerning the ethics of the experiments, led him to a profound conclusion: "Men are doomed if they act only within the alternatives handed down to them."[26]

The grimness of that prospect, the dangers of holding fast, and the immediate anticipatory survivor ethos it evokes, can give energy to explorations so desperately required by the healing professions. We can then move beyond the psychiatry of either executioners or victims, toward one that is historically grounded, formative, and candid in its own continuing self-examination. There is much call these days for deprofessionalization—not only in psychiatry but in virtually every other field of work and thought. But what is really needed—and perhaps meant by many who make that call—is detechnicization and breakout from numbing. More desirable than "deprofessionalized" healers or thinkers are men and women who are genuinely professional in their work and advocacies—who can come to a new blend of specialized knowledge and "professed" social and ethical attachments.

Ringing in our ears is Camus' insistence that "in the midst of a murderous world, we agree to reflect on murder and to make a choice." "After that," he goes on to say, "we can distinguish those who accept the consequences of being murderers themselves or the accomplices of murderers, and those who refuse to do so with all their force and being."[27] The choice, after all, is a similar for everyone—officer or grunt, professional or veteran. And a method of choosing is suggested by another of Camus' principles, that of

* The conditions necessary to this result seemed to be unquestioned authority of the experimenters and more or less complete dependency of the naïve subjects upon them.

perpetual rebellion, a formative state in which each of us can become "A man who says no," but at the same time "A man who says yes as soon as he begins to think for himself," and comes to recognize that "Man's solidarity is founded upon rebellion, and rebellion can only be justified by this solidarity." The warrior in us will hardly disappear, but are we not capable of mobilizing that "warrior"-self on behalf of the special illumination made possible by our dreadful and strangely hopeful historical moment.

Afterword

It isn't peace. And there's no honor.

> —Vietnam veterans commenting on
> the cease-fire

> Our generals . . . I obey
> When their command is righteous, but
> When evil, I shall not obey, and here,
> As in Troy, I shall show my nature free
> To fight my enemy with honor.
>
> > —Euripides' fifth-century-B.C.
> > description of a Greek veteran
> > (Achilles) bringing his war home
> > [*Iphigenia in Aulis*]

I will set my ear to catch the moral of the story
and tell on the harp how I read the riddle
> —Psalm XLIX

Is THE WAR over? A cease-fire agreement has been signed (January 1973), and the President has proclaimed "Peace with Honor." Shortly before the cease-fire, American B-52s carried out their "Christmas bombing" of Hanoi and Haiphong, two weeks of indiscriminate high-altitude "carpet bombing" employing the greatest amount of destructive power in the history of aerial warfare. Most of the world responded with strong condemnation. There was no mass protest in the United States, though there were many expressions of outrage and a compelling national campaign was mounted to raise money to rebuild Bach Mai Hospital in Hanoi. The American reaction to the cease-fire was even more equivocal, probably best characterized as joyless relief.

A few days after the announcement of the cease-fire, I met in New Haven with a group of antiwar veterans, some of whom I knew well from personal talks and rap groups. We had planned to get together a week later, but one of them telephoned to suggest that we meet right away because "the guys were having pretty strong reactions." As soon as we sat down they made it clear that the essence of those reactions was rage.

One veteran described how, right after the announcement, he found himself losing control. He broke a window in his room and drove off in his car at breakneck speed with a half-conscious intent to "smash into something"—until he was able to restrain himself and examine what he was doing and feeling. That night he had two dreams, both mostly reenactments of actual events in Vietnam: one of the men in his unit shooting Vietnamese civilians—"men, women, children, everyone"; the other of a buddy "hit by a rocket, his guts falling out . . . trying to hold them in . . . even though he was dead." The other men expressed similar combinations of reactivated memories and immediate rage, and emphasized that "what especially makes us gag is talk about peace with honor."

In softer tones another veteran said, "There is no sense of an ending. Usually a war—or anything—is supposed to have a beginning, a middle, and an end. . . . This is a false ending." He spoke of "the incredible reluctance of the country to face what did go on there," and another added that "a real ending of this war would be that America would have to come to terms with what the war has been all along."

The men went on to speak of the tendency of Americans to be more preoccupied with the return of prisoners of war than with the larger questions of war and peace. "They need heroes" was the way one put it. We talked of the desperate effort to salvage something ennobling from a degrading war—to focus on the courage and strength of men subjected to prolonged incarceration by the enemy, or on that of their wives or parents in waiting for them. The veterans had conflicted feelings about the whole matter—a mixture of sympathy for the returning POWs, whom they viewed as war victims much like themselves, along with resentment of the government's manipulation of national feelings about POWs in ways that distracted Americans from the war's truths. As one man said, somewhat uneasily, "I'm withholding emotion from them."

A few had made an attempt at celebration. "We thought, Well, it's over now. That's what we've been struggling for. Why not have a few drinks together?" But when they got to the bar, they found their hearts were not in it and left early: "We made believe we should celebrate—but it just didn't work." They noted that most other veterans they knew, including those who took no stand on the war, were also "on downs"—in low moods if not actually depressed.

An added influence on the veterans' responses was the death of former President Lyndon Johnson just before the cease-fire was signed. "We had to realize that it wasn't just him—it was the whole country—and then there was nowhere to place the rage." That rage became more diffuse, so that one of the most militant of the men could say, "I'll always be at war while I'm in this country—it's the only way to survive."

Again and again the men returned to the phrase "Peace with Honor." They pointed out that America was still at war in Laos and Cambodia; that America had a lot to do with the fighting still going on in Vietnam; that we were leaving behind various kinds of agents to engage in covert warfare throughout Indochina, and maintaining a tremendous financial and technological presence in South Vietnam. They spoke bitterly of news reports of "the last American to die in Vietnam" and then of "the first American to die after the cease-fire," which sounded to them both "like a baseball score" and "a new body count." What they were saying was that the counterfeit universe of the war had been extended into the cease-fire and beyond. Hence one man concluded: "It isn't peace. And there's no honor."

Yet they knew something had changed. Above all, their own status was suddenly different. "We are no longer dissidents against the war but just hippies" was the way one man put it. As veteran-dissidents they had standing and credibility, but as troublesome hippies they would have neither. In other words they perceived the cease-fire, in the form it took, as a negotiated interruption of war-making pre-cluding confrontation of the war—as an officially-sponsored termina-tion of their own special survivor mission as antiwar veterans. Their rage as well as their painful inner reenactment of the war had to do with their sense of being again rebuffed, this time definitively, and left to stew in their own conflicts. Their government had, as one man said, "once and for all closed the door"—shut out the truth, the possibility of illumination and of new beginning. Hence the addi-tional reaction he experienced to the cease-fire: "Was this it? Was this all?"

Yet that door could not be locked, not even fully closed. Even before the cease-fire many veterans had been thinking about and beginning to act upon the next stage of their survivor mission. Over the years they have been bringing truths about the war into many corners of American life. A number of them have been focusing on the issue of amnesty, which they sense to be inseparable from their own mission. And the six or seven of us who met in New Haven formed a new rap group for the dual purpose of exploring changing personal emotions and considering possible ethical and political directions for the immediate future—precisely the concerns of many rap groups that continue to take shape among Vietnam veterans.

Some veterans, ambivalent about having the term "post-Vietnam syndrome" applied to themselves, suggest that it is more genuinely applicable to America at large. The psychological truth of that claim lies in the combination of a cease-fire that is not quite a peace, and

the powerful war-linked residuum in the American people of confusion, guilt, rage, and betrayal. We have become a nation of
troubled survivors of a war not yet over and still just distantly perceived. We experience a continuing sense of threat, of 'immersion
in death,' and the resulting survivor conflicts can take many forms.
We have already seen the beginnings of the most pernicious kind of
survivor formulation on the part of government spokesmen: one
which attributes the prolonging of the war, and by inference the
suffering of everyone, to war opponents and protesters. That formulation combines scapegoating with still more ominous currents of
potential victimization.

But there are more hopeful directions of survivor formulation in
which error and wrongdoing can be acknowledged and the death-
and-rebirth imagery of survival called forth. In that spirit, the sister
of America's longest-held prisoner of war, a man known to be a
leader of POW 'hawks,' tells us that when her brother comes back
he will have much to learn about the social change that has occurred
in this country in his absence. "In 1964, when my brother was shot
down, there was complete faith in the government, the government
knew best. The military and the uniform were looked upon with a
tremendous amount of respect. All that has changed considerably."
Originally in agreement with him about all this, she has since joined
the antiwar and chicano movements: "The mentality that calls Vietnamese 'gooks' is the same mentality that calls brown people 'spics.'
It's the same battle." The pain and suffering surrounding the Vietnam War have made available to virtually everyone at least the
possibility of illumination and growth—if one can permit oneself
to feel and take some responsibility toward that pain and suffering.

As for me, I think I have learned a great deal. But like many others,
I remain dissatisfied both with what I know and with what I can do
with that knowledge. In pursuing the dialectic of "resistance and con-
templation" so eloquently lived out by James Douglass, I have, together with others in the arts and professions, engaged in two acts of
modest civil disobedience to protest the war. We were trying to express our own 'Nuremberg obligation,' according to the principle laid
down by American international legal authorities after World War II
at Nuremberg that citizens had the responsibility to resist war crimes
of their own government. Originally stated as applicable to everyone,

that principle has so far been applied only by victors to those they have defeated. The Indochina War, with its combination of massive American illegality and criminality, and its multiple confusions concerning victors and vanquished, would seem to be an ideal war around which to revive a more universal Nuremberg obligation.

That obligation takes one immediately to such issues as the implementation of the cease-fire accords, the sustained American intervention in Indochina and its potential for covert warfare, and, perhaps most centrally, that of unconditional amnesty for resisters, exiles and deserters.

Now Vietnam veterans are everywhere. They are an embarrassment to the country in the unanswerable questions raised by their very presence. I meet increasing numbers of them at campuses I visit in various parts of the United States. They speak with mixtures of anxiety and wisdom of their future and the country's, and of the kinds of American leadership that might emerge from the Vietnam war experience. We talk of survivor imagery in leaders being twenty years behind the times, so that the men who insisted upon "standing fast" and "staying the course" in Vietnam were filtering the situation through retained images of 'Munich' and of the disastrous results of Western European "appeasement" of Hitler in 1938. The veterans raise hard questions about whether survivor imagery from the Vietnam War will in turn be inappropriately misleading for a crisis twenty years from now. All of which suggests that wisdom does not come easily, and also that we may just have learned something from Vietnam.

The veterans I talked to sense the fragility of their own insight, psychological or political. They know themselves all too capable of embracing idols and taking wrong turnings. Looking about they see many of their veteran 'brothers' overwhelmed with bitterness or on drugs, in one way or another immobilized. They themselves experience pain that will not go away, which one of them spoke of as "an emotional devil inside of us—all of us." Like Guy Sajer, the Alsatian veteran of the German Army in World War II, they sense that "something hideous . . . entered our spirits to remain and haunt us forever."

I have two final images. One is of the chilling contrast between peace celebrations of 1945 and 1973, as flashed on the television screen: the night of V-E Day in Times Square, film clips of pure mass joy, which I know to be authentic as I was there in that crowd, a happy nineteen-year-old medical student; and Times Square after the 1973 cease-fire—the area itself now looking seedy, almost deserted, a few Vietnam veterans gathered in anger, some drinking, others apparently on drugs, most simply enraged, screaming at the camera, at the society, about having been deceived by the war and ignored upon coming back, one especially enraged black veteran shouting, "You can tell that bastard the war isn't over."

The other image was from the meeting with Vietnam veterans described above shortly after the cease-fire. We talked about whether or not one still goes on being an antiwar veteran. One of the men spoke simultaneously of continuing war abroad and his own inner struggles, and then said firmly, and not only for himself, "I'm going to be a Vietnam veteran against the war for the rest of my life."

Epilogue

Over the years, now decades, many indeed have remained Vietnam veterans against the war—by holding to certain lessons learned about war making. As they enter middle age, too many are still burdened by the traumatic effects mentioned in the new preface, and all who saw combat are likely to retain some of the painful images discussed in this book. But most Vietnam veterans have taken their places in American society, work force, and professions. Two of them who participated actively in our New York rap groups have become psychologists widely recognized for their work on psychic trauma, especially in Vietnam veterans. Others from various parts of the country have written powerful novels, stories, and poems either focused on, or profoundly informed by, their Vietnam experience. Still others serve in state and national government, including the U.S. Senate and House of Representatives, and several have been mentioned as possible presidential candidates. Our society seems to sense that Vietnam veterans have knowledge to impart.

To be sure, Vietnam combat does not inevitably result in wisdom. Some veterans find an outlet for their bitterness in denouncing our unwillingness to have used still greater firepower in Vietnam. That Rambo-like stance, with its impulse to replay the war ("This time we win!" as a character in one of the films put it), contributed of course to the Gulf War enthusiasm. But all Vietnam veterans, whatever their politics or professions, retain in some portion of their minds a sense of the horror and filth of war in general and the particular horror and filth of their war. That realization can continue to give rise to waves of Vietnam-based insight, even illumination.

One such wave, of enormous importance, has been the articulation of the experiences of American women in Vietnam. Although a very small percentage of the military force, women sent there numbered about ten thousand, the great majority of whom were involved in nursing. As medical professionals who were often older than the GIs they treated, they experienced enormous psychological pressures to suppress their own painful feelings. Their voices were slow to be heard, but during the 1980s a movement to make them be heard took place. It was initiated mainly by Lynda Van Devanter. Her 1983 book, *Home before Morning,* in which she describes her Vietnam experiences, has helped awaken many women veterans to their own feelings and struggles. But according to Rose Sandecki, the first woman Vietnam veteran to head a Vet center (part of the national Outreach Program of the Veterans Administration), there are still special barriers women face in acknowledging their post-traumatic symptoms.

With Joan A. Furey, Van Devanter edited *Visions of War, Dreams of Peace,* a 1991 anthology of poems by women, most of them Vietnam veterans. Norma J. Griffiths, in a 1982 poem, tells us what has been absent from the definition: "The 'Vietnam Vet'/people instantly conjure/their own picture/in their mind/Is it ever of/a woman?/Huddled . . . somewhere . . . /alone . . . " Another nurse, in 1987, conveys the suffering of the care-giver in attending a dying soldier: "Goodbye David—my name is Dusty./I am the last person/you will see./I am the last person/you will touch./I am the last person/who will love you./So long, David—my name is Dusty./ David/who will give me something for my pain?"

There are also poems by Vietnamese women, one of which, by Minh Duc Hoai Trinh, is about a Vietnamese death and has these haunting lines: "Tomorrow the field green with grass . . . /Oh what a lonely tomb." Lynda Van Devanter, in a 1990 poem, connects her war with the new one: "the line of soldiers marching across the screen/Wears desert sand camouflage instead of jungle green./And they're still/just/kids." She goes on to talk of "two fresh, young nurses in fatigues" who declare themselves "committed . . . highly trained . . . prepared for anything," and then adds, "A chill runs through me/My God, they/have/no/idea." When I talked with her a year later, she told me how much Vietnam had influenced her sense, at the beginning of the Gulf War, that "this is crazy!"

Compared with Vietnam a much higher percentage of troops in

the Gulf were women. With their expanding activities and involvement in dangerous tasks, they stimulated a national debate on equality of treatment in the military and whether that equality should include combat assignments. Perhaps the debate was necessary, but it has something of the grotesque about it. We do better to respond to the insights of the nurse-poets of Vietnam. Furey and Van Devanter recall quiet moments in Vietnam when a group of nurses would read poetry to one another, which "engendered in each of us a new level of compassion and understanding, and helped us to discover the true meaning of duty, honor and country. It was not commitment to a misguided cause, but rather a deep and personal commitment to universal brotherhood and Love." Norma J. Griffiths asks that we "think no more of the 'war to end all wars' but rather of the 'Peace to end all wars . . . ' "

There are already indications that Van Devanter's apprehension about Gulf War military service was justified. As I write this, just a few months after the end of their war, Gulf veterans are beginning to tell their story. From talking to a few of them I have the distinct impression that, like their Vietnam counterparts, they will be a source of special knowledge. All I spoke to condemned Saddam Hussein's aggression in Kuwait, but they varied greatly in their initial attitudes to the Gulf War—from a conviction that the war was necessary and just, to doubts and uncertainty about it, to a sense of resentment at being forced to fight a war that was wrong for America to undertake. During the buildup and the early days of the air war (which began on January 16, 1991), they were struck by the scale of the enterprise but tended to focus on their individual responsibilities, on avoiding angering their superiors, and on learning how best to stay alive when the inevitable ground fighting came.

Their first exposure to danger came when the Iraqis fired Skud missiles into Saudi Arabia, an experience, as one put it, of "complete terror." The uncertainty of where the missiles might land was combined with a special fear of the chemical warheads they were expected to carry. The always excrutiating fear of poison gas was extended to the different kinds of chemical agents they had been told about—those that paralyze the nervous system and those that cause complete blistering of exposed skin areas.

They were also apprehensive about the ground war. But when it began, the two men I spoke to from tank units were amazed at the absence of Iraqi opposition. One veteran witnessed many Iraqi tanks "burned to shreds" and told how Iraqis soldiers fled from their tanks, sometimes ineffectively firing hand machine guns, until "our tankers blew them away." He said that there was "no resistance whatsoever. . . . Almost every target they shot was just running. . . . They were just like going through training . . . with live targets." Their account was confirmed by a *New York Newsday* story of September 12, 1991, describing how we "used plows mounted on tanks and combat earth movers to bury thousands of Iraqi soldiers—some still alive and firing their weapons—in more than 70 miles of trenches."

The frustration of some American tankers at the paucity of targets led to strange behavior. Tank crews in great competition with each other over the few targets available on occasion would fire at another American tank because it was "horning in on a kill" (attempting to attack an Iraqi tank on which the first American crew had already set its sights). The first tanker "was pissed because he [the rival tanker] was shooting his target." This happened frequently enough during the second night of the ground war that many of the troops labeled that night "Fright Night" (the name of a current movie).

The scale of the American military operation seemed to create considerable chaos and danger. One veteran described how "hundreds and hundreds of vehicles, on a little two-lane road, going pretty fast" resulted in many fatal traffic accidents. All of the veterans I spoke to believe that the great majority of American fatalities resulted from either traffic accidents or "friendly fire." The latter includes being blown up by "CDUs," small golf-sized plastique explosives, a hundred or so of which might be contained in large bombs dropped by the U.S. Air Force, which American soldiers later picked up.

As in the press, veterans described the mass killing of fleeing Iraqi soldiers toward the end of the ground war as a "turkey shoot." A woman reservist observed the debris on the "highway to hell" on which that event occurred and told me, "I couldn't believe it. All the vehicles blown up from a distance—tanks, cars, automobiles, clothes, bags." There was debris of every kind, except that of human bodies, which had been removed before she got there.

Some Americans became bloodthirsty in their frustration, as in the case of a general observed by one of the veterans to have been "furious with the cease fire. He just wanted to kill people . . . destroy the Iraqis, disable vehicles—kick ass was all he wanted to do." The veteran went on to explain about the general and many others: "They trained a lot. All of a sudden they saw everything work. They wanted a chance to do the real thing."

Junior officers also were bitterly criticized. One veteran bemoaned their poor quality and told how his entire unit had been endangered by a lieutenant's incompetence, so that first the unit was "lost" and then exposed to lethal American cross fire. He said that the feeling among the troops became so strong that some of them began to make plans to kill the officer, and would surely have done so—"like they did in Vietnam"—had the war not ended so quickly.

Another veteran told me that "the whole thing was out of control" and "we didn't know basically what we were doing." Some of the troops felt so ignorant about what was going on that they would listen to news programs either on CNN or military stations six to seven times a day in order to grasp their own situation. Support troops experienced harsh conditions ("Most people don't realize how *cold* the desert can be!") and were troubled by such things as inordinate delays in mail delivery, thought to be caused by inefficiency and lack of concern. A woman veteran spoke bitterly about discriminatory treatment she and others in her unit received from the military and from other troops because they were reservists, because their unit was so small they lacked an officer to speak up for them, and possibly (though she did not emphasize this) because they were women.

Much more disturbing were certain events reported to have occurred during the ground war. One veteran described an incident
(told to him by another soldier) in which American Apache helicopters, supporting a tank unit, "saw some POWs trying to surrender."
The soldier asked the brigade commander (on an FM communications network that anyone could listen to) what to do about them,
and "the brigade commander just told the Apaches to shoot them, so
they just shot them." The same veteran also described how "MPs
handling POWs were ordered by military intelligence counterin-
telligence experts to use excessive force [meaning various kinds of
torture] as a coordinate technique to get valuable information from
important POWs, such as known terrorists." The veteran characterized the attitude as assuming that "getting any information from
them is good" and as "kind of the Oliver North syndrome."

This same veteran told how members of his own unit told him
that, while guarding an oil refinery in Iraq, they shot into the big oil
storage drums with their vulcan guns (formidable air defense
weapons) to start enormous fires in the drums. He was able to
confirm that account by observing bullet holes in drums that did not
catch fire. His understanding of the act, from talking to the men,
was a way of "everybody getting kicks" and just "fucking off." He
saw us as destroyers, more or less following in the Iraqis footsteps:
"The Iraqis were the first marauders. Then it seemed like we just
took their place. People had the attitude 'We don't care. We're
Americans. We can do what we want.' " What was dangerous, he
thought, was that our troops felt they had "complete power."

After the "victory," the same veteran observed what he describes
as extensive looting by American troops in Kuwait and Iraq and
stealing from Iraqi civilians at checkpoints—"booze,
money . . . anything they wanted." He also observed drug abuse,
colluded in by medics who made morphine or valium available. And
he spoke of such corrupt practices as people receiving medals "for
not doing anything," "a couple of cooks . . . telling me about their
bronze stars when they weren't even there," and a female medic who
saw no action, but "just for fucking the general got a bronze star,"

adding that the general is now under investigation.

There were also accounts of friction between American troops and various Arab groups. A veteran who served in the MPs expressed deep resentment toward the Kuwaitis who, he said, first welcomed American military assistance but as soon as the war was over insisted that "we had no business there." They "wanted to take over our area" and constantly sought to force their way into POW compounds in order to "kill Iraqis." Having "started out feeling sorry for them," he reversed his feelings and lost all sympathy. The Kuwaiti interpreter in his unit, after being "well paid" by Americans, began to be extremely critical of them and of American policies, insisting that he "didn't want anyone else involved but Arabs." He stirred up so much resentment that, according to the veteran, he would surely have been subjected to some kind of violence had he remained longer with the unit. The Iraqis, he said, were "cowards" because "first they raped the people of Kuwait" and then "they ran the whole time." And the Saudis, he observed, sold guns to the Kuwaitis, with members of all three groups stealing regularly from the American military, so that "any Arab posed a threat." He was especially bitter because the Kuwaitis and Saudis "were supposed to be our allies." One could say that mutual antagonism between Americans and Arab groups was inherent in the situation, just as it was in Vietnam between Americans and virtually all Vietnamese.

Veterans described to me a series of indelible images, memories conveyed by the senses, mostly but not entirely pictorial, which came to symbolize their experience. One veteran described four of these: the burning oil wells ("The smoke was so bad . . . you couldn't see your hand in front of your face—you wonder what it does to people even hundreds of miles away"); the overall destruction (images of overwhelming American fire power and of debris and dead bodies); the terror of Skud attacks (memories of fearful anticipation of different forms of gas); and finally, a more quiet image of the desert, empty except for the pieces of a small radio tower that had been destroyed by an American bombing sortie (suggesting the

absurdity of our targets of destruction and of the war in general).
Another veteran retained most strongly various smells: those of the
dead bodies of Iraqis killed in our air attacks, and the more general
smell of the desert which he associated with the emptiness of a
"dead place."

Veterans I spoke to tended to sum up the war cynically. One felt
that "we got used," meaning exploited by the different Arab groups,
and is sure that now "we'll end up giving them money [to recover]."
Another declared that the war was "useless," that he felt "no honor
in what we did—not proud of anything." He said that Saddam
Hussein "is still doing what he did before," that "we didn't accomplish anything . . . and didn't have to do this in the first place."
The female reservist spoke contemptuously of the whole project as
"a political war." The veterans also scoffed at the media's glorification of the war and its strategic brilliance. One spoke of the "bullshit" of the claim of "super tactics" and careful step-by-step
planning "because it was simply a matter of our overwhelming force
so that they [the Iraqis] didn't stand a chance."

These veterans retained at least mild posttraumatic symptoms of
anxiety, fearful dreams, and ready association of immediate events
to those of the war. One, for instance, told me how "nervous" he
became during a Fourth of July fireworks display. When I asked him
whether other soldiers he knew had such feelings and attitudes
about the war his answer was, "If they don't feel this way now, they
will later."

I cannot claim that these descriptions fully represent what men
and women experienced in the Gulf. I was told, for instance, of
many men who maintained their bravado, feelings of "being powerful and indestructible." And there are undoubtedly a vast array of
additional attitudes and emotions. Moreover, the reactions I have
mentioned emerge not only from specific characteristics of the Gulf
War but from war in general. Yet, whatever the necessary qualifica-
tions, these preliminary impressions make clear enough that for the
men and women involved there was a great deal of Vietnam in the
Gulf.

Notes

❦

PROLOGUE: ENGAGING THE AFFLICTION

1. *Crimes of War*, edited by Richard A. Falk, Gabriel Kolko, and Robert Jay Lifton, New York: Random House, 1971.

2. Murray Polner, *No Victory Parades: The Return of the Vietnam Veteran*, New York: Holt, Rinehart and Winston, 1971.

3. "Oversight of medical care of veterans wounded in Vietnam, hearings before the Subcommittee on Veterans' Affairs of the Committee on Labor and Public Welfare, United States Senate," U.S. Government Printing Office, Washington, D.C., 1970, pp. 491-510; also in *Crimes of War*, pp. 419-426, and *Commonweal*, February 20, 1970, 554-556. Vol. XCL.

4. Lifton, "Experiments in Advocacy Research," the 1971 William V. Silverberg Award Lecture, *The Academy* (Newsletter of The American Academy of Psychoanalysis), Vol. 16, No. 1, February 1972, pp. 8-13; reprinted in Jules E. Masserman, ed., *Science and Psychoanalysis, Vol. XXI: Research and Relevance*, New York: Grune and Stratton, 1972, pp. 259-271.

5. See final section of my *Death in Life: Survivors of Hiroshima*, New York: Random House, 1968, and Vintage Books, 1969; "The Sense of Immortality: On Death and the Continuity of Life," the Karen Horney Lecture, March 22, 1971 (*The American Journal of Psychoanalysis*, in press); and *The Broken Connection*, ms. For theory of symbolic immortality see *Boundaries, Psychological Man in Revolution*, New York: Random House and Vintage Books, 1970; and "On Death and Death Symbolism: The Hiroshima Disaster," *Psychiatry*, Vol. 27, August, 1964, pp. 191-210. For discussion of open personal change see *Thought Reform and the Psychology of Totalism: A Study of "Brainwashing" in China*, New York: W. W. Norton, 1961, and Norton Library Edition, 1963; and *The Broken Connection*.

6. For general discussion of "shared themes" as one of four psychohistorical models, see Lifton, "On Psychohistory," *Psychoanalysis and Contemporary Science*, Vol. 1, 1972 (Previous versions in *Partisan Review*, Spring, 1970, pp. 11-32; and *The State of American History*, ed. Herbert Bass, 1970.)

1. THE HERO VERSUS THE SOCIALIZED WARRIOR

1. See note 5 of Prologue.

2. Joseph Campbell, *The Hero With a Thousand Faces*, Meridian, 1956, p. 337.

3. Ibid., p. 337.

4. Lifton, *Revolutionary Immortality*, New York: Random House, 1968, pp. 36-37.

5. Karl Liebknecht, *Militarism*, New York: B. W. Heubsch, 1917, p. 62.

6. Campbell, op. cit., 340-41.

7. Thucydides, *The Peloponnesian War*, Penguin, 1970, Warner Translation, pp. 92, 121-22. I am indebted to Donald W. Wells' study, *The War Myth* (Pegasus, 1967) for suggesting some of these ideas and references.

8. Wells, *The War Myth*, p. 62.

9. My earlier study, *Thought Reform and the Psychology of Totalism* (New York: W. W. Norton, 1961), explores the psychology of this kind of

process, though more in relationship to total ideology in general than the warrior ethos as such.

10. Wells, *The War Myth*, p. 69.

11. I begin to suggest this hypothesis in *Death in Life,* and have elaborated it further in several public talks and in *The Broken Connection*, ms. It is discussed again in Chapter VII.

12. In Wells, op. cit.

2. AMERICA'S NEW SURVIVORS: THE IMAGE OF MY LAI

1. Quotations are from report on Vietnam Era Veterans contained in Appendix to Chief Medical Director's letter of December 22, 1970, Veterans Administration, Department of Medicine and Surgery, Washington, D.C. See also *The Unique Problems of the Vietnam Era Veterans Workshop*, VA Hospital, New Orleans, La., October 8-9, 1970, ms; *The Vietnam Veteran: Challenge for Change—Administrative Seminars in Five Cities*, Washington: Veterans Administration, U.S. Government Printing Office, 1972; *The Vietnam Veteran in Contemporary Society: Collected Materials Pertaining to the Young Veterans*, VA Department of Medicine and Surgery, U.S. Government Printing Office, 1972; and Marc J. Musser and Charles A. Stenger, "A Medical and Social Perception of the Vietnam Veteran," *Bulletin of New York Academy of Medicine*, Vol. 48, July 1972, pp. 859-869.

2. Erik Erikson, *Identity: Youth and Crisis*, New York: Norton, 1968, p. 17.

3. Polner, *No Victory Parades.*

4. "The Vietnam Veteran: Characteristics and Needs," Marcul R. Stuen, M.D. [VA Hospital, American Lake, Tacoma, Washington], and Kristen B. Solberg [VA Hospital, Fort Meade, S.D.], mimeo, for observations made from 1968 through 1971.

5. Erich Maria Remarque, *All Quiet on the Western Front,* Fawcett Crest Books, Greenwich, 1958, p. 83.

6. Lifton, "America in Vietnam: The Counterfeit Friend," in *History and Human Survival*, New York: Random House, 1970, pp. 210-37.

7. Appendix 2, Veterans Administration Memorandum from Chief Medical Director, December 22, 1970, ILIO-70-95, p. A-11.

8. Johan Huizinga, *Homo Ludens: A study of the Play Element in Culture*, Boston: Beacon Paperback, 1955, p. 91.

9. Seymour M. Hersh, *My Lai 4: A Report on the Massacre and Its Aftermath*, New York: Random House, 1970, and *Cover-Up: The Army's Secret Investigation of the Massacre at My Lai 4*, New York: Random House, 1972; Richard Hammer, *One Morning in the War: The Tragedy at Son My*, New York: Coward-McCann, 1970, and *The Court-Martial of Lt. Calley*, New York: Coward-McCann and Geoghegan, 1971; Martin Gershen, *Destroy or Die: The True Story of Mylai*, New Rochelle, N.Y., Arlington House, 1971; *Lieutenant Calley: His Own Story, As Told to John Sack*, New York: Viking, 1971; and Arthur Everett, Kathryn Johnson, and Harry F. Rosenthal, *Calley*, New York: Dell, 1971.

10. W. Barry Gault ("Some Remarks on Slaughter," *American Journal of Psychiatry*, October 1971, Vol. 128, pp. 450-54) used this term in his thoughtful discussion of factors that led to atrocity in Vietnam. His ideas both blend with and extend my own earlier observations.

11. Vietnam Veterans Against the War, *The Winter Soldier Investigation: An Inquiry into American War Crimes*, Boston: Beacon Press, 1972, p. 5.

12. Robert Butow, *Japan's Decision to Surrender*, Stanford, 1954.

13. *Winter Soldier Investigation*, p. 6.

14. *Crimes of War*, pp. 64-72.

15. This and all previous quotations in this paragraph are from Peter Bourne, "From Boot Camp to My Lai," in *Crimes of War*, pp. 462-68.

16. Hersh, *My Lai 4*, p. 11.

17. Ibid., p. 23.

18. Gershen, p. 186.

19. Ibid, pp. 186-92 (includes quotations in following sentence).

20. See Lifton, *Death in Life*, discussion of "the survivor," pp. 479-539.

21. Last two quotations, Gershen, pp. 208-09.

22. Charles J. Levy, "ARVN as Faggots," *Transaction*, October 1971, pp. 18-27, 23.

23. Gershen, p. 288.

24. *My Lai 4*, pp. 40-41.

25. Hersh, "Cover-Up," *New Yorker*, January 22, 1971, p. 54.

26. Gershen, p. 290.

27. Documented in Hammer, *One Morning in the War*; and Hersh, *Cover-Up*.

28. Gershen, p. 28.

29. Ibid., pp. 37-38.

30. Ibid., p. 297.

31. *My Lai 4*, p. 187.

32. Interview by Jerry Samuels with former GI, transcript from Canadian Broadcasting Corporation program, "Ideas," July 1971, p. 16.

33. Gershen, p. 47.

34. Ibid., p. 43.

35. Ibid., p. 45.

36. Ibid., p. 24.

37. *The Court-Martial of Lt. Calley*, p. 161.

38. Gershen, p. 17.

39. Ibid., p. 31.

40. Gershen, p. 281.

41. "Cover-Up," *The New Yorker*, January 22, 1971, p. 49.

42. Peers Committee record of Medina's recollections of Henderson's briefing, reported by Hersh, "Cover-Up," *The New Yorker*, January 22, 1971, p. 54.

43. Avery Weisman and Thomas Hackett, "Predilection to Death: Death and Dying as a Psychiatric Problem," *Psychosomatic Medicine*, May-June, 1961, Vol. 23, No. 3, pp. 232-256. See also Weisman, *On Dying and Denying*, New York: Behavioral Publications, 1972.

44. *Court-Martial of Lt. Calley*, pp. 274-76.

45. *Cover-Up, The New Yorker*, January 22, 1971, p. 64.

46. Ibid., p. 64.

47. Ibid., pp. 76, 79, and in Random House book.

48. Lifton, "My Lai and the Malignant Spiral" (statement for Congressional Conference on War and National Responsibility, February 20-21, 1970). Reprinted in Erwin Knoll and Judith Wies McFadden, eds., *War Crimes and the American Conscience*, New York: Holt, Rinehart and Winston, 1970, pp. 104-109, and in *Crimes of War*, pp. 419-29.

49. Statement by Arthur Egendorf, American Orthopsychiatric Association meeting, Washington, D.C., April 1971, transcript. pp. 19-20.

4. ANIMATING GUILT

1. Samuels transcript, p. 26.

2. *Death in Life*, p. 480.

3. Ibid., p. 48.

4. Philip Kingry, *The Labor of the Spear*, ms., p. 34.

5. *Death in Life*, p. 56.

6. Ibid., p. 482.

7. Samuels, transcript.

8. Jeff Needle, "Please Read This," circulated by New Mobilization for Peace Committee, Washington, D.C., and Vietnam Peace Parade Committee, New York, N.Y., 1970.

9. See Otto Rank, *The Double: A Psychoanalytic Study*, Chapel Hill, University of North Carolina Press, 1971.

10. *Death in Life*, pp. 485-86.

11. From "Strange Meeting," *Collected Poems of Wilfred Owen*, Oxford University Press, 1967, p. 35.

12. Alfred de Vigny, *The Military Necessity*, London: The Cresset Library, 1951, pp. 187-88.

13. Statements by Robert McLain, American Orthopsychiatric Association meetings, Washington, D.C., April 1971, transcript.

14. Stan Platke, "And Then There Were None," *Winning Hearts and Minds: War Poems by Vietnam Veterans*, p. 101.

15. See Huizinga's discussion of religious and ritual elements of warfare in his *The Waning of the Middle Ages* (New York: Doubleday Anchor, 1954), Chapters IV-VIII, and *Homo Ludens* Boston: Beacon Paperback, 1955, Chapter V.

16. Gershen, p. 43.

17. Thomas Szasz, "Drugs and Politics," *Trans-action*, January 1972, p. 406.

18. Hans J. Spielmann, "The Southeast Asian Connection," *New York Times*, Op-Ed Page (47), May 17, 1972; and Alfred W. McCoy (with Cathleen B. Read and Leonard P. Adams, II), *The Politics of Heroin in Southeast Asia*, New York: Harper & Row, 1972.

19. Sigmund Freud, *Standard Edition*, Vol. XXI, p. 131.

20. Both Buber quotations are from his article, "Guilt and Built Feelings," *Psychiatry*, Vol. XX, No. 2, May, 1957.

21. Samuels interview, p. 28.

22. *The Collected Poems of Wilfred Owen*, ed. C. Day Lewis, New Directions Paperback, 1965, Introduction.

23. *Wilfred Owen, Collected Letters* (edited by Harold Owen and John Bell), London: Oxford University Press, 1967, letters 505, 508, 512.

24. *Collected Poems of Wilfred Owen*, p. 69.

25. Buber, op. cit.

26. Michael Casey, *Obscenities*, New Haven: Yale University Press, 1972.

27. *Winning Hearts and Minds: War Poems by Vietnam Veterans*, edited by Larry Rottmann, Jan Barry, and Basil T. Paquet, Brooklyn, N.Y.: First Casualty Press, 1972. (Newer editions distributed by McGraw-Hill.)

5. ZONES OF RAGE AND VIOLENCE

1. Charles J. Levy, statement to the Subcommittee of Veterans' Affairs, Senator Alan Cranston, Chairman, December 3, 1970; "The Violent Veterans," *Time Magazine*, March 13, 1972, pp. 45-46; and personal communications.

2. Robert McLain, transcript of panel of American Orthopsychiatric Association meeting in Washington, D.C., March 22, 1971, pp. 9-11.

3. Samuels transcript, pp. 24-25.

4. See Charles Levy, "ARVN as Faggots."

5. *Death in Life*, p. 193 ff.

6. *Revolutionary Immortality*, pp. 36-37.

6. THE COUNTERFEIT UNIVERSE

1. Samuels, transcript.

2. See T. Szasz, *Law, Liberty and Psychiatry*, New York: Macmillan, 1963; and Seymour L. Halleck, *The Politics of Therapy*, New York: Science House, 1971.

3. Huizinga, *Homo Ludens*, pp. 30-31, 89-104.

4. Brecht, *Mother Courage and her Children*, New Directions Paperback, Bently translation, p. 30.

5. See Norman E. Zinberg, "Heroin Use in Vietnam and the United States," *Archives of General Psychiatry*, 26:486-488, 1972.

6. Lifton,"Protean Man," in *History and Human Survival*, New York: Random House, 1970, pp. 316-31; *Partisan*

Review, Winter 1968, Vol. 35, 13-27; and *Archives of General Psychiatry,* 1971, Vol. 24, 298-304.

7. Harrison Kohler, "Victory," *Winning Hearts and Minds: War Poems by Vietnam Veterans,* ed. by Larry Rottman, Jan Barry, and Basit T. Paquet, Brooklyn, N.Y.: First Casualty Press, 1972, p. 44.

7. GOOKS AND MEN

1. Glasser, *365 Days,* pp. 271-72.
2. Needle, "Please Read This," p. 18.
3. Levy, "ARVN as Faggots."
4. Levy, op. cit., p. 27.
5. Glasser, *365 Days,* p. 29.
6. Lifton, *Death in Life,* pp. 512-14.
7. Frances Fitzgerald, *Fire in the Lake,* Boston: Atlantic-Little-Brown, 1972, pp. 219-221.
8. James Henry Breasted, *The Dawn of Conscience,* Scribners, 1933, p. 70.
9. *The Pocket Dictionary of American Slang,* New York: Thomas Y. Crowell, 1968, p. 144.
10. *American Heritage Dictionary of the English Language,* New York: American Heritage Publishing Co., and Houghton Mifflin Co., 1969.
11. Tom Englehardt, "The War Wounded Come Home," in *Pacific News Service* release No. 35, June 21, 1971, *Dispatch News Service International.*

8. TRANSFORMATION I: FROM JOHN WAYNE TO COUNTRY JOE AND THE FISH

1. Michael Casey, *Obscenities,* New Haven: Yale University Press, 1972.
2. Needle, "Please Read This," pp. 7-19.
3. Samuels, transcript, p. 23.
4. Introduction to *America and the Asian Revolutions,* Lifton, ed., Transaction Books, Aldine Publishing Co., 1970.

5. Lifton, *Thought Reform and the Psychology of Totalism,* pp. 67-68.
6. Levy, "ARVN as Faggots," p. 18.
7. See Martin Wangh, "A Psychogenic Factor in the Recurrence of War," *International Journal of Psychoanalysis,* 1968, 49:319-22.
8. Lifton, "Protean Man."
9. Cecily Woodham Smith, *The Reason Why,* p. 36.

9. TRANSFORMATION II: LEARNING TO FEEL

1. Remarque, pp. 60-61.
2. Lifton, *Death in Life,* pp. 479-539; and "The Sense of Immortality . . ."
3. These 'subparadigms' around death are discussed in "The Sense of Immortality . . .", and *The Broken Connection,* ms.
4. Guy Sajer, *The Forgotten Soldier,* New York: Harper & Row, 1971, p. 355.
5. See Erikson's discussion of Fidelity in *Insight and Responsibility,* New York: Norton, 1964, pp. 125-28.
6. T. S. Eliot, "The Wasteland," in *The Wasteland and Other Poems,* New York: Harcourt-Harvest, 1962, p. 30.

10. TRANSFORMATION III: SELF AND WORLD

1. Lifton, "Protean Man."
2. Erik Erikson, *Insight and Responsibility,* New York: W. W. Norton, 1964.
3. Samuels, Interview, p. 25.
4. Orthopsychiatric Meetings Transcript, p. 18.
5. George Urvan, "A Conversation with Lukacs," *Encounter,* October 1971, pp. 30-36.

11. TRUTH AND PROPHECY

1. Tom Englehardt, "An Air Force Hospital: The War-Wounded Come

Home," *Dispatch News Service International* release, No. 35, June 30, 1971, p. 6.

2. Englehardt, p. 5.

3. Needle, "Please Read This."

4. Lifton, *Death in Life*, p. 487.

5. *Encyclopedia of Religion*, p. 615.

6. Lifton, *Death in Life*, pp. 480-541.

7. Lifton, "Prophetic Survivors," *Social Policy*, January/February 1972, Vol. 2, No. 5, pp. 8-15; and *The Future of Immortality*, ms.

8. *Encyclopedia of Religion*, p. 614.

9. See my discussion of mockery in "Protean Man," and "The Young and the Old—Notes on a New History," in *History and Human Survival*, pp. 317-373.

10. Lifton, "Images of Time," *History and Human Survival*, pp. 58-81. See also A. C. Welch, *Kings and Prophets of Israel*, London: Lutterworth Press, 1952.

12. ON WAR AND WARRIORS

1. John Kerry, statement before Senate Foreign Relations Committee, April 22, 1971, in Kerry and The Vietnam Veterans Against the War, *The New Soldier* (edited by David Thorne and George Butler), New York: Collier Books, 1971, p. 18.

2. Donald Kirk, "Who Wants to be the Last Man to be Killed in Vietnam," *New York Times Magazine*, September 21, 1971.

3. *Time Magazine*, October 25, 1971, p. 38.

4. Larry Rottmann, "Realization," in *A Few Moments Out of "America's Finest Hour,"* ms., p. 7.

5. Kirk, op. cit. Previous quotation from same article.

6. McCoy, *The Politics of Heroin in Southeast Asia*.

7. Norman E. Zinberg, "GI's and OJ's," *New York Times Magazine*, December 5, 1971; "Heroin Use in Viet-

nam and the United States"; and "Rehabilitation of Heroin Users in Vietnam," *Contemporary Drug Problems*, Spring, 1972, pp. 263-94.

8. See also statements and discussion before Subcommittee on Health and Hospitals of the Committee on Veterans' Affairs, and Subcommittee on Alcoholism and Narcotics of the Committee on Labor and Public Welfare, United States Senate, June 15 and 23, 1971, by Donald Juhl et al, Dr. Sidney Cohen, and Dr. George Solomon (U.S. Government Office, Washington, D.C.). See also hearings before the Subcommittee on Alcoholism and Narcotics of the Committee on Labor and Public Welfare, U.S. Senate on Military Drug Abuse, June 9 and 22, 1971 (U.S. Government Printing Office, Washington, D.C.).

Papers given at that panel included Jerome H. Jaffe, "A Bio-Behavioral and Public Health Approach to a Heroin Epidemic among Military Personnel"; Jonathan F. Borus, "Reentry: 'Making It' Back in the States," A. Carl Segal, "Army Psychiatry and the Vietnam Veteran: A Critique," Marcus R. Stuen, "Vietnam Vets as Psychiatric Patients at the VA," and my own "The Rap-Group Experience with Vietnam Veterans." See all Jaffe's talks to the Veterans of Foreign Wars, Washington, D.C., March 5, 1972, and to one National War College, Fort McNair, September 27, 1971, ms.; and George F. Solomon, "Psychiatric Casualties of the Vietnam Conflict with Particular Reference to the Problem of Heroin Addiction," *Modern Medicine*, September 20, 1971, pp. 199-215; and Gordon S. Livingston, "Medicine and the Military: Some Ethical Problems," in Maurice B. Visscher, ed., *Humanistic Perspectives in Medical Ethics*, Buffalo, New York: Prometheus Books, 1972, pp. 266-74, and "The Indo-China War and American Values," in the *Year Book of World Affairs*, 1971, Vol. 25,

The London Institute of World Affairs, London: Stevens and Sons, Ltd., 1971, pp. 26-38; and Fisher et al, Human Resources Research Organization reports pp. 12-72 (May 1972) and TR-72-9 (March 1972), Alexandria, Va.

9. *New York Times,* December 18, 1971, pp. 1 and 16; and Hersh, *Cover-Up.*

10. *Armed Forces Journal,* June 7, 1971.

11. Arthur Fink, personal communication.

12. Alfred de Vigny, *The Military Necessity,* pp. 201-209.

13. As sung by Len Chandler in late 1971 at a New York appearance.

14. Talk by Art Kanegis at "The People's Panel: A Grand Jury Investigation of Citizen Grievances and American Power," Washington, D.C., October 22, 1971. Much of this material comes from NARMIC (National Action Research on the Military Industrial Complex) reports and slide shows. NARMIC is a project of the American Friends Service Committee.

15. Fred Branfman, "The Era of the Blue Machine: Laos: 1969-," *Washington Monthly,* July 1971.

16. Branfman, "Airwar: The New Totalitarianism," *Liberation,* February-March-April, 1971.

17. VVAW, *The Winter Soldier Investigation: An Inquiry Into American War Crimes,* Boston: Beacon Press, 1972, pp. 48-50.

18. Branfman, interview transcript.

19. Branfman, "The Era of the Blue Machine," p. 13.

20. Branfman, "Airwar: The New Totalitarianism," pamphlet reprint, pp. 1-2. For the most complete study of the air war, see Raphael Littaner and Norman Uphoff, eds., Air War Study Group, Cornell University, *The Air War in Indochina,* Boston: Beacon Press, 1972.

21. Branfman, People's Panel talk.

22. Branfman, "American Bombing in Laos: The Crime Against Humanity," International Commission of Inquiry into U.S. Crimes in Indochina, second session, Oslo, June 20-25, 1971.

23. Branfman, "The Era of the Blue Machine," p. 7.

24. Branfman, People's Panel talk.

25. Branfman, "The Era of the Blue Machine," p. 5.

26. Both accounts from Branfman, *Voices from the Plain of Jars: Life Under an Air War,* New York: Harper Colophon Books, 1972, pp. 85 and 69. Author of first account unknown, of second "an eighteen-year-old woman."

27. Kanegis, People's Panel talk.

28. Last three quotations from Paul Dickson and John Rothchild, "Electronic Battlefield: Wiring Down the War," Washington Monthly, May 1971.

29. Ibid.

30. Ibid.

31. "Investigation into Electronic Battlefield Program," hearings before the Electronic Battlefield Subcommittee of the U.S. Senate Committee on Armed Forces, November 18, 19, and 24, 1971.

32. Ibid.

33. Masao Maruyama, *Thought and Behavior in Modern Japanese Politics,* New York: Oxford University Press, 1963.

34. Branfman, "The Era of the Blue Machine," and personal communication.

35. Address by General W. C. Westmoreland, Chief of Staff, U.S. Army, Annual Luncheon Association of the U.S. Army, Sheraton-Park Hotel, Washington, D.C., October 14, 1969.

36. Dickson and Rothchild, "Electronic Battlefield," p. 8.

37. Branfman, "The Era of the Blue Machine," p. 11.

38. Kanegis.

39. Westmoreland, address.

40. Hannah Arendt, "Lying in Politics: Reflections on the Pentagon

Papers," *New York Review*, November 18, 1971, pp. 30-38.

41. *New York Times*, November 16, 1971, AP dateline November 15.

42. See also Francine Gray, *"The Sugarcoated Fortress*, New York: Random House, 1972.

43. *New York Times*, late 1971.

44. Lifton, "America in Vietnam— The Counterfeit Friend," *History and Human Survival*, pp. 210-37.

45. U.S. Government Printing Office, 1971.

46. Lifton, "Images of Time," *History and Human Survival*, pp. 58-80. See also footnote in Chapter 8, p. 232.

47. *New York Times*, December 15, 1971. Quotes are from talks by Vice-President Spiro Agnew.

48. Branfman, *Voices from the Plain of Jars*, and also Betty Jean Lifton, *Children of Vietnam*, New York: Atheneum, 1972.

49. Glasser, *365 Days*, pp. 260-61.

50. Willard Gaylin, *In Service of Their Country*, New York: Viking Press, 1970.

51. *Time Magazine*, November 6, 1972, p. 23.

52. *Boston Globe*, November 2, 1972, p. 16.

53. Speech delivered February 10, 1970, reprinted in Murray Polner, *When Can I Come Home?: A Debate on Amnesty for Exiles, Antiwar Prisoners and Others*, New York: Doubleday Anchor, 1972. More argued statements of opposition to amnesty included in the book are those by Ronald Docksi, National Chairman of Young Americans for Freedom, William Rusher, editor of *National Review* magazine, and Ernest Van den Haag, adjunct professor of social philosophy at New York University. Statements generally in favor of amnesty include those of Willard Gaylin, James Reston, Jr., Martin E. Marty, Arthur Egendorf, Jr., and my own. See also James Reston, Jr., *Amnesty of John David Herndon*, New York: McGraw-Hill, 1973.

54. Allan Solomonow, *When Can I Go Home*, p. 121.

55. *Oxford English Dictionary*, 1971 edition.

56. *Oxford International Dictionary*, usage is respectively dated 1580 and 1880.

57. "Objectives of Vietnam Veterans Against the War," VVAW mailing, August, 1972, mimeo.

58. *Collected Poems of Wallace Stevens*, New York: Knopf, 1969, p. 320.

59. Johan Huizinga, *Homo Ludens*, p. 101.

60. This and above quotations are from de Vigny, *The Military Necessity*.

61. Lionel Tiger, *Men in Groups*, New York: Random House, 1969.

13. ON CHANGE

1. Photograph accompanying unsigned article, "A Trip to Hanoi," *The First Casualty*, Vol. I, No. 2, October 1971.

2. W. S. Merwin, "For Now," in Stephen Berg and Robert Mezey (eds.), *Naked Poetry*, New York: Bobbs-Merrill, 1969, p. 264.

3. Lifton, "Protean Man."

4. This and subsequent quotations concerning *areté* are from Werner Jaeger, *Paideia: The Ideals of Greek Culture*, New York: Oxford University Press, 1939, Vol. 1.

5. Huzinga, *The Waning of the Middle Ages*, p. 96.

6. Lifton, *Thought Reform and the Psychology of Totalism*, pp. 462-72.

7. *American Heritage Dictionary* (of the English Language), Boston/New York Houghton Mifflin Co., and American Heritage Publishing Co., 1969.

8. *Oxford English Dictionary*.

9. George F. Solomon, Vincent P. Zarcone, Jr., Robert Yourg, Neil R.

Scott, and Ralph G. Maurer, "Three Psychiatric Casualties from Vietnam," *Arch. of Gen. Psych.*, 1971, 25: 522-24. See also William Goldsmith and Constantine Cretekos, "Unhappy Odysseys: Psychiatric Hospitalizations Among Vietnam Returnees," *Arch. of Gen. Psych.*, 1969, 20: 78-83.

10. See Roy R. Grinker and John P. Spiegel, *Men Under Stress,* New York: McGraw-Hill, 1963. See also A. J. Glass, "Psychotherapy in the Combat Zone," *American Journal of Psychiatry.* 110:725-31, 1954; and studies from earlier wars such as T. W. Salmon, "The War Neuroses and Their Lessons," *New York Journal of Medicine,* 109:992-94, 1919; and a recent book by Peter Bourne, *Men, Stress, and Vietnam,* Boston: Little, Brown & Co., 1970, as well as Bourne (ed.), *The Psychology and Physiology of Stress: With Special Reference to Studies on the Vietnam War,* New York: Academic Press, 1969. My work owes much to these studies, but emphasizes the psychology of the survivor rather than the concept of "war neurosis" or "traumatic neurosis." See also papers by Jonathan Borus: Reentry I, II, and III, in press for *Arch. of Gen. Psych., American Journal of Psychiatry,* and *Psychiatry.*

11. Lifton, *Thought Reform,* p. 19.

12. The writings of two co-participants and colleagues in the rap-group program, Chaim F. Shatan and Arthur Egendorf, Jr., present pictures very consistent with my own. See Egendorf, "The Re-Integration of the New Soldier," ms., and "Veterans . . . the Agony and the Challenge," ms.; and Shatan, "The Grief of Soldiers," *American Report,* June 23, 1972, pp. 1, 10. "Soldiers in Mourning—Vietnam Veterans Self-Help Groups: The Post-Vietnam Syndrome," *Am. Journal Orthopsychiatry,* 1972, 42: 300-301, and "Bogus Manhood, Bogus Honour: Surrender and Transfiguration in the U.S. Marine Corps," in *Psychoanalytic Perspectives on Aggression,* Charles C. Thomas, in press. I have also learned much from many discussions with a third close colleague in the rap groups, Florence Volkman Pincus.

13. Frank Acnner, "The Confession of an FBI Informer," *Harper's,* December 1972, pp. 54-65.

14. Alexander Mitscherlich, *Society Without the Father,* New York: Harcourt, Brace, & World, 1969, and personal communication.

15. See, for instance Harvey A. Barocas and Carol B. Barocas, "Manifestations of Second Generation Concentration Camp Effects," *American Journal of Psychiatry,* in press, 1973; and V. Rakoff, J. J. Sigal, and M. B. Epstein, "Children and Families of Concentration Camp Survivors," *Canada's Mental Health,* 1966, 14: 14-16.

16. Erik Erikson, *Godkin Lectures,* Harvard University, 1972, ms.

17. *American Heritage Dictionary.*

18. Jean-François Steiner, *Treblinka,* New York: Simon and Schuster, 1968.

19. Lifton, *History and Human Survival,* p. 153.

20. Lifton, *The Broken Connection,* ms.

21. From the poem "Dogalypse," translated by Robert Bly and Lawrence Ferlinghetti, *New York Times,* November 19, 1971, p. 45.

22. See Donner, "The Confession of an FBI Informer"; and also newspaper articles: "Informer Appears Key to U.S. Case Against Six Antiwar Veterans," *New York Times,* August 14, 1972; and "What Led Anti-War Vets to Gainesville?" *the Miami Herald,* August 13, 1972.

23. *Look Magazine,* "Ellsberg Talks" (interview by J. Robert Joskin), October 5, 1971, pp. 31-34.

24. Daniel Ellsberg, *Papers on the War,* New York: Simon and Schuster, 1972, p. 33.

25. Ibid., pp. 38-39.

14. ON HEALING

1. For brief discussions of these issues of investigative involvement, see my introductions to *History and Human Survival and Thought Reform and the Psychology of Totalism*, as well as my essay, "On Psychohistory."

2. Quotations and etymological sequences are from the *Oxford English Dictionary*, Vol. 2, p. 2316, and the *American Heritage Dictionary*.

3. H. Spencer Bloch, "Army Psychiatry in the Combat Zone—1967–1968," *American Journal of Psychiatry*, 1969, 126:289-98, 289.

4. Bloch, pp. 291-92.

5. Douglas R. Bey, Jr., and Walter E. Smith, "Organizational Consultation in a Combat Unit," *American Journal of Psychiatry*, October 1971, Vol. 128, pp. 401-06.

6. William Barry Gault, "Some Remarks on Slaughter," *American Journal of Psychiatry*, October 1971, Vol. 128, pp. 450-53.

7. Bloch, p. 292-94.

8. Glasser, *365 Days*, p. 178.

9. Hearings before Subcommittee on Veterans' Affairs, chaired by Senator Alan Cranston, January 27, 1970.

10. Personal communications from George F. Solomon, Peter Bourne, A. Carl Segal, Emanuel Tanay, Gordon S. Livingston, Charles Levy, Jon Bjornson, Werner Simon, Barry Gault, and Marcus B. Stuen, psychiatrists working within and outside of the Veterans Administration, support these conclusions; as do those from Arthur Egendorf, Jr., Florence Volkman Pincus, and Robert Shaporo (psychologists), Charles Levy (a sociologist), and Murray Polner (a historian and educator), all of whom have worked extensively with veterns in rap groups and other informal settings. See also Solomon, "Three Psychiatric Casualties," and "Psychiatric Casualties of the Vietnam Conflict with Particular Reference to Problems of Heroin Addiction," *Modern Medicine*, September 20, 1971; Egendorf, "The Re-integration of the New Soldier," and "Veterans—The Agony and the Challenge"; Shatan, "The Grief of Soldiers"; Stuen, "The Vietnam Veteran: Characteristics and Needs"; Livingston, "The Indochina War and American Values"; the Veterans Administration Administrator Seminars on *The Vietnam Era Veteran: Challenge for Change*, 1971; and William Goldsmith and Constantine Cretekos, "Unhappy Odysseys."

11. Allan Wheelis, *The Quest for Identity*, New York: W. W. Norton, 1958.

12. Leslie Farber, "The Therapeutic Despair," in *The Ways of the Will*, New York: Basic Books, 1966.

13. Thomas Szasz, *The Myth of Mental Illness*, New York: Harper and Row, 1961.

14. Ronald Laing, *The Divided Self*, London: Penguin, 1960; and *The Politics of Experience*, London: Penguin, 1967.

15. Humphrey Osmond, "The Medical Model in Psychiatry: Love It or Leave It," *Medical Annals of the District of Columbia*, 41:171-75.

16. "The Sense of Immortality," and *The Broken Connection*, ms.

17. See Ernst Cassirer, *An Essay on Man*, Doubleday Anchor, 1944, *The Myth of the State*, Doubleday Anchor, 1946, and *The Philosophy of Symbolic Forms* (three volumes), Yale University Press, 1953-1957; and Susanne Langer, *Philosophy in a New Key*, Cambridge, Mass.: Harvard Univ. Press, 1942, Feeling and Form, New York: Scribners, 1953, Philosophical Sketches, Baltimore: Johns Hopkins, 1962, and *Mind: An Essay on Feeling*, Baltimore: Johns Hopkins, 1967. See also R. G. Collingwood, *The Idea of History*, New York: Oxford (Galaxie),

1956; Alfred North Whitehead, *Modes of Thought*, New York: Capricorn (Macmillan) 1958, and *Science and the Modern World*, New York: Mentor, 1948.

18. Robert R. Holt has made an interesting attempt to distinguish "Freud's mechanistic and humanistic images of man" (in Holt and Peterfreund, eds., *Psychoanalysis and Contemporary Science*, pp. 3-24). See also Daniel Yankelovich and William Barrett, *Ego and Instinct*, New York: Random House, 1970, and Thomas S. Kuhn, *Structure of Scientific Revolutions*, Chicago: Phoenix Books (Univ. of Chicago Press), 1964; and Lancelot Law Whyte, *The Next Development in Man*, London: The Cresset Press, 1944.

19. *Oxford English Dictionary*.

20. Erik Erikson, "The Dream Specimen of Psychoanalysis," *Journal of the American Psychoanalysis Association*, 1954, 2:5-56.

21. Maryse Choisy, *Sigmund Freud: A New Appraisal*, New York: Philosophical Library, 1953, p. 5.

22. Max Schur, *Freud: Living and Dying*, New York: Basic Books, 1972, pp. 50-51.

23. Lifton, *Revolutionary Immortality*.

24. Lifton, "Home by Ship: Reaction Patterns of American Prisoners of War Repatriated from North Korea," *The American Journal of Psychiatry*, April 1954, Vol. 110, 10:732-39.

25. Theodore Roethke, "The Far Field," in *Collected Poems*, New York: Doubleday, 1966, p. 200.

26. Stanley Milgram, "Behavioral Study of Obedience," *Journal of Abnormal and Social Psychology*, 1963, 67: 371-78; and "The Compulsion to Do Evil," *Patterns of Prejudice*, Vol. I, November/December, 1967 (London).

27. Quotations are from Albert Camus, *The Rebel*, New York: Knopf, 1954.

Index